20

KU-714-096

Group Dynamics in Sport
Theoretical and Practical Issues

Albert V. Carron
The University of Western Ontario

WITHDRAWN

NEWMAN COLLEGE
BARTLEY GREEN
BIRMINGHAM, 32.

CLASS   301.57
ACCESSION   95456
AUTHOR   CAR

Spodym Publishers
London, Ontario

N 0015651 5

Canadian Cataloguing in Publication Data

Carron, Albert V. (Albert Vital), 1941
    Group dynamics in sport

Bibliography: p.
Includes index.
ISBN 0-921911-04-1

1. Sports - Social aspects.   2. Sports -
Psychological aspects.   3. Social groups.
I. Title.

GV706.5.C37 1988   306'.483   C88-095100-1

© **Spodym Publishers 1988**

10 9 8 7 6 5 4 3 2 1

All rights reserved. No part of this publication may be reproduced, stored in any retrieval system or transmitted in any form or by any means, electronic or otherwise, without the prior written permission of the publisher, **Spodym Publishers,** 11 Ravenglass Crescent, London, Ontario, Canada, N6G 4J9

Preface

Finished. At last. In order to appreciate the extent of my satisfaction, you have to understand that the decision to write this book was made in early 1981. At that time, I was asked to prepare an article for *Quest* in the general area of group dynamics. In the process of preparing that article (Carron, 1981), it quickly became apparent to me that there were no books available in sport psychology or sport sociology which focused on the group. Certainly, most good texts at that time introduced selected topics such as leadership, cohesion, cooperation, and competition. But none dealt exclusively with the group or the sport team. Since my main interests lie in this area, I decided to try to pull research together from the sport sciences, psychology, sociology, and the management sciences and then interpret it for the student, coach, and teacher. Every year for the past seven, I have resolved to get started but other projects always seemed to get in the way. This past year, I was fortunate to receive a sabbatical leave from the University of Western Ontario. Consequently, I finally had the time to complete what was beginning to seem like a pipe dream.

One thing that did become obvious during the preparation of this work is that group dynamics in sport is a relatively unexplored area in sport psychology and sport sociology. This makes it fertile ground for new ideas. Hopefully, this book will help to promote more interest in the analysis of group dynamics in sport teams.

One of the main functions of the preface of a book (in my view) is to publicly acknowledge and thank those individuals who have been a help in one way or another. In this regard, I am appreciative of the efforts of my colleagues, Chella Chelladurai, Larry Brawley, Craig Hall, Kevin Spink, and Neil Widmeyer, who proofread and reacted to various chapters as they were finished.. There is not much value in going to people who are nonproductive and/or uniformed if you want worthwhile input. But productive and informed people also have their own agendas and deadlines. Consequently, proofreading the work of others is always a sacrifice.

I would also like to acknowledge the contributions of Larry Brawley and Neil Widmeyer to my understanding of group dynamics in sport. Over the past five years, the three of us have worked as a team in numerous projects. During that time, Larry and Neil have contributed immeasurably to the breadth and depth of my understanding in this area. While each of us would undoubtedly write a different book on the topic, and while the limitations in this work are mine alone, most of what I have included here has been influenced by the conversations, research, and writings of our team.

Finally, my family ... my wife Dana, and my children Wendy, Brett, Pat, Jeff, and Chris. There is no doubt that one dimensional people — whether they are religious fanatics, exercise nuts, health food kooks or of some other extreme persuasion — are terribly boring. Whatever focus preoccupies the fanatic, also tends to dominate the life of those around him or her. Conversations, behavior, plans, social engagements, start with, come back to or are influenced by that overriding single dimension. Unfortunately, a book simply cannot be completed without the author becoming something of a fanatic. It's too large an undertaking to be treated casually. So without a supportive family, a family prepared to indulge the fanaticism, a book would be unmanageable. My family consistently supported me, encouraged me, inquired about my progress, and were as pleased as I was to see this completed. Thanks.

Albert V. Carron
London, Ontario

Contents

Part 3. Member Attributes

Part 4. Group Structure

Part 7. Concluding Observations

1 Introduction

I have always believed that there was a larger purpose to basketball than individual achievements. Excellence has been defined for me in terms of the team's success. In high school, it was whether our team from a very small school in a small town could defeat the bigger, city teams. In college, it was whether a team of students who played basketball to their collective potential could compete with the best in the country. In the pros, it was whether a team without a dominant star could be the best in the world. And in the U.S. Senate, a moment of insight came when I realized that the passage of legislature, like teamwork, required getting people with different backgrounds, different interests, and different personal agendas to agree on a shared goal, and to work toward it. (Bradley, 1976, p. iii)

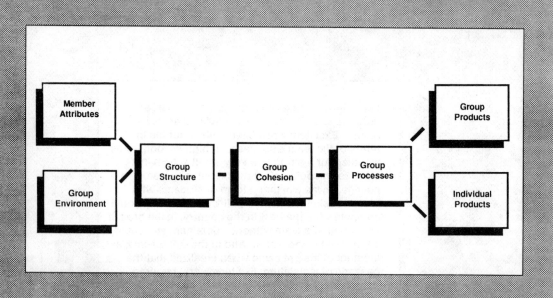

1 Introduction

The purpose of this book is to review research and theory in the area of group dynamics and interpret its application to sport groups. As the quote by U.S. Senator and former basketball player, Bill Bradley, which was used to introduce this section serves to illustrate, teamwork is important in sport teams at every level and in society in general. Membership and involvement in groups is a fundamental characteristic of our society. We enter life as a member of society's strongest and most significant group — the family. As we grow and develop, we are exposed to and influenced by other important groups in social and work settings. We attend school in groups, worship in groups, socialize, and carry out business in groups. And, of course, play, exercise, and sport are group activities. Even the so-called individual sports like wrestling, badminton, and tennis are group activities since at least two people — the minimum for a group — are required for competition. Through our interactions with other people in group situations, we influence the behavior and attitudes of other people and, in turn, are influenced. The groups to which we belong have a powerful, significant impact on our lives.

Consider the Green Bay Packers of the National Football League, for example. Between 1965 and 1967, they won three championships and the first two Super Bowl games. Subsequently, six members of the team plus the coach, Vince Lombardi, were elected to the Professional Football Hall of Fame. The Packers were, quite obviously, a highly successful team. In his book **Distant Replay,** Jerry Kramer (Kramer & Schaap, 1985) attempted, almost twenty years later, to

> We respected each other's individuality, but for those three hours each Sunday, we stopped being individuals and we became a team, dependent on each other, confident that we could depend on each other. We blocked, tackled, ran, passed, caught passes, every man contributing, and we capitalize on our similarities .... I felt that I was a part of something special, but only a part. Our sense of togetherness was so ingrained I don't think any of us ever felt that *he* won the game, that *he* was the star. We always felt it was a group effort, and it was.
> (Kramer & Schaap, 1985, p.37)

explain the powerful feeling of togetherness which flowed through the team at that time:

> *We could say goodbye to each other at the end of each season, lead separate lives for six or seven months, pursue different interests, age and change, and on rare occasions even mature, and yet the next season, as soon as we saw each other, the old feelings returned, of warmth and affection, respect and admiration. We were like the lovers in the play* **Same Time Next Year.** *Ours was an affair that endured, a bond stronger in so many ways, than marriage.* (p.34)

Anyone who has been involved with a successful sport group can also relate to Kramer's sentiments. A powerful bond is formed within the group that has vitality, that endures over time, extended separations, and even adversity. The feeling of "we" never seems to go away. How does this bond form? Why? What gives it this strength? What is it about some groups that leads to this powerful sense of unity?

There are no simple answers to these questions, no quick prescriptions. From what we know about groups, there seems to be a number of elements which sometimes seem to operate alone and at other times in combinations. In some cases, it's shared adversity. In others, it's the presence of common goals. And, shared successes. Or, a feeling that the team is more important than the individuals who make it up. But, there are no easy answers. When Jerry Kramer attempted to explain the Packers, he came up with a number of possibilities:

> The answer, the first answer, has to be Lombardi. He united us, initially, in our fear of him, our hatred of him. He was, deliberately, the common enemy, the focus of all our frustrations. If our muscles ached, it was Lombardi's fault. If our nerves were frayed, it was Lombardi's fault. The fierceness of Lombardi — combined with the smallness of the city in which we played — forced upon us a camaraderie and a closeness that, nurtured by victory, grew into love.
>
> Victory was important because victory was our measure of success ... We liked each other before we won. We loved each other after we won. We loved Lombardi, too ... And, yet our love for each other, and for our coach, was based upon more than winning, for if it had based only on winning — as athletic "love" so often is — it would have ended or diminished, when the victories ended. We went beyond loving to caring, to caring about what happened to each of us, professionally, financially, emotionally ...
>
> We cared because we respected each other, our differences and our similarities. We were so different, one eyed jacks and straight arrows, street fighters and family men, churchgoers and barflies ... We never let our differences divide us, not differences in style, nor in race ....
>
> We judged each other, not on what we did on Monday nights or Friday nights, but on what we did on Sunday afternoons, between one o'clock and four, the way each man played, the way he confronted violence, if he shrunk back or if he met and conquered it, with vigor, gusto, with intensity. (pp. 35-37)

The Kramer account of the Packers, the personal experiences of anyone who has been on a team, and the available research carried out on groups of every type serve to highlight a point made earlier — there are no simple prescriptions for the development of effective sport teams. The only common thread which does run through every successful team, however, is that the team takes precedence over the individual, the team is more important, the team, not the individual is preeminent. This sentiment is discussed in the account of every successful team, it is a part of their tradition. Kramer indicated that this was the case with the Packers in the quote used to lead off this chapter.

The Boston Celtics are also a good example. In a book written in 1976, Jeff Greenfield, observed that from 1957 to 1969, the Celtics established a record which was unique in professional sport. They won eight consecutive championships and, but for an injury to Bill Russell, might have won ten in a row. In his discussion of the team, Greenfield noted:

> The story of the Boston Celtic dynasty and the apparent durability of its success suggest some lessons ... Consider the essential irony: we live, we are told, in a competitive society, where each individual must strive for excellence on his own merits. But the success of the Celtics is based on a philosophy wholly opposed to individualism. The basic Auerbach commandment is that to win, the individual must fit in; he must subordinate his desires and skills to those of the team. He must, to use an Auerbach watchword, "sacrifice himself", in his life and on the court, to the working of the team. (p. 205)

Another equally good example is provided by the Montreal Canadiens. Their history includes the most championships in the history of the National Hockey League (23), the most consecutive championships (5), the most appearances in the final series (27), and the most years in the play-offs (56). In their book, **Lions in Winter,** Chrys Goyens and Allan Turowetz (1986) also commented on the importance of a team perspective over an individual one:

> Selke looked for three essentials in his players: a strong hockey background; a deep commitment to winning or an equally strong aversion to losing; and the sense of self-confidence, self direction and self-motivation necessary in a player who would be asked to accept the team's regimentation. He wanted his players to adopt a shared perspective, rather than just an individual one. Personal expectations, attitudes and motives had to become team expectations, team attitudes and team motives. (p. 112)

These examples serve to illustrate how important the group is in sport. In order to produce a better group — a better sport team — it is necessary to know more about their nature, structure, and dynamics.

The Reality of Groups

Historically, both the lay person and the social scientist have had difficulty understanding groups. For example, on the one hand, the lay person appears to have had difficulty determining whether groups are positive or negative, good or bad, useful or detrimental. If we examine old adages and popular bromides — the wisdom of the ages which is passed on to succeeding generations — it's easy to see how the lay person might be confused. Our old adages and popular bromides offer more contradictions than solutions (Steiner, 1972). For example, consider the following:

> Two heads are better than one
> vs
> Too many cooks spoil the broth
>
> The more the merrier
> vs
> Three is a crowd
>
> If you want things well done, do them yourself
> vs
> If you're a jack of all trades, you'll be master of none
>
> Many hands make the work lighter
> vs
> A camel is a horse developed by a committee
>
> There is unity in numbers
> vs
> A chain is as strong as its weakest link

If it's difficult to come to an understanding about the utility of groups by relying on old bromides, some help might be expected from the scientist. But, historically, social scientists also have had difficulty understanding groups. For example, scientists have debated whether groups even exist. The object of psychology as a science is to describe, explain, predict, and control behavior. But, groups are abstract; only the individual members are real. Consequently, only the behavior of individuals — either alone or in collective situations — can be directly measured. As a result, some social scientists in the 1920s even questioned the reality of groups. One represenative of this position was Floyd Allport, a prominent psychologist. Allport argued that any scientist who wished to understand human behavior should focus on the individual, not the group. In support of this position, Allport stated:

the only psychological elements discoverable are in the behavior and consciousness of the specific persons involved. All theories which partake of the group fallacy have the unfortunate consequence of diverting attention from the true locus of cause and effect, namely the behavioral mechanisms of the individual .... If we take care of the individuals, psychologically speaking, the groups will be found to take care of themselves. (p. 9).

This issue may seem to be simply philosophical to the coach or athlete who could argue "Of course, we have a team. We meet and practice, travel together, compete against other teams, have a history, and so on". And, the coach and athlete would be correct. But the issue raised by Allport is not whether an organization exists, whether it is more or less successful, and/or whether it is recognized as a distinct entity. When he questioned the reality of groups, Allport questioned whether groups were anything more than the sum of the individual members.

Consider the hypothetical case of two mixed doubles tennis teams. Allport might have argued that if the two males were identical in their ability, personality, attitude, and so on and the two females were also identical in every way, the two doubles teams would be identical. And, their behavior and performance would be identical. In short, Allport proposed that a group is a sum of its parts. If the parts are identical, the groups will be identical. If we wish to describe, explain, predict, or control the behavior and performance of the doubles tennis teams, we must describe, explain, predict, and control the behavior and performance of the individual members. Inherent in this viewpoint is the assumption that there is no special chemistry which sets off one group or team from another.

In the decades following the publication of Allport's book, psychologists, sociologists, and anthropologists have debated about the reality of groups. Currently, there is almost universal agreement that groups are "real"; that they are different from the simple sum of the attributes of the individual members; that group behavior and performance are different from individual behavior and performance. It might be useful to look at one case which was advanced from a philosophical perspective to support the conclusion that groups are real.

Theodore Mills (1984), a sociologist, pointed out that group goals are quite distinct from the set of goals established by individuals for themselves. He used the game of chess to illustrate his point. In chess, the goal of each of the two individual participants is to win; this personal goal is identical for both contestants. But, the goal of the dyad (the two contestants when they are considered together as a "group" playing chess) can't be "to win". There is no opponent for the unit represented by the two chess players considered together. So, can we assume that this unit, the two chess players as a group, has no goal? Mills argued that "on the contrary, there is an idea in the minds of the two parties which refers to a desirable state of the dyad: it is to have a high quality contest which each party wants to win, wherein play is imaginative, in which superior play does win. The group goal, as distinct from personal goals, then, is to have a good contest" (Mills, 1984, p. 94).

The point made by Mills using the chess game as an example has often been echoed by coaches and athletes. For example, in the 1987 Canada Cup Series, Canada and the USSR played four superb games. The first ended in a 3-3 tie. The next two were tied 5-5 in regulation time so in both cases sudden-death overtime was necessary. One of these overtime games was won by the USSR, the second by Canada. In the final game, Canada scored a goal within the final two minutes of the third period to win 6-5. Prior to the last game, Mike Keenan, the coach of the Canadian team commented, "there's a synergism involved in this and it has taken the game to greater levels than ever before. The chemistry in both teams and what it has brought out in each other is incredible. Both have been challenged to the ultimate and it has brought out the very best in both. To play at this level, the best players in the world have played as well as they've ever played. They're enjoying it. You can see it in their faces (quoted in Kernaghan, 1987, p. C1). The synergism referred to by Keenan is identical to the "group goal" discussed by Mills.

Another example of the synergism between two competitors was provided by Ken Dryden, a former goaltender for the Montreal Canadiens. In his autobiography, Dryden stated that "a good opponent [is] a rare and treasured thing for any team or player... By forcing you to to be as good as you can be, such an opponent stretches the boundaries of your emotional and playing experience ... It is why good players and good teams, good enough to stand alone, stand straighter and more vividly with a good opponent" Dryden, 1983, p. 127).

Mills, Keenan, and Dryden were essentially discussing the same thing. There's no doubt that the two opponents in any competition have the identical goal of winning. But, they also share a common goal of playing a satisfying game. And the fact that they share a common goal is evidence of the reality of groups. In summarizing his discussion, Mills pointed out that "two points need emphasis. First, the group goal is not the simple sum of personal goals, nor can it be directly inferred from them. It refers to a desirable state for the group, not simply a desirable state for individuals... the second point is that the mental construct of the group goal resides not in some mystical collective mind, but in the minds of group members... It may be shared by most or all group members, but since many other ideas are shared, that is not its distinction. What sets the concept of group goal apart is that in content and substance it refers to the group as a unit — specifically to a desirable state of that unit" (p. 95).

Groups are real. They have goals, aspirations, character, and a personality different than the simple sum of the goals, aspirations, character and personality possessed by individual group members. Further, individual behavior is different in group situations. The influence of the group can lead to increased conformity, deviance,tenacity, or many other behaviors individuals might not exhibit when alone. Similarly, individual performance is different in group situations. Frequently, individual athletes who cannot or do not stand out by themselves are outstanding in a group situation. Groups can make a difference.

The Group Defined

If groups make a difference, it is important to understand what is meant by the term. Definitions are useful because they help to highlight specific features of a concept. It shouldn't be surprising that since groups are so complex, a number of definitions have been offered. Some examples include:

[*a set of*] *mutually responsive individuals (Steiner, 1972, p.5).*

a collection of individuals whose existence as a collection is rewarding to the individuals (Bass, 1960, p. 39).

its members share norms about something ... [including] norms concerning the roles of the group members ... These distinctive features of a group — shared norms and interlocking roles — presuppose a more than transitory relationship of interaction and communication (Newcomb, 1951, p.3).

The face-to-face interaction of two or more persons in such a way that members are able to recall the characteristics of the other members accurately...Some additional characteristics of small groups that provide further definition of the concept and serve to distinguish the small group [include] ...frequent interaction ... *the development of a* group personality ... *the establishment of* group norms.. coping behavior ... role differentiation ...interdependent goals... *The final unique characteristic of small groups is something called the* assembly effect bonus. *This refers to extra productivity that is caused specifically by the nature of groups (Burgoon, Heston, & McCroskey, 1974, pp. 2-5).*

two or more more persons who are interacting with one another in such a manner that each person influences and is influenced by each other person (Shaw, 1981, p.8).

a set of individuals who share a common fate, that is, who are interdependent in the sense that an event which affects one member is likely to affect all (Fiedler, 1967, p.6).

A sport team is a special type of group. Consequently, it possesses some of the specific features presented in the above definitions but not others. Some of the more important characteristics of the sport team as a group are a collective identity, a sense of shared purpose, structured patterns of interaction, structured methods of communication, personal and task interdependence, and interpersonal attraction (Carron, 1980).

A football team can be used to illustrate each of these definitional components. For example, a collective identity exists when individual team members, opponents, and other nonteam members all view the group as a unit distinguishable from other units: "We are teammates on the University of Xebec Scullers." The sense of shared purpose or objectives readily develops from the strong task-oriented nature of the sport. With a football team, this can vary from an awareness and agreement on short-term objectives (attend weight-training sessions) or long term ones (reduce the number of yards penalized in the upcoming season).

Numerous examples are available for the structured patterns of interaction that exist within a team. The interrelated blocking assignments for various offensive lays and the defensive responsibilities under different alignments are unique task interactions within any specific team. Any newcomer to a football team requires some time to become completely familiar with the specific system. Similarly, the distinctions made implicitly or explicitly between rookies and veterans early in training camp (locker room assignments, uniform distinctions, hazing practices) is an example of the patterned social interactions existing within any sport team.

The language of football generally — blitz, drive block, fly, curl, trap — and the specific manner in which it is selectively used on particular teams provides one example of a structured mode of communication. The specific terminology used to convey particular offensive and defensive assignments (R-221, Man, Z-Curl) is another. Although members of a team can readily translate these apparently meaningless symbols into something meaningful, a nonteam member or uninitiated observer cannot.

Personal and task interdependence are inherent within the nature of the sport itself; the rules of sport dictate the size, general structure, and organization of the sport team. Thus, an individual cannot play football alone; a specific number of players is permitted on the field at any given time; there are general rules on how they must be aligned; interaction with opponents must conform to certain standards, and so on. In essence, each team member is dependent on his or her teammates if competition is going to occur.

Finally, although there are documented exceptions, interpersonal attraction generally evolves from sport team participation. Friendships are usually present to some degree on most teams. However, interpersonal attraction is neither necessary nor sufficient to define a sport team.

These characteristics — collective identity, a sense of shared purpose, structured patterns of interaction, structured methods of communication, personal and task interdependence, and interpersonal attraction — help to provide some insight into the nature of a group.

Group Dynamics

If we use an intramural basketball team as an example, it should be apparent that the group undergoes a number of changes throughout its life cycle. When it forms, members are assigned or assume group roles within a short period of time, e.g., organizer, playmaker, peacemaker, social organizer. Over time, as the team develops, it increases in cohesiveness and becomes more effective in carrying out its objectives. Those objectives might be to compete in high quality games, or to enjoy a weekly social outing, or to have a weekly excuse to go to the campus pub — or all three. Also, the team's objectives might change over time as it responds to the changing interests of members and strives to maintain its membership. The important point here is that in order to develop and maintain itself as an effective group, the intramural basketball team will be dynamic, not static. It will exhibit energy, vitality, and growth.

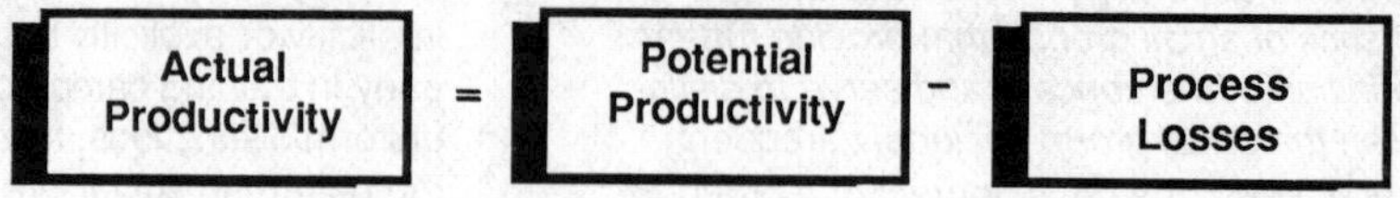

$$\boxed{\text{Actual Productivity}} \; = \; \boxed{\text{Potential Productivity}} \; - \; \boxed{\text{Process Losses}}$$

Figure 1.1 Steiner's model of group effectiveness

The term *group dynamics* has been used to describe the energy, vitality, and activity of groups (Carron & Chelladurai, 1981). It was originally introduced by Kurt Lewin to represent two principal, fundamental processes associated with group involvement. One of these, cohesiveness, is the activity associated with the formation, development, and maintenance of the group. The word cohesion comes from the Latin word *cohaesus* which mean to cleave or stick together. So, if a group exists, it must be cohesive to some extent (Donnelly, Carron, & Chelladurai, 1978). And, some of the energy, vitality, activity of the group will be directed toward developing and enhancing group cohesion.

The second component of group dynamics, locomotion, is the activity associated with productivity and the performance, output of the group. Sport groups such as intramural basketball teams have social and performance objectives. This is also true of fraternities, bridge clubs, and work crews. The most important goals and objectives may be different from one group to another and may even change in the same group over time. They may be formally set out in a constitution or simply assumed because they have become an accepted group practice over an extended period. Whatever their origin or however formally they are set out, some of the energy, vitality, and activity of the group will be directed toward enhancing group task and social cohesion. The factors which are associated with enhanced group cohesion and locomotion, in turn, are associated with the increased effectiveness of the group.

Group Effectiveness[1]

All groups strive to be effective. But, effectiveness takes on different meanings for different groups. A police force might judge itself effective if the community has a low crime rate, an effective sorority could be one that maintains its annual membership, while an effective investment club is likely to be one which makes money for its members.

What makes a sport team effective? Is it finishing first in the standings or is it simply having more wins than losses? In both of these instances, effectiveness is equated to the performance outcome. Since a sport team competes with other teams, its *performance outcome* is dependent upon not only its own performance but also upon the performance of its opponents. Thus to judge a team's effectiveness by its performance outcome is somewhat misleading and, at times, unfair. A better indicator of team effectiveness is *team performance*. Team performance refers to how well the team carries out (executes) its tasks. Some examples of team performance include minimizing the number of turnovers in basketball, maximizing the number of shots on net in hockey or team handball, and increasing the percentage of successful passes in soccer or football.

A simple and popular model of group effectiveness was advanced by Ivan Steiner (1972). A schematic representation of this model is presented in Figure 1.1. As Steiner pointed out, *actual productivity* is the performance that is attained whereas *potential productivity* is the performance that might be obtained based upon the relevant resources present in the group. The group's resources include the knowledge, ability, and skills of the individual players, their respective level of training, the adequacy of their equipment and so on. The actual steps, actions, or behaviors taken individually or collectively by group members to carry out the group task represent the *group processes*. When individuals work in groups, communication, coordination, and interaction are necessary. These can be relatively ineffective and losses in efficiency occur. Steiner proposed that the two major sources of losses which occur in any group are the result of faulty

---

1. The following is taken from Carron & Widmeyer (1987). I would like to thank Neil for providing me with permission to reproduce material which was developed by him for that project.

coordination and reduced motivation.

Steiner's model can be illustrated with a hypothetical example of a tug-of-war team. In the case of a two-person team, each individual might be able to pull 100 kg. Thus, the potential productivity of the group based on the group's resources is 200 kg. However, the group would likely pull less than this — possibly 180 kg. — because of the inability of the two people to coordinate their efforts and/or because each person might expect the other to carry the main load. Therefore, the group would have experienced a process loss of 20 kg.

As a group increases in size, its potential productivity increases. A volleyball team that keeps 30 members throughout the season has a greater likelihood of having the necessary resources to handle almost every situation. There will always be enough players for scrimmages, replacements will be available in case of injuries, specialized lineups can be used against certain teams, and so on. But, with an increase in resources, there will also be an increase in the number of problems associated with effectively and efficiently managing the group. With 30 players, it is more difficult for the coach to run an effective practice in which all of the players are active. Frequent personal communication with each individual player is difficult. If lineups are rotated, the players will not be as familiar with each other. Also, and more importantly perhaps, social loafing can increase — with increased numbers in the group, individual team members may suffer a loss in motivation and personal accountability.

The application of Steiner's model to the effectiveness of sport teams in general is illustrated in Figure 1.2. In this example, Team A will be more effective than Team B if:

> **A. It possesses greater relevant resources but experiences fewer process losses, or**
>
> **B. It possess greater relevant resources but experiences approximately equal process losses, or**
>
> **C. It possesses approximately equal relevant resources but experiences fewer process losses.**

In professional sport where the desire for league parity has lead to efforts to equalize team resources (e.g., the weakest team drafts first), the reduction in process losses is crucial. In amateur sport, where coaches have limited control over their resources (they generally coach the talent available and have very little

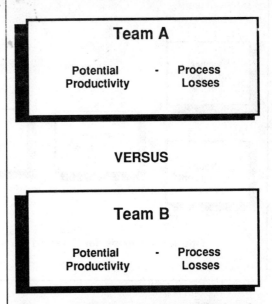

Figure 1.2 The application of Steiner's model for understanding the effectiveness of sport teams.

opportunity to supplement or change their roster during a season), the reduction in process losses is crucial. How can process losses be reduced? How can group effectiveness be increased?

Research in psychology, sociology, anthropology, and business has been concerned with these questions since their origin as sciences. Fortunately, information is available to provide the coach with some guidelines and insights. The presentation of this information is the objective of this book. In order to more effectively communicate that information, it is useful to represent a model for the sport team as a group.

A Model for Sport Groups

A model is a representation — a simplified representation — of reality. Providing a model to represent the sport team offers some advantages and disadvantages (Carron, 1984). One disadvantage which might be obvious is that any model, because it is a simplified representation, can never adequately portray the total phenomena. Model builders are like the fabled three

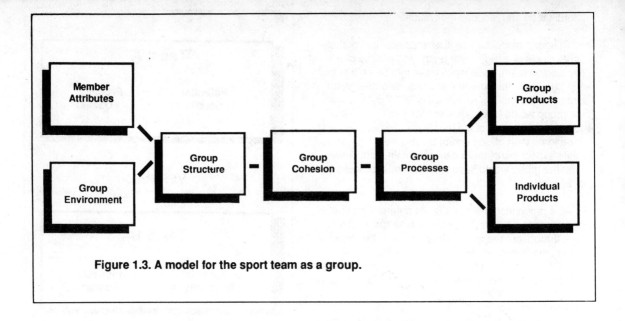

Figure 1.3. A model for the sport team as a group.

blindmen who were placed at different parts of the elephant and asked to provide a description. Each was a good scientist and provided a completely reliable and objective description. But, none of the individual descriptions was adequate as a portrayal of the total elephant. A second disadvantage is that human behavior is dynamic while models tend to present a static picture — a photograph rather than a video. For example, if a group is more cohesive, there is an increased tendency for members to more readily accept their group roles. In turn, role acceptance by group members enhances group cohesiveness. All of this is a dynamic, ongoing process. A model cannot readily capture the dynamic relationship.

There are advantages to the use of a model. One advantage is that complex topics can be simplified and more readily explained and understood. If the group is so abstract that early psychologists even questioned its existence, how can any sense be made out of it without a simplified representation? A second advantage is that assumptions can be more readily drawn about how the individual components of the complex phenomena are related. In the case of the group, for example, a model might permit us to make assumptions about the interrelationship of role clarity, role acceptance, group cohesion, and group performance. And, finally, a model can help clarify what is known and unknown about a phenomena, and, consequently, provide some direction for further research. Again, if we take the group as an example, a model might serve to highlight the fact that we know very little about the

role of density and group size.

The model for a sport group which was used as the organizational framework for this book is presented in Figure 1.3. This is a linear model consisting of inputs, throughputs, and outputs. The outputs, the major consequences in effective sport teams are individual products such as performance, satisfaction, and adherence and group products such as performance, stability, and morale. The throughputs are the group's structure, processes, and cohesiveness. Finally, the inputs are the individual group members, and the nature of the group environment. In this book, information pertaining to each of these components as well as its relevance for the effectiveness of sport groups is presented and discussed.

Prologue

There are 19 chapters in this book and they are presented in seven sections: introduction, group environment, member attributes, group structure, group cohesion, group processes, and issues and problems in groups. The first section, which contains the present chapter, serves to introduce the concept of a group. The remaining six sections deal with the major factors influencing group formation, group development and group functioning. An analogy which helps to outline specifically how each of the other six sections (and the remaining 18 chapters) are related to one another is the purchase and operation of a bicycle.

Group effectiveness is influenced by environmental factors. Similarly, the relative effectiveness of 3-speed, 10-speed, and mountain bikes also depend on environmental factors such as the terrain on which they will be used. A 10-speed is impractical to deliver newspapers, a mountain bike is ineffective for the Tour de France. In the three chapters in the second section, factors associated with the group's environment are introduced.

Groups are made up of individual members and the attributes of those members directly influence the group's effectiveness. A bike is also composed of a number of component parts which represent its "resources". It should be obvious that the resources which are used to construct different bikes vary in both number, function, and quality. For example, there are over a thousand components for some bikes, the components for a standard bike differ from those for a mountain bike, and it's possible to spend either a minimal or a large amount of money for the same component. Not surprisingly, the quality of a bike is strongly influenced by the quality of its component parts. This same truism also applies to groups — the quality of a group is strongly influenced by its component resources. In the four chapters of the third section, factors associated with member attributes and group effectiveness are discussed.

In every bike, the various parts are put into position according to their functions and roles — the component parts make up the bike's structure and foundation. Groups also have a formal structure which develops when its members assume positions and take on different functions and roles. The five chapters in the fourth section are concerned with the develop-ment of group structure.

When the bike is put together, each part is tightened into place. Also, care is taken to insure that the wheels don't rub on the frame, that the gears work smoothly, that oil is applied where necessary. In short, the bike is drawn together into a tight integrated unit. This process is analogous to the development of group cohesiveness. Cohesiveness is the bond which accounts for the fact that many individuals with differing needs, personalities, motives, and goals can be formed together into one strong effective group. In the two chapters in the fifth section, the issues associated with group cohesiveness are discussed.

The construction of the bike is not an end in itself. It is put together for performance — for some purpose such as competing, socializing, working, or recreating. During the periods it which it is used, the bike's effectiveness is influenced by many different interdependent (related) processes. Some of these, for example, involve regular maintenance such as putting oil on the chain and air in the tires, insuring that the gears operate in a smooth coordinated fashion, and so on. These functions are associated with the process of operating the bike. A group also forms for some purpose such as competing, socializing, working, or recreating. And, during the period in which it is engaged in its activities, various group processes also influence its effectiveness. The three chapters in the sixth section focus on group processes.

The single chapter in the seventh section deals with some issues in the area of group dynamics and offers some suggestions for future consideration. It isn't really the equivalent of a owner's manual for a bicycle but in order to continue with the analogy, we can refer to it that way.

In the weeks before the 49ers won Super Bowl XIX, some sports writers were wondering if [Joe Montana] had a sore arm. He hadn't been throwing deep ... So when the stories appeared in the Bay Area newspapers about his not throwing deep, I visited him at the 49ers' complex in Redwood City. "Are you going to start throwing deep?"
He never batted an eye. "No", he said.
"Why not", I pressed. "Is your arm sore?"
"No, my arm's not sore; I can throw deep", he said. "But we don't have any plays to throw deep. We never practice throwing deep."
"How come?"
"Look at our practice field here", he said. "Most teams have two full hundred-yard fields, one grass and one artificial turf. But, we only have one field that's half grass and half artificial turf. When it rains in December here, the receivers have to wear either artificial turf-shoes or grass shoes, depending on which half of the field we're practicing on. If we practiice on the grass half, the receivers don't want to run on the the artificial turf with cleats. If we practice on the artificial-turf half, the receivers don't want to risk falling on wet grass with artificial-turf shoes. When we practice plays, we put the ball on what would be the twenty-five yard line, so I've only got about thirty yards to work with. You can't throw deep in thirty yards. Even in the pregame warmup, it's the same situation. You only have half the field to work with. That's why I don't throw deep". (Madden, 1986, p. 34-35)

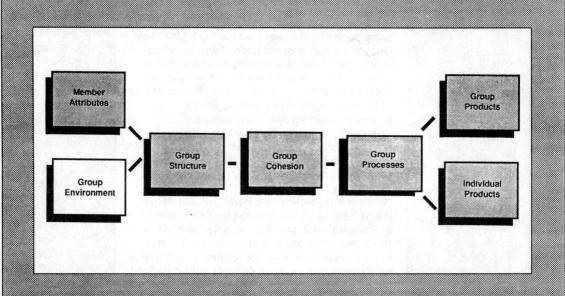

2 The Nature of the Group Task

In order to understand the group and judge its effectiveness, we must first understand its task. Does a ballet troupe really have anything in common with a football team as the quote used to open this chapter suggests? Probably not. But, if ballet and football were similar, then it should be possible to identify similarity in things other than "moves" and "tights" — in factors such as group development, group structure, measures of group effectiveness, for example.

What about group development? It seems unlikely that the group develops in the same way in ballet troupes and football teams. Because of the specialized nature of the sport, football teams become subdivided into offensive, defensive, and specialty units. Typically, each of these units has its own coaches and the bonding which occurs within a unit can often make it seem independent of the other units. Buddy Ryan, the former defensive coordinator for the Chicago Bears stated that he didn't work for Mike Ditka, the head coach. He was hired by the Bears' management before Ditka arrived, he coached the defensive team, and Ditka managed the offense. Like most football teams, Ryan's defense developed a special closeness to each other and to their coach.

What about the group's structure and group roles? Again, it seems unlikely that ballet troupes and football teams are similar. The hierarchy which exists in ballet troupes and the preeminence of the prima ballerina have no parallel on football teams.

> A cloud, no larger than a man's athletic support, has come over football. It was first noticed by television sportcasters who observed that many of the "moves" made by football players were as graceful and airborne as ballet. From this analysis it was an easy step to discover that both football players and ballet dancers wear tights and are more emotional than people who play a man's game, such as golf. This in turn led to perceiving the linemen as the corps de ballet, the quarterback as the prima ballerina, and the coach as the choreographer --Diaghilev with cleats. (Nichol & More, 1980, p. 141)

And, finally, the measures of group effectiveness are quite different. In football, quantitative measures — yards gained passing and rushing, number of first downs, pass completions, and points scored — reflect the team's effectiveness. In ballet, the assessment of the performance is qualitative. Peterson (1986) emphasized this point when she stated that "dancers are involved in the process of making art. They are part of the magic of theatre ...The only score card that the audience might see after the performance is a 'review' in a local paper, where any comparison of this performance to another will be based solely on the experience and opinion of the reviewer, not a record sheet" (p.49).

So, a dance troupe and a football team are different. This information might be the scientific equivalent of observing that birds can fly. It is also likely that in terms of group development, group structure and/or group processes, badminton teams, rowing teams, basketball, and track and field teams differ from each other as well. And, from ballet troupes and football teams. Consequently, problems arise in any attempt to explain, predict, or control group behavior and performance across these different situations. In order to provide some general prescriptions for different sport groups, researchers have felt that it is necessary to better understand the group task.

In the attempts to take into account the nature of the group task, three approaches have been adopted:

a) the development of standard group tasks for laboratory research, b) the categorization of group tasks on the basis of their different aspects or dimensions, and c) the classification of tasks into categories on the basis of the group processes required for their execution (Shaw,1981).

Standard Group Tasks

Zander's Group Goal Setting Research

Typically, standard group tasks have been developed for use in laboratory studies so that group processes can be examined under controlled conditions. For example, Alvin Zander was interested in gaining a better understanding of the conditions which influence goal setting in groups. In sport, some teams have a national championship as their goal from the moment they begin their season; other teams simply aspire to a winning record. And, in other teams, team goals are less important to the members than personal goals. In order to know why these differences exist, it is necessary to know more about the goal setting process. This was emphasized by Zander (1971) who pointed out: "the ability to interpret behavior in working groups would be considerably improved if there was a better understanding of the conditions that determine why a group chooses one goal rather than another, a reasonable goal rather than an unreasonable one" (p. 1).

For his program of research, Zander used a shuffleboard-like task. This consisted of a board 12 ft. long containing a channel along its length which was wide enough for a wooden croquet ball. Holes were drilled in the floor of the channel. The hole in the middle of the board was identified as Number 10; other holes numbered from 9 to 1 were set a regular intervals above and below the Number 10 hole. The task of the group was to move the ball along the channel by pushing in unison on a 6-ft. aluminum pole. After a number of practice shots, the group member's were given a private ballot to record the score they believed that the group would achieve on the next trial. This represented the *member's aspiration for the group*. A discussion followed in which this same question was considered until a group consensus was reached. This represented the *group's level of aspiration*.

The parallel between this laboratory situation and what frequently occurs in sport groups is obvious. A story told by Jack McCallum (1988) about an incident that occurred in an 1988 NBA playoff series between the Detroit Pistons and the Chicago Bulls helps to illustrate this point:

> Piston point guard Isiah Thomas was shooting around and talking to the Cleveland Cavaliers' Ron Harper ... when Chicago point guard Rory Sparrow happened by. Harper told Sparrow that the Pistons were going to send the Bulls on summer vacation. No, said Sparrow, it's Detroit that should be packing its bags. "You know why you won't win?" said Sparrow to Thomas. "Because you got too many egos on that team". The comment infuriated Thomas. "I ran right back and told my teammates," he said after the game. "It fired us up". (p. 23)

The Detroit Pistons' team members had aspirations for themselves and for their team. Also the team as a whole came to a consensus on on the style of play for the final game. When it appeared that there were possible discrepancies and even conflicting aspirations within the team, consensus was reached on group aspirations and expectations.

Research Using the Prisoner's Dilemma Game

Another laboratory task, the *prisoner's dilemma game,* has been used to examine issues associated with trust, conflict, and cooperation within groups. The name of this game is derived from a life-like situation in which two people are taken into custody for interrogation. For the sake of example, these two individuals can be referred to as Larry and Neil; their crime, publishing bad research. There is little doubt that both are guilty but a confession is necessary in order to insure that there is a conviction. Without a confession, both can go free. The two prisoners are separated and given a choice; confess or remain silent. A confession has dramatically different consequences than silence — and, the difference increases if either of these options is selected by one but not the other individual. This is illustrated in Table 2.1.

If both Larry and Neil confess to the crime, they each receive a 5 year sentence. If neither confesses and both remain silent, however, they both go free. If Larry confesses (which helps the prosecution) and Neil remains silent, Larry will go free and Neil will be sentenced to 10 years. Conversely, if Neil confesses and Larry remains silent, Neil will go free but Larry will receive a 10-year sentence. The dilemma faced by each prisoner is apparent: a confession could lead to freedom or a moderate sentence of 5 years. On the other hand, silence could lead to freedom or a 10-year sentence.

There are no direct parallels in sport to the prisoner's dilemma game. But, there are numerous instances where difficult decisions must be made, where group cooperation and consensus are integral to group solidarity, and, where trust is fundamental. Often, individuals must decide whether to operate in their own interests or in those of the group. Either individual and team performance or the relationships between group members may be affected. Consider, for example, the dilemma about perform-ance which is presented in Table 2.2. On a basketball team, two outstanding shooters — Jeff and Chris — must decide whether passing to each other will be in their best interests in the long term. Should Jeff pass or not pass? Will Chris pass or not pass? If both pass freely to one another, they may each average 16 points a game. If Jeff passes freely while Chris doesn't, Chris could average 24 points a game; Jeff only 8. And, finally, if neither passes freely, the total offense wouldn't be as effective. Consequently, Jeff and Chris might each average only 11 points a game.

Table 2.1 The prisoner's dilemma.

		Larry	
		Confess	Remain Silent
Neil	Confess	Both Larry and Neil Receive 15-Year Terms	Neil Goes Free and Larry Receives a 10-Year Term
	Remain Silent	Larry Goes Free and Neil Receives a 10-Year Term	Both Larry and Neil Go Free

Another example is provided by an article by Jill Lieber (1987) entitled "I Will Be Ostracized". In this article, Lieber chronicled the growing lack of trust on the part of one football player during the 1987 NFL Players' Strike. This lack of trust ultimately led the player to a realistic dilemma similar to that faced by participants in the prisoner's dilemma game:

Linebacker Tim Green was the only Atlanta Falcon regular to play in all three replacement games held during the NFL strike. As he looked ahead to his teammates returning to work this week, he feared the worst. "I will be ostracized", Green said...

When Atlanta voted to strike, Green went along with the crowd ... Green and his room-mate, Jim Costello, a linebacker on injured re-serve, walked the picket line side by side. Costello carried a sign that read: THE ONLY GOOD SCAB IS A DEAD SCAB.

After a few days Green began to question the strike. "When I heard the negotiations were caught up in free agency, I started to see a lot of inconsistencies," he says. "[Union Chief] Gene Upshaw called free agency both a

bargaining tool and an American right. Which was it?"

The pro-union pronouncements ... started to ring hollow ."The union reps gave us the truth as they knew it," Green says. "It's dangerous for people to accept what is told them by a biased source"..... Green grilled his agent ... He consulted family friends ..

Green lay awake at night trying to sort things out .... "I didn't want to come out of the strike saying ... that it was a waste of time and money".

So Green phoned five of his closest friends on the Falcons and explained why he was breaking rank.

"The players have told me that I'm not their teammate anymore," Green says. (p. 61)

In a manner similar to subjects in the prisoner's dilemma game, Green had to decide whether it was in his best interests to protect the group position or to operate independently. His eventual decision was based, in part, on a lack of trust — a feeling that the union pronouncements were not accurate. Ultimately, he came to the conclusion that staying on strike was not in his best interests so he went back to work.

Implications for the Effectiveness of Sport Groups

The group goal setting task and the prisoner's dilemma game represent only two of the standard tasks which have been used in the laboratory research to examine group processes. Some other examples include a trucking game developed by Morton Deutsch and Robert Krauss (1960) to study cooperation, competition, and conflict; a homeostatic balance task used by Simo Salminen and Pekka Luhtanen (1987) to study coordinated group activity; and, a group motor performance maze used by Diane Gill (1979) to compare individual and group performances. These standardized laboratory tasks provide insight into the dynamics that occur in intact sport groups. Research with standardized laboratory test also provides the opportunity to systematically examine group problems under controlled conditions. Their limitations lie in the fact that they do not — in fact, cannot — capture the dynamic conditions which exist in sport groups. But, given that the amount of research carried out on sport groups is so sparse, research from standardized tasks and other nonlaboratory contexts is invaluable for the insights it provides.

Dimensional Analysis of Group Tasks

Marvin Shaw (1981) has defined dimensional analysis as "an attempt to specify task differences along a variety of relatively independent dimensions or continua" (p. 363). A dimensional analysis is based on the assumption that tasks can be distinguished by such characteristics as monotony versus variety or significance versus nonsignificance. Thus, for example, athletes prefer scrimmages and games to repetitive drills and instruction. There is greater variety in the former; more monotony in the latter. Similarly, athletes with important team roles are more motivated to perform well than athletes with roles that are not very significant. Understanding the task an athlete is trying to perform can provide insight into why he or she is not performing effectively.

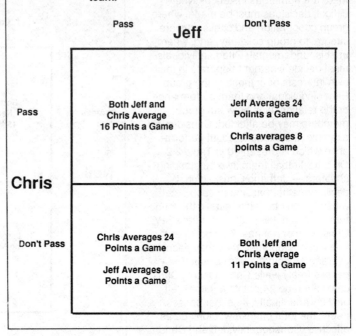

Table 2.2 A dilemma of two star players on a basketball team.

	Jeff	
	Pass	**Don't Pass**
Chris **Pass**	Both Jeff and Chris Average 16 Points a Game	Jeff Averages 24 Points a Game Chris averages 8 points a Game
Don't Pass	Chris Averages 24 Points a Game Jeff Averages 8 Points a Game	Both Jeff and Chris Average 11 Points a Game

One of the more comprehensive dimensional analyses of group tasks was undertaken by Richard Hackman and Greg Oldham (1980). Their model is presented in Figure 2.1. According to Hackman and Oldham, each task can be assessed on the basis of *specific job characteristics*. The presence of these job characteristics contributes to *critical psychological states* in the individual. In turn, the critical psychological states lead to positive *outcomes* in terms of performance and satisfaction.

The specific characteristics included by Hackman and Oldham are skill variety, task identity, task significance, autonomy, and feedback. Skill variety represents the degree to which the individual must use a variety of different activities, talents, or skills to carry out the task. Thus, a swimmer who is involved in an individual medley event has more opportunities for variety than a swimmer who is involved in an event requiring only one stroke. Similarly, a football team might pass only 10% of the time when it's on offense. Consequently, that team's offensive linemen have less opportunity to develop their pass protection blocking talents and skills than linemen on teams where the distribution of passing and running plays is equal.

Task identity represents the degree to which the

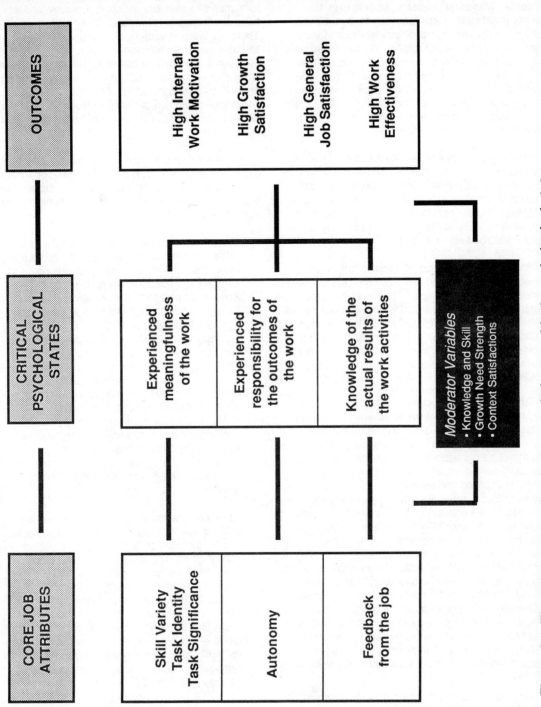

Figure 2.1 The relationship of task characteristics to critical psychological states (Adapted from Hackman & Oldham, 1980)

individual has the opportunity to complete a whole, identifiable task from beginning to end with a visible outcome. Whenever division of labor is high, task identity is reduced. Thus, team sports, by their very nature, provide the individual with less task identity than individual sports; on a team, different individuals carry out different tasks. Similarly, there is relatively greater task identity in the sprints in track than there is in the relays. But, it should be emphasized that task identity in sport is relative. Sport is high in this dimension in contrast to workers in industrial settings; e.g., workers on an assembly line.

The third job characteristic identified by Hackman and Oldham, task significance, refers to the degree to which individuals feel that their activity is important. Backup goaltenders in hockey, backup quarterbacks in football, and the nonstarters on a basketball team may have difficulty accepting their roles if they are not perceived to be very important.

As Figure 2.1 illustrates, if a task is high in skill variety, task identity, and task significance, the work is considered to be meaningful. However, "a person can experience the work as meaningful even if one or two of these task characteristics are quite low" (Hackman & Oldham, 1980, p. 79). The second runner in a relay rates low in skill variety, and task identity. However, the task is high in task significance and, therefore, would undoubtedly be perceived as meaningful.

The fourth job characteristic listed in Figure 2.1 is autonomy. As the name suggests, autonomy represents the degree to which the individual can use personal discretion and operate independently without excessive rules, regulations, or supervision. In professional hockey, for example, coaches like the joint role of coach and general manager because of the increased autonomy which results. Autonomy is also associated with a critical psychological state — experienced responsibility for outcomes of the work. Hackman and Oldham pointed out that "as autonomy increases, individuals tend to feel more personal responsibility for successes and failures that occur on the job and are more willing to accept personal accountability for the outcomes of their work" (Hackman & Oldham, 1980, pp. 79-80). In a group situation, diffusion of responsibility may occur. If one individual is present, there is autonomy and complete responsibility for the outcome. When two individuals are present, independence is reduced and responsibility is shared.

The final task characteristic included by Hackman and Oldham is feedback - the degree to which the job provides the individual with direct and clear information about performance effectiveness. This is not feedback from a coach or teammate; it's feedback about performance from the activity itself. A tennis player who is serving has clear information about performance effectiveness. In sport generally, athletes have direct access to feedback about performance. There are isolated exceptions — a golfer hitting to an elevated green, a shortstop upended while completing the double play, or a basketball player run off the court while shooting a layup. But, these are exceptions, they are not inherent in the sport. As Figure 2.1 illustrates, knowledge of the actual results of the work activity is derived from feedback and is a critical psychological state.

The three psychological states, in turn, contribute to motivation, satisfaction, and effective performance. Although they developed their model for business and industrial settings, Hackman and Oldham noted that it does have application in sport:

It is ironic that the three psychological states often characterize games played for pleasure better than they do work in organizations. Consider, for example, the game of golf. Knowledge of results is direct and immediate: the player hits the ball and sees at once where it goes. Moreover, tallies of scores for each hole played are kept, providing cumulative and comparative data about performance effectiveness. Experienced personal responsibility for the outcomes is clear and high, despite the tendency of golfers sometimes to claim that the slice was due to someone whispering behind the tee, or perhaps to a little puff of wind that came up 100 yards down the fairway just after the ball had been hit. Experienced meaningfulness also is high, despite the fact that the task itself is mostly devoid of cosmic significance ....

So, in golf, the three psychological states are present, and internal motivation among regular golfers is usually quite high. Indeed golfers exhibit an intensity of behavior that is rarely seen in the workplace: getting up before dawn to be first on the tee, feeling jubilation or despair all day depending on how well the morning round was played, sometimes destroying the tools and equipment of the game — not out of boredom or frustration with the work (as is sometimes seen in industrial settings) but rather from anger at oneself for not playing better. (pp. 74-75)

A final consideration in the model presented in Figure 2.1 is the moderating role played by individual differences in knowledge and skill, the need for growth, and "context" satisfaction. Thus, for example, autonomy probably wouldn't be motivating to a young gymnast just learning a routine; close supervision and repeated instruction from a coach would be preferable. On the other hand, an experienced gymnast might be highly motivated by this same situation. Similarly, some individuals have a strong need for growth — to face new challenges, learn, and develop. Consequently, variety in experiences and opportunities are motivating for them. Others prefer the status quo. Two figure skaters, for example, could differ completely in the degree to which they would like input into the development of their routine. The final moderator, "context" satisfaction, is an acknowledgement by Hackman and Oldham that the job characteristics listed in Figure 2.1 are relatively unimportant if the person is dissatisfied with some critical aspect of the job. In 1987, Paul Coffey, an All-Star defenseman and former winner of the Norris trophy as the league's outstanding defenseman refused to play for the Stanley Cup champion Edmonton Oilers until his contract was renegotiated. Coffey believed that he was underpaid relative to other defensemen of comparable or lesser ability in the NHL.

Implications for the Effectiveness of Sport Groups

Dimensional analysis is an attempt to identify specific criteria which serve to differentiate among various tasks or jobs. The dimensional analysis developed by Hackman and Oldham identified five task aspects which influence internal motivation, general satisfaction, performance effectiveness, and growth satisfaction. Although the model was developed for industrial and business settings, it also has a great deal of relevance for sport groups. For example, skill variety is essentially the same as skill development. And, a number of researchers (e.g., Alderman and Wood, 1976) have identified skill development as one of the two most powerful incentives for participation in sport and physical activity.

Similarly, autonomy, which contributes to feelings of responsibility and self determination, is the basis for intrinsic motivation — motivation which arises out of personal interest rather than because of rewards or inducements provided by others. As Garvie (1981) has emphasized, "*intrinsic reasons for participation ... are the central contingencies of sport continuance*" (p. 6). Providing autonomy enhances intrinsic motivation. This is not intended to suggest that athletes in team settings should be permitted to operate independently. What it does mean is that athletes should be given opportunities for input whenever possible. Halliwell (1978) provided a number of suggestions on how this might be done: consulting athletes if a code of behav-

ior is established, permitting athletes to direct some aspect of practice or training program, having athletes monitor the team's behavior code, getting athletes involved in the development of a goal setting program.

Task identity and task significance are also important. Sport groups, by their very nature, require committed role players — setters in volleyball, the sixth person on a basketball team, the checking line in hockey. Athletes, like workers in an office, have to feel that the role they are assigned is meaningful in order to feel satisfied and to carry it out with optimal motivation. The perception of meaningfulness can be enhanced or reduced depending on how the coach interprets the responsibility for the athlete and for the team.

Feedback is typically available in most sport situations. Ready access to video recorders can supplement the knowledge of results the athlete receives directly.

Typology of Tasks

Shaw defined a task typology as "a set of categories into which group tasks can be sorted, more or less exclusively" (p. 362). Task typologies are developed because it is assumed that behavior and performance may be better understood if the situation in which it occurs is better understood. The presence of the top four sprinters in the world almost guarantees the success of a relay team. However, the presence of the No. 1 and No. 2 ranked players in the world doesn't necessarily guarantee the success of a tennis doubles team. Why? The answer probably lies in the nature of the two tasks. Tennis requires much more coordination over a longer period of time than the sprint relay. Consider this within the frame-of-reference presented in Figure 1.1. In the sprint relay, the actual productivity of the group is almost solely a product of its potential productivity because coordinative activity (and, therefore, the opportunity for process losses) is minimal. Conversely, in tennis doubles, more coordination is necessary and, therefore, there is greater opportunity for process losses to have an impact. Thus, both the coordination and the resources are important.

Task Typologies Used in Sport Research

Many of our most durable stereotypes — and the research questions that they have stimulated — have had a basis in the implicit assumption that the task makes a difference. For example are team sport athletes more extroverted? Individual sport athletes more introverted? Are athletes in contact sports more aggressive? Athletes in racquet sports more cerebral?

In order to answer these and other questions, a large number of different typologies have been used in research in sport situations. For example, in a study of the personality traits of athletes, Schurr, Ashley, and Joy (1977) compared team and individual sport athletes. These two general categories were further subdivided into parallel sports (sports where direct aggression against an opponent isn't possible), and direct sports (sports where direct aggression against an opponent is possible). Finally, the individual parallel sport category was further subdivided into long duration events and short duration events. (The results of this study are discussed in Chapter 5.)

A slightly different typology was used by Chelladurai and Saleh (1978) to examine whether athletes in different types of sports have different preferences for coaching behaviors. Two main dimensions were considered: dependence and variability. Insofar as the dependence dimension is concerned, various sports were classified according to whether they are interdependent (interaction and coordination among individuals is essential for performance effectiveness) or independent. The dependent and independent sports were then categorized on the basis of the variability dimension — the degree to which the task requires the athlete to adjust to environmental changes. Low variability is present in closed tasks such as the high jump — the stimuli the athlete faces are stable and unchanging. High variability is present in open task such as rebounding in basketball — the athlete must respond to a constantly changing environment.

A sport activity typology, which was also based on the degree of task interdependence of athletes during performance, was used by Carron and Chelladurai (1979). They were interested in developing a framework to help explain why cohesion is beneficial to team performance in some instances but of little consequence in others. (This work is discussed in the last section of this chapter.)

In their typology, Carron and Chelladurai distinguished between independent sports, coactively dependent sports, reactively and proactively dependent sports, and interactively dependent sports. In independent sports, no coordinative activity is required for group success. Bowling, archery, and rifle shooting are examples. In coactively dependent sports such as rowing, individual group members carry out the same task simultaneously. Any coordination required comes from a common source. In reactive-proactive sports, individual activity occurs in sequential fashion. A baseball pitcher and catcher or a setter and spiker in volleyball are good examples. For proactive

Table 2.3 Steiner's task types.

Type of Task	Description	Sport Group Example
Additive	Group output results from the addition of individual outputs.	The team score for wrestling
Compensatory	Group output is the average of individual outputs	A group of officials judging gymnastics
Disjunctive (Eureka)	Group output is an "either-or" solution; one individual output is used	A group of players computing batting averages
Disjunctive (Noneureka)	Group output is judgmental and one individual output is used	A group of coaches selecting an All-Star team
Conjunctive (Unitary)	Group output is the result of the combined efforts of all and no division of labor is possible	A mountain climbing team
Conjunctive (Divisible with Matching)	Group output is the result of the combined efforts of all and a division of labor is possible	A volleyball team.

dependence, the individual who initiates the action must depend on others to complete the action. And, for reactive dependence, the individual who completes the action must depend on others to initiate it. Thus, the setter in volleyball is proactively dependent on the spiker while the spiker is reactively dependent on the setter. Finally, in interactively dependent tasks, group members are mutually dependent on each other for group effectiveness. The ball or puck is passed back and forth between group members.

Steiner's Task Typology

The most comprehensive typology of task has been advanced by Ivan Steiner (1972). When Steiner developed this typology, he felt that research in group dynamics was dying out due to an inability to make sense out of the widely differing results:

> By 1950 the empirical investigation of group productivity had outdistanced theory, and each new study tended to stand aloof from the others. Literature reviews had become encyclopedic listings of discoveries that appeared somehow to belong in the same abstract category, and one investigation was piled on top of another. In retrospect, it seems clear that this chaotic state of affairs reflected two notable deficiencies in the early work: investigators had tended to pay little attention to the demands that tasks impose upon groups, and they had often attempted to investigate productivity without examining the processes by which groups become productive. In the absence of evidence concerning these two important matters, neither programmatic research nor integrative theory was very feasible. (pp. vii-viii)

The typology of tasks developed by Steiner is based on three main questions. The first concerns whether the task is *divisible* — can it be broken down in subunits — or *unitary* — no subtasks are present. A sprint relay team performs a divisible task. There is the lead-off runner, the fourth or anchor runner, and the second and third runners. On the other hand, a rowing team carries out a unitary task; all the rowers perform the same task at the same time.

The second question concerns whether the group product is measured by *qualitative* or *quantitative* standards. Figure skating and gymnastics are sports in which quality is the most important criterion for judging performance effectiveness. On the other hand, weightlifting and track and field are sports in which performance effectiveness is measured through quantitative standards. How much? How fast? How high?

The third question concerns *how the individual inputs are combined* to yield the group's product. Six ways are possible — each of which corresponds to a specific task-type identified by Steiner. These are summarized in Table 2.3.

When the group output is determined by summing the individual outputs, the task is referred to as *additive*. This is the case when team scores are obtained at wrestling, gymnastic, and track and field meets. A specific number of points is given for each individual performance. These points are then summed to determine a team total.

In the case of *compensatory tasks*, the group product is obtained from the average of the individual member inputs. This is what occurs when gymnastics events, diving competitions, and figure skating competitions are judged. The scores of the various judges are pooled and an average value is obtained — sometimes after eliminating the highest and lowest value. In some tasks carried out by groups, a problem must be solved and only one solution is taken from all the possibilities raised by group members. The answer is either right or wrong. This type of task is referred to as *eureka disjunctive*. A group of baseball players calculating the batting averages of individual team members is one example. All the players may start to calculate the average of any single player. But, when one player has the solution, the group's task is completed.

In *noneureka disjunctive tasks*, a judgmental problem must be solved by the group. Again, only one solution is adopted by the group from all of the possibilities raised by group members. In this case, consensus within the group is necessary because any potential solution might be debated. This is the type of task faced by a panel of national team coaches when they try to select a final roster for international competition. The merits and limitations of the different athletes must be evaluated in terms of the overall good of the team. Some decisions are obvious such as the inclusion of a Maradonna on Argentina's national soccer team or a Gretzky on Canada's national hockey team. However, as the team roster comes close to being completed, the decisions about who should be included and who should be left out become more difficult.

Unitary conjunctive tasks are not very prevalent in sport. All members of the group must complete the task or contribute to the group's product in order for the group to finish. Also, no matching of individuals to roles is possible. Consequently, the group is only as strong as its weakest member. An example which is sometimes used is mountain climbing; every member of the team must successfully complete the climb. A poor climber with inadequate technique or poor conditioning will hold the group back.

In the case of *conjunctive tasks divisible with matching*, all members must complete the task in order for the group to be successful. However, a division of labor is possible — individuals can be matched to the tasks which best match their skills. This is more typical in sport situations. Athletes may be designated as setters and spikers in volleyball, a specific blocking scheme may be used in football to capitalize on individual talents or to compensate for lack of talent, and/or a basketball offense may be developed around the exceptional skills of one or two players.

Implications for the Effectiveness of Sport Groups

There are two major advantages inherent in any task typology. One of these is that a typology helps to identify those factors within a situation which are most important. In Chapter 1, it was pointed out that group productivity is a function of the positive impact of the resources available in the group membership and the negative impact of the losses which occur due to faulty group processes (see Figure 1.1 again). Steiner's task typology permits some reasonable assumptions about the emphasis that should be placed on each of these components in different situations.

As one example, the group's resources — the talents, skills, and abilities of individual group members — are more important than the group processes in unitary disjunctive tasks than they are in compensatory tasks. Having one very weak member on a mountain climbing expedition (a unitary disjunctive task) could destroy the group. On the other hand, having one very weak official at a diving competition (a compensatory task) might not have a major impact on the overall quality of the officiating.

A second major advantage inherent in any typology is that it helps to clarify when comparisons across tasks, sports, or situations are useful. Can a volleyball coach benefit from the general approaches used by a rowing coach to develop an effective team? Or, are their sports so different that the relative importance placed on group resources and/or group processes are completely different?

One example of where knowledge of the task provides insight into the relative importance which

should be attached to group processes was provided by Carron and Chelladurai (1979). In a discussion on the role of cohesion in sport, they noted that in some instances group cohesion seems to be beneficial to performance; in others, it's of little consequence. In an attempt to reconcile these contradictory findings, Carron and Chelladurai began by categorizing sports according to the type of task interdependence present during competition. Their typology (which was presented earlier) included a distinction between independent sports, coactively dependent sports, reactively-proactively dependent sports, and interactively dependent sports.

They also utilized a typology for coordination which was originally developed by Thompson (1967). Thompson proposed that coordination in groups can be achieved in three ways: by standardization, by planning, and by mutual adjustment. In coordination by *standardization*, a set of fixed rules, schedules, or routines is developed prior to competition. These are practiced repeatedly until every group member becomes familiar with them. Coordination by standardization is used for team gymnastics, figure skating pairs, rowing crews, and synchronized swimming teams. Prior to competition, team members are completely familiar with what is expected.

In the case of coordination by *planning*, various plans for action are established and practiced repeatedly prior to competition. This is the approach taken when coaches lay out different formations and strategies for the corner kick in soccer, the powerplay in hockey, the double play in baseball. Because situations are dynamic and because the opposition adjusts when the same plan is used every time, a number of contingencies are developed. These various contingencies serve as guidelines for the athletes during competition.

Finally, coordination by *mutual adjustment* occurs in those instances in sport where standardization and preplanning aren't possible. For example, the general strategies that might be effective in a 2-on-1 or 3-on-1 break in basketball can be discussed and practiced. But, the situations in a game are almost never the same as they are in practice. Therefore, mutual adjustments must be made by the athletes.

Carron and Chelladurai suggested that cohesion contributes to group performance by improving group interaction and coordination in those instances where mutual adjustment is essential. In independent tasks such as bowling, archery, or rifle shooting, almost no coordinative activity is necessary. In independent sports, any coordination necessary is achieved by standardization (see Figure 2.2). Thus, cohesion is

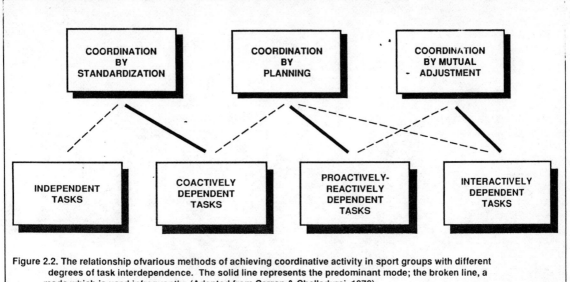

Figure 2.2. The relationship of various methods of achieving coordinative activity in sport groups with different degrees of task interdependence. The solid line represents the predominant mode; the broken line, a mode which is used infrequently. (Adapted from Carron & Chelladurai, 1979)

relatively unimportant for group performance because the opportunities for process losses due to faulty task coordination are almost nonexistent.

In coactively dependent sports such as rowing and synchronized swimming, the most prevalent method of achieving coordination is standardization. Also, some planning is necessary to prepare for emergency situations which arise during competition. Therefore, again group cohesion is not a critical factor group success.

In reactively-proactively dependent sports such as baseball, coordination can be achieved by planning and mutual adjustment. However, the most dominant method is planning. Thus, again, cohesion is not critical for group success.

Finally, in interactively interdependent sports such as basketball, volleyball, soccer, hockey, some coordination can be achieved by planning. But, the dynamic nature of these sports means that coordination by mutual adjustment is essential. Thus, group cohesion becomes an important factor in the reduction of process losses through poor coordination and, therefore, is important for team success.

3 Group Size

The quote by James Michener which introduces this chapter clearly highlights one of the problems associated with a large group size. Increasing the number of freshmen recruited and retained on the roster does increase the probability that the necessary resources for team effectiveness are available (and are not available to a competitor). However, in the situation outlined by James Michener in the above quote, not all of the recruited

> Each year he would recruit some ninety freshmen, even though he knew that he would ultimately find places for no more than sixteen or seventeen. He signed up the extras, he told his associates, "so that Woody and Bear and Ara can't get their hands on them". (Michener, 1976, p. 177)

Steiner also presented a conceptual framework for considering group size.

Steiner's Framework

Steiner's hypotheses related to the interrelationship between group size and the group's potential productivity and efficiency are presented in Figure 3.1. It is evident that with an increase in group

freshman could be retained on the team roster. And, of those who were retained, only a limited number would have the opportunity to eventually compete. Thus, one pertinent question concerning group size is "What is the optimal number of extra competitors to retain for the team?"

In social psychology, questions about group size had their origin in questions about the optimal size of problem-solving groups and work crews. If a problem must be solved, it is beneficial to know whether one individual can do the job as well as or better than two. If two people are better than one, what about three, four, five ..? At what point is one more "too many"? Historically, there has been considerable research devoted to these questions. However, the results of that research fell into what Ivan Steiner (1972) referred to as a "chaotic state of affairs" (p.xiii). In an attempt to provide a frame of reference and to put some order into the chaos, Steiner developed the task typology which was outlined in Chapter 2. He also considered questions about group size in light of his formula for group effectiveness which was presented in Figure 1.1; namely that Actual Productivity is equal to Potential Productivity minus the Losses Due to Faulty Group Processes.

size, the potential productivity (the amount of resources available) of the group increases. But, this occurs at a decelerating rate. That is, when the number of group members increases, the resources that are available also increases — but only to a point. Eventually, as group size continues to increase, the resources available to the group plateau. A hockey coach, for example, might normally keep 18 players on the team's roster — three regular forward lines, three regular defense pairs, two goaltenders, and one role player. However, the coach might conclude that this contingent of players failed to provide the team with sufficient flexibility to make adjustments for special situations. Consequently, he or she might add additional players — a penalty killing unit, offensive specialists, an extra goaltender ...... At some point all of the players that could possibly be used would be available. There would be no purpose in continually adding more players (resources) because a plateau would be reached.

As the group size increases, it also becomes more difficult for the coach to coordinate practices, to use all the players in games, to provide instruction to

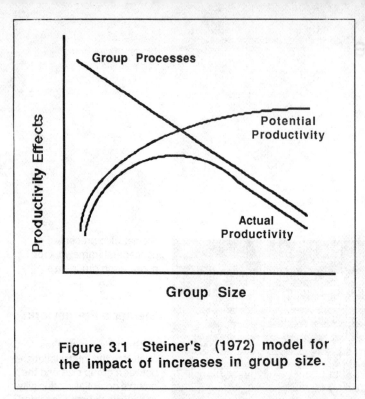

Figure 3.1 Steiner's (1972) model for the impact of increases in group size.

The relationship between group productivity and relative individual productivity is the result of two factors. First, increases in group size lead to increases in the problems associated with coordinating the efforts of a group of people. Second, increases in group size also lead to a decrease in personal accountability and a decline in personal motivation. This phenomenon which is referred to as *social loafing* is discussed later in the chapter.

The Group Task

As indicated above, the questions about group size had their origin in problem solving groups and work crews. Is one individual as effective as two? Are two people as effective as three? And so on. The answer to the question "what number is best?" is "it depends on the group task". On some tasks, greater size is better; on others, one good individual is more effective than a group. The work by Ivan Steiner on a taxonomy of tasks which was discussed in Chapter 2 (see Table 2.3 again) went a long way toward shedding light on the question of when and why groups are more or less effective than one individual operating independently. Table 3.1. presents a summary of the relationship of individual resources to group productivity using Steiner's taxonomy as a frame of reference.

As the summary in Table 3.1 illustrates, it is possible that on some tasks an increase in group size may not necessarily lead to an increase in group effectiveness. This is the case in what has been referred to as an *eureka disjunctive task*. These are tasks in which the solution to the problem is usually yes-no or either-or. A group of individuals sitting down to calculate individual batting averages is an excellent example. When one competent individual has calculated the correct solution, it is readily apparent to the group. Therefore, that solution is also readily assumed as the group's solution. Because the most successful individual's score is adopted by the group, one intelligent, competent member is at least as effective as a group. In fact, one person may even be more effective than a group. A single person can work more quickly and with less interference because there is no need to communicate strategies and discuss progress. And, if the group possesses only mediocre mathematicians and no calculators, its solution might not be correct.

all of the players in practices, and to communicate effectively with everyone. It would also become more difficult for each player to interact with every other player. As a result, with increases in resources there is also a decrease in process efficiency (see Figure 3.1 again).

Not surprisingly, increased size influences the absolute output of the group and the relative output of each individual group member. Figure 3.1 illustrates this effect. Steiner proposed that as group size continues to increase, the absolute productivity of the group increases initially and then shows a decrease. Eventually, the group becomes so large that it cannot effectively carry out its task. The relative productivity of each individual member also declines systematically with increases in group size. An example which illustrates this relationship is a volleyball team. If twelve players were kept on the roster, the team would be able to scrimmage effectively, run specialized drills for setters and spikers, and so on. The team would be better off than if only six players were retained on the roster. In a twelve-person roster, however, each individual player would have less opportunity to spike, set, or work with the coach than in a six-person roster. The relative productivity of each individual would decrease.

Table 3.1 The impact of the group's size and task on its productivity.

Type of Task	Impact of Group Size	Sport Group Example
Additive	Increases in group size lead to increases in the team's effectiveness	The team score for wrestling
Compensatory	Increases in group size lead to increases in the team's effectiveness	A group of officials judging gymnastics
Disjunctive (Eureka)	One competent individual is sufficient; increases in group size do not always increase	A group of players computing batting averages
Disjunctive (Noneureka)	One competent individual may be sufficient but creases in group size produce a broader perspective which increases group efectiveness	A group of coaches selecting an All-Star team
Conjunctive (Unitary)	Increases in group size lead to decreases in group effectiveness	A mountain climbing team
Conjunctive (Divisible with Matching)	Increases in group size lead to increased group effectiveness if the members are matched to the appropriate subtasks	A volleyball team.

either-or or yes-no. The questions of who is the best player in the National Basketball Association would be one example. Also the question of which athletes should be chosen for a World Cup Soccer team is another example. These problem solving situations are referred to as *noneureka disjunctive tasks*. A variety of approaches to the problem and/or solutions are possible. In noneureka disjunctive tasks, increases in group size lead to increases in resources and a broader perspective. Thus, a large group should be more effective than a small group or single individual. However, a group may not be as effective as one highly competent person because one person working alone doesn't need to convince, justify, explain, or achieve consensus. So, using a group rather than one competent individual might be a disadvantage.

So, even if the individual and the group arrived at the same solution, the individual would be more efficient in terms of time.

Another situation in which increases in group size may be detrimental to group effectiveness is with a *unitary conjunctive tasks.* The group is only as strong as its weakest member. All members contribute to the group product and/or must complete the task in order for the group to finish. Mountain climbing teams are an example. In the case of unitary conjunctive tasks, the group's performance will match the performance of the weakest member — if one person can't complete the task, the group doesn't complete the task.

There are some problems in which an increase in group size may or may not be beneficial — depending on the circumstance. This is the case with problems that are not philosophical in nature -- the solution is not

There are also instances where increases in group size always lead to increased group effectiveness. One instance where this would be the case is in those tasks Steiner described as *additive* — the group score is arrived at by summing the scores of the individual members (see Table 3.1 again). A single rower, for example, can never cover the same distance in the same time as a pair of rowers; the total number of problems solved by a group will always be greater than the number solved by one individual.

Another instance where this is the case is *compensatory tasks.* The group's performance is achieved by averaging the results from individual group members; e.g., judging in diving or gymnastics events. One highly competent individual may be more accurate than the group but, generally, the group as a whole outperforms a substantial number of its members.

A third instance in which increases in group size lead to increases in group effectiveness is with *divisible conjunctive task.* Most sport teams fall under this category. Specialization is required and individuals must carry out specific group roles; e.g., setter and spiker in volleyball, pitcher and catcher in baseball. In this case, a larger group is much more effective providing that (a) the individuals can be matched to the appropriate tasks and (b) the group is not too large.

Group Performance

One of the earliest reported studies on the impact of group size on group performance was the classic Ringelmann research. "Ringelmann's interest lay in determining the relative efficiency of work furnished by horses, oxen, men, and machines in various agricultural applications ... In each case, his concern seems to have been the following: Which machine, method, or animal type is most efficient in actual use?" (cited in Kravitz & Martin, 1986, p. 937). Using a variety of additive tasks, Ringelmann compared the performance of individuals against that of groups of varying sizes. His results are summarized in Table 3.2.

A coordination link represents the interaction between two people. A problem that arises with increasing group size is that it becomes increasingly difficult for each individual to interact with every other individual — either in a task or social context. If one person is operating alone, there is no interaction, no need to work in a coordinated fashion, or to be concerned with the feelings of someone else — there are no coordination links. As the group increases in size, the number of coordination links increases drastically. The number of possible two-person links in groups of varying size can be determined with the following formula:

$$\text{No. of Coordination Links} = \frac{N^2 - N}{2}$$

In a 2-person group, there is one link, in 3-person groups, there are 3 links, and in 8-person groups, there are 28 coordination links. Thus, in comparison to a 2-person group, an 8-person group has 4 times the resources to draw upon but 28 times as many links to coordinate.

Using individual productivity as a baseline, Ringelmann computed group efficiency. Assuming that one person worked at 100% efficiency, then the individuals in the 2-person groups worked at 93% of their potential, the individuals in the 3-person groups at 85% of their potential, the individuals in 4-person groups, at 77%, and the individuals in the 8-person groups at 49% of their potential. There was an increasing loss of efficiency with increasing group size.

The decrease in relative individual productivity with increasing group size is probably the result of two factors. One of these is that it is difficult to coordinate the efforts of larger groups of people. The second is that it is more difficult to motivate individuals when personal accountability is reduced. In an attempt to determine whether Ringelmann's results could be reproduced and to determine which of these two factors was more important, Allan Ingham, George Levinger, James Graves, & Vaughn Peckham replicated the Ringelmann study in 1974.

In two different studies, subjects were tested alone and in groups of 2, 3, 4, 5, and 6 people. In the first study, Ingham and his colleagues

Table 3.2 A summary of Ringelmann's reseasrch on the impact of group size on group productivity (Adapted from Kravitz & Martin, 1986 and Steiner, 1972)

No of Participants	No. of Coordination Links	Relative Performance Per Worker	Group Productivity	Process Losses
1	0	1.00	-----	-----
2	1	.93	1.86	.14
3	3	.85	2.55	.45
4	6	.77	3.08	.92
5	10	.70	3.50	1.50
6	15	.63	3.78	2.22
7	21	.56	3.92	3.08
8	28	.49	3.92	4.08

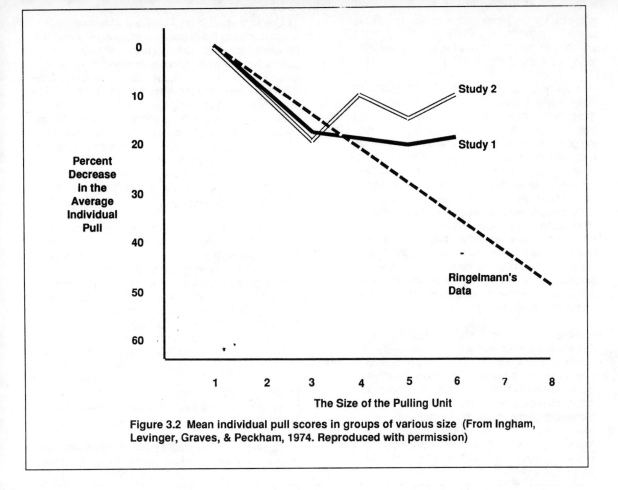

Figure 3.2 Mean individual pull scores in groups of various size (From Ingham, Levinger, Graves, & Peckham, 1974. Reproduced with permission)

found results similar to those reported by Ringelmann for groups up to the size of three people (see Figure 3.2). That is, if a single individual can be considered to be working at 100%, the individuals in two person groups worked at 91%; the individuals in three person groups, at 82%.

The purpose of the second Ingham et al. study was to determine the relative contribution of motivation and coordination to the process losses which occur with increasing group size. Again, subjects were tested alone and in groups of 2, 3, 4, 5, and 6 people. However, in every instance, only one subject was actually tested. In the conditions where 2, 3, 4, 5, and 6 people were involved, the balance of the group was made up of confederates of the experimenters. The subject was placed in the front of the line and the confederates assumed positions behind. All the appropriate sounds of effort were made by the confederates but, in reality, the subject pulled alone.

As Figure 3.2 shows, the results of Study 2 were almost identical to those found in Study 1. That is, there was a decline in relative individual productivity in groups up to the size of three people and then a plateau occurred. More importantly, these results showed that coordination was not the most important factor in the process losses. The decline in relative individual performance was primarily the result of a loss in motivation. Presumably, with groups of increasing size, there is a decreasing sense of personal accountability and, therefore, a decrease in motivation.

In any discussion of the group size - group performance relationship, it is also necessary to take into account not only the group task but the group goal. There are some sport situations in which the group goal is quantity or speed — doing more and/or doing it faster is better. This is the case with a relay race. This type of goal has been referred to as *maximizing*. There are other situations in which accuracy and/or precision are the group goal — greater quality is better. Synchronized swimming or team gymnastics are an example. This type of goal has been referred to as *optimizing* (Steiner, 1972).

A study by Frank and Anderson (1971) illustrates how the group goal, group size, and the nature of the group task all interact in a unique manner. They found that on the one hand, when the group had a maximizing goal (i.e., more is better) and a disjunctive task (i.e., the group product is equal to that of the best group member), increasing the group size enhanced the group's productivity. This is a result which seems quite logical. As Table 2.1 shows, if a group of people were brought together to calculate batting averages for all the players in a league, the more people present, the faster the task would be completed. The presence of more good mathematicians would have a positive impact on the group's ability to complete the task accurately. And, increasing the group size would increase the likelihood that a good person or good people would be present.

On the other hand, Frank and Anderson also found that when the group had a maximizing goal in a conjunctive task (i.e., a task in which the group product is equal to that of the worst member), increasing the group size led to a decrement in group performance. Again, this result seems reasonable. In mountain climbing (which is a conjunctive task), one weak member can detract from a team's effectiveness. Increasing the size of a climbing team increases the probability that one or more poor climbers will be added to the team.

One final result in the Frank and Anderson study which highlights the importance of taking into account the group task, size, and goal is related to member satisfaction. Frank and Anderson reported that when group size was increased, the subjects working on the disjunctive tasks found the situation more pleasant; the subjects working on the conjunctive tasks found it more unpleasant. When the addition of individuals can contribute to group effectiveness (which is the case with disjunctive tasks), an increased number is viewed positively by the group in general. But, when the addition of new members represents a potential liability (which is the case in conjunctive tasks), their addition is viewed negatively.

There is also evidence that both the nature and amount of cohesiveness that develop are influenced by the group's size. In a study which used a divisible conjunctive task, basketball, Widmeyer, Brawley, and Carron (1988) manipulated the number of members on teams and examined the subsequent effects of this on task and social cohesion and performance. Participants in a 3 on 3 recreational basketball league were initially matched on ability and then formed into teams consisting of either three, six, or nine members. The results revealed that task cohesion was greatest in the 3-person teams and lowest in the 9-person teams. On the other hand, the 6-person groups had the highest social cohesion and also were the most successful (see Figure 3.3),

Apparently, in the smallest teams it was easiest to develop consensus and commitment around common

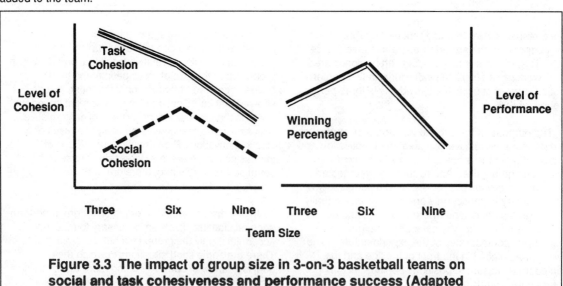

Figure 3.3 The impact of group size in 3-on-3 basketball teams on social and task cohesiveness and performance success (Adapted from Widmeyer, Brawley, & Carron, 1988)

group goals and objectives. But, with no substitutes available, there was not enough opportunity to develop social cohesiveness or to compete successfully against the 6-person groups. The largest groups, on the other hand, had too many resources available which hindered the development of their task cohesion, social cohesion, and their ability to compete effectively. The curve for performance success in Figure 3.3 is very similar to the hypothesized curve for productivity proposed by Steiner and illustrated in Figure 3.1.

Social Loafing

The reduction in individual effort when people work in groups versus when they work alone has been referred to by Bibb Latane' and his colleagues as *social loafing* (Harkins, Latane',

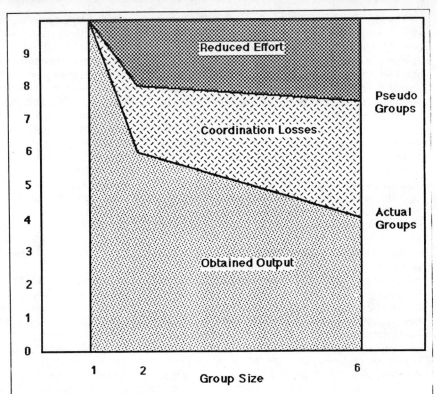

Figure 3.4 Social loafing and coordination losses in groups.(From Latane', B. Williams, K. & Harkins, S. Many hands make light the work: The causes and consequences of social loafing. *Journal of Personality and Social Psychology* 1979, *37,* 822. Copyright 1987 by the American Psychological Association. Adapted with permission.)

& Williams, 1980; Latane', 1981; Latane', Williams, & Harkins, 1979; Williams, Harkins, & Latane', 1981). As they also pointed out, the phenomenon of social loafing seems to contradict many popular stereotypes. One popular stereotype is, of course, that many hands make the work lighter. Another stereotype which is held in sport is that a sense of solidarity and commitment to the team leads athletes to put in a special effort in order to not let teammates down. Social loafing also contradicts social psychological theory. It has been repeatedly documented that when others are present — either as spectators or as coactors — individual performance in simple, well learned tasks will improve. Thus, the presence of others could be expected to enhance, not diminish individual performance.

Since social loafing does appear to contradict previous research and common assumptions, it also raises a number of questions. First, how generalizable is the phenomenon? Social loafing has been demonstrated in the laboratory by Ingham and his colleagues

with the task of rope pulling. Does it occur in other tasks? And, under other conditions? Second, what about real teams competing in actual sport situations? Does social loafing occur? Third, what are the factors which contribute to social loafing? Can social loafing be reduced?

Generalizability of Social Loafing. Social loafing has been observed in other laboratory tasks by Latane' and his colleagues. For example, in one study, Latane' et al. (1979, Experiment 2) had subjects produce as much sound as possible by shouting. The noise level produced was assessed in dynes per cm^2 under three conditions: alone, in actual groups of two and six people, and in pseudogroups of two and six people. The subjects wore blindfolds and headsets so that they couldn't hear or see each other. In the pseudogroup condition, the subjects believed that they were shouting in a group but they were actually recorded alone.

The results are presented in Figure 3.4. The line along the top indicates the potential productivity — the potential noise level based on individual capability. The area at the bottom of the figure represents the obtained output from individuals in actual groups. Finally, the area at the top of Figure 3.4, is the output obtained in the pseudogroups — the effort exerted by individuals when they thought they were performing in a group but were actually alone. This represents the amount of loss due to social loafing. In a two-person group, individuals shouted at 82% of their potential; in a six-person group, at 74%. On the basis of these results as well as others with different tasks, there is no doubt that the phenomenon of social loafing is generalizable across a variety of group tasks (e.g., Petty, Harkins, & Williams, 1980)

Social Loafing in Sport Teams. At first glance, it seems possible that social loafing might not occur in sport teams. The strong commitment that individuals have made to their team, the experiences and sacrifices that they have shared, and the significant, important goals that they hold in common might help to keep motivation at a high level. And, working with strangers on a lab task undoubtedly influences coordination and motivation. Ingham et al. (1974) raised this point in the discussion of their results with the tug-of-war task:

Since the groups used in our experiments were quasi-groups, incoordination problems would probably be greater than in established groups who are used to working together. One might ask whether the discrepancy between actual and potential productivity would be reduced if our subjects had been team members on the same rowing crews. (p. 383)

In an effort to test this possibility, Ingham et al. examined the performance times of rowing crews from Olympic Games held in the period 1952 to 1964. They found that the coxed fours were only 13% faster than the coxed pairs and that the eights were only 23% faster than the pairs. Although, there are differences in boat size, water displacement, and so on, it must be assumed that social loafing occurs in real sport teams in actual competitive situations.

Sharon Huddleston, Susann Doody, and Karen Ruder (1985) also found evidence of social loafing in a sprint relay. After female athletes were timed running a 55-yard sprint alone, they were formed into a 4-person team for a shuttle relay. One half of the groups were provide with information about the phenomenon of social loafing under the assumption that this insight might help to alleviate the problem. It had no effect. Performance times over the 55-yard distance were faster when the athletes ran alone than when they ran in teams.

Charles Hardy and Bibb Latane' (1988) reasoned that social loafing effects "may be restricted to tasks that are seen as unimportant, meaningless, or lacking in intrinsic motivation, performed by relative strangers in noncompetitive situations" (p. 109). In order to examine this possibility, they tested high school girls attending a cheerleading camp. The cheerleaders were required to don earphones and blindfolds (to control sensory feedback) and were then tested alone or in pseudopairs. In the pseudopairs situation, the cheerleader was led to believe she was performing with a partner but she was actually alone. The results showed that social loafing was present; the cheerleaders produced only 94% as much noise when they were in pairs as they did when they performed alone.

Factors Contributing to Social Loafing. When it became evident that social loafing occurs across a number of group tasks, interest was generated in trying to pinpoint some of the causes. A number of possibilities were raised. These are summarized in Table 3.3. Two tested by Harkins Latane' and Williams (1980) were the *allocational strategy* and the *minimizing strategy*. With the allocational strategy, it is assumed that individuals are motivated to work as hard as possible overall. But, their best effort is saved for those times when they perform alone because the individual trials are the most beneficial personally. If this is the case, individual swimmers who only swim on relay teams (i.e., they don't swim any individual events) could be expected to put out as much effort as swimmers who swim individual events only. All personal effort could be allocated to the single event.

With the minimizing strategy, it is assumed that individuals are motivated to get by with the least amount of effort possible. Working in a group reduces identifiability and accountability, and as a consequence, personal motivation is diminished.

As was the case in studies discussed above, the Harkins et al. subjects wore headsets and blindfolds. A hand clapping tasks was used and they were tested alone or in pseudogroups of two people. There was no support for the supposition that social loafing results from an allocation of effort. The authors concluded that the results were "easily explained by minimizing strategy, where participants are motivated to work only as hard as necessary to gain credit for a good performance or to avoid blame for a bad one" (Harkins et al., 1980, p. 263-264).

Table 3.3 Explanations advanced to account for motivation losses in groups (Adapted from Harkins, Latane', & Williams, 1980 and Orbell & Dawes (1981)

Factor	Explanation
Allocation Strategy	Individual members are motivated to work hard but their best effort is reserved for when they work alone because it is most beneficial.
Minimizing Strategy	Individual members are motivated to get by with as little effort as possible in groups because there is minimal personal accountability
Free Rider Effect	Individual members reduce their personal efforts because they feel they are dispensable
Sucker Effect	Individual members reduce their personal efforts because they do not want to provide a free ride to other less productive group members

Another explanation (see Table 3.3) offered to account for the motivation losses which occur in groups is the *free rider effect* (Orbell & Dawes, 1981). The free-rider effect occurs when individual members reduce their personal efforts because they view themselves as dispensable. With the addition of more group members (resources), there is an increase in the number of competent individuals available in the group. Consequently, group members conclude that someone else is better qualified or more capable of doing the job. Consequently, they reduce their own efforts.

The free-rider effect was observed by Kerr and Bruun (1983) in a series of experiments using conjunctive (the worst score in the group defines the group's performance) and disjunctive tasks (the best score in the group defines the group's performance). The high ability subjects worked harder in the disjunctive tasks and showed a free-rider effect in the conjunctive tasks. Conversely, the low ability subjects worked harder in the conjunctive tasks and showed a free-rider effect in the disjunctive tasks. It was also found that member motivation decreased with increasing group size even when individual contributions could be identified.

The final explanation presented in Table 3.3 is the

sucker effect (Orbell & Dawes, 1981) In this case, individual members reduce their personal efforts in a group endeavor because they don't want to "play the sucker" and provide a free ride for less productive group members. The individual doesn't want others to profit from his or her contribution without making a contribution themselves.

Evidence that the sucker effect does operate in groups was provided by Norbert Kerr (1983). He had subjects work alone or in pairs on a disjunctive task (the best of the two individual scores is the group score). Feedback on performance was manipulated so that one group of subjects believed that they were working with a person of high ability who was failing. Their performance decreased substantially relative to when they worked alone. Apparently, the low ability subjects weren't prepared to be a sucker and shoulder the load for a free-riding high ability workmates.

Kerr also found evidence for the free-rider effect. The subjects in another group were led to believe that they were working with a person of high ability who was succeeding. Again, their performance decreased substantially relative to when they worked alone. In this case, the low ability subjects were prepared to take a free ride on the efforts of their high ability workmates.

In both instances where subjects worked with a partner of high ability (able/fails and able/succeeds), they reduced their own efforts. Interesting, Kerr also found that no drop in individual performance occurred when the subjects were led to believe they were working with a person of low ability who was failing.

What all of the above research shows is that individuals lose motivation when they work in groups. These losses are greatest when the group members perceive that their contributions are either (1) not identifiable, (2) dispensable, or (3) in disproportion to the contributions of other group members. When individual input to the group product can be monitored directly, social loafing is reduced. When an individual's input is perceived to be essential to the group's performance, social loafing is reduced. And, finally, when an individual's input is considered to be appropriate relative to the input of other group members, social loafing is reduced.

Member Adherence

In fitness classes, the size of the group can influence the adherence and attendance of individual members. This was illustrated in a study by Carron, Brawley, and Widmeyer (1988) when they monitored 47 fitness classes varying in size from 5 to 46 members. A drop out was defined as any individual who missed two consecutive weeks (six classes) in the 10-week session. After subdividing the classes into four categories — small (5 to 17 members), medium (18 to 26 members), moderately large (27 to 31 members), and large (32 to 46 members) — Carron et al. analyzed two measures of attendance. One of these was adherence — the percentage of individuals who did not drop out of the class during the 10-week session. The second was attendance — the percentage classes attended by those individuals who did not drop out. As Figure 3.5 shows, a curvilinear relationship was present. Both adherence and attendance were highest in the smallest and largest classes; they decreased in the medium and moderately large classes.

Carron et al. suggested that one possible reason for their results was that larger and smaller classes provide participants with social advantages not available in medium-sized groups. The largest classes represent the greatest opportunity to meet attractive and interesting others; the smallest classes represent the greatest opportunity for familiarity. As a result, social attractiveness of the classes might have influ-

enced adherence and attendance. Another possible reason suggested was that the instructor's role is clearest for both the instructor and the participant in the largest and smallest classes. In large classes, an approach consisting of group reinforcement is expected by members and provided by the instructor; in small classes, an individual reinforcement approach is expected by members and provided by the instructor. As a result, dissatisfaction with the instructional mode used by the instructor might have influenced adherence and attendance in the moderate size classes.

Group Morale

Research in management science, sociology, and psychology has consistently shown that the size of the group influences social psychological aspects of group life. On the basis of his review, Neil Widmeyer (1971) concluded that increases in group size have a major impact on individual satisfaction and group morale (see Table 3.4). For example, one outcome obviously associated with an increase in group size is reduced individual participation and feelings of responsibility. On a volleyball team with six members, the participation of the individual athletes at practices and games would be 100 percent. As the size of the roster increases, the absolute participation and feeling of responsibility for the group's welfare would decrease in

each athlete. Initially, this might be viewed favorably since each individual would have some opportunity for a rest and the burden placed on any one person would be reduced. But, with further increases in group size and the resultant decrease in individual participation and responsibility, satisfaction and group morale would decrease.

Increases in group size and the resulting decrease in individual participation are also associated with a number of other factors. For instance, it is more difficult to give each individual personal attention and involve them in the social activities of the group. Also, opportunities for personal instruction are reduced — as anyone who has been in large physical education classes can testify. Instruction becomes more group-oriented. Not surprisingly, the amount of reinforcement and rewards provided to each individual also decreases. Each of these contributes to reduced individual satisfaction and

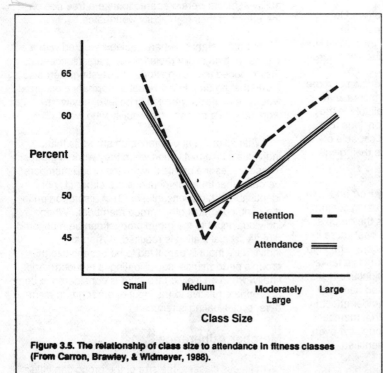

Figure 3.5. The relationship of class size to attendance in fitness classes (From Carron, Brawley, & Widmeyer, 1988).

Table 3.4 The impact of group size on member satisfaction and group morale (Adapted from Widmeyer, 1971)

Factor	Impact of Group Size on the Factor	Individual Satisfaction and Group Morale
Member Participation	Decreases with an increase in group size	Decreases with a decrease in participation
Density and Crowding	Increases with an increase in group size	Decreases with an increase in density and crowding
Feelings of Responsibility	Decreases with an increase in group size	Decreases with a decrease in in feelings of responsibility
Attention Provided	Decreases with an increase in group size	Decreases with an increase in attention provided
Instruction Provided	Decreases with an increase in group size	Decreases with a decrease in in instruction
Reinforcement Provided	Decreases with an increase in group size	Decreases with a decrease in in reinforcement
Opportunities to Meet Attractive and Interesting Others	Increases with an increase in group size	Increases with an opportunity to meet attractive and interesting others
Feelings of Personal Threat & Inhibition	Increases with an increase in group size	Decreases with an increase in feelings of personal threat & inhibition
Communication	Decreases with an increase in group size	Decreases with a decrease in in comunication
Leadership	Participation in leadership decreases	Decreases with a decrease in in participation

anxiety occur. And, this contributes to reduced individual satisfaction and lower group morale.

One of the few positive outcomes of an increase in group size is that there is also an increase in opportunities available to meet other people who are perceived to be interesting and attractive. In a dyad — a pairs team in figure skating or rowing, for example — there is only one other person available in the group for friendship and communication. If the two members of group don't like each other, the group offers little in the way of social satisfaction. As the group increases in size, the number of potential friends who are available also increases.

As groups become larger, there is also a necessity for leadership to become more centralized and autocratic. The coach of a soccer team with 25 members on its roster is more likely to to be autocratic and authoritarian than the coach of a soccer team with 12 members. Individual input into decision making is not only more difficult to coordinate in larger groups, it is less efficient to solicit it. The group can experience "paralysis of analysis" if an overly democratic approach is used.

lower group morale.

As Table 3.4 also shows, if the sport group becomes excessively large, increased density and feelings of crowding result. And, feelings of anxiety and inhibition also occur. These two outcomes can easily be illustrated with an exercise class which grows from 30 to 50 people or a badminton team which adds six members to its roster. The amount of space available for workouts/practices is reduced. Consequently, it's difficult for the individual participant to relax and focus solely on the activity. The participants are constantly aware of the presence of others and the possibility of contact or collision. Performance in dense, crowded situations is inhibited and feelings of

The impact of group size on the social psychological aspects of group involvement was also discussed by Paul Hare (1981). He suggested that four conditions must be present for any group to be successful:

1. The group members must share a common identity and have a commitment to the group;

2. The group members must have the necessary skills and resources;

3. Group norms and roles must be clearly established and a feeling of solidarity must be present; and,

4. Group leadership and control must be adequate.

According to Hare, each of these is influenced by a change in group size. For example, as groups increase in size, the group members' identification with the group and their commitment to its values are reduced. More skills and resources are present but the contribution of each individual group member is reduced. Group norms and individual roles must be more clearly defined and, as a result, flexibility is reduced. It is also more difficult to maintain the solidarity of the group. Finally, leadership becomes more centralized and authoritarian; individual involvement in decision making is reduced.

From a social psychological perspective, there are some positive benefits which result from an increase in group size. However, the overall evidence supports a conclusion that members of larger groups are less satisfied with their experiences. Also, the general group morale is lower.

Implications for the Effectiveness of Sport Groups

It may be apparent from the preceding discussion that increasing group size *generally* has the following consequences:

1. Group productivity initially increases, then decreases,

2. Relative individual productivity decreases,

3. Social loafing increases,

4. Individual satisfaction and group morale decrease.

As a consequence, it should be easy to establish general prescriptions about group size for sport groups. However, this isn't the case — primarily because it's so difficult to reach consensus on what constitutes the size of a sport group.

This point was made by Neil Widmeyer (1971) who pointed out that there are three possible indices of group size in sport and physical activity. One is the number of people on the playing surface at one time

Using this criterion, for example a basketball team would consist of five members a tennis team, one or two. Another index of group size is the number of individuals in uniform during competition. League rules and budget considerations usually influence this number. The team roster for competition might be ten to twelve athletes for a basketball team; four to six for a tennis team. A third possible index is the total number of athletes on the roster. Many athletes practice with a team during a season but never have the opportunity to compete against another team. One basketball team might have 25 athletes on its roster while another might have only 15. Using these three measures, it could be concluded that a basketball team had five, 10 to 12, or 15 to 30 athletes. Obviously, if a researcher or coach was interested in determining how team size influences other variables such as adherence, absenteeism, satisfaction, or cohesion, the measure used could affect the answer obtained. So, what constitutes an appropriate group size?

Bray, Kerr, and Atkin (1978) felt that the *principle of functional group size* should be the most important consideration insofar as group size is concerned. The functional group size for any activity is represented by the number of people necessary to carry out the group's activities. As the number of group members increases beyond this functional complement, the number of nonparticipants also increases. And, the four consequences listed above also follow. A similar point about the optimum group size was made by Thelen (1949). He advocated that groups should adopt the *principle of least group size*. The basis for this principle is that a group should be just large enough to include sufficient members with the social and task skills necessary to carry out its activities.

In sport situations, the principles of functional group size and least group size would provide support for the suggestion that — all things being equal — a sufficient number of individuals should be retained in order to practice efficiently and effectively. What this means is that the necessary resources would be available to scrimmage in team sports and compete in individual sports. Consequently, a basketball team should retain 10 to 12 members; a volleyball team should retain 12 to 14 members, a wrestling team, 20 to 24 members (approximately 2 individuals per weight class). This would insure that there wouldn't be a large number of individuals inactive at any given time. Opportunities for individual instruction, reinforcement, and reward would also be available. And, the amount of individual participation and high feelings of personal responsibility, commitment, and accountability to the group would be present.

be present.

It is important to keep in mind that the application of the principles of functional group size and least group size are not a fixed standard. They can vary from group to group and sport to sport. For example, there is evidence that very large groups usually form into smaller subgroups (e.g., Baker, 1981). Sometimes this might even occur because of the organizational structure adopted. A football team provides a good example. Traditionally, large rosters are maintained in this sport and the total roster is generally subdivided into smaller units each of which has its own coach. A total squad of 40 people might be subdivided into an offensive unit, a defensive unit, and in some cases a special unit associated with the kicking game. These units represent subgroups within the total team roster. Each of these subgroups can have all of the characteristics of a separate group — leadership, roles, structure, and so on. Thus, a football team of 40 may not differ substantially (insofar as functional size and "extra" group members is concerned) from a basketball team of 12 to 15 people.

The application of the principles of functional group size can also vary from one team to another within the same sport. Football again provides the best example. On one team of 40 athletes, the coaches might decide to use some of their best athletes on both offense and defense. On another team of 40 athletes, the coaches might decide to have their personnel specialize on either offense or defense. From a social and a productivity point of view, there is considerable difference between a single group of 40 and a group of 40 that contains two subgroups with 20 members each. In the case of the first team, the principles of least group size and functional group size might lead the coaches to conclude that they had at least 15 players too many on the roster. These 15 would be nonparticipants who could become dissatisfied and detract from group morale. Therefore, it might be best to release them. On the other hand, an entirely different conclusion might be reached in the case of the second team. As a result of the specialization between offense and defense, the coaches might conclude that there were no unnecessary "extras".

One of the most problematic areas associated with group size is social loafing. There is good evidence that individuals do not work as hard in groups as they do alone. And, as the size of the group increases, the amount of social loafing on the part of each individual group member also increases accordingly. A theory of social impact has been advanced by Latane' (1981) to account for this phenomenon. According to Latane', each new member in a group has marginally less *social impact* on that group. There is a law of diminishing returns. When one individual is the target of social forces — a rowing coach urging an all out effort, for example — the social impact is concentrated. But, when other individuals are added to the boat, the impact of the social forces becomes divided among the group members.

The one factor that appears to reduce the degree of social loafing is accountability — the identifiability of individual effort and productivity. Any technique that can be used to increase individual accountability and to identify the contributions of each individual to the group effort should serve to reduce social loafing. In track and swimming relay teams, for example, the contribution of each individual can be assessed by obtaining lap times. This should serve to reduce social loafing. In football, basketball, hockey, and soccer, performance can be measured or evaluated through the use of video. This also should serve to reduce social loafing. Williams, Harkins, & Latane' (1981) emphasized this point when they used a football example to illustrate importance of identifiability to reduce social loafing:

> Football lineman, for instance, receive relatively little in the way of fan attention or media coverage. Unsung heroes, they work in obscurity while their efforts seem to go unnoticed by all but their running backs and a few linemen on the other team. Our present research might suggest that this lack of identifiability would lead these players not to exert themselves as strenuously as their more visible teammates. However, successful coaches work hard to counteract this tendency. For example, at Ohio State University ... movies of each play and players were taken from isolated cameras and viewed by the entire coaching staff and players after each game. The staff screened and graded each play and computed the average percentage of perfection of each individual, a score known to teammates and helping to determine whether a player would start the next game. Also, weekly press luncheons were called to announce "lineman of the week" honors and the award of "buckeye" decals to adorn players' helmets signifying their 110% effort on the field to teammates and crowd. (p. 311)

Not every coach has the resources and budget necessary to undergo this type of comprehensive evaluation program. However, some attempt should be made in group activities to heighten identifiability and accountability. They reduce social loafing.

In summary, there is no doubt that size is a two

edged sword in any sport group. Every coach likes to have considerable resources available. Size provides a larger talent pool, greater flexibility, and protection in the event of injury, dropout, or absenteeism. But, size brings problems in management, morale, and individual satisfaction.

4 Group Territory

Territoriality is also a relevant issue relating to the group situation. For many sport teams, the stadium, rink, or court becomes so intertwined with the identity of the team that it is often difficult to separate one from the other. Yankee Stadium. Maple Leaf Gardens. Boston Gardens. Each of these brings to mind an image of its team.

The actual layout or physical structure of the team's "territory" can also influence the interaction between fan and athlete. Roger Kahn's (1971) description of Ebbets Field, the home of the Brooklyn Dodgers, provides a good example:

Ebbets Field was a narrow cockpit, built of brick and iron and concrete, alongside a steep cobblestone slope of Bedford Avenue. Two tiers of grandstand pressed the playing area from three sides, and in thousands of seats fans could hear a ball player's chatter, notice details of a ball player's gait and, at a time when television had not yet assaulted illusion with the Zoomar lens, you could see, actually

The court had every conceivable deficiency. The baskets were hung against the end walls, which meant that those of us accustomed to using them mastered the art of dashing headlong at the wall, planting our right foot high against the planking, and vaulting upward toward the basket, ending high above the rim so that we could then dunk the ball downward. This was a shot fairly hard to stop by a bewildered defender who had never before seen such a court.

The ceiling was unusually low, with a wide, heavy rafter right above the basket, and we became expert in speeding down the floor, and with maximum force slamming the ball vertically upward so that it caromed back down through the basket. This, too, was a shot difficult to stop if you were not accustomed to it.

On this bizarre floor the Doyleston Boys' Brigade fielded teams with far more than normal skills. We once went for a period of three years without losing a home game, even though we played teams that had better reputations and much taller players. At the time I thought we were pretty good, but now, looking back on those years, I realize that even superlative opponents would have required about three-quarters of a game to familiarize themselves with our peculiar floor and its strange rules. (Michener, 1976, p. 4)

see, the actual expression on the actual face of an actual major leaguer as he played. You could know what he was like! (p. xi-xii).

The sport team's territory — its court, stadium, or rink — can also provide it with advantages during the competition. For example, in professional baseball, the "Green Monster" — the left field wall in Boston's Fenway Park — continues to confuse visiting outfielders and intimidate visiting pitchers. In the Boston Gardens during basketball games, fans are seated almost on the court itself. This continues to produce feelings of crowding among opponents of the Celtics'.

In amateur sport, the problems posed by the home team's territory can be even greater. Many facilities are built for multiple purposes — and sometimes sport wasn't one of them. Consequently, a home team's territory can often give new meaning to the phrase "home court advantage". The story told by James Michener (1976) in the quote used to introduce this chapter is an excellent example. There is no doubt that Michener's home court was uniquely advantageous. However, there has been a long-standing belief that the home team has an advantage — even when the playing surface is generally the same from from one location to another; e.g., a hockey rink or basketball court. Thus, its not surprising that this issue has been the topic of considerable research with amateur and professional teams.

Home Advantage

The research on home advantage has yielded quite different results depending on whether the focus has been on the regular competitions held during the course of the season (league play) or whether the focus has been on playoff games. Thus, these two are discussed separately.

Regular Season Competition. Table 4.1 contains a summary of research carried out on the impact of home advantage during regular competitions. It should be apparent that in terms of winning percentage, the results are clear. In every sport, at both the college and professional level, the home team enjoys an advantage which translates into a favorable winning percentage. The superiority of the home team's winning percentage varies from 53% in professional baseball (Schwartz & Barsky, 1977) to 70% in college basketball (Varca, 1980). This difference in success is substantial when the number of games in a season is considered.

The question of why this advantage is present has produced three general explanations: learning factors including a lack of familiarity with an opponent's playing surface, physiological factors including the debilitating effects of travel, and psychological factors including the positive influence of a friendly audience (Schwartz & Barsky, 1977).

The *learning factor* -- familiarity with the home playing surface, a lack of familiarity with an opponent's — is important. The Green Monster in Boston or the home court of the Doyleston Boys' Brigade which was described by Michener would require some adjustment. In a close contest, errors due to a lack of familiarity with the playing surface could prove to be decisive. However, familiarity does not appear to be the most important reason. This was the conclusion arrived at by Barry Schwartz and Stephen Barsky (1977) after analyzing the winning percentages of home and visiting teams in professional baseball, basketball, and hockey, and college and professional football. They found that

The home advantage is more dramatic where conditions of play are most uniform. Not only are hockey rinks and basketball courts everywhere almost identical in size and shape, they are also smaller than baseball and football fields, so that the basketball or puck is, for all players, always in clearer view relative to the physical background. Moreover, lighting and climatic conditions are more uniform in indoor sports. All this means is that the home advantage is greatest where arena as well as field of play variations are least, not most, conspicuous. (p. 650)

The second series of factors thought to contribute to the home advantage are *physiological* in nature. Fatigue and the disruption of sleeping and/or eating routines are associated with travel. In a close contest, these disruptions could be decisive. Schwartz and Barsky (1977) also concluded that physiological factors are not the most critical. The reasoned that if the physiological factors are the primary factor, they should become more significant as the season progresses. Injuries start to take their toll and fatigue accumulates. However, in every sport examined by Schwartz and Barsky, there was no major difference in the home team's win-loss superiority in the first half versus the second half of the season.

The factors which seem to be most important in contributing to home advantage are *psychological* in nature. Essentially, the home team receives more social support from the crowd. It receives more reinforcement for any positive behavior. On the other hand, an extraordinary performance from the visiting team may be followed by silence. The result is that the home team is generally more motivated and aggressive. It out hustles and outworks its opponent to obtain the crowd responses associated with approval.

Most of the performance differences between visiting and home teams found by Schwartz and Barsky were in the offensive statistics. For example, in baseball, there were no differences in the defensive statistics of errors, double plays, walks, or strikeouts. But, the home teams were superior in the rate of runs scored (i.e., runs scored as a function of the number of times at bat), extra base hits, total hits, and runs as a proportion of hits. In hockey, home teams were superior in terms of shots taken, goals scored, number of assists and number of assists per goal. And, finally, in basketball, while home teams obtained more rebounds (a defensive measure), they also took more shots and scored more points. Schwartz and Barsky felt that the superiority of the home team on offense should be expected because

Table 4.1 Research on home advantage in various sports for regular season competitions.

Sport	Comparison	Result	Reference
Baseball			
Professional	Winning Percentage	Home team wins 53%	Schwartz & Barsky (1977)
Professional	Winning Percentage	Home team wins 56%	Edwards (1979)
Professional	Balloting for All-Star teams	Home attendance influence votes received	Aamodt (1981)
Basketball			
College	Winning Percentage	Home team wins 64%	Schwartz & Barsky (1977)
College	Winning Percentage	Home team wins 70%	Varca (1980)
College	Functional vs dysfunctional aggression	Home team had more steals, rebounds, blocked shots; less fouls	Varca (1980)
College	Fouls following crowd's antisocial behavior	Home team had more fouls/min after the crowd's antisocial behavior	Thirer (1979)
Football			
Professional	Winning Percentage	Home team wins 58%	Schwartz & Barsky (1977)
Professional	Winning Percentage	Home team wins 54%	Edwards (1979)
College	Winning Percentage	Home team wins 60%	Schwartz & Barsky (1977)
Ice Hockey			
Professional	Winning Percentage	Home team wins 64%	Schwartz Barsky (1977)

these are precisely the kinds of activities most likely to elicit the approval of a friendly audience. The most casual observation will show that local spectators everywhere reach their highest point of enthusiasm when the home team is at bat or in control of a basketball or puck. The mere possibility of offensive success is enough to excite a crowd. Superb defensive plays, on the other hand, only create a stir after they occur. (p. 652)

In short, the home team's offense has a greater likelihood of producing a favorable crowd response. Consequently, there is increased hustle and aggres-

A study by Phillip Varca (1980) also provides support for the view that the differences in success at home versus away can be attributed to psychological factors such as greater aggressiveness, hustle, and intensity. However, Varca found that aggression on offense versus defense is not as important as whether the aggression is functional or dysfunctional. Functional aggression includes behaviors such as rebounds, steals, and blocked shots — skills which facilitate effective performance. On the other, hand, dysfunctional aggression includes fouls — behaviors which detract from effective performance.

The college basketball teams studied by Varca were considerably more successful at home than on the road with a winning percentage of 70% at home. Also, the home teams were more functionally aggressive. They had more steals, rebounds, and blocked shots. At the same time, they committed fewer fouls — the measure of dysfunctional aggression. These results are not inconsistent with the Schwartz and Barsky contention that increased aggressiveness on the part of the home team to secure the social support of the crowd is the basis for the home advantage.

There is also a home advantage for an athlete when it is time to the vote for an all-star team. Aamodt (1981) found that baseball fans tend to vote for players from their home team. Consequently, teams with the greatest home attendance have more players selected. Aamodt's also examined whether these results were an artifact in the data. That is, it might be expected that the best players play well so, therefore, more fans come out to watch them and, therefore, they receive more votes. Home attendance was correlated .52 with team wins. Thus, there is no doubt that fans do come out if the team is successful. However, home attendance was not significantly correlated with individual All-Star player statistics such as batting average(.03), home runs (.28), runs batted in (.19), or runs scored (.05). Thus, the better players don't always play in front of the bigger crowds.

Playoff Competitions. The home crowd wants to be rewarded for its loyalty with championships. But, there is also some evidence that the home crowd isn't always a benefit in championship series. A preoccupation with the home crowd may even be detrimental to performance in the playoffs. Roy Baumeister and Andrew Steinhilber (1984) looked at winning percentages at home and away during championship series in professional baseball and basketball. In a seven-game championship series, Games 1, 2, 5 and 7 were played at the home of the team that had the superior record throughout the regular season. Thus, the home advantage summarized earlier in Table 4.1 might be expected to be even stronger in the playoffs since the stronger team plays more games at home.

For their analyses, Baumeister and Steinhilber excluded all four-game sweeps since they represent a clear superiority on the part of one team. They reasoned that any advantage from playing at home should appear in close competitions, not in one-sided mismatches. (Interestingly, of the ten 4-game sweeps in baseball, five ended with a home victory, five with a visitor victory. Of the seven 4-game sweeps in basketball, five ended with a visitor victory, two with a home victory.)

Games 1 and 2 in baseball and Games 1 to 4 in basketball were used as baseline measures in the two sports. This baseline measure of home team success was then compared with the winning percentage in the last game (which might have been Game 5, 6, or 7) as well as with the winning percentage in Game 7 for those series which went all seven games. The results are summarized in Table 4.2.

In the initial games (the baseline measure), the home team won 60.2% of the time in baseball and 70.1% of the time in basketball. This advantage in favor of the home team is comparable to results reported for the regular season (see Table 4.1 again). However, as the championship series progressed and neared completion, the home advantage seemed to

reverse itself and become a disadvantage. When the final game was either Game 5, 6, or 7, the winning percentage for the home team dropped to 40.8% in baseball and 46.3% in basketball. When the championship series was tied at three games each, the home advantage virtually disappeared. The home team won only 38.5% of the time in both baseball and basketball.

In an attempt to determine whether this startling reversal of the home advantage was due to the home team choking or to the visiting team excelling, Baumeister and Steinhilber analyzed individual performances in the baseline games and the seventh game. They chose errors in baseball as the measure of choking because, unlike pitching or batting, it is not directly influenced by the other team. An error, by definition, is a poor performance that, in the judgement of the official scorer, should have been handled successfully. In basketball, free throws were used. This is also an individual performance measure which is not mutually determined by the athlete and an opponent. Therefore, it is also a relatively good measure of choking.

It was expected that for all of these measures, the home team should have an advantage. In the World Series, for example, the home team is much more familiar with the playing surface and its idiosyncracies. It has had a full season of games in the stadium whereas the visitors have only played three previous playoff games. In basketball, the home team isn't subject to the same harassment and distractions while shooting free throws. Nonetheless, despite these advantages, members of the home team performed more poorly in Game 7 than members of the visiting team. In baseball, for example, in the initial games (the baseline measure), the home team committed less errors than the visitors (.65 versus 1.04 per game) and had more errorless games (33 versus 18 games). But, in Game 7, the home team committed more errors than the visitors (1.31 versus .81 per game) and had fewer errorless games (6 versus 12 games). In basketball, the home and visiting teams were approximately equal in the initial games (the baseline measure). The home team shot 72% from the free throw line, the visitors, 73%. In Game 7, however, while the visitors stayed about the same (74%), the home team dropped to 69%. On the basis of these results, Baumeister and Steinhilber concluded that the reversal of home advantage in Game 7 was primarily due to choking on the part of the home team, not improvement on the part of the visiting team.

According to Baumeister (1985), the underlying reason for the home team's choke is that athletes become preoccupied with what he referred to as self-presentation — how they will perform, look to others,

Table 4.2 Winning teams in home versus away games in championship series.

Sport	Comparison	Game Winners			Reference
		Home	Visitor	%	
Professional Baseball	Games 1 & 2	59	39	60.2	Baumeister & Steinhilber (1984)
	Game 7	20	29	40.8	
	Last Game	10	16	38.5	
Professional Basketball	Games 1 & 2	115	49	70.1	Baumeister & Steinhilber (1984)
	Game 7	19	22	46.3	
	Last Game	5	8	38.5	
Professional Hockey	Games 1 & 2	129	111	53.8	Gayton, Matthews, & Nickless (1987)
	Game 7	31	28	52.5	
	Last Game	7	5	58.3	

be perceived by others, be described by others. Everybody has self presentation concerns. A young child in a race may simply want to avoid looking foolish; another may want to be first and be "the fastest in Grade 6". When an event increases in importance, concerns with self-presentation also increase. When there is an opportunity to claim a desired identity — "champion", "winner", "best", "smartest" — concerns with self presentation also increase. And, when there is an opportunity to claim a desired identity in front of a sympathetic, supportive audience, concerns with self presentation are maximal.

Baumeister suggested that as a result of the heightened concerns with self presentation, athletes begin to pay too much attention to what they are doing and how they are doing it. Instead of performing their skills automatically, they begin to concentrate on a step-by-step execution. The result is that performance becomes poorer. Baumeister pointed out:

The pressure, the chance for self-redefinition and the audience all encourage choking by the home team. Most pro athletes are tough and experienced enough to cope with one or two of these factors during the season. But the combination of all three — found chiefly in championship play — is psychologically different from regular season play. That may be why it is so rare for a team to win a championship the first time it qualifies for the playoffs. And, it is not surprising that even seasoned athletes become self-conscious and choke. (p. 52)

A study carried out by Gayton, Matthews, and Nickless (1987) did not find a home disadvantages in championships for professional hockey (see Table 4.2 again). The home advantage in terms of winning percentage was 53.8% in the initial games, 52.5% when Games 5, 6, and 7 were considered as the last game, and 58.3% when the series went to a deciding seventh game.

Gayton and his colleagues suggested that a possible reason for the differences in home advantage (disadvantage) between baseball/basketball and hockey might lie in differences in the attentional demands of these sports. Baseball and basketball both have periods where the athletes can pause and reflect — and thereby adopt what Robert Nideffer (1985) has referred to as a narrow internal attentional focus. When an athlete is concerned with self-presentation, stress, or the pressures of the situation, he or she is in a narrow internal focus of attention. Hockey is a fast paced game which provides very few opportunities to become fixed in an narrow internal focus. Consequently, there is less chance that a concern with self-presentation will develop. This explanation is speculative, however. More research is necessary to provide definitive answers about the severity and the causes of the home disadvantage in championship series.

The Correlates of Territoriality

Territoriality represents a perception of proprietary rights over a physical space. There are a number of factors associated with group territoriality. One of the most important of these is *group morale and individual satisfaction*. Territoriality provides a feeling of permanence and stability so all groups work to establish their own territory. Team logos are placed on the stadium or rink, team mascots are adopted, and special locker room areas, eating areas, and clearly identified practice fields are set out. Athletes also establish their own personal space or territory in locker room areas, on team buses, and at practice fields or rinks. They also defend that territory against intruders. In his book, **The Game**, Ken Dryden (1983) discussed this phenomenon:

> I walk towards the rear of the bus and, just past halfway, turn to the left ... Others come on to the bus turning in right or left, apparently at random. But nothing is random. Just as it is in the dressing room, we each have a seat that is ours ... we sit where we do because if we didn't, we might sit in a seat important to someone else. And sitting where we do as much as we do, gradually where we sit becomes important to us ... At training camp, and a few times each year when injuries bring two or three new players to the team, it can be a problem. For new players, unfamiliar with our habits, sit anywhere, and one person in the wrong seat means someone else in the wrong seat until a simple chain of confusion becomes a mess. While most of us hover near our occupied seats wondering what to do and where to go, not quite willing to admit that a particular seat matters to us, someone will usually come along and say something — "Hey, get the fuck outa my seat" — to straighten out the problem. (pp. 112- 113)

Another correlate of territoriality is *control*. Irwin Altman (1975) pointed out that a spatial location does not become part of a group's territory until the group can exert some control over it over a period of time.

The nature of the control and the length of time over which the group exerts it have a direct influence on the development and extent of the group's sense of territoriality (see Table 4.3).

Primary territories are "owned and used exclusively by individuals or groups...[they are] clearly identified as theirs by others, are controlled on a relatively permanent basis, and are central to the day-to-day lives of the occupants" (Altman, 1975, p. 112). If a sport team has the exclusive use of a locker room, practice field, stadium, dormitory, or weight lifting facility, this represents their primary territory. A primary territory is actively controlled by a group and access by nongroup members is prevented. This is the evident on some college campuses where the football team prevents all public use or student activity in its stadium, practice area, or weight training room.

Secondary territories are those "places over which an individual or a group has some control, ownership, and regulatory power but not the same degree as over primary territory" (Altman, 1975, p. 117). In high school sport, a number of teams may share the same facility — a locker room, gymnasium, or playing field. If they do so at the same time (e.g., by splitting the area in half), certain boundary markers become demarcation lines between the groups. These might be very actively defended and any intrusion could be met with hostility and conflict.

This occurs in ice hockey and football, for example. The center line is a well accepted boundary separating the territories of the two teams for the pregame warmup. No movement into an opponent's territory is permitted. In hockey, if a puck goes into an opponent's territory, it must be left there to be returned at the convenience of the opponent. Anyone who ventures into the other team's territory risks a confrontation. George Plimpton (1978) illustrated this point:

> We wheeled around in our half of the ice, the Flyers in theirs. There was no communication between the two teams; indeed, the players seemed to put their heads down as they approached the center line, sailing by within feet of each other ... [Pettie] told me about a pregame warmup in one of the Soviet-NHL series, in which our teammate Wayne Cashman had spotted a Russian player coming across the center line to chase a puck; Cashman had intercepted the Russian and checked him violently into the boards. "Well, the guy was in the wrong place" Pettie said when I expressed my astonishment. "He should have known better".(p. 35)

Table 4.3. The nature of group territory (Adapted from Altman, 1975).

Type of Territory	Level of Group Control	Duration of Control by the Group	Sport Example
Primary	Control is high and direct. Access to others is restricted. There is a very high probability that the territory will be defended.	Control is long term and permanent. Ownership may be involved.	A team's locker room, stadium, or the parks of professional teams.
Secondary	Control is moderate. The group is a habitual user of the territory and is identified with it.	Control is short term and temporary	Practice fields, locker rooms, and parks shared by more than one team.
Public	Control is low. The group may exert some control while it is using the space but it loses all control when it gives it up.	Control does not exist or it is of minimal duration.	Public tennis courts, university gymnasia during "free time", public parks.

Full scale brawls have been initiated because one player crossed over the red line into an opponent's zone during a pregame skate. One of the most publicized examples of territoriality in hockey occurred in a 1987 NHL Stanley Cup Series between the Philadelphia Flyers and Montreal Canadiens. Some Canadien players stayed on the ice after Philadelphia had completed its warm up. They "invaded" the Philadelphia territory and shot pucks into the open net for good luck. When they were spotted by a Flyer both teams returned to the ice and a battle royal between the two teams resulted.

The third category, *public territories,* have a "temporary quality, and almost anyone has free access and occupancy rights" (Altman, 1975, p. 118). In university gymnasia, individuals or groups may arrive to play basketball. If the courts are occupied by other individuals or groups, the newcomers are able to join the game. In public tennis courts, it is universally understood that players must alternate on the the courts after a set number of games or fixed period of time. In both of these instances, the individuals or groups have some occupancy rights and some control but these are only temporary.

Another correlate of territoriality is *signs and symbols.* These are used to separate a home territory from the territory of other groups. In an early, classic study, William Whyte (1943) observed that different street gangs used graffiti on buildings, sidewalks, and signs to mark off their territory from their rivals. The amount of graffiti present increased with increasing proximity to a group's base.

In sport teams, the signs and symbols representing territoriality may consist of posters, names over lockers, ornaments, and slogans. Or they may consist of trophies and flags symbolizing past successes. In their description of the Montreal Forum, the home territory of the Canadiens, Chrys Goyens and Allan Turowetz (1986) outlined the impact of these types of symbols:

> Unlike the teams that have made the Forum great, the building itself is squat and functional ... Inside, the Forum is just another hockey rink at first glance. If you've visited any area of size in the National Hockey League, the impression here will be one of overwhelming sameness ... it could be the Forum in Ingle-

wood, California, or the Capital Center in the middle of nowhere between Baltimore and Washington. Second glance will uncover a series of visual clues that indicate the familiar and the fabled.

The stylized CH will be the first reminder of what this building has meant to the sport. But that isn't the key to the Forum either ... Where is the real Forum? Look up. Straight above your head, in the rafters. There you'll find the real Forum. There, high above the ice, they hang Silently. To call them just pieces of cloth is like describing an Arras tapestry as just another wallhanging ... Only the Forum holds twenty-three separate white panels on which these words are written in blue with red trim: "Montreal Canadiens, Stanley Cup Champions". (pp. 15-16)

The signs and symbols marking territoriality are quite important individually and collectively. Laboratory and field studies have shown that group morale and individual satisfaction are higher, feelings of being crowded are reduced, and a territory is considered to be more pleasant when it becomes personalized through the use of signs and symbols (e.g., Baum & Valins, 1977; Edney & Uhlig, 1977).

Another correlate of territoriality is *status*. Territory represents dominance; the greater the status of the individual or group, the greater the amount of territory it marks out (e.g., Durand, 1977). Group territory does not grow in direct proportion to group size, however. In fact, as groups grow in size, there is an increasing tendency for them to take over less space per member (Edney & Jorden-Edney, 1974). Also, with increasing group size, the boundaries for the group's territory become more permeable, less clearly defined (Edney & Grundmann, 1979). For example, a soccer team of 15 members might jealousy guard its one practice field. Intruders would be asked to leave. However, if that soccer team expanded to 45 members and used three fields, it would probably be easier for intruders to use a corner of one field. A pair of students might throw a baseball in one corner, sit and watch practice, or carry out individual exercises.

Implications for The Effectiveness of Sport Groups

Individuals and groups have a psychological need to develop a proprietary attitude about the physical space that they occupy. And, when control over territory is established, there is an increased likelihood

that the individual or group will defend it against intruders. In fact, the greater the perception of control or ownership over a territory, the greater is the tendency to aggressively defend it.

Feelings of territoriality have a positive influence on individual satisfaction, group morale, and even team performance. Thus, it is important for a sport team to enhance the sense of territoriality at "home" and to reduce the impact of the visiting team's territoriality "away from home".

At home, territoriality can be highlighted by signs and symbols including team logos, posters, ornaments, flags, and so on. Cheerleaders and mascots are obviously effective. The use of the team colors in dressing rooms, on buses, and so on is also useful. And, sounds — the home team's theme song, band, and unique cheers — also enhance territoriality. The specific elements producing territoriality aren't important — they are largely symbolic. In fact, the symbols that designate one team's territory might even be inappropriate in another context. What is important is that a sense of home territory should be established and maintained

Not surprisingly, many successful teams have developed a sense of territoriality by emphasizing and highlighting their tradition. The description of the Montreal Forum presented earlier is one example. The championship pennants and the pictures of former stars and teams which hang in the Forum serve as a link to the Canadiens' past.

Tradition can be developed even when the organization is relatively young. If the alumni have status and are given important roles in the organization, a tradition develops. Many amateur sport organizations use their alumni in a variety of roles — as coaches, fund raisers, administrators. Annual picnics, golf tournaments, and other social functions can be used to strengthen the link between the alumni and the organization. Pictures of former teams and outstanding athletes can be prominently displayed. All of these techniques are useful in establishing and maintaining an organization's tradition.

The evidence presented earlier shows that with the exception of the playoffs, there is a home advantage in sport. Home teams win more often than visiting teams. Also the work of Schwartz and Barsky indicates that this home advantage is due primarily to psychological factors, not to learning factors or to physiological factors. Thus, an attempt must be made to reduce the psychological impact of competing away from home.

One example of this was presented in the movie **Hoosiers**. The coach, played by actor Gene Hackman, brought his team into the huge auditorium where they were scheduled to compete for the state championship. The dramatic difference between that auditorium and their own high school gym seemed to produce feelings of awe, reverence, and intimidation in the athletes. After a few moments of observation, Coach Hackman took out a tape measure and, with the help of one of the team members, proceeded to measure the width of the court, the height of the basket, and so on. When he was finished, he paused and then concluded that the playing surface was identical to the one they had always played on. The simplicity of his approach effectively made the point for his athletes.

Another approach which is effective is to have managers and trainers arrive early and set out uniforms and equipment in the locker room. Team slogans or symbols can be prominently displayed. Then when the athletes arrive, the dressing room has the familiar appearance of home.

In amateur sport, the quality of the visiting team's dressing room is often poor and this can detract from the team's mental preparation. In order to eliminate any distractions, anxiety, stress, or negative impact produced by the home team's facility, many visiting coaches choose to dress in a neutral site and then travel directly to the competition.

If the visiting team's playing surface is rich in tradition, it is helpful to visit it early — well before the competition begins. Rookies or athletes who are unfamiliar with the facility can then act as tourists, satisfy their curiosity, and get over any feelings of reverence or intimidation. When the competition begins, the psychological impact of the home team's arena, court, or stadium is reduced.

The study by Baumeister and Steinhilber (1984) clearly shows that a new psychological situation is produced in a championship series. With a championship close at hand, the home advantage can disappear because athletes become too preoccupied with self-presentation. They begin to pay too much attention to what they are doing and how they are doing it. Consequently, their performance becomes poorer.

Athletes will always be aware of the situation and its importance, it makes no sense to down play its significance. A championship is not just another game. However, clearly, no attempt should be made to overemphasize it's importance. Emphasis should be placed on doing the routine and the familiar — doing the things associated with previous successes.

Interestingly, many professional sport teams depart from this principle when they take their athletes to a hotel in their own city during a championship series. This eliminates some of the advantages of being at home — contact with family, and familiar eating, sleeping, and practice routines. But, it also reproduces most of the conditions associated with being a visiting team. Possibly this also eliminates the home disadvantage found by Baumeister and Steinhilber. Until there is further research on the extent and nature of the home disadvantage in championship series, there is no way of knowing for certain.

3 Member Attributes

At first appearance ... the Canadiens look an immensely compatible team; compatible personally and professionally, sharing special skills and common goals, at once capable of great joy and great satisfaction, a team that, by and large, seems genuinely to like each other. A second look and it might not seem the same -- unconnected pockets of English conversation, or French, in dressing rooms, airports, at team meals; best friends ... that divide by language; the highly publicized "incidents" that seem to embroil the team so frequently. But take a third and closer look and it will look different again. These are not divisions, because they don't feel like divisions; they are unconscious and unintended, and almost always unnoticed ... we know there are differences, we just don't think they are that important. (Dryden, 1983, p. 24)

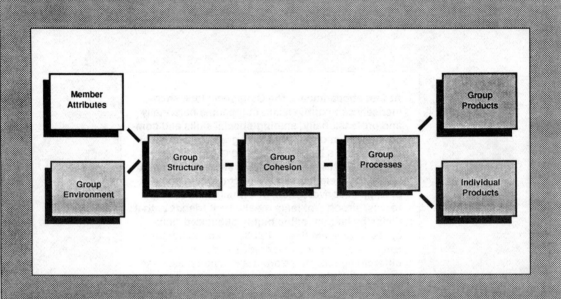

5 The Nature of Group Composition

During World War II, a series of conferences were attended by what was referred to as The Big Three — Franklin Roosevelt, Joseph Stalin, and Winston Churchill. The purpose of these meetings was to negotiate the terms of cooperation between the Allies in their war efforts and then, the terms for peace in Europe following the war. It is doubtful that any group could have had three more contrasting group members. They differed in personality, motives, political ideology, attitudes, and even in energy and physical health since Roosevelt's health was rapidly deteriorating by 1944. Differences also were present within The Big Three in the way in which they were able to get along with each other. For example, Joseph Alsop (1982), Roosevelt's biographer, noted that Roosevelt and Churchill became very close personal friends and that that close friendship "was the cornerstone of the Western alliance throughout the war... a partnership of the war leaders of two great nations like no other one can think of in history" (p. 243). This type of close friendship between two group members has the potential to destroy a three-person group — particularly if the other dyadic relationships within the group are not as positive. And, in The Big Three, they weren't. The relationship between Stalin and Churchill was cool. They were cordial, they respected each other, but there was also mutual suspicion and no friendship in their relationship. Similarly, the relationship between Roosevelt and Stalin was also marked by cordiality and mutual respect but not friendship. Nikita Khrushchev (1970) pointed out in his autobiography that "Stalin was more sympathetic to Roosevelt than Churchill because Roosevelt seemed to have considerable understanding

During the 1950s the Jackie Robinson Brooklyn Dodgers were outspoken, opinionated, bigoted, tolerant, black, white, open, passionate: in short, a fascinating mix of vigorous men. (Kahn, 1973, p. xi)

of our problems ... in disputes during the working sessions in Teheran, Stalin often found Roosevelt siding with him against Churchill" (pp.222-223). So, here was a group composed of men of completely different personalities and political ideologies who established interpersonal relationships that varied markedly in their friendship. As a group, they were responsible for establishing and maintaining the framework for cooperation between the superpowers and their Allies. Despite their personal differences and the differences in their interpersonal relationships, they operated as a cohesive, effective group. And, the fact that they did testifies to the complex nature of groups.

Although the Big Three could never be described as a typical group, it did have aspects in common with every other group including sport teams. Like every other group, it was composed of independent individuals. Like every other group, those individuals brought a wide range of attitudes, motives, abilities, previous experiences, and other characteristics to the group situation. And, like every other group, those differences among the group members could have split the group. But, they didn't. Not surprisingly, researchers have been intrigued by the impact of group composition and member characteristics on group effectiveness. What are the conditions under which personal differences are ignored or even used as elements to build a better group? What are the conditions under which these differences destroy the fabric of the group? In short, how does group composition influence group cohesion and group effectiveness?

Group Composition Defined

Initially, it may be helpful to look at what is meant by group composition and list the approaches that have been used to study it. Shaw (1981) defined it as "the relationships among the characteristics of individuals who compose the group" (p. 454). In a similar vein, McGrath (1964) defined it as "the properties represented by the aggregate of persons who are members of a given group at a given time" (p. 72). The properties referred to by McGrath also represent the resources of that group, the attributes that the group can draw upon to carry out its functions.

A group's resources — the attributes that the group can draw upon — include the group members' physical size and body type, mental and motor abilities, attitudes, aptitudes, motives, needs, and personality traits. In addition, group members can differ on social identifiers such as age, education, race, sex, and social status. One of the most frequently examined issues in group dynamics research has been the relationship between group composition and group effectiveness.

The Bass Model

One frame of reference developed to illustrate the role that group composition plays in group effectiveness is presented in Figure 5.1. In this model, which was proposed by Bernard Bass (1980), the relationship between group resources and the group performance is set out. Other factors which influence that relationship as well as the causal links between them are also outlined.

Good teams are composed of good athletes. But as Figure 5.1 shows (Link 1), various types of interaction processes modify the impact that the team resources (properties of the team) have on task performance. Two teams with the identical resources would differ in effectiveness if the teamwork in one was characterized by competition and rivalry while the teamwork in the other was characterize by cooperation and mutual sacrifices. Interaction processes are the dynamic activities of the group: coordination, cooperation, competition, information sharing, goal setting, communication, and so on. They are so fundamental to effective group performance that Bass made them the first link in his model. No sport team can be very effective if the various interaction processes are poor.

According to Bass, the team's properties can be considered in two categories: *biographical characteristics* and *abilities*. Biographical characteristics include the sex, age, race, and religion of the members. In the quote which introduced this section, Ken Dryden made reference to the biographical differences which were present on the Montreal Canadiens. He also pointed out that, in the case of the Canadiens, these differences did not detract from the effectiveness of the team. There are also sport teams where biographical characteristics such as race have divided the team.

The second property of the team, the abilities of the individual members, is of two types: the general abilities of the athletes and their task relevant abilities. A volleyball coach may begin the year with the best 12 athletes in the school; the general abilities within the team would be high. On the other hand, if none of the athletes had ever played volleyball before, their task relevant abilities would be low.

Forces outside the group have a significant influence on the way in which the group operates. They influence both the interaction within the team (Link 3b) as well as the team's properties (Link 3a). For example, budget considerations might mean that the size of a team must be limited. Or if the competition is held at a remote site access to equipment, facilities, or information might be restricted. These are the types of problems faced by Olympic teams, for example. Because of budget and space restrictions, the number of athletes, support personnel (coaches, doctors, trainers, therapists) is restricted. The host country can also limit the opportunity to practice at the facility. Track athletes who are most comfortable with a specific coach, athletic trainer, or doctor might have their access restricted during the Games. All these conditions which are imposed on the team by outside forces can detract from the team's effectiveness.

Successes and failures feed back and influence the conditions imposed on the team (Link 4). Successful teams have access to more money and greater recruiting budgets; unsuccessful teams often have to cut back.

Link 5 illustrates the relationship between individual performance and team performance. Not surprisingly, in almost every sport team, the proficiency of the individual members is the major factor contributing to team effectiveness. The degree of relationship varies across sports, of course. For example, Widmeyer and Loy (1981) found a correlation of .77 between women's individual tennis ability and their doubles team success. Jones (1974) reported correlations of .70 in men's tennis, .80 in women's tennis, .91 in football, .94 in baseball, and .60 in basketball. These studies are discussed in greater depth in Chapter 6.

The positions of group members can influence their

performance (Link 6). The positions of group members are of two types: social and task or physical position. Social positions refer to the status hierarchy in the group. On some teams, for example, the presence of a number of equally dominant, high status individuals might lead the coach to appoint a number of cocaptains rather than one captain. All of the individuals would operate more effectively than would be the case if two or three high status individuals were not given proper recognition. Task or physical position refers to whether a group member is central or peripheral in the team. Thus, for example, point guards in basketball are the hub of the offensive action. If they don't like to lead, make decisions, or serve as the catalyst for the offense, their play and the team's will suffer.

Links 7, 9, and 12 are straightforward. The abilities of the team members directly influence their individual performances (Link 7). When the saying "It's hard to make a silk purse out of a pig's ear" was coined, the author probably had Link 7 in mind. An individual's ability also influences his or her social and task position in the group (Link 12). Individuals who are more capable are put into the skilled positions. Similarly, individuals with more experience and/or leadership skills are generally asked to serve as team captains and cocaptains. Finally, the abilities of the team members also represent the resources of the group (Link 9).

The task and social positions of members are a property of the team (Link 8). A team with three captains establishes different patterns of communication than a team with one captain. Each captain plays a leadership role within the group. Similarly, a team with one outstanding athlete who becomes the focus for the team's offense or defense is different from a team which distributes those responsibilities equally.

Biographical factors influence a variety of elements within the team. For example, age, which is a biographical factor, not only influences the ability of the individual (Link 10a), it also has an impact on the position assigned to that individual (Link 10b). All things being equal, a first- or second-year player in high school will have less talent than a senior. Consequently, the senior will more likely be placed in a high profile, important position within the group. Also, if a team is composed largely of seniors, its properties are different than a team composed of a mix of seniors and sophomores (Link 11).

It is apparent that in the model, the resources of group are considered to be important for effective team performance. However, it should also be apparent that high individual skill is not sufficient by itself.

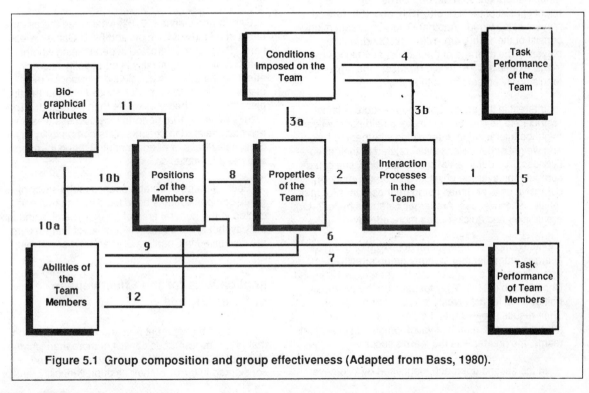

Figure 5.1 Group composition and group effectiveness (Adapted from Bass, 1980).

Bass emphasized this point when he stated that "team performance logically should depend on the performance of its individual members. Yet this dependence is modified by the interaction process among members, which in turn is affected by the conditions imposed on the team and various properties of the team, as a team. In turn, these properties and conditions can be linked to the attributes of individual team members" (p. 453). So, even with high grade silk, a high quality purse may not result.

The Widmeyer and Loy Perspective

Another frame of reference for considering group composition was proposed by Neil Widmeyer and John Loy (1981). This is summarized in Table 5.1. They suggested that the properties of sport groups can be considered from three perspectives: in terms of the amount of a resource possessed by the *average group member*, in terms of the *variability* in resources present among group members, and in terms of the degree of *compatibility* between and among members.

When the first approach is used — looking at group composition in terms of the average amount of an attribute present in the group — the focus is on the quantity of the property present and its influence on group performance. Thus, one Davis Cup tennis team might consist of the 1st, 8th, 15th, and 40th ranked players in the world. Another Davis Cup team might consist of the 12th, 14th, 16th, and 22nd ranked players. The average of the individual rankings (which in this example is 16) would represent the amount of tennis ability present on both teams.

Interest in the amount of group resources is not restricted to ability. For example, a field hockey coach might be interested in determining whether the height and weight of her defense was related to their effectiveness. In order to answer this question, she could compute the average physical size of a number of defensive units and then compare those units for their relative effectiveness. Are larger defenses better? Or, are smaller and quicker ones more effective?

One example of the general approach of using the average team member to study group effectiveness was adopted in a research study reported by Klein and Christiansen (1969). They focused on the personality trait of need for achievement in basketball players. Their results showed that the greater the amount of average achievement motivation present in basketball teams, the greater was the team's success.

In the second approach mentioned by Widmeyer

and Loy, the variability in the team resources is emphasized. In the two Davis Cup tennis teams introduced earlier, the differences among the players in ranking would represent the variability in ability present. What Davis Cup team might be expected to be more successful — the one with players ranked 1, 8, 15, and 40 (i.e., the team which is relatively heterogeneous in ability) or the one with players ranked 12, 14, 16, and 22 (i.e., the team which is relatively homogenous in ability)? When Widmeyer and Loy examined this general issue with female tennis players, they found that homogenous teams were more effective.

The third approach involves looking at the compatibility of the members in terms of some property considered to be important for group effectiveness. Shaw (1981) referred to this as the *assembly effect,* "the variations in group behavior that are a consequence of the particular combination of persons in the group, apart from the effects produced by the specific characteristics of group members" (pp. 211-212). In the two Davis Cup tennis teams, a doubles pair comprised of individuals ranked 8th and 15th would contain slightly more ability than a doubles team comprised of individuals ranked 16th and 22nd. However, if the higher ranked individuals had conflicting playing styles or didn't like each other personally, they might be completely ineffective as a doubles pair.

Carron and Garvie (1978) investigated the assembly effect in a study of Olympic and FISU Games wrestlers. They were interested in determining whether coach-athlete compatibility in personality had any effect on the athlete's absolute performance (final placement) or relative performance (whether the final placement was better or worse than expected). The results revealed that performance success was only minimally related to coach-athlete compatibility in the personality traits of need for control, need for affection, and need for inclusion.

Each of these three approaches to the study of group composition has been used in research conducted in the general area of group dynamics and in the psychology of sport. The results of that research are discussed in Chapters 6, 7, and 8 respectively.

Implications for the Effectiveness of Sport Groups

It should be apparent from the above discussion that (a) team resources consist of more than just the ability of the players; (b) team resources can be considered in terms of their amount, variability, and/or

Table 5.1 Three perspectives for considering group composition (Adapted from Widmeyer & Loy, 1981).

Component	Description
Amount of Group Resources	The focus is on the average or total amount of skills and attributes present. The fundamental question is whether the presence of more positive skills and attributes in more group members produces a more effective group.
Variability in Group Resources	The focus is on the variability in the skills and attributes of the group members. The fundamental question is whether groups composed of individuals with similar or dissimilar attributes are more effective.
Compatibility in Group Resources	The focus is on the fit between group members in terms of their personal attributes and skills and/or on the fit between the individual's skills and attributes and the task requirements. The fundamental question is whether complementarity between individuals and/or between individuals and their tasks influences group effectiveness.

compatibility; and, (c) team resources are not necessarily directly related to team success. The first point seems obvious. The attributes that individuals bring to a team — the team resources — include physical size, body type, strength and speed, mental and motor abilities, attitudes, aptitudes, motives, needs, and personality traits. Each of these can influence the social and the performance environment of the group.

Insofar as the second point is concerned, there is a tendency to consider a team's resources in terms of the average amount available. This is neither the only way to approach team resources nor the best. For example, Michael Jordan of the NBA Chicago Bulls is acknowledged to be one of if not the most dominant players in the league. As Curry Kirkpatrick (1987) noted: "Evidence is that Jordan's status in the NBA is nearing mythical proportions. In a sense, he's more of a cult figure within the league than he is out of it. That's how good he is .... The sad thing here is that since the day Michael arrived... the other Bulls have, for the most part, been awful" (p. 94). If a rating system was available for individual basketball ability, the Chicago Bulls might rank very high as a team simply because of the presence of Michael Jordan. But, despite Jordan's talent, the Chicago Bulls have been only moderately successful.

Not only is variability important, compatibility is also crucial. As another example, Jordan, Isiah Thomas of the Detroit Pistons, and Magic Johnson of the Los Angeles Lakers are perennial All-Stars. Therefore, it might reasonably be expected that these three players would be outstanding together. This has not been the case. In an All-Star game in Jordan's initial year, he had minimal opportunities to handle the ball and scored only seven points in 22 minutes. "The infamous 'freeze-out' was widely considered the work of the Johnson-Isiah Thomas axis. Johnson and Thomas deny the "freeze-out" theory, but NBA veterans were reputedly offended by what they perceived as hot-dogging by Jordan in the slam dunk contest" (Kirkpatrick, 1987, p. 96).

Finally, insofar as the third point is concerned, the Bass model illustrated in Figure 5.1 highlights the fact that there are a number of factors which moderate the relationship between group composition and group effectiveness. Group processes are a major consideration — rivalry vs cooperation, cohesion vs conflict, communication effectiveness, leadership effectiveness, and so on. All of these influence the degree to which the group resources will contribute to group effectiveness.

6 The Amount of Group Resources

Teams are composed of individuals. And, the skills, abilities, energies, and personal characteristics that those individuals bring to the group represent the amount of the team's resources. The team's resources are represented by either the average or the summed total of the attributes of individuals in a group. Thus, from an ability perspective, if three members of a hockey line scored 21, 18, and 15 goals, their line's resources in this attribute would be a total of 54 goals or an average of 18 goals per person. In this chapter, the group's resources are considered in two broad areas: the psychosocial characteristics of group members and their ability.

> I think in the '60s and '70s teams were looking for "basketball players" —basketball skills only ... You had to know how to play basketball; they weren't as interested in athletic ability as we are today. The whole thing has changed in the past 10 to 12 years, to the point where now coaches look for physical specimens. I don't say that coldly. We're looking for great athletes. A big guy — he's strong, he's filled out, he runs, he jumps. Then we teach him how to play the game. (Pat Riley quoted in Newman, 1987, p. 50)

Psychosocial Attributes of Members

On the basis of commonsense or intuition, two contrasting conclusions seem plausible about the relationship of the psychosocial attributes of group members to group effectiveness. On the one hand, it seems reasonable to expect that some personal qualities will be more positively related to team effectiveness than others. Sociability, extroversion, achievement motivation, conscientiousness, enthusiasm, empathy, intelligence, and dominance are all potentially positive attributes for any group member. Conversely, timidity, suspicion, depression, jealousy, and a lack of self-control are all potentially negative attributes. Thus, it seems plausible that if a large number of members possessed the positive attributes (and in large amounts) and only a few members possessed the negative ones (and in small amounts), the team should be more effective.

On the other hand, however, it is also intuitively reasonable to expect that the psychosocial attributes of individual team members are unrelated to team performance. People are complex — they possess a large number of attributes in differing degrees and combinations. Kluckhohn and Murray (1949) emphasized this point when they observed that each individual is like all other people, like some other people, and like no other person. All of us are intelligent to some extent; we're like every other person in this regard. Some of us are even identical in intelligence. But, our intelligence in combination with all of our other traits makes us unique; we are like no other person. And, we bring that uniqueness to the group. Two individuals who are both high in ability may or may not make a good doubles team.

The difficulty in determining the relationship of individual psychosocial attributes to team effectiveness was highlighted by Ivan Steiner (1972) who noted that:

> Any single individual may be regarded as a composite of many attributes. He possesses certain skills to a high degree and others in meager measure; he is well informed about some topics and ignorant of others; his

...ation of ...at may be patterned ...ans are multifaceted ...f whom may resemble one ...th respect to one property but may ...ssimilar with respect to another. For this reason, research dealing with group composition always requires a simplification of unmanageable complexities. (pp. 106-107)

There is no doubt that the interrelationship of the group members' psychosocial attributes (as one aspect in group composition) is complex. However, one researcher who has attempted to simplify the unmanageable complexities mentioned by Steiner has been Marvin Shaw (1981). After conducting a comprehensive review of the available research for his classic book, **Group dynamics: The psychology of small group behavior,** Shaw concluded that the "personality characteristics of group members play an important role in determining their behavior in groups. The magnitude of the effect of any given characteristic is small but taken together the consequences for group processes are of major significance" (p. 208).

Social and Work Groups

Much of the earliest work on group resources was carried out with social and work groups (not sport teams). The most important attributes identified by Shaw (and their relationship to effectiveness in social and work groups) are presented in Table 6.1. As Shaw pointed out, the relationship may be small but there seems to be little doubt that the presence of certain positive *interpersonal attributes* and the absence of other negative interpersonal attributes contributes to group cohesion and group effectiveness. The most important interpersonal attributes for group effectiveness are an orientation toward people, social sensitivity, empathy, sociability, and good judgement. If more group members possess these in large degree, the group is positively affected. Insofar as the negative interpersonal attributes are concerned, Shaw concluded that when group members are attracted to things (as opposed to people), it detracts from group cohesion and group effectiveness.

There are also a number of *personal attributes* which are associated in a positive way with activity within the group, the development of cohesiveness, and group effectiveness. These include intelligence, dependability, integrity, responsibility, self reliance, personal adjustment, emotional control, and emotional stability. Conversely, a number of negative personal attributes detract from group effectiveness

— a lack of conventionality, anxiety, neuroticism, and a tendency toward depression.

Finally, Shaw identified a number of attributes which are associated with involvement in *leadership* roles within the group. These are intelligence, authoritarianism, dominance, assertiveness, and ascendency. In every instance, if group members possess these to a large degree, they are more active within the group and assume a more prominent role in the group's leadership.

Sport Groups

In the context of sport, there are two avenues of research which have indirectly or directly dealt with the impact of the psychosocial attributes of the athletes within a team on team effectiveness. One of these is descriptive in nature and is concerned with whether *team and individual sport* athletes differ in personality. Potentially, there are two underlying mechanisms which might be in operation (Kroll, 1970). One is that is that a process of natural selection is at work. Those athletes who have the personal qualities necessary to be effective members of a particular type of sport group select and stay (or are retained), the others leave. The second is that group experiences help to develop certain personal qualities within the athlete.

Obviously, any link between the personal characteristics of the athlete and the effectiveness of the group is indirect. But, if personal characteristics such as intelligence, social sensitivity, dependability, and so on are important for social and work group effectiveness, there is no reason to believe that the same or similar personal attributes are not equally important in sport groups.

Team versus Individual Sport Competitors. The analysis of the personality traits of team and individual sport athletes as well as a sample of nonathletes was undertaken in a comprehensive study by Schurr, Ashley, and Joy (1977). A total of 1956 college males were tested. The athletes consisted of those individuals who had participated in intercollegiate sport programs. This group was also categorized into letter winners and nonletter winners and according to the type of sport in which they participated. One categorization consisted of the distinction between *team* (e.g., basketball) versus *individual* sports (e.g., golf). These two categories were further subdivided into *parallel* sports — direct aggression is not possible against an opponent (e.g., tennis, volleyball) — and *direct* sports — direct aggression against an opponent is possible (e.g., football, wrestling). And, finally, in addition to the team versus individual and parallel versus direct sport classification, the individual sport athletes in parallel sports were subdivided into *long duration* events (e.g., cross country) and *short duration* events (e.g., gymnastics).

Major differences in personality were found by Schurr, Ashley, and Joy between nonathletes, individual sport athletes, and team sport athletes A summary is presented in Table 6.2. It is apparent that the team sport athletes differed from the individual sport athletes in a number of qualities which should lead to increased team cohesion and improved team effectiveness — extroversion, dependence on others, and lower sensitivity. In addition, the individual sport athletes also possessed a number of qualities which should lead to more effective involvement in their groups — independence and low anxiety for example. The key word in both cases, however, is "should". While these traits are positive and, therefore, should lead to improved group effectiveness, there is no direct evidence to demonstrate this link.

Individual Orientations in Groups. A second avenue of research does permit more direct inferences to the group composition-group effectiveness issue. It is concerned with whether the *individual orientation* of group members influences team effectiveness. The orientation or motivation of an individual or a team is an important determinant of group effectiveness. Motivation, a theoretical concept, is used to represent the selectivity, the intensity, and the persistence in behavior.

Table 6.1 The influence of various traits on group involvement (Adapted from Shaw, 1981)

Trait	Impact on Group Involvement
Members with High Intelligence	Are more active. Are more popular. Are less conforming. Are in leadership roles
Authoritarian Members	Are more demanding. More readily conform
Members with High Social Sensitivity	Are more readily accepted. Enhance group effectiveness
Members Interpersonally Ascendent	More readily assume leadership roles More frequently engage in group activities More readily conform Contribute to group cohesion Are more popular Have more impact on decisions
Dependable Members	More readily become leaders Enhance group effectiveness
Members High in Conventionality	Inhibit group effectiveness
Members High in Anxiety	Inhibit group effectiveness
Members High in Personal Adjustment	Enhance group effectiveness

Thus, for example, if one athlete chooses to train while a second does not, this choice (i.e., different selection) is considered to be a manifestation of motivation. Also, if two athletes are training and one works harder than the other, this effort (i.e., greater intensity) is also considered to be a manifestation of motivation. Finally, if two athletes are training and one continues after the other has stopped, this persistence (i.e., greater duration) is also considered to be a manifestation of motivation.

Motivation provides both the focus (selection) and the energy (intensity and duration) for behavior. Thus, theorists in group dynamics have assumed that it is possible to determine the nature and strength of a

group's primary goals by examining its motivation. And, because a distinction is made in group dynamics research between individual motives and group motives, both of these perspectives have been examined. Group motivation is discussed in Chapter 16.

One of the more important contributions relating to individual motivation in groups was made by Bernard Bass and his colleagues (Bass, 1962; Bass, Dunteman, Frye, Vidulich, & Wambach, 1963; Dunteman and Bass, 1963). Their work was based on the assumption that individual behavior in group situations is a product of the person's needs and motives. In fact, Bass et al. even stated that the group is

Table 6..2 A comparison of team sport and individual sport athletes (Adapted from Schurr, Ashley, & Joy, 1977)

Focus Groups	Personality Differences
Team Sport vs Individual Sport	*Team Sport Athletes* are: more extroverted, dependent, and alert-objective *Individual Sport Athletes* are: less anxious and more sensitive-imaginative
Team Sport vs Nonathletes	*Team Sport Athletes* are: more extroverted, dependent, and higher in ego-strength *Nonathletes* are: higher in abstract reasoning
Individual Sport vs Nonathletes	*Individual Sport Athletes* are: more independent and objective *Nonathletes* are: more anxious and higher in abstract reasoning

"merely the theatre in which certain generalized needs can be satisfied" (p. 102). In short, Bass and his colleagues proposed that people get involved in group activities to satisfy their individual needs.

There are some slight differences in perception about the significant types of needs which individuals want satisfied in group situations. Hollander (1967), for example, has stated that two main clusters of needs are predominant: task motives and affiliation motives. The task motives are associated with the group's goals and objectives. When a group is engaged in activities which are task oriented — playing basketball, practicing with an elite team — the individual members' task needs are fulfilled. The affiliation motives are associated with social needs and interpersonal relationships. Thus, when group members have an opportunity to socialize with one another before or after practice and to develop and maintain friendships through the competition, their social needs are fulfilled.

Bass and his colleagues proposed that in addition to a task and affiliation motive, group members also have a self motive — an orientation toward personal rewards and goals. Again, by way of example, if the self motivation of a team of basketball players was predominant, they would be satisfied with good personal statistics even if the team was unsuccessful.

The influence of affiliation and task motivation on the success and satisfaction experienced by 1200 college males participating on 144 intramural basketball teams was examined by Martens (1970). The task and affiliation motives of each athlete were assessed by a questionnaire which was administered prior to the season. The average response for each team was then computed. On the basis of these average scores the teams were categorized as low, moderate, or high in task motivation and as low, moderate, or high in affiliation motivation. The team's win-loss record was used as the measure of success and the degree of team satisfaction was obtained by averaging the individual responses to a post season questionnaire.

Martens found that the two motives were quite distinct in their effect upon performance and satisfaction. The teams that were high in affiliation motivation were less successful but were more satisfied than teams that were low in affiliation motivation (see Figure 6.1). Thus, when affiliation motivation — a concern with developing and maintaining warm personal relationships within a group — is relatively high on a team, that team's performance effectiveness and ultimate success suffers. From an individual perspective, however, this doesn't seem to be too important; the members are satisfied with their group experiences.

Martens also found that teams that were high in task motivation were more successful and more satisfied than the teams that were low in task motivation. So, when task motivation — an orientation toward the group's performance goals and effective completion of the group task — is high on a team, that team's performance effectiveness and ultimate success benefits. And, in turn, the individuals are more satisfied with their group experience.

A number of other authors have also examined the personal orientation of group members and its relationship to group effectiveness (see Table 6.3). For example, in results consistent with Martens, Cooper and Payne (1967) found a correlation of .72 was present in soccer teams between the high task motivation of coaches and trainers and team success. Subsequently, Cooper and Payne (1977) also reported that athletes on more successful soccer teams were more task oriented and less self and affiliation oriented than athletes on less successful teams.

Implications for the Effectiveness of Sport Groups

There are a number of psychosocial attributes which contribute to effective group performance in social and work groups. Similarly, there are also a number of psychosocial attributes which detract from group effectiveness. Unfortunately, however, psychosocial attributes are partly a product of heredity and partly a product of daily social experiences and learning. Consequently, they develop (and change) very slowly over time. Thus, it's unrealistic to expect that a six-month or

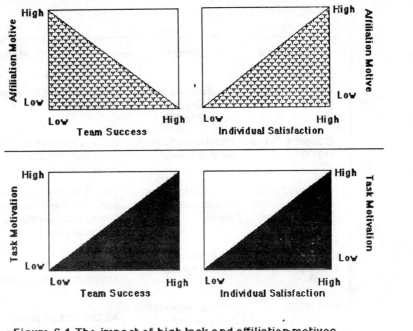

Figure 6.1 The impact of high task and affiliation motives in group members on team success and individual satisfaction (Adapted from Martens, 1970).

one-year athletic season can have a major impact on a team member's psychosocial attributes. It is possible, however, for a coach to emphasize the importance of behaving in a manner consistent with these specific attributes, reinforce the positive behaviors when they occur, and discourage any negative manifestations. In addition, it must be kept in mind that more successful sport teams seem to contain members who are high on task motivation. The task — the performance goals and objectives of the team — must be consistently emphasized through group goal setting programs (see Chapter 16).

Individual Ability

Social and Work Groups

Among the earliest work which examined the relationship of individual ability to group performance was carried out by Comrey and his colleagues (Comrey, 1953; Comrey & Deskin, 1954a, 1954b) using a manual dexterity task called the Purdue Pegboard Task. It was found that pairs of subjects

assembled more pegs than the most proficient individual member. That is, absolute performance was always better in the group situation. However, this absolute score was substantially less than twice the number that an average individual could assemble alone. Social loafing occurred and each individual was not as productive in the group situation. When the pairs were required to proceed alternately so that each member contributed 50% to the group's total, the group's performance was highly correlated with the performance of the least competent individual. In this instance, the group was limited by its weakest member. In tasks requiring less coordination or where the task demands were modified to permit the more proficient individual in the pair to contribute more than 50%, the group's performance was more highly associated with the more proficient individual's performance.

Research results have consistently demonstrated that a relationship exists between the amount of resources in the group (the level of ability of individual group members) and group problem solving (Heslin, 1964; Mann, 1959: McGrath & Altman, 1966). But, as the discussion in Chapters 2 and 3 emphasized,

Table 6..3 Participation orientation in sport.

Authors	Group	Results
Cooper & Payne (1967)	Coaches and trainers in English football teams	Teams with high task motivation were more successful
Cooper & Payne (1977)	Athletes on English football teams	Players on more successful teams were more self oriented and less task and affiliation oriented
Martens (1977)	Male college intramural basketball teams	Teams high in task motivation were more successful and more satisfied. Teams high in affiliation motivation were less sucessful and more satisfied.
Carron, Ball, & Chelladurai (1977)	Male college ice hockey teams	High task motivation was associated with satisfaction with team performance
Bird (1977)	Female Division I and II female volleyball teams	All coaches perceived their leader behavior as task oriented. In Division I, athletes on winning teams perceived their coaches as more person-oriented; athletes on losing teams perceived their coaches as more task oriented. In Division II, the reverse was true.
Klein & Christiansen (1969)	Three person basketball teams	Teams higher on achievement were more successful
Widmeyer (1977)	Three person basketball teams	Task, affiliation, and self motivation were not related to team sucess
Stogdill (1963)	Ohio State football team	High drive combined with cohesion improved team performance
Arnold & Straub (1972)	College varsity basketball teams	Successful teams scored higher on task motivation in postseason. No differences in preseason

the nature of the relationship is strongly influenced by three factors: the group task, size, and goal.

Sport Groups

In sport teams, the most relevant attribute (resource) that group members can bring to the situation is physical skill and ability. And as might be expected, there is a good relationship between the average amount of individual ability present and team effectiveness. For example, in a laboratory study in which a motor maze task was used, Diane Gill (1979) found that the average ability of a two-person group and the discrepancy in their ability correlated .54 in one experiment and .64 in a second with group performance.

Neil Widmeyer and his colleagues (Widmeyer and Gossett, 1978; Widmeyer, Loy, & Roberts, 1979, Widmeyer & Loy, 1981) have carried out a number of studies examining the member resources-group effectiveness question. In an early study, of male tennis doubles teams, Widmeyer, Loy, and Roberts (1979) found a correlation of .54 between the ability of the individual members and team performance. In a second study comparing the relationship of cohesion and ability to success in intramural basketball teams, Widmeyer and Gosset found that team member ability correlated .73 with team success.

In a third, more comprehensive report, Widmeyer and Loy had two independent raters judge the skill of eight female tennis players in the serve, volley, forehand, and backhand. Win-loss records were assessed for the 28 teams which resulted when the 8 players were combined in all of the possible combinations. The results showed that the average ability of the two players was related to the team's effectiveness. The correlations for the individual components were .30 between the doubles team's forehand ability and team success, .42 for the doubles team's ability to serve and team success, .61 for the doubles team's ability to volley and team success, and .79 for the doubles team's backhand ability and team success. The correlation between overall individual tennis ability and team success was .77.

Probably the most extensive investigation of the relationship of individual ability to team success in different sports was carried out by Jones (1974). He used available individual statistic in professional tennis (singles rankings), baseball (runs batted in and earned run averages), basketball (points, assists, rebounds), and football (points for and against). These statistics were then correlated with team effectiveness as represented by rankings and win-loss records. Team effectiveness and individual skill and ability were correlated .70 in men's tennis, .80 in ladies tennis, .91 in football, .94 in baseball, and .60 in basketball.

The fact that the highest relationship found by Jones was in baseball and the lowest was in basket-ball is consistent with what would be predicted from Steiner's proposition that actual productivity is a product of the potential productivity of a group minus the losses due to faulty group processes. Faulty group processes result primarily from the inability of group members to coordinate their efforts efficiently and effectively. In baseball, the amount of coordination required on offense and defense is relatively small so the potential losses due to faulty group processes in any team would be small. Consequently, the team with the best actual productivity (win-loss record) should most frequently be the one with the best potential productivity (i.e., the best players). In the Jones study, this was the case as reflected in the very high correlation of .94.

In basketball, greater coordinative team play is required on offense and defense. Thus, individual talent by itself (potential productivity) is not as strongly related to actual productivity. The ability to play well together (i.e., to minimize the process losses) is important. This was also reflected in the relatively lower correlation of .60 found by Jones.

Implications for the Effectiveness of Sport Groups

Although the correlations between individual measures of ability and team performance are not perfect (i.e., the best individuals don't always produce the best team), there is sufficient strong evidence to support the view that coaches should always select on ability first. Diane Gill (1984) emphasized this point in her summary of the research on the relationship of individual ability to team ability:

Perhaps the most basic finding is that research supports our common belief in the general individual ability-group performance relationship; the best individuals make the best team. No evidence suggests any reason for selecting any but the most skilled or capable individual performers. (p. 325)

7 The Variability in Group Resources

The variability in group resources — or homogeneity versus heterogeneity as it is also called — has been the topic of considerable research in a wide variety of groups. And, depending upon the nature of the group and its task, variability has been considered to be beneficial, detrimental, or even both. As one example, Alvin Zander (1982), a psychologist who has extensively researched and written on groups, pointed out that homogeneity is beneficial to group development because it:

> If you take a shot or make a move to the basket that isn't successful, then you should have passed off to [Michael] Jordan. But if you constantly ignore your own shot in an all-out effort to set up Jordan, then you are not providing him with substantial support. It's a problem the [Chicago] Bulls have struggled with all year. (McCallum, 1988, p. 34)

> encourages a group sense. Birds of a feather flock together, and create a more distinct entity when they do. People too form a better unit if they are alike, and an effective leader develops oneness within a set by encouraging likeness among members. To do this, she recruits persons who will interact well because of similar purpose, background, training, experience, or temperment. She pays special attention to their basic values (what they feel they should or should not do) because similarity in values plays a major part in determining who associates with whom and who remains within an organization. Persons whose beliefs do not fit together well have a hard time forming a strong group, as has been observed in school boards, management committees, or fraternities. (p. 3)

Zander was referring to homogeneity in psychological attributes. Commonsense indicates that homogeneity in physical skills and attributes might not always be desirable. When World Cup or All-Star teams are selected for international competition, for example, heterogeneity of skill is considered to be essential. The performance of sport teams is enhanced by the presence of different individuals who have the skills to play different roles. No soccer team or hockey team or basketball team could hope to be successful if each team member possessed identical skills. This point was highlighted by Carron (1981) who noted that

> The division of responsibility present on sport teams — setter and spiker in volleyball, blocking and pass receiving in football, playmaking and rebounding in basketball — requires heterogeneous skills if the team is to be successful. (p.250)

Carron was referring to heterogeneity in the variety (i.e., the type or breadth) of skills present in a team. As a third example, it is also possible to have heterogeneity in the absolute amount of skill each team member possesses (i.e., the depth of skills). Extreme heterogeneity in ability can present special problems for a group. One of them is illustrated in the quote used to introduce this chapter. The exceptional talents of Michael Jordan produce what Jack McCallum (1988) referred to as a damned-if-you-do, damned-if-you-don't dilemma. His teammates are criticized for not helping Jordan enough, for letting him carry the team. They are also criticized for trying to do too much, for taking too many shots (unsuccessful shots) when he is so much more capable.

Finally, Richard Hackman and Greg Oldham (1980), two industrial psychologists, have pointed out that homogeneity can be both negative and positive for work group productivity:

> On the one hand, if members are too much alike, some of the special advantages of having a team are lost, including the special expertise and perspectives that different individuals can bring to the task and the chance for people in the group to learn new skills ...Yet excessive heterogeneity also can impair group effectiveness because insufficient "common ground" among members makes communication difficult and provides for less-than-needed interchangeability among members. (p.177)

It is useful to examine the conditions under which heterogeneity and homogeneity are beneficial, detrimental, or unimportant.

Social and Work Groups

On the basis of their research in business and industry, Hackman and Oldham (1980) provided four generalizations related to the composition of a work groups and group effectiveness. The first is that the team members should have *high levels of relevant expertise* on the task. While this seems to go without saying for almost every group situation, it is often difficult to ensure that it occurs. Most group leaders simply have to make do with the pool of talent available. In industrial psychology, however, considerable time and effort have been spent in the development of inventories for personnel selection. So, it is often possible in work groups to match individual preferences and abilities with specific tasks.

A second Hackman and Oldham generalization is that the *group should be sufficiently large* to carry out the task, but not larger. The issue of group size was discussed in Chapter 3. The rationale for retaining a large number of athletes on a team is obvious; the greater the number of athletes on a roster, the greater are the resources available. The rationale for not retaining too many athletes was also discussed in Chapter 3. As the team increases in size, coordination and communication problems increase. The process losses resulting from poorer communication and poorer coordination also increase (see Figure 3.1 again). A team must have enough players to compete and practice. But, as the size of a roster increases, the number of individuals who are not playing, who are inactive at practice, and who have limited access to

their coaches also increases. A reduction in size means that less resources are available but the process losses associated with reduced coordination and communication are also reduced.

A third principle advanced by Hackman and Oldham is that in addition to their task-relevant skills, individual group members should also possess *moderate levels of social skill*. Although performance-oriented groups such as sport teams have the task as their primary focus, they are nonetheless, social units. Individuals with limited social skills can increase the problems associated with communication and coordination thereby increasing the process losses.

The fourth and final principle is that the group should possess *both homogeneity and heterogeneity* in the characteristics of its members. Homogeneity enhances communication while heterogeneity limits it. The link between homogeneity and communication represents the basis for the Hackman and Oldham proposition that some similarity among members will contribute to group effectiveness. At the same time, however, heterogeneity among group members insures that varied perspectives, skills, and attitudes are brought to the group. These varied resources help the group — as long as the group members are able to work together.

The homogeneity versus heterogeneity issue has also been approached from the point of view of the group task (Steiner, 1972). Table 7.1 contains an overview. In *additive* tasks — a track team, for example — the group product results from the combined efforts of the group members. Thus, the question of homogeneity versus heterogeneity is largely irrelevant. If one team has more competent members than another team, its output will be better; if it has more incompetent members, its product will be poorer. The variability among members is not an issue except to the degree that poorer members drag the group down.

The issue of homogeneity versus heterogeneity is also largely irrelevant in compensatory tasks, those tasks in which the group product is the average of the results from individual members. Judging in gymnastics or diving is an example. Ultimately an average score representing the pooled evaluations of the individual judges is used. So, as was the case with additive tasks, the important issue is the competence of all of the judges, not the variability among them.

Steiner has suggested that heterogeneity of ability has the tendency to establish higher levels of productivity when the task is *disjunctive*. When a group of coaches is faced with a problem that either involves an

Table 7.1 Steiner's task types and productivity when the group's resources are homogeneous versus heterogeneous

Type of Task	Production Effects	Homogeneity versus Heterogeneity
Additive	Group output results from the addition of individual outputs; e.g. tug of war	Homogeneity versus heterogeneity is irrelevant
Compensatory	Group output is the average of individual outputs; judging of diving	Homogeneity versus heterogeneity is irrelevant
Disjunctive (Eureka)	Group output is an "either-or" solution; one individual output is used; calculating batting averages	Heterogeneity is best because there is an increased likelihood that individuals with the requisite skills will be available
Disjunctive (Noneureka)	Group output is judgmental and one individual output is used; e.g., selecting an All-Star team	Heterogeneity is best because there is an increased likelihood that individuals with the requisite skills will be available
Conjunctive (Unitary)	Group output is the result of the combined efforts of all and no division of labor is possible; e.g. a mountain climbing team	Homogeneity is best because no single group member will hold back the group
Conjunctive (Divisible with Matching)	Group output is the result of the combined efforts of all and a division of labor is possible; e.g., a volleyball team	Homogeneity is best if individual skills are matched to the task
Discretionary (Variable)	Group output is the result of an autocratic, delegative, or democratic decision.	Homogeneity versus heterogeneity is irrelevant

either-or solution (*eureka disjunctive* tasks) or is philosophical in nature *noneureka disjunctive* tasks, heterogeneity is better than homogeneity. Varied resources and approaches can be brought to the same question. There is a greater chance that somebody will have the skill and expertise to solve the problem.

In the case of *unitary conjunctive* tasks, such as mountain climbing, all group members participate equally and contribute to the group product. Thus, the group is only as strong as its weakest link. Homogeneity is an advantage in this case "because it permits a high level of potential productivity and is less likely

than heterogeneity to generate dissatisfaction among superior members of the group" (Steiner, 1972, p. 112).

This is not the case with *divisible conjunctive* tasks on the other hand. These types of tasks require a specialized division of labor. The process of assembling any sport team is an example. Both offensive and defensive specialists, rebounders and playmakers, and spikers and setters are required. Consequently, heterogeneity in the team's membership increases the likelihood that individuals with more specialized resources will be available. And, if the specialized skills of team members can be matched to the task demands, the group's performance is more effective.

Finally, in the case of *discretionary* tasks, there are a variety of ways in which the group can arrive at the solution to a problem (Forsythe, 1983). The four most frequently used — autocratic, participative, consultive, delegative — are discussed in detail in Chapter 13 (see Table 13.6). Since one individual makes the decision for the group in the autocratic, consultive, and delegative approaches, homogeneity versus heterogeneity is irrelevant. The democratic approach is similar to the approach used in compensatory tasks. So, again, the issue of homogeneity versus heterogeneity is irrelevant.

Sport Groups

In social and work groups, there is a high degree of flexibility in terms of the assignment of individuals work together. This same level of flexibility isn't always present in sport teams; a coach usually must work with the talent available. Possibly this is one of the reasons why the issue of heterogeneity versus homogeneity has received so little attention in motor skills research. The research which has been carried out has focused on the impact of differences in the depth of ability (i.e., the amount of skill group members possess) rather than the breadth of abilities (i.e., the variety of skills members bring to the group).

In one study, Diane Gill (1979) tested female college students on a motor maze task in two experiments in the laboratory. The scores obtained by individuals practicing alone were used to form a range of average ability groups. For example, when two individuals with poor scores were combined, they represented a group with low ability; when a person with a high score was partnered with a person of low ability they represented a group of average ability; and, when two individuals with good scores were combined, they represented a group with high ability.

These same groups were examined from another perspective as well; in terms of the discrepancy in ability in the group. Thus, the partners low-low and high-high in ability represented groups with a low discrepancy in ability; the low-high partners represented a group with a high discrepancy. Also, the situation was manipulated by Gill in two experiments to insure either cooperation or competition.

In the first experiment, Gill found no relationship between the discrepancy in ability and group performance under cooperative or competitive conditions. Good and poor performance could not be explained by

the fact that individuals were in groups that were homogeneous (low-low, moderate-moderate, high-high) or heterogeneous (low-high, moderate-low, moderate-high, etc.) in ability. However, in her second experiment which involved a cooperative task, Gill did find a correlation of .31 between discrepancy in ability and group performance. The groups that were heterogeneous in ability were more effective.

In a study by Neil Widmeyer and John Loy (1981) with female tennis players, homogeneity in ability was positively associated with team effectiveness. The number of team losses decreased as the discrepancy in the ability between the two partners decreased. This finding was most noticeable in the case of homogeneity in the ability to serve ($r = -.38$), followed by the volley ($r = -.38$), the backhand ($r = -.31$), and the forehand ($r = -.11$). The heterogeneous teams had a winning percentage of 45%; the homogeneous teams, a winning percentage of 55%.

Widmeyer and Loy observed that "many would predict the opposite findings arguing that the heterogeneous teams should do better because they have a high ability person who can play the majority of shots. The results suggest that these female tennis players adopt a very egalitarian strategy when playing with their partners and thus their game is not marked by 'poaching' or any other form of overplaying by the better players. It could also be that the homogeneous teams are directing the majority of their shots to the weaker player on heterogeneous teams. Support for these two assumptions lies in the fact that the total ability of the weakest player was more positively related to team performance outcome ($r = .74$) than was the total ability of the best player ($r = .49$)" (p.27).

Spillover Effects in Heterogeneous Groups

Working in a heterogeneous group can also have a positive influence on the subsequent performance of the weaker individual. This is referred to as a *spillover effect* (e.g., Dunnette, Campbell, & Jaastad, 1963; Goldman & Goldman, 1981; Silverman & Stone, 1972). The spillover effect seems to be due to both learning and motivation. The lower ability person not only learns new strategies and techniques but the task is approached with renewed interest and energy.

A study by Florence Goldman and Morton Goldman (1981) helps to illustrate the spillover effect in a classroom context. High school students were tested on a problem-solving task in three sessions. In the initial session, the students worked alone and on the basis of their performance were categorized as high, medium, or low in ability. In a second session held two weeks later, the students either worked alone or in pairs. Every possible combination of ability group was included — high-high, high-medium, high-low, medium-low, etc. Then, in the third session which was held two days later, the students again worked independently.

Goldman and Goldman had initially expected that the experience of working in a group would be beneficial to the performance of all subjects. This wasn't the case. For high ability and moderate ability subjects, there was no difference between working in groups and working alone. In the case of the low ability subjects, however, performance was better in the group situation. Also, when homogeneous and heterogeneous group involvement was contrasted with working alone, the low ability subjects in the heterogeneous groups were the only ones to show a positive effect. Working with someone more knowledgeable was a benefit. Goldman and Goldman noted that "in general, students indicated that because of the peer group experience they became aware of new arguments, details, and strategies and were helped to correct errors in their understanding ... and that due to these sessions they may have had incentives to improve their performance" (p. 88).

Implications for the Effectiveness of Sport Groups

In most sport situations, the division of responsibility present insures that heterogeneous skills are necessary if the team is to be successful. Volleyball involves blocking and setting, basketball involves playmaking, shooting, and rebounding, football involves blocking, tackling, passing, running, and receiving. Each of these sports profits from having a division of labor which permits different individuals to focus on developing very specific skills and abilities.

One exception to this list of sports in which heterogeneity is advantageous seems to be tennis doubles teams. Widmeyer and Loy found that teams made up of women of medium ability were superior to teams composed of a high and a low ability player.

In physical education classes, heterogeneity may be advantageous. The work of Goldman and Goldman showed that working in heterogeneous groups can have a spillover effect for low ability individuals. When they return to independent activities, their performance is enhanced. This has been attributed to the learning of new strategies and techniques as well as to the increased motivation acquired during the group experience with more competent individuals.

8 The Compatibility of Group Resources

Essentially, compatibility reflects the ability of an individual to function effectively and in harmony with other people and/or in the situation. A mesh or fit is present in attitudes, personality, and/or skills. In sport groups as well as in other social situations, compatibility contributes to increased individual satisfaction and performance effectiveness. The quote from Tretiak (1987) which was used to introduce this chapter, highlights the essence of compatibility in sport. The three linemates, Kharlamov, Mikhailov, and Petrov, worked so well together that they formed what Tretiak felt was the best line in hockey history. Tretiak also felt that part of the reason for their compatibility was the similarity in important attributes:

> What distinguished this trio was their thirst for goals. They did not care who got the credit for a goal or an assist, the important thing was to score. They could not bear defeat ... Each trusted his linemates as he would himself ... they were picky about their game. To play carelessly, not giving it their all, was not their style. They could not do it. (p. 63)

However, compatibility isn't simply similarity; individuals may be quite different and still be compatible with each other. Tretiak also highlighted this aspect of compatibility when he pointed out that Mikhailov "was not as talented as Kharlamov ... not as powerful as Petrov" (p.62). Their talents complemented one another. In fact, an example which highlights complementarity is the nursery rhyme: "Jack Spratt could eat no fat, his wife could eat no lean; so betwixt them both they licked the platter clean". The Spratt family, like the Kharlamov line,

> It is impossible to talk about [Valery] Kharlamov without mentioning Boris Mikhailov and Vladimir Petrov. Valery's superb linemates helped him to discover his talents. It seems that they were born to meet and become the greatest hockey line in history. (Tretiak, 1987, p. 62)

not only held some things in common, they possessed other attributes which served to complement one another.

Perspectives on the Compatibility in Groups

In the study of compatibility in sport teams, the principal focus has been on coach-athlete compatibility. Athlete-athlete compatibility has generally been considered under the topic of group cohesion (with interpersonal compatibility being one of the factors associated with the development of group cohesiveness). Two main approaches have been used to study the nature and effects of coach-athlete compatibility. In one of these approaches, FIRO Theory, the *needs and personalities* of the coach and athlete have been contrasted. In the second approach, the specific *behaviors* of the coach and the athlete have been examined.

The FIRO Theory

FIRO Theory (it rhymes with Cairo and means Fundamental Interpersonal Relations Orientation), which was developed by William Schutz (1958, 1966), begins with the premise that *people need people*. Schutz pointed out that human beings have interpersonal (social) needs which are as important as their biological needs for sustaining health. These interpersonal needs are satisfied through the development and maintenance of compatible relationships with other people. The three principal interpersonal needs identified by Schutz are *inclusion, control,* and *affection.* Schutz also proposed that in interpersonal relationships, people not only need to express inclusion, control, and affection, they need to receive these from others. Thus, there are six components which make up the interpersonal elements in FIRO theory: expressed inclusion, wanted inclusion, expressed control, wanted control, expressed affection, and wanted affection. These are assessed through a paper and pencil test, FIRO-B (Fundamental Interpersonal Relations Orientation-Behavior), which assesses the degree to which an individual engages in these behaviors in social situations. A description of the six behaviors is presented in Table 8.1.

Inclusion is a need which is manifested in such interpersonal behaviors as associating, mingling, joining, and communicating. It is a behavior which is fundamental to any interpersonal relationship; if the other person is not considered to be significant enough to be "included" (either psychologically or physically), then no interpersonal relationship is possible. Individuals high in the need to express inclusion, actively seek out relationships, communicate freely, and indicate to others that they are significant and important. Individuals who are high on wanted inclusion behavior have a high need to be with others, to be considered significant and important, to be included in the activities of others.

Control is behavior associated with the decision making process between people; it is reflected in power, authority, dominance, influence, and leadership. Individuals high in the need to express control are dominant in their behavior. They actively seek out leadership roles and positions of power and influence in interpersonal relationships and group situations. On the other hand, individuals who are high in wanted control have a strong preference to let others make the decisions, to follow the rules set out for them.

Finally, affection is behavior associated with feelings of love, affiliation, friendship, and cohesion. Individuals who are high in expressed affection actively show their love, liking, and friendship to others. On the other hand, those individuals who are high in wanted affection have a great need to be liked, loved, and/or friends with others.

It is possible for a coach or athlete to exhibit any one

Table 8.1   Schutz's Fundamental Interpersonal Orientation theory (Adapted from Schutz, 1966)

Dimension	Description
Inclusion: to belong, associate, mingle, communicate, and join	*Wanted Inclusion* is a need to be included in the activities of others, to associate with others, to be considered significant *Expressed Inclusion* is a need to include others, to actively join and associate with others, and to indicate to them that they are significant
Control:: to exert power, leadership, authority, and dominance	*Wanted Control* is a need to have others control, lead, influence, dominate, or handle authority *Expressed Control* is a need to control others, to lead and influence them, to take charge and exert leadership
Affection: to love, like, affiliate with others, cohere, be affectionate	*Wanted Affection* is a need to be liked, loved, friendly with others, to have others provide affection *Expressed Affection* is a need to give others love and affection, to extend friendship

of four behavioral patterns insofar as the giving and receiving of inclusion, control, or affection is concerned: receiver only, originator only, high interchanger, or low interchanger. A *receiver only* is a person who wants others to provide a specific behavior but does not express that behavior to others. An example of this is an athlete who looks to others for leadership on a team but declines any opportunity to lead. An *originator only* is a person who has a preference for expressing but not for receiving a behavior. An athlete who is comfortable leading but is uncomfortable when others are trying to exert influence or power illustrates this behavioral pattern. When a person has a high preference for both giving and receiving a behavior, they are referred to as a *high interchanger.* This is illustrated by the person who wants and gives a great deal of affection. And, finally, the fourth behavioral pattern, a *low interchanger,* reflects behavioral isolation. This person has no desire to either express or receive a behavior. Track athletes who prefer to work out alone — they don't want other athletes to practice with them and they reject all invitations — are an example of a low interchanger for inclusion behavior.

A Behavioral Approach

In the behavioral approach, the frequency with which specific behaviors occur in practices or games is tabulated by direct observation or through the use of videotapes. Some typical questions might be: Is the coach frequently critical? How often is praise used? Does the coach spend a great deal of time talking or do the athletes have frequent opportunities to practice? From a compatibility perspective, the relative frequencies of these various behaviors are then compared with athlete preferences, satisfaction, and performance. Typical questions in this regard are: Is the relative frequency with which a coach gives positive encouragement associated with athlete satisfaction? When the coach spends a great deal of time talking, does team performance suffer? The behavioral approach to the study of coach-athlete compatibility is discussed in detail in Chapter 13.

Implications for the Effectiveness of Sport Groups

Compatibility exists when there is a fit, a complementarity in needs and behaviors among group members. Compatibility influences group effectiveness. Marvin Shaw emphasized this point when he noted that "when group members have personality attributes which predispose them to behave in compatible ways, the group atmosphere is congenial, the members are relaxed, and group functioning is more effective. On the other hand, when member attributes lead to incompatible behaviors, members are anxious, tense, and/or dissatisfied, and group functioning is less effective" (p. 238).

Sport is a unique activity in terms of the degree of control and power held by the coach. Thus, compatibility is often a matter of the athletes making a greater effort to conform to the needs and personality of their coaches. Many athletes, because of the nature or strength of their own personality have difficulty with

this. Those who are incompatible or who don't conform often quit the sport (Pease, Locke, & Burlingame, 1971).

Bryant Cratty (1983) has suggested that one way to capitalize on a coach-athlete differences is to assign an athlete whose personality does not coincide with that of the coach to another coach on the same team. He also proposed that on individual sport teams different coaches with different psychological attributes (e.g., a tranquil versus an emotional coach) should be used to motivate athletes at critical times. The key ingredient seems to be flexibility — having the ability to adapt to different situations and different athletes.

The Dimensions of Compatibility

Although compatibility is most often viewed as the fit between individuals, it's much broader than this. It is also the property of the relationship between an individual and the role he/she must play in the group, and between an individual and the demands of the task (Schutz, 1966). Compatibility between individuals has already been introduced. The Kharlamov line is a good example. Their interpersonal compatibility contributed to their effectiveness. Incompatibility between an individual and a role could exist if a quiet, reserved, withdrawn individual was appointed team captain. The leadership demands in the role of captain might be overwhelming. Insofar as person-task compatibility is concerned, specific tasks require specific dispositions. The individual must possess these dispositions in order to be effective. The Spratts, Jack and his wife, are a good example. Each was highly suited to his/her specific task. Thus, when the composition of the group is looked at in terms of the compatibility of the resources, the focus is on the fit between individuals, the fit between individuals and their role responsibilities, and the fit between individuals and the demands of the task.

Interpersonal Compatibility

Personal Needs. A considerable amount of attention has been directed toward the question of whether compatibility — the fit between individuals — contributes to group effectiveness in social and work groups. It was pointed out previously that compatibility represents complementarity of needs. An individual who prefers to lead complements the preferences of an individual who prefers to be led. Not surprisingly, the general consensus is that the mesh or fit between people is important for group effectiveness. On the basis of his work, Argyle (1969) concluded that "there

Table 8.2 Sources of incompatibility in dyads in studies using Schutz's FIRO-B.

Authors	Group	Results
Carron & Bennett (1977)	College athletes and coaches from various sports	Affection and control were factors but inclusion was the most important contributor to incompatibility
Horne & Carron (1985)	College athletes and coaches from various sports	Affection, control, and inclusion did not discriminate between compatible and incompatible coach-athlete dyads
Carron (1978)	College students	Coaches were perceived to exert high control but little affection or inclusion. Athletes were perceived to be the recipients of control and also perceived to exert little affection or inclusion
Pease, Locke, & Burlingame (1971)	Junior high school baseball players	Coach-athlete incompatibility was not associated with athletes being cut from the team. Coach-athlete incompatibility in control and affection were associated with athlete decisions to leave the team.
Carron & Garvie (1978)	Olympic wrestlers	Coach-athlete compatibility in con trol, affection, and inclusion were not related to performance.
Carron & Chelladurai (1981)	High school wrestlers & basketball players	Coach-athlete compatibility in control, affection, and inclusion were not related to cohesiveness in wrestlers. Compatibility in control was related to cohesiveness in basketball players.

expected that compatibility in the area of control would be most important. Again, the results supported this prediction. Individuals compatible in their preference for control behavior consistently selected one another as a potential traveling companion. A summary of studies which have used Schutz's FIRO-B to assess interpersonal compatibility are presented in Table 8.2.

A number of studies have been undertaken by my colleagues and me to examine the sources of coach-athlete incompatibility (e.g., Carron, 1978; Carron & Bennett, 1977; Carron & Chelladurai, 1978, 1981; Carron & Garvie, 1978; Horne & Carron, 1985). These are also summarized in Table 8.2. In the earliest study

are three results of incompatibility — the meshing is poor, the interactors do not enjoy the interaction or like each other, and task performance is poor" (p.204).

In one of his early studies, Schutz (1966) examined the relationship between interpersonal orientations and dyadic relationships in a fraternity. Sociometric questionnaires were administered to assess each individual's preferences for roommates and traveling companions. Also, each individual's behavioral preferences for inclusion, control, and affection were assessed using FIRO-B (see Table 8.1 again). Because selecting a roommate involves a relatively long-term commitment, it was expected that compatibility in all three dimensions would be important. Schutz's results supported this prediction. Individuals compatible in their preferences for inclusion, control, and affection consistently selected one another in the sociometric questionnaire. Because selecting a traveling companion involves only a limited commitment that terminates within a short period of time, Schutz

(Carron & Bennett, 1977), all of the coaches at a Canadian university were approached and asked to identify the athletes with whom they were compatible and those with whom they were incompatible. The compatible group were those athletes who satisfied a gestalt definition of most coachable and least disruptive — who were furthest removed from being "problem athletes". The coaches were also asked to identify the athletes who caused the greatest problems, who were on the opposite end of the spectrum.

All the athletes and the coaches were tested on Schutz's FIRO-B scale to obtain compatibility measures for inclusion, control, and affection. Although control and affection were contributors to compatibility, inclusion behavior was the most important. The relationship in the incompatible dyads was characterized by relatively detached, withdrawn, isolated behavior (i.e., a lack of inclusion) on the part of both the coach and athlete. This result is consistent with the suggestion made by Tutko and Richards (1977) that if a coach has "an athlete who suffers from the same problem as the coach, there is a very high probability that the coach will be unable to handle the player successfully or communicate with him effectively" (p. 74).

In a later study by Horne & Carron (1985), the question of compatibility versus incompatibility was approached from the athlete's perspective. Intercollegiate athletes were asked to rate their overall relationship with their coach on a 9-point scale. Neither control, affection nor inclusion was an effective predictor of coach-athlete incompatibility.

The question of who holds the perception of incompatibilty — the coach or the athlete — might be quite critical to continued involvement in sport (see Figure 8.1). Pease, Locke and Burlingame (1971) pointed out that when athletes are cut from the team, it is the result of the coach' perception. When athletes quit a team, it is a result of their personal perception that the situation is unattractive. When Pease and his colleagues studied athletes who were cut from baseball teams, they found that compatibility with their coaches on the FIRO measures was not a factor. The coaches did not center out those athletes with whom they were incompatible and cut them from the team. A different picture emerged when athletes who quit the team were studied. Players who quit were incompatible with their coaches in control and, to a lesser extent, affection.

Ability. There is no doubt that compatibility in ability is one important aspect of group success. The Kharlamov example discussed at the beginning of the chapter is one example. Good doubles teams in badminton and tennis are another. If the skills and attributes of one individual mesh and complement the skills and attributes of the other, the team is more successful. What isn't clear across different sports is what similar skills the individuals should possess and what skills should be complementary. In some sports the answer seems intuitively obvious. On a compatible hockey line, all three of the individuals must be similar in skating ability. A poor skater can't keep up with the two good skaters. But a line with three playmakers and no checker wouldn't be effective. So, complementarity in the skills of playmaking and checking are essential.

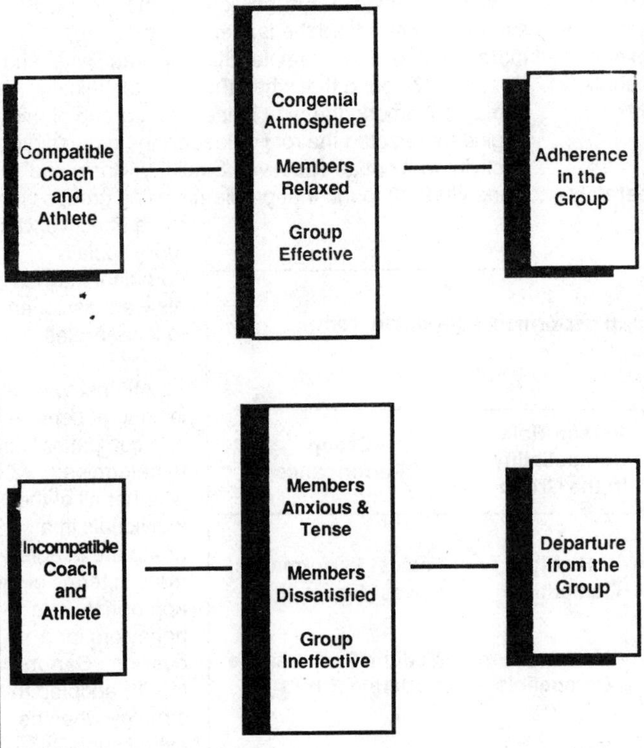

One of the only studies to assess the relative importance of the fit of different abilities to team success was carried out by Widmeyer and Loy (1981). This research was introduced earlier. Widmeyer and Loy compared the importance of compatibility in the serve and volley versus compatibility in the forehand and backhand using women's doubles tennis teams. Compatibility in the forehand and backhand was more important (r = .78) for team effectiveness than in the serve and volley (r = .51). However, the authors cautioned that this result could have been particular to the sample tested. The women players who were tested had a tendency to play at the baseline rather than to come to the net in a serve and volley style.

Compatibility with Group Roles

A second aspect of compatibility discussed by Schutz concerns the relationship between the dispositions of individual group members and the roles they must fill in the group. A number of examples serve to illustrate this aspect. A young Canadian hockey player was told that he would have to be the "enforcer or policeman" on the team if

Figure 8.1 The consequences of coach-athlete compatibility.

he hoped to play regularly. He didn't want to be a fighter. Moreover, he saw himself as a potential goal scorer. So he left that team for another one. As a second example, an outgoing, people-oriented athlete was asked to help two first-year athletes make the transition from high school to university. She took on this responsibility and successfully provided a complete orientation for both first-year athletes. And, as a final example, an outstanding basketball player in her senior year was approached by her coach and asked to assume more of a leadership role; the rest of the team was very young and inexperienced. Although the athlete tried, she was always uncomfortable directing and encouraging others. And, her own play seemed to suffer. The time and energy spent trying to fill the leader's role detracted from her concentration.

A laboratory study which illustrates the importance of person-role compatibility was reported by Liddell and Slocum (1976). They selected their subjects using the control dimension of Schutz's FIRO B. The subjects were then assigned to groups of five people to solve communication problems. In the task, a wheel network, one person occupies a central position (in the hub of the wheel) while the remaining four people are in peripheral positions. The people in the periphery must direct their communications through the hub, they can't communicate directly with each other. So, the person in the central position has a very dominant role with a considerable amount of control; the people in the peripheral positions have passive roles with minimal control.

Three groups were created: compatible, moderately compatible, and incompatible. In the compatible group, an individual with a high need for control was placed in the central position and four individuals with a low need for control were placed in the peripheral positions. All group members occupied a role which was completely compatible with their personalities. In the incompatible group, a person with a low need for control was placed in the central position and four individuals with a high need for control were placed in the peripheral positions. In this case, all group members occupied roles completely incompatible with their personalities. In the moderately compatible group, the hub and each of the four peripheral positions were occupied by a person who had been randomly selected in terms of control. Thus, from the perspective of person-to-role compatibility, this group fell between the other two.

Liddell and Slocum found that the compatible group arrived at decisions faster and made less errors than both the moderately compatible and the incompatible groups. The moderately compatible group was the next most effective. They arrived at decisions faster and made less errors than the incompatible group (see Table 8.3).

When the high status individual in the group assumes or is assigned the leader role, the group is more effective. For example, Slusher, Van Dyke, and Rose (1972) found that when the most technically competent among the nine leaders of a group of thirty engineers rejected the role of leader, the group's productivity was not as effective. Similarly, Shaw and Harkey (1976) found that problem solving groups were more effective when more socially dominant individuals were assigned to leader roles.

Another way of looking at person-role compatibility is to determine whether all of the individuals in a group are in agreement in terms of the appropriate role behaviors for a position. Carron (1978) adopted this strategy when he asked subjects to indicate the appropriate role behaviors for coaches and

Table 8.3. Person- role compatibility and group performance (Adapted from Liddell & Slocum, 1976)

Occupant of Central Position	Occupants of Peripheral Positions	Person-Role Compatibility in the Group	Group Performance
High Need for Control	Low Need for Control	Highly Compatible	Fastest Performance Fewest Errors
Moderate Need for Control	Moderate Need for Control	Moderately Compatible	Medium Performance Moderate Errors
Low Need for Control	High Need for Control	Highly Incompatible	Slowest Performance Most Errors

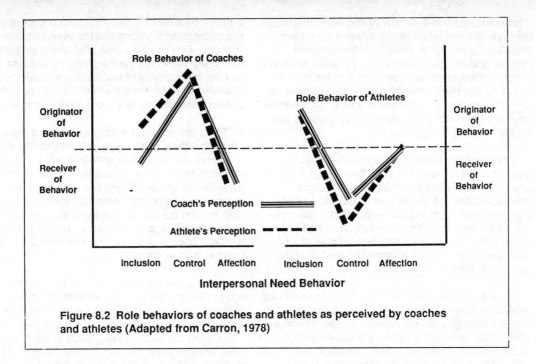

Figure 8.2 Role behaviors of coaches and athletes as perceived by coaches and athletes (Adapted from Carron, 1978)

athletes. He found that both coaches and athletes perceived that the coaching role involves exerting a high level of control and being passive in terms of initiating interactions with athletes and developing warm personal friendships. The athlete's role was perceived to involve very little control and also to be passive in terms of initiating interactions or establishing a friendship with the coach. These results are illustrated in Figure 8.2.

These perceived role behaviors could contribute to coach-athlete incompatibility. If both the coach's and the athlete's role involve being passive in terms of initiating interactions and developing friendships, the athletic situation would be cold and impersonal. It must be kept in mind, however, that interpersonal relationships are a product of both the personality of the individuals and the nature of the situation. Early in a group's development, the situation has the strongest influence on interpersonal interactions. Both the coaches and the athletes could be expected to behave in a manner consistent with their role expectations. As the group develops, the personal dimension and the personalities of the coaches and athletes assume more importance. Consequently, in well established teams, incompatibility would more likely be the product of differences in personality rather than differences in appropriate role behaviors.

Compatibility with The Task

One area in which the relationship of person to task compatibility and individual effectiveness has been tested is personnel selection. The rationale for matching individuals to jobs on the basis of their personality dispositions was highlighted by Schutz (1966):

> jobs may be classified according to their interpersonal requirements... For example, the essence of a salesman's job, ordinarily, is wide and frequent contact with people, or high inclusion. The politician's role involves high control in that when in office he exercises power over a large number of constituents, but he also may be voted out by them; therefore his constituency has a kind of collective control over him. The expectations for a military officer as far as his relations to subordinates is concerned, may be described as low affection, exemplified by the 'no fraternization' dictum interposed between officer and enlisted man. (p.67)

Schutz found support for his expectations in a number of studies.

In sport, skill is the ultimate criterion. Nonetheless, there has been a longstanding interest in whether specific psychosocial attributes are associated with athletic success. In a number of studies, differences between elite and lesser skilled athletes have been identified. It isn't clear, however, whether these psychosocial attributes were already present when the athletes entered into the sport (and assisted them to rise to an elite level) or whether they developed in the elite athletes over time. Whatever their origin, performance at a high level is characterized by a unique psychosocial profile (Morgan, 1979).

The positive mental health profile of elite athletes that was originally identified by William Morgan (1979) is presented in Figure 8.3. According to Morgan, athletic success at the elite level is associated with a high degree of vigor, and low amounts of tension, depression, anger, confusion, and fatigue. This has been referred to as the *iceberg profile* because while the vigor of elite athletes is above the median of the population, the other factors are below.

A number of other studies have also examined elite athletes including gymnasts (Mahoney & Avener, 1977), racquetball players (Meyers, Cooke, Cullen,& Liles, 1979), wrestlers (Highlen & Bennet, 1979), and divers (Highlen & Bennett, 1983). Although there were slight differences from one study to the next, some similarities also emerged across the studies. The elite athletes were superior in self confidence, were less anxious, used positive performance imagery to a greater extent, and were better able to block out negative thoughts. Although personnel selection in sport based on the presence of positive personality traits is intuitively appealing, the evidence available isn't sufficiently conclusive to permit this.

Implications for the Effectiveness of Sport Groups

An increased knowledge of training methods and skill development has led to progressive improvements in the strength, endurance, and skills of the modern athlete. They are now better prepared than in any other period in the history of sport. Talent identification has also improved. Professional teams who hoped to improve quickly needed the draft; amateur teams needed to recruit. In order to elevate the draft-recruitment process beyond a simple

lottery, it became necessary to better understand the requirements of the sport and the ingredients for success. This led to the task analyses of different sports, increased knowledge about the requisite skills, and the development of techniques of assessment. Consequently, if there is a science associated with the addition of resources to a team, it falls in this area.

The art of coaching is associated with trying to insure that there is interpersonal compatibility in the resources available. The answer to which two or three individuals will work well together in terms of their personalities and/or abilities seems to lie largely in the realm of trial and error. Putting together a successful front court in basketball, a defense in soccer, a forward line in hockey, or a scrum in rugby comes with coaching experience — knowing the personnel and knowing the demands of the sport.

Insuring that the right personnel fulfill the proper roles in the group — insuring that there is person-role compatibility — is also a coaching art. The loudest most dominant individual in the group doesn't necessarily make the best captain. But, if group roles are filled by individuals who do not have the necessary status or skill, group effectiveness suffers.

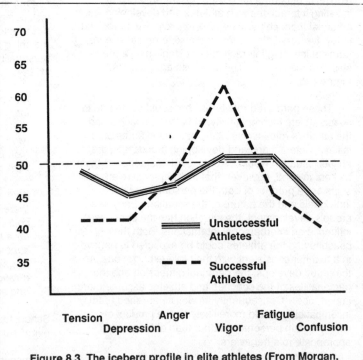

Figure 8.3 The iceberg profile in elite athletes (From Morgan, 1979. Reproduced with the permission of the publisher)

4   Group Structure

You're not going to see teams win five straight world championships any more unless you have a very strong organization. The only way to do it is to sign a DEave Winfield for ten years, and sign a Rickey Henderson for five years, and sign a Don Mattingly for five years. Now you have three key players all signed for at least five years. Then you have to work around those three positions. You do it cleverly. You have to get the type of young players you need for your shortstop of the future, your third baseman of the future. And you take a chance for a year or two that you won't win while you're molding your young players, helping them improve ....

I don't give a damn what you say, you take a guy from another organizationand he doesn't always fit in. He has different techniques, different habits, different coaching and instruction. It's important to have a certain chemistry on a baseball team, to have players who have played together for a few years and who know each other intimately, on the field and off. (Martin & Pepe, 1987, p. 146-148)

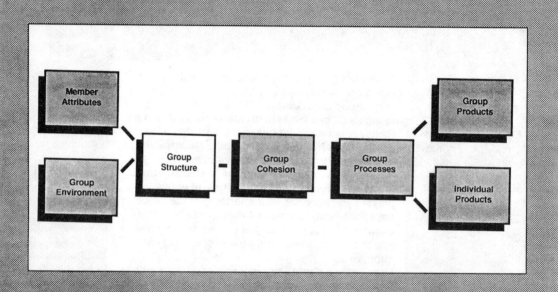

9 Group Development

If you consider the situations in which you participate in sport and physical activity, it is quickly apparent that there are a large number and variety — competitive sport, fitness classes, physical education classes. In each instance, the collection of individuals may differ in many important aspects — in terms of the number generally present, the extent to which there is social interaction, the level of intimacy, the degree to which there is an interest in the success of the group, the amount of mutual help and assistance provided, and the extent or frequency that the participants refer to the whole as "we" and to other social bodies as "they". In short, the collections of individuals present in these various sport and physical activity settings may differ markedly in the degree to which they constitute a "group".

The need to distinguish between a group and a collection of individuals (a crowd) has frequently been emphasized by group dynamicists. Although they may look similar, a group is quite different from a crowd of people who are together, doing the same thing at the same time. Alvin Zander (1982) emphasized this point when he observed that:

A number of persons jointly engaged in an activity — traveling on a sightseeing tour, picking apples in an orchard, working in a personnel department, attending a seminar — are not necessarily a group but it may become one. We know that people have formed a group when they talk freely, are interested in the achievement of their set as a whole, feel that associates are helpful, try to assist colleagues, refer to their collectivity as "we"

> Somewhere along the line you have to make them realize that nothing is going to happen unless it's done as a team. Not one thing is ever going to happen ... A team can't be a good team without great individuals, but it all happens within the framework of a team concept. (Ditka & Pierson, 1986, p. 236)

and to other social bodies as "they", and faithfully participate when members gather. A body of people is not a group if the members are primarily interested in individual accomplishments, are not concerned with the activities of other members or see others as rivals, and are often absent. (p. 1-2)

In short, group dynamics theory — and common sense — dictates that groups must be distinguished from collections of individuals. In fact, common sense also suggests that various sport groups (competitive sport teams, intramural sport teams, fitness classes) should be distinguished from each other. Their objectives are different, their sizes are different, the purposes of the participants are different ..... the list is endless. So, given the number, variety, and dissimilarities among groups, how is it possible to study groups in a general sense? How is it possible to generalize across groups?

The study of groups, while difficult, is not impossible because, despite their differences, there are also some strong similarities present across even the most widely differing groups. These similarities lie in the general way in which groups develop, in the structure that is characteristic of all groups, and in the types of interactions that occur within and between groups. In the five chapters in this section group development and group structure are discussed.

The Nature of Group Development

Numerous theories have been advanced to account for group development. In fact, in their review, Hill and Gruner (1973) identified over 100. Essentially, these theories fall into three general categories. In one general category, the stages in group development are considered to occur in a *linear* fashion; in the second, group development is thought to be *pendular* in nature; and, in the third, a *cyclical* pattern is assumed (see Figure 9.1). The major difference between each of these lies in the changes in the nature and amount of cohesion over time (Carron, 1984).

The Linear Perspective

In the linear perspective of group development, it is assumed that the group changes, progressively develops, and moves through different stages. Critical issues arise in each successive stage and when they are successfully dealt with, the group moves on. One example of a linear model was advanced by Bruce Tuckman (1965). Tuckman initially reviewed 50 studies in a search for common interpretations on how groups develop. On the basis of his analysis, he proposed that all groups go through four stages as they develop and then prepare for and carry out the group's task. These were referred to as: *forming, storming, norming,* and *performing.* Subsequently, Tuckman and Jensen (1977) modified this original proposal and added a fifth stage, *adjourning.* The Tuckman and Jensen perspective on group development is presented in Table 9.1.

In the first stage, forming, the group members become familiar with each other and begin to identify the group's task. A fraternity group that makes the decision to enter a team in an intramural basketball league would go through this stage — even though all of the individuals belong to the same fraternity and know each other well. It would still be necessary for them to become familiar with each other's skills and abilities and to determine what offensive and defensive systems that the team should use. The forming stage is essentially an orientation phase.

In the second phase, tension and conflict arise in the group as interpersonal disagreements occur, resistance to the group leader develops, and members begin to question the group's approach to the task or the task itself. In the case of the fraternity team, "storming" might be reflected in disagreements about how the offense or defense should be run, who should make the decisions on substitutions, who should do most of the shooting, and so on. During the storming stage, various group members attempt to resist the group's influence and impose their preferences on the group.

Following the storming of stage two, the group begins to draw together again in the third phase, norming. Group roles and group norms are established for both social relationships and task productivity. A dominant person, an outstanding player, or even a senior member of the fraternity might become assertive within the team and be acknowledged as the leader. Other group roles would also be assigned or assumed — peacemaker, comedian, social director, playmaker, shooter, for example. Essentially, the norming stage, is characterized by cooperation, cohesiveness, and consensus on the group's goals and objectives.

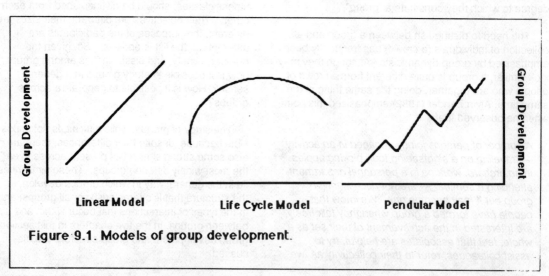

Figure 9.1. Models of group development.

Table 9.1 Stages in group development (Adapted from Tuckman & Jensen, 1977)

Stage	Interpersonal Characteristics	Task Characteristics
Forming	Individuals become familiar with each other and bonds develop within the group	Members determine what the group task is and what methods are suitable to carry it out
Storming	Tension develops and conflict occurs among members and with the leader	Resistance arises to the group methods and the group task
Norming	Cohesiveness and group harmony develop and group roles are established	Task cooperation among members is prevalent
Performing	Relationships are stabilized	The group's orientation is on productivity and per-
Adjourning	Member contact decreases and emotional dependency among individual members is reduced	The task is completed and the duties of members are finished

one stage is variable for different groups. One group might spend a considerable amount of time in the forming stage but pass quickly through the storming stage. Another group might be just the opposite; the forming stage might be brief but the storming stage prolonged. And, third, all effective groups must go through the various stages. If a group hopes to be productive, it must form, storm, norm, perform, and ultimately, when production is completed, adjourn.

The Pendular Perspective

In the pendular models of group development, the shifts which occur in interpersonal relationships during the growth and development of the group are highlighted. It is assumed that a group doesn't continue to develop in a consistent linear pattern from the moment it forms. There are periods of conflict, tension, dissatisfaction; these reduce the cohesiveness of the group. Budge (1981), for example, proposed that as the group develops it swings (shifts, oscillates) from being cohesive to separating to being cohesive to separating and so on.

The life of any sport team has numerous examples which help to illustrate how a pendular model of group development is in operation. Table 9.2. presents two such case histories. One comes from the book, **A Season on the Brink,** by John Feinstein (1987). During the 1985-86 season, Feinstein was given complete access to Coach Bobby Knight and the Indiana Hoosiers. He attended practices, team meetings, and games, traveled with the team and recorded what he saw and heard. That season might be considered successful by most sport team's standards, but in 1986-87, the year after Feinstein was with them, the Indiana Hoosiers won the NCAA National Championship. The bulk of Feinstein's book deals with 1985-86 but in an epilogue he does present an overview of the championship year. The quotes in Table 9.2 overlap both seasons. Interestingly, while Feinstein's project wasn't undertaken as a scientific endeavor, **A Season on the Brink** is an excellent example of quality field research with an intact sport group.

In the fourth stage, performing, interpersonal relations are stabilized and the group's energy is directed toward successful execution of the group task. The fraternity team's leader, peacemaker, playmaker, and shooter know and accept their roles. In the performing stage, the team becomes completely focused on achieving team success.

When the group's task has been completed, there is a termination of duties, a reduction in dependency on the group, and possibly the break up of the group. This is referred to as the adjourning phase. It would occur — at least in terms of playing basketball together — in the fraternity team when the basketball season was through. The roles that the various fraternity members filled on the team such as leader, comedian, and so on would disappear with the breakup of the team. When the team members went back to just being members of the fraternity, the roles and responsibilities developed in that context would prevail.

Three important points should be highlighted about the Tuckman and Jensen schema. First, the five stages are sequential. That is, one stage must be successfully reached before the group passes on to the next. Second, the duration of time spent at any

Table 9.2. An example of the pendular model of group development in a basketball setting (the Indiana Hoosiers as described by John Fenistein, 1987) and a hockey setting (Team Canada as described by Ken Dryden & Mark Mulvoy, 1973).

Stage	Description	Team Canada	Indiana Hoosiers
Orientation	Cohesion and feelings of unity are high; the athletes share many common feelings, anxieties, aspirations	**Practices Start.** "One surprise aspect of the first week of practice was the absolute lack of temper flare-ups -- like high sticks -- between people who go out of their way to knock each other down during the regular season ". (p. 27)	**Practices Start.** "In college basketball, no date means more than October 15. On `that day, basketball teams allaround the country begin formal preparation for the upcoming season". (p. 27)
Differentiation and Conflict	The group physically and psychologically subdivides into smaller units; conflicts often arise as athletes compete for positions on the team	**Preseason Practices Continue.** "All of us desperately want to play on Saturday night because it is Game 1` of a historic event. It will mean so much to be one of the best seventeen and two -- that is, seventeen skaters and two goaltenders". (p. 32)	**Preseason Practices Continue.** "November is the toughest for any college basketball team. The excitement of starting practice ... has worn off, asnd practice has become drudgery .... There is just day after day of practices - - the same faces, the same coaches, the same drills, the same teammates". (p. 59)
Resolution and Cohesion	Cohesion increases as group members share common concerns and feelings as they prepare to face a commom threat	**The First Game.** "After we finished our work, Sinden names the lineup for the opening game. Before we left the ice, Red Berenson, one of the centers, told Sinden and Ferguson to get lost for a couple of minutes .. 'Look', Red said to us ... 'we have thirty-five outstanding hockey players here right now but only nineteen will be dressing tommorow night. It's no disgrace not to be playing ... This is a team of thirty-five men. Let's keep it that way'". (pp. 41-42)	**The First Game.** "The tension in the locker room was genuine. Al the remindrs about Miami, all the memories of last season, not to mention the memories of the forty-eight practices that had led to this afternoon combined to create a sense of dread". (p. 96)
Differentiation and Conflict	Team Unity is weakened as different individuals are rewarded or punished, `setting them off from the group	**During the Season.** " I practiced this morning with the Black Aces and tonight I'll be in the stands with them. The Black Aces of a hockey team are the spares ... As expected, the Black Aces were flat at practice. Disappointed, down, depresed, none of us is used to watching a game from the stands". (p. 60-61)	**During the Season.** " The locker room would not have been much quieter if Kent State had won the game .... Mentally, Knight had decided he needed Hillman and Smith in place of Robinson and Brooks. They were deep in the doghouse .... After [the team] showered, he blistered them one more time. Ønly three players had pleased him". (p. 102)

The Cycles of Differentiation and Conflict And Resolution and Cohesion Alternate Throughout the Season

Termination	If the season has been successful, feelings of cohesiveness are high. If the season has been unsuccesful, feelings of cohesiveness are	The Championship Game. "We were exhausted emotionally. Exhausted physically. Totally spent. I just looked around the room: everyone's uniform was soaked with sweat. I felt really proud .. for all of us. I didn't know more than a handful of them six weeks ago, but now I felt that I knew everyone of them in a way you rarely know anyone. We had gone from the heights to the depths -- and now we were back on top again". (p. 178)	The Championship Game. "They jumped on each other, pummeled each other and cried .... Finally they went back to the locker room. When there was quiet Knight spoke briefly. 'What you did', he told them, 'was refuse to lose. You've ben that kind of team all year'". (p. 348)

The second example comes from the book **Face-off at the Summit** by Ken Dryden and Mark Mulvoy (1973). It is the result of a diary maintained by Dryden during the 1972 Canada-Russia hockey series and then developed into a book in collaboration with Mulvoy. The year 1972 marked the first opportunity for professional hockey players from North America to compete against European amateurs. From the mid-1950s, the Russians had enjoyed a clear superiority over Canadian amateur hockey teams in international exhibitions, in the Olympics, and in World Cup championships. Canadian sport fans felt that the Russian's success was achieved against inferior opposition. Thus, in 1972 when an All-Star team of professionals was selected from the National Hockey League, popular consensus was that "Canada's best" would soundly beat the Russians 8-0 in the eight-game series. Many Canadians considered the outcome of the first four games (which were played in Canada) a national disaster. The Russians led the series with two wins, one loss, and a tie. Team Canada eventually won the series with four wins, three losses and one tie. The winning goal was scored in the eighth and deciding game with only 34 seconds left to play.

As Table 9.2 shows, cohesion is assumed to be relatively high in the first stage of the pendular model of group development. When a group first comes together, it is a period of *orientation* and general feelings of team unity arise from the common expectations, experiences, anxieties, and aspirations that all the prospective team members share. In the Team Canada and Indiana Hoosier examples, the feelings of unity might have been a result of the sacrifices that all athletes made during the summer, e.g., training. Or, it may have been the result of the common goals and aspirations that the athletes had for the upcoming competition/season. The essential point is that when the team first gets together, there is a relatively high feeling of unity.

Following the orientation period, the pendulum swings and there is *differentiation and conflict*. Differentiation refers to the fact that the group physically and psychologically subdivides into smaller units and conflicts arise as athletes compete for a limited number of positions on the team. In many sports, breaking the total group into smaller units for practice is a natural consequence of the way the sport is organized; offense versus defense, forwards versus defense, setters versus spikers, and so on. The Team Canada quotation in Table 9.2 serves to highlight the potential conflicts that can arise from competition for a starting position on the team; the Indiana Hoosier quotation highlights the drudgery, monotony, and feelings of boredom which arise when a team is confronted with constant early season practices and no games. Both examples help to illustrate the decline in cohesion and team unity which follows the orientation period.

Inevitably, the group draws together again as the pendulum swings forward in the opposite direction. This is what is referred to as *resolution*. In sport groups, resolution usually occurs when the team is about to meet an opponent. Competition within the group decreases and consensus is reached on general team goals and objectives. In the Team Canada quotation, a respected team member has reminded the total group about the importance of group solidarity. In the Indiana Hoosier example, the shared aspirations for the present season and the memory of a failure in the previous season both contribute to team unity in terms of a common shared anxiety — the fear of not doing well.

As the season progresses, the above sequence is repeated — differentiation and conflict are followed by resolution and cohesion which are followed by differentiation and conflict which are followed by resolution and cohesion. The group continues to grow and develop over the course of the season but there are pendular shifts until the team dissolves. Examples are presented in Table 9.2 which serve to illustrate these pendular shifts.

When the team is successful, the final pendular swing is toward high cohesiveness. In fact, Carron and Ball (1977) have shown that success is a much better predictor of eventual cohesiveness than cohesiveness is of eventual success. When teams win, the feelings of cohesiveness are extremely high, when they lose, they're low. The Team Canada quotation in the Table 9.2 best serves to illustrate this; feeling of closeness accompany team success.

Another example of a pendular model of group development is one developed by William Schutz (1966). The main elements in Schutz's theory — the need for inclusion, the need for control, and the need for affection — were introduced in Chapter 8 (see Table 8.1 again). Schutz proposed that all groups from dyads to the largest groups must sequentially and successfully handle problems in the areas of inclusion, control, and affection. A different interpersonal problem is predominant in different phases during the group's development. Schutz emphasized that "these are not distinct phases ... these problem areas are *emphasized* at certain points in a group's growth. All three problem areas are always present but not always of equal salience" (p. 171).

Schutz's model is similar to a linear perspective. However, it is pendular because it is assumed that the three problem areas reappear during the life of the group. Thus, when a group has gone through the sequence of inclusion - control - affection, it begins another cycle.

Initially, problems of *inclusion* predominate. These problems center around how much communication, interaction, and involvement different individuals want with each other and with the group. Obviously, if the majority of individuals want little or no interaction, communication, or involvement, the chances that they will form and develop into a strong group are minimal. On the other hand, if the majority of members want and express a great deal of inclusion behavior, the group has a solid foundation from which to proceed.

The second problem area is characterized by issues relating to *control*. Group members must resolve who will make the decisions, how the group will be led, and where the primary power and influence will lie. The control phase in Schutz's model of group development is similar to the storming stage in the Tuckman and Jensen model.

Finally, as the group develops, interpersonal concerns in the area of *affection* arise. These center around how friendly, intimate, or affectionate group members want to be with each other.

Schutz proposed that when a group breaks up (disintegrates), it does so in a reverse sequence — affection — control — inclusion. Affection is the last to develop in the group; it is the first to go. After the decline in affection, issues relating to control, power, and influence begin to decline in importance. Eventually, group members simply don't care "who's in charge". Finally, contact, communication, and involvement decline to the point where the members no longer meet as a group.

The Cyclical Perspective

The main element in the cyclical approach to group development is the assumption that as a group develops, it psychologically prepares for its breakup. The life cycle models have their origin in counselling, psychotherapy, and clinical settings where groups are established for relatively short periods of time. During their existence, intimacy, dependence, and affiliation among group members may be high. Since members know that the group's existence is temporary, however, eventual group disintegration is always a dominant consideration. As the group comes closer to the time of its breakup, there is a great deal of activity centered around maintaining the group or reconfirming its vitality.

The life cycle model can be illustrated by the example of a member of the family who is about to leave on an extended trip. There are numerous reminiscences about earlier shared experiences. There is a great deal of "busy work" which essentially serves to occupy the family so that they can avoid thinking about the departure. There are periods of high communication followed by periods of silence. Communication may be awkward. Previous family (group experiences) are evaluated favorably.

A cyclical perspective also has relevance for groups in sport and physical activity. For example, fitness classes last for approximately eight to ten weeks, school intramural teams often play 15 to 20 games, municipal recreation leagues last for the duration summer, winter, or fall season. Even professional sport teams have a fixed season and then the group separates. There is no doubt that a sport team doesn't usually begin at the most preliminary stages of group development when it reforms the following season. Nonetheless, it does have a fixed life cycle.

A model proposed by Garland, Kolodny, and Jones (1965) is typical. It includes five stages: (1) *pre-affiliation*: individuals explore the possibility of joining together in a group; some potential group members decide not to become involved; (2) *power and control:* group members define, formalize, and test intragroup relationships; subgroups may form; (3) *intimacy*: interpersonal relationships become intensified; cooperation and sharing are strong; (4) *differentiation*: cohesion is high; acceptance of the individuality of other group members is strong; and, (5) *termination*-separation: social interactions and communication center around maintaining the group; there is reminiscence and evaluation of past group activities.

An example of the life cycle model is illustrated in a study by Jaroslav Cikler (1966). He charted the actual group development and eventual break up of fourteen 11-year old boys who met to play soccer. Table 9.3 presents an overview of the dominant activities that were evident as the group formed, competed together,

and then began to disintegrate.

The overriding consideration which drew the 14 boys together initially was their interest in soccer. This interest became the catalyst for their formation into a group. It also became the factor which drew the boys into a cohesive group. In the early stages, the structure within the group was very basic. Teams were divided by two captains who were elected by the total group. The role of team captain tended to be rotated among four different individuals while the composition of the two teams tended to vary from one day to the next. Also, all of the boys retained some input into the composition of the two teams. Conflicts and disagreements were minimal. In short, the total group developed some structure (e.g., dominant individuals, captains) but the two teams that were formed to compete were spontaneous and unstructured.

Over time, the overall group became mu   more

Table 9.3 Characteristics in the rise, development, and breakup of a youth soccer group (Adapted from Cikler, 1966)

Stage	Duration	Dominant Characteristics
Preaffiliation ↓ Power and Control	One Year	Mutual interest in soccer was the factor bringing the group together. Play was spontaneous. Group members voted on team captains with four individuals receiving the most votes. Team captaincy alternated among the four. Two captains always chose the teams. Team composition varied considerably from competition to competition. Team members had input into the team composition. Disagreements were minimal and were settled by the captains.
Intimacy ↓ Differentiation	Six Months	Interest in soccer and insults from nongroup members were both factors in holding the group together. Captains introduced training techniques; sometimes practices were held instead of games. Two individuals assumed the captaincy by acclamation; toward the end of the period electionswere no longer held. Team composition varied only minimally Group norms and roles were stabilized. Disagreements began to dominate the play
Termination	Six Months	Interest in soccer began to disappear; interests outside the group increased in importance. The teams split into two distinct subgroups. Conflicts and disagreements developed between the two subgroups and spred within each subgroup.
Separation	After Two Years	One captain moved, the other began to play with another team. Team members no longer met to play soccer

structured. Practices were often held instead of games in order to improve the quality of play of all group members. Eventually, elections were no longer held — captains selecting the two teams simply assumed the leadership role. Ultimately, the number of individuals in this role was reduced from four to two and the composition of the two teams became stabilized. The number of disagreements increased and began to dominate the play.

After approximately a year and a half, the group began to disintegrate. Interest in soccer began to fade and members of the group began to develop interests outside the group. Possibly it was due to the fact that the original group of 14 was now, for all intent and purposes, two group of 7. Possibly it was due to the increased emphasis on playing well, e.g., practices and training sessions. Or possibly it was due to the conflicts and disagreements that arose during games. It's even possible that other factors such as increasing age, changing interests, added responsibilities outside of the group were the main "causes" and all of the factors observed by Cikler were "effects". Whatever the origin, the group began to break up and after approximately two years it was extinct.

Implications for the Effectiveness of Sport Groups

One of the major advantages gained by understanding the stages in group development is that their sudden appearance is less threatening. For example, prior knowledge that a storming phase will usually occur in groups will likely insure that a volunteer organizer of a summer sport team will not be devastated when his or her team "rebels". As another example, understanding group development should also lead a coach to realize that it takes time for group members to readily assume the necessary group roles.

A second advantage is that it is also possible for a group leader (e.g., coach, captain, organizer) to enhance group effectiveness by emphasizing certain behaviors which are appropriate to a particular stage of group development. For example, if the Tuckman and Jensen model is used (see Table 9.1 again), a team leader could expect his/her group to go through five stages: forming, storming, norming, performing, and adjourning. The first stage, forming, is a period of orientation, a characteristic of every team when it first comes together. Team members must become familiar with each other, friendship bonds must develop, the group's performance and behavioral norms, its goals and objectives, and the offensive and defensive systems must be learned.

Coaches can attempt to reduce the amount of time their teams spend in the forming stage with a wide variety of strategies. Bringing new players into training camp early, providing a play book prior to the season, posting team rules and regulations, and pairing new players with experienced players in training camp are some examples. Rookie nights and initiation rituals can also be used to facilitate the entry of new additions into the social structure of the group. During the forming stage, the team's goals and objectives and any performance standards and rules for conduct are clearly spelled out.

Some coaching behaviors may be inappropriate during the forming stage (Lasnier, 1979). These include requiring players to express their opinion in public, using excessive authority (i.e., abusing authority) since it could lead to resentment and aggression later, and forcing new team members to assume important team responsibilities.

Organized, highly competitive sport is generally assumed to be an autocratic endeavor. The coach or team leader sets the standards — "My ways or Trailways [Bus Lines]" — and the athletes accept them. Thus, a storming stage is not as prevalent in competitive sport teams as it is in more democratically-organized groups. Nonetheless, feelings of tension, anxiety, and frustration can develop in the early stages of the team's development. The length of the storming stage and its negative impact may be reduced by personalizing the coaching process as much as possible. Experienced coaches do this by outlining their expectations and any contingencies (i.e., conditions). It is also useful to remember that minor conflicts, disagreements, and differences of opinion are a natural aspect of group development. Thus, it's not necessary to force a positive team climate every time that a disagreement arises among team members (Lasnier, 1979).

In the norming stage, group roles are more clearly established and group cohesiveness develops. Role clarity and role acceptance are influenced strongly by communication and cohesiveness. Clearly outlining an athlete's responsibilities within the team helps to insure that there is a clear picture of what is expected. Also, however, role acceptance is improved if both the athlete and the team understand what is expected. For example, many basketball teams have a "sixth person" who comes in from the bench to replace one of the starters and carry out a specific function (i.e., a role). It may involve shooting for 3-point baskets, checking an opponent who is on a scoring streak, or quarterbacking the offense. If the athlete and the team have a clear understanding of the role responsibilities of the sixth person, there is a greater likelihood that that athlete will readily carry out the assignment — and that there will be minimal interference or obstruction from teammates.

In the performing stage, interpersonal relationships are stabilized and productivity and performance are emphasized. During this period, the focus should be on group goals, group aspirations, and group accomplishments. Individual goals are highly effective as a motivator but care must be taken to insure that they don't compete with team goals. In fact, many professional sport teams no longer include bonuses for individual accomplishment. It has been observed that these often detracted from the team's effectiveness — particularly late in a season when individual sacrifices might be necessary for team success.

The social aspects of group involvement are an integral aspect of group life in the performing stage. Cohesion associated with strong friendships and positive interpersonal relationships helps to unite a team. And, the presence of social cohesion is related to the presence of task cohesion (Widmeyer, Brawley, & Carron, 1985). As long as social cohesion doesn't become as important (or more important) than task cohesion, it will be a positive force in the group.

The adjourning phase is smoother if team activities are scheduled for the off-season period. These could be related to an off-season training program, e.g., weight training, aerobics. Or they could be more social in nature, e.g., barbecues, dances. If contact is maintained with the athletes during the off-season, the "team" orientation is maintained. Consequently, the forming stage at the beginning of the next season is smoother.

Member Turnover

Typically, in all organizations including sport, an issue which has attracted more attention than group development has been member turnover. Interscholastic, intercollegiate, professional, and amateur sport teams continue to function year-after-year. However, there is a regular turnover in the team's composition as a result of graduation, resignation, retirement, promotion, transfer, and dismissal. This is the case even in highly successful professional sport teams. For example, Grant Fuhr, the goaltender for the Edmonton Oilers, winners of the Stanley Cup in four of the five years between 1984 and 1988, observed that "every year, there's a turnover — three or four

guys every year, it seems like ... That's life in the NHL" (quoted in Wiley, 1988, p. 68) Fuhr's impressions of the Oilers seem to be applicable for the NHL as a whole — McPherson (1976) reported that there is an average of 5.88 player changes per team per year.

In studies of organizational effectiveness in nonsport settings, it has repeatedly been shown that the replacement process is time consuming. The recruitment, training, and assimilation of new personnel is also expensive. Effective communication among group members is adversely affected. Established routines are disrupted. And, group productivity and group effectiveness generally suffer (e.g., Caplow, 1964; Evan, 1963; Shelley, 1964).

A number of researchers have examined the implications of personnel changes in a sport organization in terms of (1) team performance, (2) the consequences for the organization if the turnover occurs in management (coaches, general managers) or among the athletes, and (3) the consequences for the organization if the turnover occurs in specific playing positions, e.g., goaltenders versus forwards in hockey, infielders versus outfielders in baseball, quarterbacks versus defensive backs in football.

The Replacement of Management

In amateur sport, when things don't go well, the coach usually makes changes in the athletes on the roster. This isn't always the case in professional sport. As Roger Neilson stated, "when things aren't going well, the team feels it has to do something. Usually, it's fire the coach" (quoted in Kernaghan, 1988, p. C-1). Unfortunately, Neilson can probably be considered somewhat of an expert since he is a former coach with Toronto (where he was fired twice in one season), Buffalo, Vancouver, and Chicago.

There is evidence that firing the coach isn't necessarily the best solution. A considerable body of research shows that there is a negative relationship between the replacement of a coach or manager and team effectiveness. Teams that change their coaches and managers a great deal are less successful than teams that don't (see Table 9.4). The only exception appears to be professional hockey.

One possibility examined by Nancy Theberge and John Loy was that an internal change (i.e., the manager is replaced by someone already working in the organization) would be less disruptive than an external change. When they examined the records

Table 9.4 The relationship between managerial turnover and team effectiveness

Sport	Period Examined	Results	Reference
Baseball			
Professional	1921-1941 1951-1958	Higher managerial turnover was associated with lower team effectiveness (r = -.43)	Grusky (1963)
Professional	1949-1968	Higher managerial turnover was associated with lower team effectiveness (r = -.54)	Loy (1970)
Professional	1951-1960	Higher managerial turnover was associated with poorer win-loss, league standing, and games behind first-place; no differences between internal versus external changes	Theberge & Loy (1976
Basketball			
College	1930-1970	Higher coaching turnover was associated with lower team effectiveness (r = -.24	Eitzen & Yetman (1972)
Ice Hockey			
Professional	1950-1966	Managerial change was unrelated to organizational effectiveness	McPherson (1976)

of managers in professional baseball between 1951 and 1960, they did find that manager turnover adversely influenced organizational effectiveness in terms of the percentage of games won, standing in the league, and the number of games behind the first place team. They also found, however, that an internal change was no better than an external one.

Care must be taken in the interpretation of these general findings. There is no doubt that managerial turnover is associated with a lack of team effectiveness. But, correlational data do not provide any real insight into causation. When a seat belt sign comes on in an airplane, the ride generally gets rougher. But it would be unreasonable to ask the pilot not to turn the sign on in order to insure a smooth flight. The turbulence is associated with the seat belt sign, not caused by it.

This line of reasoning was emphasized by Gamson and Scotch (1964) who pointed out that the relationship between manager turnover and team success can be interpreted in three ways. One of these is that teams that frequently turn over their managers are less successful. The causal interpretation here would be that too frequent a turnover in management causes a lack of team success. A second possibility is that managers are incompetent so they are replaced. The causal interpretation here would be that an incompetent manager causes poor team performance so the manager is replaced. A third possibility is that the manager is a simply a scapegoat — the manager is the seat belt sign in the airplane of sport. The interpretation here is that some other factor or factors are the cause of the turbulence, but the manager, like the seat belt sign is eliminated. Gamson and Scotch tested these alternatives but couldn't find clear support for any one of the three. Nonetheless, they stated that their own preference was the scapegoating alternative.

The Replacement of Team Members

In the introduction to this section, a quote by Grant Fuhr, goaltender of the Edmonton Oilers, testified to the annual replacement of team members in professional sport. Fuhr felt that three or four players per year were replaced on the Oilers — a figure slightly under the 5.88 average in the league as a whole (McPherson, 1976). Turnover or member replacement is a fact of life in all sport. The turnover may be due to injuries, trades, the draft, or retirements and it affects some teams in some sports more than others.

A comparison of the rate of turnover across three

sports was made by Schwartz (1973, reported in Loy, McPherson, & Kenyon, 1978). Turnover was defined as the ratio of players used by a team in a season who were not present in the previous season divided by the total number of players used by a team. Schwartz's data were obtained from teams in the National Basketball, Baseball, and Football Leagues for the 1960-1969 seasons. He found that baseball had the highest turnover (.403) followed by basketball (.367), and football (.334).

Not only does the rate of turnover vary across sports, within a sport it is related to team effectiveness. Teams that have the highest rate of turnover on their rosters, are the least successful. A summary of these studies is presented in Table 9.5. As was the case with manager turnover, the only exception to the generalization about athlete turnover and team effectiveness is professional hockey (McPherson, 1976).

Four points should be emphasized about these findings. The first, which was mentioned above, is that the data on player turnover and team effectiveness are correlational. Thus, they are subject to the same limitations and reservations Gamson and Scotch raised about the managerial data on turnover. It isn't possible with correlational data to conclude that one factor caused another.

The second point is that too little turnover in a playing roster can also be a problem for team effectiveness. For example, baseball manager Billy Martin (1987) suggested that without turnover, motivation can diminish and compla-cency can develop on a team:

Long-term contracts are often harmful. I'm not saying it's true with all players, but it is with many of them. They lose incentive, their motiva-tion, if they have a long-term contract. Subconsciously, they just don't seem to try as hard.

If a guy is a fringe player and it's time to sign him to a new contract, I'd like to see baseball just let him go. Bring in somebody else, somebody who won't cost as much money and who is hungrier, who is not set in his ways with all those bad habits. I'm not talking about a Don Mattingly or a Dave Winfield or a Ricky Henderson. Keep them. But get rid of the fringe players, just keep turning them over. That will stop all that nonsense of threatening the manager and the owner. (p. 148)

A third, related point is that there is an optimal time for player turnover; if player turnover is either too fast or too slow, a team's effectiveness suffers. This point is well illustrated in a study by Donnelly (1975, reported in Loy, Theberge, Kjeldsen, & Donnelly, 1975). He examined the relationship between player turnover in professional baseball and the number of games behind first place. The operational definition for player turnover was the duration of time to *half-life*, the duration of time required for the team to be reduced (through player changes) to one half of its original complement. Thus, a team roster might contain 40 athletes in 1988. Through trades, retire

Table 9.5 The relationship between athlete turnover and team effectiveness			
Sport	**Period Examined**	**Results**	**Reference**
Baseball			
Professional	1960-1969	Higher athlete turnover was associ-ated with lower team effectiveness (r =-.51)	Schwartz (1973)
Professional	1951-1960	Higher athlete turnover was associ-ated with poorer win-loss (r = -.54), league standing ((r = -.55) and games behind first place (r = -.57)	Theberge & Loy (1976)
Basketball			
Professional	1960-1969	Higher athlete turnover was associ-ated with poorer team effectiveness (r = -.47)	Schwartz (1973)
Football			
Professional	1960-1969	Higher athlete turnover was associ-ated with poorer team effectiveness (r = -.54)	Schwartz (1973)
Ice Hockey			
Professional	1950-1966	Athlete turnover was unrelated to organizational effectiveness	McPherson (1976)

ments, injuries, and other factors, only 20 of those original 40 members might still be present on the roster in 1990. In this case, the duration to half-life would be two years. Donnelly found that there was an inverted-U relationship between the duration of time to half life and team success.

The final point is that turnover in some positions is undoubtedly less disruptive than turnover in other positions. If an individual has a peripheral role on the team, his/her departure has less impact than the departure of an individual who occupies a more critical, central position. Theberge and Loy's (1976) study with professional baseball supported this proposition (although McPherson's (1976) study with professional hockey did not).

Implications for the Effectiveness of Sport Groups

Both managerial and player turnover are associated with less effective team performance and productivity. The major problem in interpreting these findings was raised above — the correlational nature of the data. It would be a mistake to assume that the frequent changes in managers or players are the major source of a team's poor performance; to assume that if less changes were made, the team would be more successful. When a team is unsuccessful, the organization feels that it must take some steps to improve. Trades, firings, and/or moving players back and forth from a minor league affiliate are obvious strategies. If a trade is made but it doesn't work then a demotion is possible. If that doesn't work, then the coach might be fired or a player released. If those don't work, another trade might be made. And, so on. Successful teams have less need to make these types of changes. Why tamper with a good product?

Notwithstanding the difficulty of determining what's cause and what's effect, it is reasonable to assume that some permanence in coaching is best. If a coach is going to have any impact, that impact is more likely to be felt over the long term rather than a short term. Interestingly, Eitzen and Yetman (1972) found that there is an inverted-U relationship between coaching stability and team success:

Coaches who left after eight or nine years tended to leave as winners in comparison with their early years. Coaches whose tenure lasted ten, eleven, or twelve years were split evenly into those whose records were improving and those whose records were deteriorating. For those coaches whose longevity at one post exceeded twelve years ... every year but one

showed a disproportionate number of coaches ending their career at a school with last-half records poorer than their first. (p. 115)

When coaches stay at one institution for a long period of time, they have an opportunity to build a program and their record improves. Subsequently, their record tends to level off and, eventually, it declines. This decline may be due to complacency, decreasing motivation, or some other factors. Whatever its causes, there is an optimal tenure for coaches as there is for team members (Donnelly, 1975).

A final point which should be raised is that the studies with sport teams that have examined the member turnover and team effectiveness issue have focused on one measure of effectiveness — win-loss record. There are a number of other indices of effectiveness which might be influenced by turnover including individual and team morale, job satisfaction, costs associated with moving, training, and accommodating new personnel, and the number of spectators in attendance (McPherson, 1976).

The latter measure, the number of spectators in attendance, may seem like a strange barometer of organizational effectiveness. However, in professional sport, spectator attendance is possibly the ultimate criterion of effectiveness. And, player turnover adversely influences spectator attendance. A case study which clearly illustrates this point is the Canadian Football League. In 1987, the league was in danger of folding. And one of the primary reasons cited for the declining attendance was excessive player turnover. As Reilly (1987) noted:

You can't tell the players without a scorecard — except of course in the CFL, where you can't tell the players even with a scorecard. Because teams are desperate to win ... turnover is outrageous ... "The people who make money out of the CFL are the airlines" says John Hudson, a vice-president of Labatts. "They run a shuttle business like you cannot believe .... In baseball the rosters are pretty much frozen after April 1. The guys you see are the guys you'll see all year. The CFL better freeze the roster or it'll never have identity between the players and fans. (pp. 40 & 43)

Whether turnover causes organizational ineffectiveness or whether turnover occurs because the organization is ineffective isn't clear. What is clear is that there are no major benefits associated with large turnovers but there are numerous potential problems.

10 The Elements of Group Structure

Group development is closely associated with the emergence of a group structure. There are four components which most clearly reflect the emergence and presence of a group structure (Shaw, 1981). The first of these is group *position* — the place or location of the individuals in the group. In the quote used to introduce this chapter, three key positions involved with the field goal in football are discussed: the kicker, the ball holder, and the center (snapper).

> No matter how good a kicker is, he's no better than his holder and snapper. It takes all three . The holder needs sure quick hands. He's got to be able to catch the snap without bobbling it, then get the ball down quickly, spotting it with the index finger of his rear hand while getting his front hand out of the kicker's way .... The snapper, the center who snaps the ball back, is even more important than the holder ... Every good snapper knows where to position the laces in his grip so that the rotation will bring the ball into the holder's hands with the laces away from the kicker. (Madden & Anderson, 1986, pp. 170-171)

Different teams in different sports have different positions. Thus, a hockey team differs in structure from a basketball team and both differ from a soccer team. Anyone attempting to describe the unique characteristics or structure of these particular sport groups might begin by describing their positions.

A second element which makes up the structure of a group is status. The positions in any group or on any team vary in terms of their *status* — their power, prestige, and importance to the group. In the quote above, Madden suggested that the center who snaps the ball is more important than the holder. Later in his book, Madden also stated that the position of quarterback is the most important in terms of a football team's ultimate success:

> In the NFL, quarterback is still the most important position. If you don't have a quarterback, your team won't be a winner. (Madden & Anderson, 1986, pp. 35-36)

In every group, different positions are associated with different status. Consequently, knowledge of status differences also provides insight into the group's structure.

A third element which reflects the presence of structure in a group is group *roles*. A role is an expectation for the behavior of an individual who occupies a specific position in the group. Teams (or subgroups within teams such as the snapper, holder, and kicker football), work groups, social groups, organizations, corporations, and societies in general establish behavioral expectations for the occupants of different positions. The appearance of those different roles within the group contributes to the emergence of a unique group structure.

The fourth element is group *norms.* They are the standards for behavior that is expected of members of the group. Norms reflect the the organization's (or group's) consensus about the behaviors that are considered acceptable.

The interrelationship of group positions, status, roles, and norms to group structure can be illustrated by the example of a group of fraternity members who decide to establish an intramural basketball team. Even though the individuals are all members of the same fraternity, a specific structure will emerge within the basketball team. Part of that structure will be represented by the positions that the different individuals hold; e.g., center, guard, forward. Part of that structure also will be represented by the roles filled by different individuals. These might include the "coordinator" who acts as liaison between the team and the central administration for intramurals, the "task specialist(s)" who introduces the offensive and defensive systems to the team, and the "social director" who serves as a catalyst for the social activities after the game. Part of the team's structure also will be represented by the fact that the various positions and roles have different status, prestige, and importance. And, finally, norms will slowly evolve for the behavioral standards group members consider appropriate ... attendance at practice and games ... the amount of effort expected during games.

In the this chapter, two of the four elements of group structure — position and status — are discussed. Group roles and norms are discussed in Chapters 11 and 12 respectively.

Positions Within the Group

Importance of Position in a Group

The phrase "being in the right position at the right time" serves to illustrate the commonly held belief that our physical location can make a difference. Not surprisingly, therefore, group dynamicists have frequently examined the impact that position in the group has on individuals and on group processes. And, they have found evidence that supports the commonly held belief that position does make a difference. As one example, Strodtbeck and Hook (1961), in a comprehensive study of jury selection, found that a foreman was more frequently chosen from one of the two persons seated at the ends of the table. As another example, Steinzor (1955) found that "if a person happens to be in a spatial position which increases the chances of his being more completely observed, the stimulus values of his ideas and statements increases by virtue of that very factor of his greater physical and expressive impact on others" (p. 349). (This has come to be known as the *Steinzor effect*.)

The cause-effect nature of group position and social impact aren't clear. It may be that more dominant individuals gravitate to more dominant positions. It is also possible that more dominant positions generate more dominant impressions on the group. There is evidence to support both views. For example, Hare and Bales (1963) found that the occupants of more prominent seats had more dominant personality profiles. Also, Sommer (1969) observed that when individuals were selected to lead small group discussions, they more frequently selected seats at the head of the table. So it is likely that the certain individuals do seek out certain positions.

However, in some studies, the impact of the individual differences in personal attributes has been controlled by rotating individuals among different positions while holding the content of their opinion constant. The value attached to an opinion was found to vary with the position of the speaker (e.g., Steinzor, 1955). In short, some positions have the potential to make a greater impact on the group — no matter which individuals occupy them.

Importance of the Central Positions in Sport Teams

In sport, a frequently examined question has been whether the general formal structure of a team and the specific location of different positions are associated with different status, prestige, importance, or reward for the sport participant. One issue, for example, is whether there is a greater likelihood that individuals will be nominated as the MVP of a team if they are catchers versus outfielders in baseball, goaltenders versus defensemen in hockey, forwards versus guards in basketball, and setters versus spikers in volleyball.

One of the earliest studies concerned with this issue was reported by Oscar Grusky (1963). Grusky began with the premise that: (1) the formal structure of an organization establishes major offices or positions and the primary responsibilities for the occupants of the positions; (2) the positions in a group vary according to their spatial location, the type of task the occupant performs, and frequency of interactions with other positions; and, (3) certain positions, because of their responsibilities and the behaviors required, increase the likelihood that the occupant will develop leadership skills and assume a leadership role.

According to Grusky, "all else being equal, the more central one's spatial location, : (1) the greater the likelihood dependent or coordinative tasks will be performed, and (2) the greater the rate of interaction with occupants of other positions" (p. 346). In short, he felt that organizational positions could be distinguished on the basis of whether they were central, high-interaction positions or peripheral low interaction positions. He also felt that the occupants of central, high-interaction positions would be more frequently selected as most popular, more respected, and more frequently promoted to executive positions in the organization.

Baseball, the sport that Grusky studied, can be used as an example to illustrate these points. The formal structure of the game dictates that there are nine positions; catcher, pitcher, first base, etc. The responsibilities for each of these positions are well established. Pitchers, pitch, catchers catch, the centerfielders are in the outfield between the other two fielders, and so on. The position of catcher differs from the position of rightfielder in a number of significant ways: proximity to the main flow of activity, amount of involvement in the play on every pitch, and opportunity to interact verbally and/or engage in coordinated team play with other team members. Consequently, the opportunities to provide leadership, to assume a leadership role, and to learn leadership skills are also different.

Grusky proposed that in the organization of baseball, more individuals who had been in central, high-interaction positions as players would be recruited as managers. In order to test his proposition, he examined the backgrounds of the total population of field managers of major league baseball teams for the periods 1921-41 and 1951-58. The central, high-interaction positions were defined as catchers and infielders; the peripheral, low-interaction positions as pitchers and infielders. Grusky found that the majority of managers (76.9%) were recruited from central high-interaction positions rather than from peripheral, low-interaction (23.1%) positions. The highest percentage were former catchers (26.2%) followed by shortstops (14.0%) and third basemen (13.1%).

A number of other studies replicated or extended Grusky's work into other areas and other sports. Some of the areas examined included the recruitment of college coaches, the selection of team captains in high school and university, and the selection of most valuable players. Other sports examined included football, basketball, field hockey, and ice hockey. Essentially, the results of these other studies were consistent with those reported by Grusky (see Table 10.1). One exception was a study by Tropp and Landers (1979) which was concerned with leadership, team captaincy and interpersonal attraction in field hockey. Tropp and Landers suggested that their results might be explained by the fact that centrality is not a useful concept in highly dynamic sports.

Although Breglio (1976) found that individuals in peripheral positions in baseball were more frequently recruited to umpiring positions, he considered this to be consistent with Grusky's propositions. The task demands of umpiring require the individual to be independent and aloof. These are the characteristics developed in the peripheral positions. Therefore, if the responsibilities and behaviors acquired during competition serve to prepare the individual for another position in the organization, then umpires should come from the peripheral positions.

Overall, it seems reasonable to conclude that position does make a difference. Being in a high interaction central position enhances a player's chances of being selected team captain, being selected as the most valuable player, and being recruited into a management position.

An Alternate Perspective

The concept of centrality does not necessarily refer to a geographical location in the middle of the total group — the hub in the center of the wheel. For example, Hopkins (1964), in a discussion of how influence works in groups, argued that "centrality designates how close a member is to the 'center' of the group's interaction network and thus refers simultaneously to the frequency with which a member participates in interaction with other members and the number and range of other members with whom he interacts" (p. 28). In this instance, centrality is viewed as the center of the interaction network, not the physical center of the geographical boundaries of the group.

This perspective makes sense. In the case of an army, the command post is the hub of activity (i.e., central) but it is not in a geographical location midway between command and the front line. In short, in a wide variety of situations, the most central location in terms of interaction, leadership, and criticality is at the extreme of the physical boundaries of the group or organization. Feld (1959), in a study of command responsibility in military organizations, stated that "the wider the responsibility, the more remote the post ... In so far as command responsibility increases, the proper station will be progressively to the rear" (p. 17-18). Adams and Biddle (1970) also pointed out that "the teacher's spiritual and temporal home seems to be the center front of the room".

On the basis of this general line of reasoning, Chelladurai and Carron (1977) proposed an alternate model to account for the importance of different positions in group structure. This model contained two dimensions: *propinquity* and *task dependence*.

The first dimension, *propinquity,* consists of the combined attributes of (1) *observability,* the extent to which a position provides its occupant with knowledge of ongoing events, and (2) *visibility*, the degree to

Table 10.1 The relationship between position in a sport team and organizational rewards.

Sport	Results	Reference
Baseball		
Professional	Managerial recruitment was greatest from high interaction positions (73%)	Gusky (1963
High School	Selection of team captains was greates from high interaction positions (93%)	Loy and Sage (1968)
College	Selection of team captains (69%), most valuable players (54%) and managerial recruitment (72% was greates from high interaction positions	Sage, Loy & Ingham (1970)
Professional	Recruitment of umpires was greatest from low interaction positions	Breglio (1976)
Basketball		
Professional	Recruitment of coaches was greates from central positions (71%)	Klonsky (1975)
Football		
College	Selection of team captains was greatest from central positions (51%)	Sage (1974)
College	Recruitment of head coaches was greatest from central positions (65%); assistant coaches from peripheral positions (51%)	Massengale & Farrington (1977)
Professional	Recruitment of coaches was approximately equal from central and peripheral positions	
Ice Hockey		
Professional	Recruitment of general managers (67%), coaches (74%), captains (76%) and cocaptains (78%) was greatest from central positions	Roy (1974)

which the occupant of the position is seen and watched by individuals in other positions (including opponents). Thus, for example, a catcher is in a position to observe everything that happens on the playing field; everything occurs in front of him or her. So this position has high observability. Similarly, a quarterback in football and a playmaking guard in basketball are also in positions with high observability. In the same vein, the catcher, the quarterback, and the guard are also high in visibility — they are located in a position which insures that they are in the focus of a large number of other players on the playing surface. Thus, all three positions would rate high in the propinquity dimension even though none is geographically central.

The second dimension, *task dependence*, refers to the degree of performance interaction, the extent to which the occupant of the position interacts with the occupants of other positions. The positions discussed above, the catcher in baseball, the quarterback in football, and the guard in basketball would all control the play on the playing surface and interact continuously with other positions. Consequently, all three would rate high in the task dependence dimension.

When the positions of baseball are classified according to these two dimensions, a catcher is high in both, the infielders are moderate in both, and the outfielders are relatively low in both (see Figure 10.1). When the data reported in the previous studies of baseball (see Table 10.1) were re-analyzed, it was observed that leadership, status, and rewards were highly related to the degree of propinquity and task dependence present in a position. A summary is presented in Table 10.2. Catchers, who are highest in these two dimensions, were also highest in team captaincy, MVP, and recruitment to management positions. Outfielders, the lowest in these two dimensions, were least frequently the recipients of these organizational rewards.

Implications for the Effectiveness of Sport Groups

One of the major implications is that position can make a difference. The relationship between status, prestige, leadership, rewards, and position within the group does appear to be cyclical in nature. That is, individuals with dominant personalities and assertive leadership qualities more readily seek out positions of prominence in the group environment. They sit at the head of the table. They select positions where they can be seen and heard more easily. At the same time, however, certain positions lead more readily to status, leadership, and prestige within the group. A more prominent position contributes to the perception that the occupant of that position is more dominant, has opinions and viewpoints which are more valuable to the group, and should be accorded more status and prestige. As Shaw (1981) has pointed out:

The structure of the group, once established, is largely independent of the particular individuals who compose the group. A given position is accorded a given status regardless of the person who happens to occupy it. (p.265)

Since this is the case, it may be important for coaches and managers to be most concerned about the personal qualities of individuals who occupy the prominent positions in the team; the personal qualities of individuals in peripheral positions may be less important. On high school and elementary teams, individuals with the best work ethic and leadership qualities should be put in the central, high-interaction positions, e.g., guard in basketball, quarterback in football, catcher in baseball, setter in volleyball, center in hockey. Other athletes with less favorable personal qualities could be used in the relatively more peripheral positions. In this way, the more positive qualities of the individuals in the high-interaction positions would have a beneficial impact on the team. And, the less favorable personal qualities of those individuals in the peripheral positions would have less negative impact on the team.

For university and professional sport teams, during periods of recruitment and/or the draft, the personal qualities of individuals who will occupy the prominent

Table 10.2 The recruitment of managers /coaches and the selection of team captains and most valuable players on the basis of playing position (From Chelladurai & Carron, 1977. Reproduced with permission of the publisher)

Categories	Grusky (1963) 1	Sage, Loy, & Ingham (1970) 2	Loy & Sage (1968) 3	Sage, Loy & Ingham (1970) 4	Sage, Loy, & Ingham (1970) 5	Average from All Studies
I Catchers	26.2%	27.0%	27.3%	15.5%	12.9%	21.8%
II Infielders	12.2	11.0	16.7	13.3	10.4	12.7
First Base	11.2	12.6	0.0	9.9	8.9	8.5
Second Base	10.3	8.6	20.0	13.8	9.8	12.5
Short Stop	14.0	17.1	40.0	14.6	11.8	19.5
Third Base	13.1	5.8	6.7	14.8	11.1	10.3
III Outfielders	5.3	1.8	2.2	6.4	6.4	4.4
Left Field		1.0	0.0	6.1	4.9	3.0
Center Field		4.5	6.7	10.5	11.5	8.3
Right Field		0.0	0.0	2.5	2.9	1.4

* Selection of (1) professional baseball managers, (2) college coaches, (3) interscholastic team captains, (4) intercollegiate team captains, and (5) most valuable players.

positions should be scrutinized. An outstanding athlete who is also a social maverick may be tolerable in a peripheral position but completely disruptive in a central position.

The position that individuals are in relative to each other can also influence the nature and amount of their interaction and communication. For example, Sommer (1969) has shown that specific seating arrangements are closely associated with certain activities (see Table 10.3). Individuals in competitive situations prefer a face-to-face or distant (i.e., across and at the opposite end of the room) arrangement. On the other hand, individuals engaged in cooperative activities prefer a side-by-side arrangement. Coacting individuals — those working on the same task but independent of one another — prefer to be seated in a distant position.

On a sport team, little attention is usually paid to locker room arrangements. The situation for Indiana basketball described by Feinstein (1987) is typical of most sport teams:

The locker closest to that door is Alford's — a coincidence, since players inherit empty lockers the way they inherit empty chairs at pregame meal. (p. 74)

Although locker assignments are generally ad hoc with no attention paid to the specific assignments of specific individuals, it might be useful to consider otherwise. For example, if teammates are in competition — for a scoring title, the same position on the team, or leadership roles — and that competition has the potential to destroy the cohesion of the team, it would be beneficial to assign them lockers in close proximity. This might not eliminate the competitiveness entirely but it would increase their interaction and communication. Moreover, a distal arrangement only serves to contribute to or maintain the competitive orientation.

Status Within the Group

The Nature of Status

It was pointed out in the introduction to this chapter that when individuals come together in a group and begin to interact, differences among them begin to appear. This differentiation not only leads to the occupation of different positions, it also leads to the emergence of differences in status.

Status exists because of differences in beliefs, perceptions, and/or evaluations. These beliefs, perceptions, and/or evaluations influence the interactions among group members. For example, age is a characteristic perceived (believed, evaluated) to be associated with higher status in some cultures. As another example, in some cultures, different occupations are accorded more status; e.g., judges have higher status than professors. So in a group context, older individuals (or judges) would be perceived to have greater status. In turn, this perception would influence the nature and the amount of interactions between them and other group members.

A number of studies have clearly demonstrated that sport and physical activity are viewed as high status activities among adolescents. For example, when Abraham Tannenbaum (1960) examined the attitudes of high school juniors toward different types of male students, he

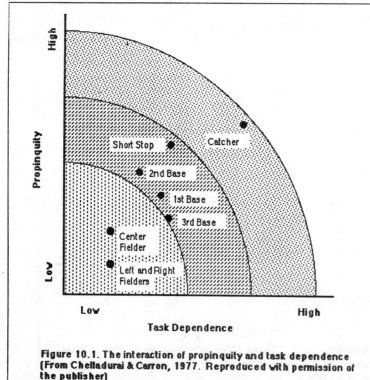

Figure 10.1. The interaction of propinquity and task dependence (From Chelladurai & Carron, 1977. Reproduced with permission of the publisher)

Table 10.3 The relationship of position to interaction and communication (Adapted from Sommer, 1969).

Configuration	Dominat Activities	Configuration	Dominat Activities
	Conversing Coacting		Conversing Cooperating
	Conversing Cooperating		Coacting Competing
	Coacting Competing		Coacting Competing
	Cooperating		

backgrounds, and by those individuals more heavily involved in sport. In terms of the type of school attended, greater importance was attached to sport by adolescents in smaller schools and schools with a more rigid authority structure. Finally, greater importance was attached to sport in smaller communities, rural communities, and communities with larger numbers of families living in poverty.

The Correlates of Status

A number of terms have often been used interchangeably with status. Some of the more popular include authority, power, social influence, and importance. These are not simply synonyms for status but, rather, are other elements in the group's structure that are closely associated with status differences. Further, they not only contribute to status, they also emerge as a result of status differences. For example, individuals in authority positions in the team (e.g., an elected captain), are generally accorded higher status than other team members. Similarly, individuals with high status (e.g., a team member with exceptional ability or experience) are generally elected to positions of authority.

Authority. The hierarchy for authority (and associated status) varies from one team to the next. Consider, for example, the two hierarchies illustrated in Figure 10.2. In the upper example, the pyramid is steeper and the status of the head coach is clearly greater than that of the three assistants, who have equal status. Greater coaching authority, prestige, power, and importance lie in the hands of one person — the head coach. Similarly, among the athletes, the pyramid is also quite steep with differentiation existing between the one captain and three assistant captains. There are also differences in status between veterans and rookies.

In the lower example, the pyramid is relatively flat for both the coaches and the athletes. The two co-head coaches have equal status, power, authority, and prestige. (One might be responsible for the offense, the second for the defense.) There are two assistant coaches with equal status. Among the athletes, three co-captains share the leadership role and no distinction in status is made between veterans and rookies.

found that the rankings from the most to least acceptable were:

1. Brilliant nonstudious athlete
2. Average nonstudious athlete
3. Average studious athlete
4. Brilliant studious athlete
5. Brilliant nonstudious nonathlete
6. Average nonstudious nonathlete
7. Average studious nonathlete
8. Brilliant studious nonathlete

In a classic study carried out in ten high schools in Illinois in 1957 and 1958, James Coleman (1961) found that status in males was most closely associated with involvement in sport (see Table 10.4). When Coleman's research was later replicated in the 1970s by Stanley Eitzen (1976), similar results were obtained.

Eitzen also found that a number of individual, school-related, and community-related factors influenced the sport-status relationship. Among the individual factors that were important were age, race, socioeconomic background, and degree of involvement in sport. Greater importance was attached to sport involvement by younger adolescents, by non-whites, by individuals from lower socioeconomic

Table 10. 4 Activities asociated with status among adolescent males and females (Adapted from Eitzen, 1976)

Reference Group	Criteria for Status	Average Ranking Coleman (1961)	Average Ranking Eitzen (1976)
Ranking to be Popular with Boys	Be an athlete	2.2	2.06
	Be in the leading crowd	2.6	2.10
	Be a leader in activities	2.9	2.82
	Have high grades	3.5	3.73
	Come from the right family	4.5	3.98
Ranking to be Popular with Girls	Be an athlete	2.2	1.94
	Be in the leading crowd	2.5	2.12
	Have a nice car	3.2	2.81
	Have high grades	4.0	3.87
	Come from the right family	4.2	3.89

An authority hierarchy seems to develop in all task groups — whether they have formalized leaders such as coaches and captains or not. Joseph Berger and his colleagues have referred to this as a *status organizing process* (Berger, Fisek, Norman, Zelditch, 1977). They suggested that a status hierarchy — the organization of the group according to status differences — results logically from members' expectations for future performances. Those individuals who are expected to contribute the most to the group's effectiveness are accorded the greatest status.

Earlier in the chapter, an example was used of a group of fraternity members who decided to establish an intramural basketball team. It was pointed out that even though the individuals were all members of the same fraternity, a specific structure would evolve within the basketball team which was specific to that group. Part of that structure would result from a status organizing process. If the group wanted to be successful, its members would most likely accord the greatest status to those individuals expected to contribute the most to future performances. If the group wanted to have a good time socially, the individuals with the greater social skills would be accorded the greater status and authority.

It is preferable for the formal status hierarchy (e.g., captains, co-captains) to be identical with the informal status hierarchy (e.g., the most competent group members). Otherwise, group effectiveness suffers (e.g., Haythorn 1968; Slusher, Van Dyke, & Rose, 1972). For example, in the hierarchy illustrated in the top half of Figure 10.2, the one head coach has greater authority than the three assistant coaches. But, if one of those assistant coaches was held in considerably higher esteem because of ability and contributions than the head coach, there could be resistance to the head coach's decisions among the assistant coaches and the athletes. Similarly, if one veteran player not in a formal leadership role was held in much greater esteem than the captain or co-captains, the team's effectiveness could suffer.

Power. Power is "the capacity to produce intended and foreseen effects on others" (Wrong, 1979, p. 21). As is the case with other correlates of status, power both contributes to and results from status. Individuals who have status in the group — coaches, captains, outstanding players — have the capacity to influence other group members. And, similarly, possessing power in the group leads to status.

In the most comprehensive analysis of power — which was provided by John French and Bertram Raven (1959) — it is assumed that there are five sources of power in small groups (see Table 10.5). *Expert* power results from knowledge, expertise, and competence at the task. Group members are influenced and will more readily follow the directions of more competent group members. In a sport group, the coach is generally the most knowledgeable. In the quote in Table 10.5 which is used to illustrate expert power, Kareem Abdul-Jabbar commented on the expertise of his former coach, John Wooden, and the impact that this had on the team's confidence. Holding expert power made it easier for Wooden to lead.

Another source of power associated with status in the group is called *coercive.* It results from threats, the possibility of having a reward withheld, or punishment. If a group member has the capacity to inflict some penalty on other group members, that power can help to produce desired outcomes. In the example presented in Table 10.5, Ken Stabler, recounted an incident which occurred in high school where one of his coaches used coercive power — physical punishment. According to Stabler, Coach Jones'' coercive power became a deterrent to missing practices.

Reference power exists when an individual is well liked and respected by other group members. In the quotation presented in Table 10.5, Coach John Madden emphasized the need for assistant football coaches to have the affection and respect of the group of athletes that they coach. Without it, the players would not respond to the coach's leadership.

In the status hierarchies illustrated in Figure 10.2., those individuals at the top of the pyramid have the greatest power; the organization has appointed them to be in charge. When power exists because of rank or position, it is referred to as *legitimate.* Legitimate power is almost synonymous with status — the greater the legitimate power, the greater the status and influence. In the quotation presented in Table 10.5, Jim Plunkett discussed a struggle between the head coach of the San Francisco 49ers, Monte Clarke, and the general manager, Joe Thomas. As the quotation illustrates, Thomas had more legitimate power, Clarke had to leave.

The fifth source of power which comes from and contributes to status is referred to as *reward.* As the name suggests, it is power which results from control over rewards and payoffs. If an individual has the power to reward other group members, he/she will have a major impact on the group. In the final quotation in Table 10.5, Ken Dryden outlined how his coach, Scotty Bowman, used praise and public recognition as a motivator for the fringe players on the roster.

In all of the examples used above, the focus is on coaches. In any sport team, they generally have the greatest status and the greatest power. However, high status athletes on the team also may possess these same sources of power. In fact, in some instance, a high status athlete may have more power than the coach.

Personal Attributes. Since status in groups develops because of differences in beliefs, perceptions, and evaluations, it is influenced by culture. A Caucasian has high status in some cultures, low status in others. Age is a significant correlate of status in some situations but not in others. In an attempt to categorize the personal factors which contribute to the evolution of status differences in groups, Joseph Berger and his colleagues distinquished between *specific-status characteristics* and

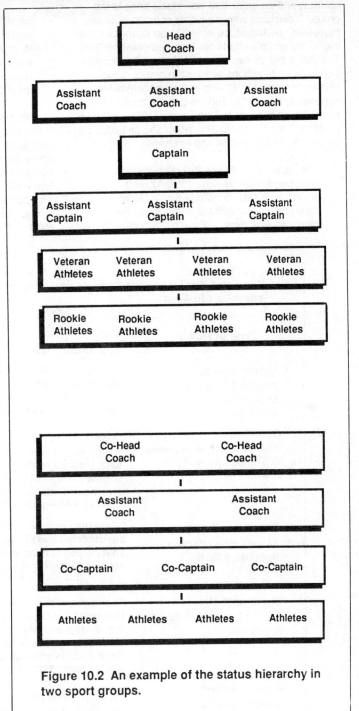

Figure 10.2 An example of the status hierarchy in two sport groups.

diffuse-status characteristics (Berger, Fisek, Norman, Zelditch, 1977).

Specific-status characteristics represent the skills,

abilities, and expertise that individuals bring to the group. Individuals who are highly competent or are perceived (evaluated, expected) to be strong contributors to the group's efforts are awarded greater status. The status that comes from ability also influences the individual's interactions outside the group. Sport heroes, for example, have status with teammates, opponents, the media, and the general public. This is evident in an account by Don Cherry (1982), a former coach with the Boston Bruins, about the demands on Bobby Orr for autographs and interviews:

> The social part [of Orr's life] left him little pleasure, simply because the fans were always after him. Solitude was virtually impossible, what with the demands of the media and the fans .... Even his own players

would bug him. Before a game other players would send him sticks to be autographed for their fans or their uncles or cousins .... Working with Orr, for me, was like being a museum curator [with an] extremely valuable piece of art. (Cherry & Fischler, 1982, pp. 166-167)

Diffuse-status characteristics are attributes, which in the absence of specific indices such as ability, contribute to the development of perceptions, beliefs, and expectations about competence at the task. In contact sports, new recruits who are unknown to the team will likely be given some status immediately if they possess exceptional size. If their subsequent performance doesn't meet with early expectations, that status will vanish. Similarly, an unknown, well-dressed

---

Table 10.5 The French and Raven sources of power illustrated in coaching situations.

Type of Power	Example
Expert Power Results from competence, knowledge, and expertise at the task	"[Coach John Wooden] used his mind and he understood the game totally. The best he could do was the best there was ... our confidence in him never wavered" (Abdul Jabbar & Knober, 1983, p. 152)
Coercive Power Results from threats, warnings of danger, and punishment	"Coach Jones took me into his office and closed the door ... 'Bend over and grab your ankles, Snake,' he said. I looked between my legs and saw him standing behind me with a paddle that looked like a cricket bat. He whacked me .... I didn't skip practice anymore." (Stabler & Stainback, 1986, pp. 33-34)
Reference Power Results from affection, from being liked	"More than anything else the assistant coach has to be respected and liked by the players in his group. That rapport is important ... he's got to wear well. If he doesn't, he'll turn off the players. They'll stop listening to him". (Madden & Anderson, 1986, p. 208).
Legitimate Power Results by virtue of rank or position	"Control was the operative word. [Coach Monte] Clark had control of the 49er operations, which meant drafting, trading and coaching ... Thomas wanted control of the first two ... Monte refused to give up his power. He knew what he was doing. Thomas fired him." (Plunkett & Newhouse, 1981, pp. 144-145)
Reward Power Results by virtue of control over rewards and payoffs	"[Coach Scotty Bowman] works them hard in practice, watching them, telling the press how hard and well they are working, making them feel they are earning their place on the team. Given a chance, usually at home, they give back an inspirational game." (Dryden, 1983, p. 41)

male who enters a poolroom with his own pool cue will likely be treated with deference and respect — at least initially.

Diffuse-status characteristics can also be attributes which cause the group to expect very little in the way of competence in the task. A quote from Ken Stabler (1986) on the training camp of the Oakland Raiders illustrates this:

One rookie came into camp with a huge jigsaw puzzle. That guy might as well have posted a sign that read: I AM NOT RAIDER MATERIAL. (Stabler & Stainback, 1986, p.4)

In addition to specific-status and the diffuse-status characteristics, an individual's actual *behavior* also contributes to the awarding of status. People who are assertive in groups, who behave in a dominant or aggressive way are also given greater status initially. Whatever the source — behavior, specific-status characteristics, or diffuse status characteristics — when individuals are perceived, believed, or expected to contribute to the group's effectiveness, they are accorded greater status. In turn, this greater status is accompanied by greater authority in the group (Greenstein & Knottnerus, 1980).

Situational Factors. A number of characteristics within the situation are also associated with status. *Spatial position* is one. As Brown (1965) pointed out "for Americans the spatial positions of *above* and *in front of* clearly imply superiority of status" (p. 78). In the previous section, it was pointed out that some team positions — playmaking guard, quarterback, catcher — have greater innate status than others.

Symbols are other types of situational characteristics which are associated with status. Team jackets, crests, pennants, uniforms, and titles are all symbolic. And, all can serve the purpose conferring status. Goyens and Turowetz (1986) emphasized this point in their commentary on the status attached to certain team uniforms:

Whether it be the Yankee pinstripe ... or perhaps the Kelly green with white trim of the Boston Celtics ... there is something instantly recognizable about the uniform colours of a special team in a particular sport. Few will argue that Yankee pinstripes represent baseball at its finest over the twentieth century. The same glory is attached to the Boston green and white in professional basketball. In professional hockey it is ... the red-white-and-blue of [the Montreal Canadiens]. (pp. vi-vii)

The status attached to various symbols can increase or decrease over time and according to circumstances. For example, the more successful sport franchises at any given time are readily identifiable by the number of young children wearing replicas of their jersey. With success, a jersey becomes fashionable, with a lack of success, it almost disappears. As another example, the value of an autograph from very incompetent professional athletes may have little value when they are still participating, but may increase in value after their retirement.

Implications for the Effectiveness of Sport Groups

In every group, a status hierarchy inevitably develops. Status is a primary element in group structure and fundamental to group development. As groups develop into strong goal-oriented cohesive units, differences in status among group members appear. Therefore, even if it seemed desirable to have a sport group in which all members were equal in status, it simply wouldn't be possible. If a group exists, status differences are present. The answer, therefore, is not to try to eliminate status differences in the group but, rather, to either use them to produce a more effective group or to prevent them from detracting from the group's effectiveness.

Establishing *group congruency in status* is one factor which is important in terms of preventing status from detracting from group effectiveness. The term *group congruency* has been adopted to represent the degree to which there is equality in ranking among the various parameters associated with status in a group. In sport groups, these parameters might include age, education, years of experience, ability, access to special privileges, income, power, and authority. Too wide a discrepancy in the parameters associated with status can produce problems by detracting from the social and task cohesion of the group. And, group performance suffers.

The presence of too large a difference between high- and low-status individuals can also produce problems. Consequently, group leaders should try to avoid wide differences in status in their groups (Zander, 1982). If this isn't possible, efforts should be directed toward reducing the inhibitions produced by group incongruency. Any of a number of approaches are possible: (1) encouraging high-status group members to take initiatives to increase communication and interactions, (2) providing opportunities for group social activities, (3) structuring locker room and room assignments, travel arrangements, and seating at team meals to force more integration, (4) outlining in public the importance of the roles filled by the lower-status individuals in team success.

Another related factor which is also important in terms of group effectiveness is the congruency between the status and esteem hierarchies. Although status and esteem are similar, they do represent different elements in the group's structure. In order to differentiate between them, Bernard Bass (1980) used the terms *formal organizational structure* and *informal organizational structure*. A status hierarchy is a product of the formal organizational structure. A person who is elected or appointed team captain has a position of higher rank and greater status in the formal organizational structure. Thus, in the hierarchies illustrated in Figure 10.2, the differences in status associated with being a team captain versus a co-captain versus a team member are a product of the formal structure. Another more informal hierarchy may develop in the group based on the esteem members have for specific individuals. This esteem could be the result of exceptional ability — the most competent athletes in the group are generally held in highest esteem.

Group effectiveness is influenced by the degree of congruence between the status hierarchy and the esteem hierarchy (e.g. Haythorn, 1968; Shaw & Harkey, 1976). The group will be more effective if the higher status individuals are also those individuals who are held in the highest esteem in the group. Conversely, incongruency between the status and esteem hierarchies produces conflicts and detracts from group effectiveness. According to Bass (1980):

This is readily explained. The tendency to lead is greater among those of higher status as well as those of higher esteem. Suppose that the person of higher esteem in a group is not the same as the member with highest status. The occurrence of two or more individuals with equal leadership potential is likely to promote conflict in interaction. For instance, the higher status of the foreman of a department

permits him to serve as a leader. But if the most esteemed member is someone other than the foreman, this other member of the department also has the potential to influence the team. As long as the foreman and the most esteemed department member agree on the solutions to the group's problems, no conflict occurs. But if disagreement arises between these two members, both of whom have power to influence the department, conflict is likely. (pp. 470 -471)

Two possibilities can exist in groups in regard to the status and esteem hierarchies. The first is that they are *congruent* — the same person has the highest status and esteem. The second possibility is that they are *incongruent* — one person has the highest status position, another the highest esteem. Also, high esteem in a group can result from two different sources. One general source is the *positive personal attributes* which contribute to group effectiveness; e.g., ability. A second is the *negative personal attributes* which detract from group effectiveness; e.g., a carouser and/or a "club house lawyer".

These four possibilities taken in combination are

Table 10.6 Status-esteem congruency and the basis for esteem in sport groups.

| | Congruency in Status & Esteem | |
	Congruent	Incongruent
Positive Personal Attributes	**Highly Desirable** Retain the Status Quo	**Moderately Desirable** Recruit the High-Status Person into the Leadership Process
Negative Personal Attributes	**Highly Undesirable** Remove From the Captaincy and/or From the Team	**Undesirable** Remove from the Team

(Row group label: **Basis for Esteem**)

illustrated in Table 10.6. The implications for group effectiveness and the most appropriate course of action for a coach or team leader are different for each of the options. For example, the upper left hand box reflects a situation in which there is congruency between the esteem and status hierarchies (the same person has high status and high esteem) and the basis for the esteem is positive personal attributes (e.g., a good work ethic). In this case, it doesn't make sense to do anything. The status quo represents the best possible scenario and, therefore, shouldn't be disturbed.

The situation illustrated in the lower left hand box also reflects a situation in which there is congruency between the status and esteem hierarchies. However, the basis for the esteem is negative personal attributes. An example of this combination would be a team captain held in high esteem for his carousing. This combination represents the worst possible scenario. One solution might be to remove the individual from the team. If this isn't possible, at a minimum, the team captaincy should be removed.

The upper right hand box reflects a situation in which there is incongruency in status and esteem (different individuals have high status and high esteem) and the basis for the esteem is positive attributes. In this case, it makes sense to include the high esteem individuals in leadership roles or to include them in the leadership process.

The final possibility, the bottom right hand box in Table 10.6, represents a negative scenario. In this case, there is incongruency between the status and esteem hierarchies and the esteem results from qualities which are detrimental to effective team performance. The best solution might be to remove the individual from the team — even if that individual also happens to possess high ability. The negative behavior coupled with the position of high esteem could have a negative impact on the behavior and attitudes of other team members.

11 Group Roles

A role is a *shared expectation* for behavior. The individuals who occupy a role such as group leader know in general terms what types of behaviors are expected from them. They know that they are expected to be dominant, serve as a spokesperson for the group in certain instances, and exert influence when it is necessary. At the same time, the group has these same or similar expectations for the behavior of the individual who occupies the leader role.

> Everyone knew his job ... We were a big, strong team that was not very mobile, so Freddie gave us a system that would work for us. It wouldn't have worked for Montreal or one of the more skilled teams, but it did for us. He used to say, "Give a guy a small job and make him do it very, very well". (Bobby Clarke, quoted in Swift, 1987, p. 97)

requirements of their role. Some personal interpretation is always possible, but the individual's behavior must be generally consistent with what is prescribed by the role. Otherwise, the overall group performance suffers.

The expectations for behavior that a group, an organization, or society-in-general has for any individual who occupies a specific role can be quite broad. Nonetheless, if the individual strays outside these broad prescriptions, there are repercussions. Take for example, the role behaviors considered appropriate for a college coach. At times there doesn't seem to be any limit to what is termed acceptable behavior for coaches during a game. But that's not the case. Certain behaviors become widely publicized because they fall outside a range perceived to be appropriate to the role. This was the case when Woody Hayes, the football coach at Ohio State, punched an opposing player in a moment of frustration. He was subsequently removed from his job. This was also the case when Indiana basketball coach Bobby Knight threw a chair across the gymnasium during a loss to Purdue. In both cases, public criticism was widespread. While the behavior of Hayes and Knight doesn't seem to differ a great deal from the similar actions of other coaches in other situations, they were sufficiently different from society's expectations for the college coaching role that the two became the object of considerable criticism.

There is probably no other group in which role behaviors are so integral to group effectiveness as a sport team. As the team develops, offensive and defensive systems are established and role clarity is insured by clearly outlining the responsibilities for each individual in each position. And then, they are repeatedly rehearsed and reinforced to perfection in daily practices. This point is illustrated in the quote used to introduce this chapter. Bobby Clarke, a member of the Stanley Cup winning Philadelphia Flyers recalled that his coach, Fred Shero, introduced a system which became the basis for the Flyers's success. All of the players had a specific role in that system and Shero insured that they knew it completely.

There is a direct parallel between a role on a sport team and the role in a drama production. Whatever the individual's talents — and there are good actors and poor actors just as their are good athletes and poor athletes — each individual must operate within a system, a production, or an overall plan and carry out the

The Nature of Group Roles

Formal and Informal Group Roles

Within every group, there are two general categories of roles: formal and informal (Mabry & Barnes, 1980). *Formal roles* are those which are directly established by the group or organization. Many of the formal roles within a sport team are the result of the way in which the leadership hierarchy is set out. For example, Figure 10.1 illustrates two different hierarchical models insofar as the formal leadership roles of coach, assistant coach, team captain, and assistant captain are concerned.

There are also a number of formal performance roles in a sport team which result from the specific offensive and defensive systems used. The Clarke quotation about the Philadelphia Flyers is one example of the presence of formal performance roles. Other examples include the setter and spiker in volleyball and the power forward, point guard, and small forward in basketball. Every sport team, as an organization, requires specific individuals to carry out these types of specific roles. The roles are so important to the success of the group that individuals are either trained or recruited to fill them.

The *informal roles* in a team evolve as a result of the interactions that take place among the group members. Some examples of the informal roles that often emerge on a sport team include leader (which may or may not be the team captain), policeman or enforcer, social director, and team clown. The expectations for behavior for individuals who occupy these types of informal roles are not as well established as is the case with formal roles but they are present.

The role of policeman (or enforcer) on professional hockey and basketball teams is interesting in that it can be either a formal or an informal role. Athletes most suited to the role often inherit the responsibility. However, it is assumed that a team can't be successful without someone in the policeman's role. Consequently, players are specifically recruited to carry out this responsibility. The role of the policeman, intimidator, or enforcer in professional hockey can be illustrated with two quotes. The first, by Goyens and Turowetz (1986), makes reference to the Montreal Canadiens's John Ferguson:

> Another aspect of the team dynamic that the novice might find curious is the place held by the so-called "team policeman" ... The player who fights for his teammates, or is at least willing to drop his gloves so that less pugilistic players are free to do what they do best, is as essential to a team as any other player. "We all have our jobs on a hockey team," said Yvan Cournoyer. "And we respect a player who does his job because he is bringing something special to the team. John was a rough and hard hockey player because the Montreal Canadiens needed a player like that. Without him, and guys like Terry Harper and Ted Harris on defense, we would not have been as good as we became". (pp.200-201)

The second, by Ed Snider, owner of the Philadelphia Flyers, is also in reference to the necessity of having someone competent to fill the role of policeman:

> We didn't invent fighting in hockey, we inherited it ... The Big Bad Bruins used to beat up on us regularly. And I remember going into Montreal those first couple of years and watching John Ferguson kick the crap out of all our little Frenchmen. We had a line of Andre Lacroix, Simon Nolet and Jean-Guy Gendron. I asked Keith Allen, "What's this?" I was told, "Ferguson's their policeman." I asked, "Why don't we have a policeman?" He said, "We do, but he's not as tough as their policeman." So I decided, as long as I own this team, we will not be intimidated again. We're an expansion team, and we may not have superstars, but I'm sure as hell not going to sit by and let my guys get beat up, too. (Quoted in Swift, 1987, p. 92)

Whether they occupy formal or informal team roles, athletes very quickly become aware of their role carry out the requirements of that role contributes to group ineffectiveness.

Implications for the Effectiveness of Sport Groups

In order to insure that there is a link between the individual team member's roles, role performance, and group effectiveness — in other words, to insure that group members don't repeatedly fail to carry out their group assignments — other conditions must also be present (see Figure 11.1). One of these is that there must be *role clarity*. That is, the athletes must clearly understand their responsibilities.

It was pointed out earlier that formal roles are those established by the group or organization; informal roles evolve as a result of the interactions which take place within the team. Role clarity is greater in the case of formal roles. Even in the case of formal roles, however, the specific responsibilities associated with a role must be clearly spelled out. This insures that there are no misunderstandings. The occupants of a role generally have a different perspective of the requirements of that role than other members of the group (Merton, 1957). A hockey player who has a policeman's role or is assigned to a checking line may view himself as a playmaker or goal scorer. And, overall team effectiveness will suffer.

Another link in the relationship between individual roles and group effectiveness is *role acceptance.* Athletes must be satisfied with their responsibilities. In an attempt to determine what aspects of a role are associated with role satisfaction, Genevieve Rail (1987) tested 60 administrators and coaches involved in amateur sport programs. She found that no matter what level the individuals worked at — local, provincial, or national — the same four conditions were critical for satisfaction. One of these is the opportunity to use *specialized skills or competencies.* Thus, an athlete may be required to fulfill a role that initially seems unattractive. A defensive specialist is less visible than an offensive specialist. If the role occupant understands that specialized skills and competencies are required in the role, role satisfaction is enhanced.

Another contributor to role satisfaction is *feedback and recognition.* The defensive specialist is less visible than other members of the group. When feedback and recognition are provided for the role occupants, satisfaction is increased; when they are not, satisfaction diminishes.

A third, related factor is *role significance.* If the role is critical or perceived to be critical to team success, the occupant is more satisfied. In a quotation presented earlier, John Ferguson's role as a policeman on the Montreal Canadiens was outlined. Ferguson knew that his role was viewed as significant and important for team success, as the following quote shows:

> It was really important to me that the guys felt that way. One year the Canadiens veterans voted me the most valuable

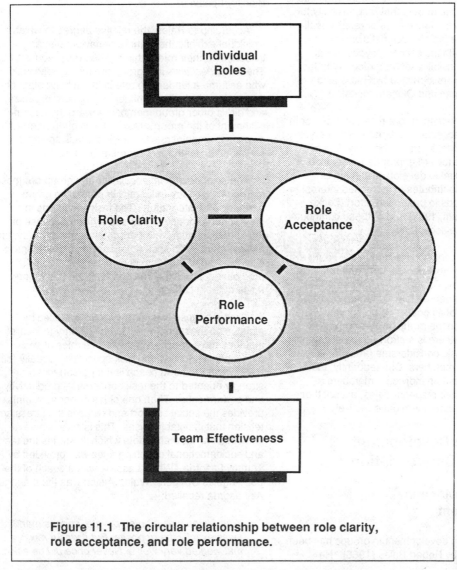

Figure 11.1 The circular relationship between role clarity, role acceptance, and role performance.

111

*player and that was the year Cournoyer led
the team in scoring. What impressed me was
that in the Canadiens scheme of things you
could be a leader not only as a goal scorer but
also as an aggressor.* (Quoted in Goyens &
Turowetz, 1986, p. 201)

The fourth condition identified by Rail was *autonomy*. It may be possible that autonomy isn't as important for role satisfaction in athletes as it was for the
administrators and coaches studied by Rail but, this
seems unlikely. It may be recalled that in Chapter 2, a
model developed by Richard Hackman and Greg
Oldham was presented (see Figure 2.1 again). Hackman and Oldham proposed that satisfaction, motivation, and work effectiveness are the product of three
psychological states: (1) the relative meaningfulness of
the work, (2) the degree of personal responsibility for
the outcome, and (3) the knowledge of results available. Autonomy is the job characteristic which is
directly associated with the second psychological
state, personal responsibility for the outcome. In fact,
each of the other factors identified by Rail is also
present in the Hackman and Oldham model.

An effective goal setting program can improve both
role clarity and role acceptance. Goal setting serves
four important functions: it directs the individual's
attention and actions toward appropriate behaviors, it
motivates the individual to develop strategies to
achieve the goal, it contributes to increased interest in
the activity, and it leads to prolonged effort (Locke,
Shaw, Saari, & Latham, 1981). All of these contribute
to role clarity and role acceptance.

The level of *task cohesion* present in the group also
influences role clarity, role acceptance, and role
performance (Brawley, Carron, & Widmeyer, 1987).
Task cohesion is the degree to which the group is
united in the pursuit of its goals and objectives. When
there is consensus on the group goals and how to
achieve them, when there is a strong general commitment to the group task, considerable pressure is
placed on individual members. Consequently, there is
greater group pressure on individual members to
clearly understand their responsibilities, accept those
responsibilities, and carry them out effectively.

Role Development
and Differentiation

Individual Behavior and
Role Development

The nature of role development in groups has been
studied extensively by Robert Bales (1966). He
observed that the prevalence of certain behaviors is
associated with the appearance of different group
roles within task-oriented groups. The three general
types of behaviors identified by Bales were: activity,
task ability, and likability. Behavior directed toward
standing out from others is referred to as *activity*. On
a basketball team, for example, speaking out frequently in the dressing room, encouraging others and
cheerleading during a game are some examples of
activity behavior. *Task ability* is behavior which helps
the group achieve its goals. As the name suggests,
task ability, is synonymous with expertise. Finally,
likability is behavior directed toward the development
and maintenance of socially satisfying relationships.
Arranging group parties, coordinating social activities,
and acting as a peacemaker are some examples of
likability behavior.

According to Bales, the relative degree to which an
individual exhibits these three behaviors has an
influence on their role within a group (see Figure 11.2).
The *task specialists* in a group are those individuals
who assume a leadership role in the achievement of
the group's goals. They influence, support, organize,
and direct other group members toward the accomplishment of the group's task. This is often referred to
as an instrumental role because the task specialist
serves as an instrument for team success.

The *socioemotional specialists* in a group are those
individuals who are influential in promoting group
harmony and integration. The task specialists in a
group often produce stress and tension because of
their preoccupation with performance, productivity, and
achievement. The socioemotional specialist helps to
diffuse some of the tension by providing support,
promoting team unity, and emphasizing the importance of team cohesion.

Although these two informal roles are filled by
athletes on the team, many teams also try to insure
that they have coaches in the formal roles of socioemotional specialist and task specialist. Usually (but
not always) the head coach is the person most
strongly oriented to the task concerns — productivity
and performance. Then one of his or her assistants
provides the social support and diffuses the stress and
tension that inevitably arises. This is an effective
combination. One anecdote which illustrates the task
and socioemotional coaching roles was provided by
Tommy Lasorda. When Lasorda was a coach of the
Los Angeles Dodgers, Walter Alston was the manager.
As Lasorda recalled:

*Walt Alston was a quiet, private, serious man.
I was exactly the opposite. But it was a mix
that worked very well ... Never once did he ask*

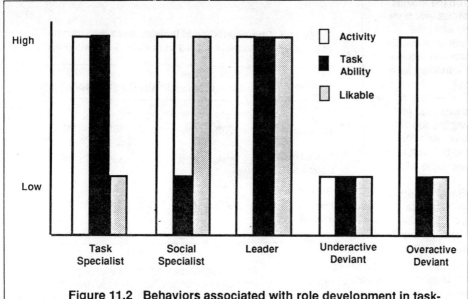

Figure 11.2 Behaviors associated with role development in task-oriented, problem-solving groups (Adapted from Bales, 1966).

On the basis of a reanalysis and review of earlier research concerned with group leadership and role differentiation, however, Lewis (1972) concluded that the two roles are often integrated. And, when they are, when one person fulfills both the task specialist and the socioemotional specialist roles, he or she has an an overall *leadership role* in the group (see Figure 11.2 again). When this occurs, leadership within the group is more effective. Individuals who occupy both the task and social roles simultaneously are considered to be exceptional leaders — the people referred to in the so-called "great man theory of leadership.

The final two roles in Figure 11.2 are the *overactive deviant* and the *underactive deviant*. Individuals who are "club house lawyers", who exhibit high activity behavior but low task ability and likability behaviors, occupy the role referred to as the overactive deviant. Finally, an underactive deviant is low on all three behaviors. There is very low prevalence of this type of individual in social and work groups and sport teams.

Role Differentiation in Sport Teams

The process by which role differentiation occurs to produce task specialists and socioemotional specialists in sport teams was examined by Roger Rees and Mady Segal (1984). They had members of two intercollegiate football teams identify the individuals who contributed the most to group harmony. Rees and Segal viewed these athletes as the socioemotional leaders. The team members were also required to identify the individuals who were the best players. These athletes were considered by Rees and Segal to be the task leaders.

me to change or to tone down my enthusiasm, and never, ever, did he appear threatened by my close relationships to the Dodger players. (Lasorda & Fisher, 1985, p. 174)

Another example is provided by John Feinstein's (1987) account of an incident in which Bobby Knight criticized Daryl Thomas, one of his athletes:

Knight walked out onto the floor. He was drained. He turned to Kohn Smith. "Go talk to Daryl," he said. Knight knew he had gone too far with Thomas, and undoubtedly he had regretted many of the words as soon as they were out of his mouth. But he couldn't take them back. Instead he would send Smith, who was as quiet and gentle as Knight was loud and brutal, to talk to Thomas. (p. 7)

The original research on role differentiation and leadership led to the conclusion that only the two informal leadership roles of task specialist and socioemotional specialist emerge as the group develops (e.g., Bales & Slater, 1955). These two roles were also viewed as incompatible with each other. The preoccupation of the task specialists with performance produced tension and stress. Consequently, socioemotional specialists emerged to insure that the group doesn't disintegrate.

The task leaders on the football team came almost exclusively from the first string players while the socioemotional leaders were equally balanced between first and second string. Interestingly, considerable role integration was present — 55% of the individuals who were listed among the top 10 individuals as task leaders were also listed among the top 10 socioemotional leaders. All of the athletes who occupied both roles were first string players (see Table 11.1).

When Rees and Segal looked at the impact of experience on role involvement, they found that task leaders were drawn from the total spectrum of the team: senior (33%), junior (56%), and sophomore (11%). On the other hand, the socioemotional leaders were almost exclusively the senior players on the team (90%). When individuals were listed in both roles, they were generally seniors (73%). It seems that ability is the most important qualification for a task leader on a sport team. Being on the first string is essential, years of experience on the team is not. On the other hand, years of experience is an essential prerequisite be a socioemotional leader. Being on the first string is not important, but being a senior is.

Table 11.1 Characteristics of individuals in leadership roles in sport teams (Adapted from Rees & Segal, 1984)

Role	1st String	2nd String	Senior	Junior	Sophomore
Task Leaders	100%	0%	33%	56%	11%
Socioemotional Leaders	50%	50%	90%	10%	0%
Great Man Leaders (Both Task & Social)	100%	0%	73%	18%	9%

The Systematic Multiple Level Observation of Groups

Robert Bales early research with groups led him to believe that most of the interactions and communication which occur within groups — and the group roles which result from those interactions and communications — are related to task and social concerns. More recently, however, he developed a new system for coding the content of group interactions and communications. It is referred to as SYMLOG — Systematic Multiple Level Observation of Groups (Bales, 1980; Bales, Cohen, & Williamson, 1979).

According to Bales, the social interactions which occur within a group can be categorized in three dimensions. One of these is an *Up-Down* dimension. It reflects the fact that the interactions and communications which occur within a group can be rated according to the degree of dominance or submissiveness present. A second dimension which is referred to as *Forward-Backward* measures the degree to which interactions and communications are expressive (emotional) or controlled. And, finally, the *Positive-Negative* dimension represents the degree to which friendliness versus unfriendliness is present in group interactions and communications. The combination of these three different dimensions produces 26 possible group roles. Although SYMLOG has not yet been used with sport groups, it does represent a useful way to study the development and emergence of group roles.

Implications for the Effectiveness of Sport Groups

Despite the existence of formal leadership roles such as captain, cocaptain, and assistant captain, interactions within the group will lead to the emergence of informal leadership roles. The two most important are the task specialist and socioemotional specialist. The most desirable outcome is if (a) the same person or people occupy both roles and (b) they are in formal leadership roles. In this case, the status and esteem hierarchies discussed in Chapter 10 are in agreement (see Table 10.6 again). If the task specialists do not have a formal leadership role (e.g., captain or assistant captain), they should either be given one or included in the leadership process.

Although the socioemotional specialist may seem to be unimportant or irrelevant in task-oriented groups such as a sport team, this is not the case. The socioemotional specialists play a valuable role in diffusing some of the tension and stress which develop as the group works toward its goals and objectives. They enhance task and social cohesion. The only danger is if the socioemotional concerns become more important than the task concerns. Kept in perspective, however, the socioemotional specialist contributes significantly to group effectiveness.

Role Conflict

The Nature of Role Conflict

Role conflict exists when, despite the presence of consensus on a desired goal or outcome, a role occupant doesn't have sufficient ability, motivation, time, or understanding to achieve that goal. Every coach wants his or her athletes to do a good job, to help the team, to contribute to team success. This is constantly conveyed directly and indirectly to the athlete. But, an athlete may lack the necessary skills. Or be confused because the behaviors associated with "doing a good job" may vary either between coaches or from one instance to the next. This is clearly illustrated in the story that Don Cherry, a former coach of the Boston Bruins, related about one of his former players, Al Secord:

> Sinden always liked fighters, which is why I couldn't understand why Secord didn't make a hit with him. After I left the Bruins, I ran into Al one day in Boston and he was really depressed. "I don't understand what the Bruins are doing to me," he said. "I'm on the bench. I asked why I wasn't playing and they told me, 'Because you're not playing your game, you're not playing aggressive and not hitting.' So naturally, I go out and be aggressive and start hitting and naturally I get a few penalties. Then they bench me again. I say, 'Why aren't I playing?' They say, 'Because you're getting too many penalties.' My head is all screwed up". (p. 193)

Three types of role conflict are possible: intrarole, interrole, and person-role (Cherniss, 1980). Intrarole conflict exists when there are contradictory demands within the same role (see Figure 11.3). These contradictory demands could be either self-imposed by the person playing the role (the role taker) or placed on the individual by the members of the group (the role senders). The quotation about Al Secord is a good example of intrarole conflict. The contradictory demands in his case seemed to have originated almost entirely from the role senders — the coaching staff and management.

Interrole conflict exists when an individual must play two or more roles and the behavioral demands of one role are incompatible with the behavioral demands of the second role. The incompatibility might exist because the expected role behaviors are inherently in contradiction. A playing coach is often in a position of interrole conflict. The coach is both a member of the team and a part of management. The expectations for behavior in competitive situations and in social situations is not the same as it is for other team members.

Student-athletes in big-time athletic programs also are often in a position of *interrole conflict.* When Alabama's legendary coach, Paul "Bear" Bryant (1974) discussed the problems associated with being a student and an athlete, he felt that the solution was straightforward:

> I used to go along with the idea that football players on scholarship were "student-athletes", which is what the NCAA calls them. Meaning a student first, an athlete second. We were kidding ourselves, trying to make it more palatable to the academicians. We don't have to say that and we shouldn't. At the level we play, the boy is really an athlete first and a student second. (p. 325)

But, obviously university professors and administrators view the priorities for the two roles differently. Consequently for individuals in big-time athletic programs, the role of being an athlete is frequently in conflict with the role of being a student.

Person-role conflict exists when a role requires certain behaviors that the person doesn't have the motivation or ability to carry out. (This same issue was also discussed in Chapter 8 in regard to compatibility of the person with his or her group role.) The examples of person-role conflict in sport are numerous. In 1987, for example, George Bell of the Toronto Blue Jays was the American League Most Valuable Player. When he arrived at spring training in 1988, the Blue Jays indicated they intended to use him in the designated hitter role (DH). He was extremely unhappy with his new role and his motivation suffered. As his agent Randy Hendricks pointed out:

> I guess the best way to describe it is that he feels a big arrow has been shot into his ego ... The designated hitter is generally regarded as one-half of a player ... it's a blow to George's pride. I could see if this thing gets out of hand that the Blue Jays might want to trade him. (London Free Press, 1988, p. C-2)

Athletes in amateur sport who are unhappy with their role — who experience person-role conflict — often quit the sport (Volp & Keil, 1987). Professional athletes often demand to be traded. Or they air their grievances with the team in the media.

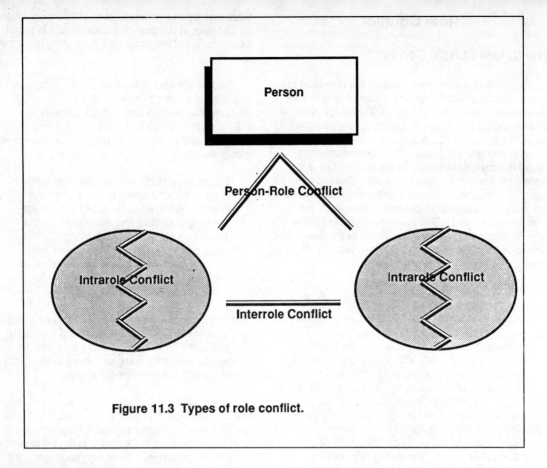

Figure 11.3 Types of role conflict.

Role Conflict and the Female Sport Experience

One issue which has attracted considerable attention is the question of whether female athletes experience role conflict. Highly competitive sport requires strength, speed, fitness, and long hours of practice and dedication. It also reinforces attributes such as aggression, assertiveness, and dominance. These are qualities which traditionally have been highly valued and encouraged in males but not in females. Consequently, a number of researchers reasoned that females involved might find that the role of athlete was incompatible with femininity.

A comprehensive investigation by George Sage and Sheryl Loudermilk (1979) focused on this question. A sample of 268 female college athletes from 13 colleges and universities was used. All were good athletes; the overwhelming majority considered themselves average or above average in ability when they were between the ages of 14 and 17 years. Only 20 percent of these athletes reported that they had

experienced a large degree of role conflict.

Type of sport involvement also makes a difference. For example, Sage and Loudermilk classified the various sports as *feminine* (tennis, golf, swimming, and gymnastics) or *masculine* (softball, basketball, volleyball, field hockey, and track and field). They then found that a fewer number of females involved in feminine activities experienced moderate to severe role conflict (34%) than females involved in the more stigmatized masculine activities (41%). A number of other studies have also found that females in stereotypical feminine activities experience less role conflict than females in stereotypical masculine activities (e.g., Anthrop & Allison, 1983; Jackson & Marsh, 1986).

Role Conflict and Psychological Burnout

Burnout is a psychological condition which is characterized by apathy, ineffectiveness, and emotional exhaustion (Maslach, 1976). When it occurs in individuals in the people-oriented professions —

medicine, teaching, coaching, and social work for example — they lose positive feelings, sympathy, and even respect for their clients. They experience physical, emotional, and mental exhaustion. As a consequence performance and productivity suffer and the "burned out" individual may even withdraw from the situation permanently.

The work of Maslach and his colleagues has been important in gaining an understanding of the nature of psychological burnout (Maslach, 1976, 1982; Maslach & Jackson, 1981a, 1981b; Maslach & Pines, 1977). The Maslach Burnout Inventory has been used in research to measure both the frequency and the intensity of three manifestations of burnout (see Table 11.2): emotional exhaustion, depersonalization, and diminished feelings of personal accomplishment.

Emotional exhaustion exists when the coach feels overwhelmed by all of the responsibilities and work associated with the job. Certainly, every coach occasionally feels that there isn't enough time available for all that must be done — planning and attending practices, scouting, and meetings with other coaches, and dealing with the media, parents, athletes, and university officials. The list seems endless and feelings of emotional exhaustion can develop. It isn't the presence of this feeling that signifies burnout, however. It's the frequency and the intensity of the feeling. How often is it present? How intense is the feeling? If the feelings are extremely intense and if they seem to be present constantly, the coach is suffering from psychological burnout.

Depersonalization is characterized by a lack of personal feelings for the athletes — they are simply numbers or bodies to be dealt with. As was the case with emotional exhaustion, depersonalization isn't an all or none feeling. Because of the pressures of time and other commitments, all coaches have lowered sensitivity for the personal concerns of their athletes at certain times. When the lack of interest increases in frequency and intensity however, burnout has developed.

Finally, diminished feelings of *personal accomplishment* represent a belief that few worthwhile things have been accomplished, that the coach has not been generally successful. Psychological burnout develops when the coach begins to constantly doubt that he or she has made a contribution and/or been successful.

Although burnout is not as severe in the coaching professions as it is in other people-oriented professions, it is present. A number of sources of burnout have been identified. For example, situational factors (including the number of hours of contact with athletes and a lack of team success) were found to be more important than personal factors by Wilson and Bird (1984). And, Caccese and Mayerberg (1984) found that female coaches experienced higher levels of emotional exhaustion and lower levels of personal accomplishment than male coaches. But, the most important factor might be role conflict.

Susan Capel, Becky Sisley, and Gloria Desertrain (1987) noted that there is considerable potential for both interrole conflict and intrarole conflict in coaches at the high school level because (1) they have many organizational and administrative tasks in addition to coaching, (2) those who are also teaching experience an overload of demands in terms of time and effort to do a good job in both teaching and coaching, (3) those who are not teaching (so that the coaching job is considered part-time) also experience an overload of demands to do a good job in both coaching and their other profession, (4) interrole conflict

Table 11.2 The manifestations of psychological burnout (Adapted from Maslach & Jackson, 1981b)

Name	Description	Example
Emotional Exhaustion	Feelings of being emotionally overextended and exhausted by the work and the responsibilities	Coach constantly feels overwhelmed by the time needed to prepare practices, teach, recruit, counsel athletes, etc.
Depersonalization	Lack of feelings of personal concern for the recipients of the services or instruction	Coach feels apathy about the general progress, health, interests, and concerns of athletes
Diminished Personal Accomplishment	Low feelings of personal competence and sucessful achievement	Coach feels he/she has not been sucessful, has not had many accomplishments

can arise because the skills, attitudes, and require-ments of coaching and teaching are vastly different, (5) within the coaching role, intrarole conflict can arise because of the different expectations held by parents, athletes, administrators, and the community (e.g., a winning team has high priority in the community; educational outcomes have a high priority with parents and administrators).

In order to assess the impact of both role conflict and role ambiguity (a lack of role clarity or understand-ing of the requirements of the role) on psychological burnout, Capel and her colleagues studied 235 male and female high school coaches. These coaches varied in the number of years they had been a head coach, their number of years of experience as an assistant coach, number of sports coached, and enrollment in their school. Half coached boys teams, the other half coached girls teams.

Capel and her colleagues found that the absolute frequency and the intensity of burnout were low relative to other people-oriented professions. For those coaches who did experience burnout, however, role conflict and role ambiguity were more important than any of the other factors considered. Simultane-ous involvement in the dual roles of teacher-coach either leads to overload or the two roles are inherently incompatible. Whatever, the basis, role conflict is an important factor in psychological burnout.

Implications for the Effectiveness of Sport Groups

Coach. Athletic Director. Student. Counselor. Mother. Daughter. One person could play each of these roles (and others) simultaneously. Humans are social animals and, consequently, involvement in a large number of groups is inevitable. And equally inevitable is the assumption of different roles in these groups. William Shakespeare probably expressed it best in his play **As you like it:**

> All the world's a stage. And all the men and women merely players. They have their exits and their entrances. And one man in his time plays many parts. (Act II, Scene 7)

Unfortunately, the general behaviors considered appropriate for each of these roles can be quite different. Consequently, role conflict can arise — the role occupant doesn't have sufficient ability, motiva-tion, time, or understanding of the role to produce the behaviors expected.

Although there are no definitive solutions for role conflict, some approaches suggested from other problem areas in sport have relevance and could be used. For example, Andreas Volp and Udo Keil (1987) observed that one effective means of dealing with intrapersonal conflict is through *cognitive restructur-ing*. An underlying assumption for engaging in cogni-tive restructuring is the need for cognitive consistency. "All organisms prefer to live in a state of equilibrium, a state of cognitive balance. Whenever this equilibrium is threatened, cognitive inconsistency or dissonance arises, which is perceived as tension or conflict ... This is always the case when elements within a cognitive field are inconsistent with each other. The individual then takes steps to reduce conflict and restore the equilibrium (Volp & Keil, 1987, p. 359).

In the process of cognitive restructuring, two strategies are possible. An individual can devalue one of the roles. Thus, a coach might reduce the impor-tance (i.e., relevance) of her teaching role if the behaviors in that role were in conflict with her coach-ing. An individual can also bring different roles into balance (i.e., harmony) by decreasing the differences among the component parts of each role. Thus, a coach might emphasize the fact that his coaching is teaching; that elite athletes are similar to elite students (i.e., graduate students); that recruiting in athletics is like recruiting in graduate programs; that scholarships for outstanding athletes are comparable to scholar-ships for outstanding students. This altered perspec-tive would help to reduce conflict between the two roles.

When Volp and Keil compared elite athletes with medium and lesser skilled athletes, they found that the elite athletes exhibited the least intrapersonal conflict. The elite athletes also made the greatest use of cognitive restructuring strategies, particularly by increasing the harmony among potentially conflicting elements. From these results, Volp and Keil suggested that

> competing successfully at a high level requires the athlete to cognitively restructure incoming information to reduce conflict that might otherwise be an obstacle to performance ... A successful athlete seems able to align himself or herself with the demands of the sport. The harmonization of conflicting cognitions seems to be a functional method of coping with contradictions inside the cognitive field ... that might otherwise impair motivation and performance. (p.372)

There are other techniques in addition to cognitive restructuring which might be useful for reducing role conflict. For example, since the primary cause of\burnout is role conflict, the same techniques might be useful in both cases. In his discussion on alleviating athlete burnout, Keith Henschen (1986) suggested (a) scheduling time-outs, (b) increasing participation in decision-making, (c) assuming control of outcomes, and (d) planning mental practices.

Scheduling time-outs involves setting up periods away from the situation. A coach may feels overwhelmed by the pressures and stresses associated with teaching and coaching simultaneously, with planning and attending practices, meeting athletes, the media, parents, and other coaches. It could be beneficial to have his or her major teaching load scheduled in a term after season. Or to timetable in a specific day, morning or evening, or even a period away from the concerns of the role. One example of how this has been done is illustrated in the case of Mark Howe of the Philadelphia Flyers:

> The life of Mark Howe does not revolve exclusively around hockey. Says Ginger Howe, ... "Mark doesn't bring the game home, except at playoff time, when he gets pretty tense ... In the summer, we go to our Jersey shore, fish a lot from the boat ... And on the boat, hockey talk is taboo. If you have nothing but hockey, you go crazy". (Knight, 1987, p.3).

A time-out can vary in type, timing, and duration depending on the constraints of the situation. There are no fixed prescriptions except that time away from a role does help reduce role conflict.

Increasing the participation of others can also help to reduce role conflict. Since role conflict arises because the role occupant doesn't have sufficient ability, time, motivation or understanding, the recruitment of others to fill these gaps can alleviate some of the problem. Increased participation may be accomplished in either of two ways: by sharing responsibilities among available group members or by increasing the number of group members. As was pointed out in Chapter 3, increasing the group's size produces increases in group resources.

A third possibility is to attempt to assume greater control over outcomes. Role expectations evolve from both the individual (the role occupant) and the group or organization (role senders). By attempting to gain greater control, the role occupant can insure that the behavioral demands (either self-imposed or from others) for the role are not beyond his or her capabilities. One way to gain greater control is by negotiating compromises. For example, an athlete could attempt to have the coach alter the factors producing the greatest stress or pressure. Similarly, a coach might negotiate with the administration to reduce some responsibilities producing role conflict.

When Henschen suggested the use of mental practice, his primary concern was for the alleviation of burnout in athletes, not the reduction of role conflict. Nonetheless, a number of psychological techniques including mental practice might be useful for role conflict. Role conflict is associated with feelings of stress, tension, frustration, anger, mental and physical fatigue, and so on. The psychological skills emphasized in a good mental skills program include goal setting, arousal management, imagery, concentration, self affirmation, parking, energizing, and stress inoculation (see Albinson & Bull, 1988). Each of these can also be used to reduce the negative feelings associated with role conflict.

12 Group Norms

The nature of group norms is clearly illustrated in the quote used to introduce this chapter. Norms are the standards for behavior that are expected of members of the group. They are descriptive, evaluative, informal, unobtrusive, internal, flexible, and stable (Forsythe, 12.1. Insofar as the *descriptive* function is concerned, norm outlines the group's beliefs about the standards for behavior considered appropriate. Norms also serve an *evaluative* function. Essentially, they reflect the values or standards that govern the behaviors of group members who occupy different positions, possess different status, and/or occupy different roles. As such, group norms represent the organization's or group's consensus about what is considered acceptable. Norms are also *informal* and *unobtrusive* — they are not specifically or overtly set out by the group. Gradual changes in individual behavior occur over time until a consensus is achieved about what is appropriate. Because they are not specifically set out as rules or laws, norms are most evident when they are violated. Nonetheless, norms are *internalized* by individual group members so that adherence occurs primarily because of the satisfaction this produces rather than the fear of sanctions. Some *flexibility* is also present and minor deviations from a norm are acceptable. Finally, norms are *stable*; they emerge slowly over time and are resistant to change.

The *Club de Hockey Canadien* did not immediately stand the NHL or the sports world on its ears. The Fabulous Flying Frenchmen were just one of many teams, no more, no less. But they were an organization that would eventually develop ... a winning tradition by stressing the importance of success. One would assume that most work organizations naturally generate such strong beliefs and commitments among their employees. The truth is that these qualities take years to cultivate. In the case of the Canadiens, those athletes and administrators not willing to commit themselves to the degree considered necessary for success were selectively eliminated from within the organization. (Goyens and Turowetz, 1986, p. 28)

Because norms reflect existing group values, the group evaluates individual behavior and judges it to be acceptable or unacceptable, satisfactory or unsatisfactory. Acceptable behavior is rewarded or approved through verbal appreciation, elevated prestige, increased group acceptance, and recognition. On the other hand, unacceptable behavior is sanctioned by verbal criticism, ostracism, physical abuse, or even rejection from the group (Crosbie, 1975).

Thus, for example, as the structure of an intramural basketball team emerges, group expectations (i.e., norms) develop around such behaviors as the average number of shots taken by any one player in a game. And pressure is placed on individual members to conform to this group norm. If a team member violates the norms — continually takes more shots than is deemed appropriate — he or she will be sanctioned. The sanctions might take the form of criticism or ostracism, i.e., the other team members might begin using a derogatory nickname such as "Gunner" to try to rely the message or they might stop passing the ball. Depending on the persistence of the behavior, its seriousness, and the cohesiveness of the group, the norm violator might even be rejected from the team.

Table 12.1 The nature of norms (Adapted from Forsythe, 1983).

Aspect	Description
Descriptive	Norms represent the standards for behavior is a group
Evaluative	Norms establish priorities for different behaviors marking some out as more valuable than others
Informal	Norms are not formally adopted by the group but result from a gradual change in behavior until a consensus is reached in the group
Unobtrusive	Norms are taken for granted and only become an important issue when they are violated
Flexible	Minor deviations from norms are generally permitted
Internalized	Norms are internalized by individual group members. Adherence results primarily from satisfaction produced rather than fear of sanctions
Stability	Norms develop slowly over time and are vary resistant to change

The Nature of Group Norms

Types of Norms

Four general types of norms have been identified by Mott (1965). These are summarized in Table 12.2. A *prescribed norm* serves to specify which behaviors are considered appropriate for group members. The norm for productivity — the concept of a fair day's work — would be one example of a prescribed norm. In Table 12.2, the norm for productivity is illustrated in a quote by Dave Poulin, captain of the Philadelphia hockey team.

The expectations that emerge which reflect behaviors not considered appropriate are referred to as *proscribed norms*. Essentially, they represent the flip side of a prescribed norm. Loafing involves behaviors which are contrary to a good work ethic. Similarly, being clean shaven and well groomed — the behaviors used as examples in Table 12.2 — are the opposite of unshaven and poorly groomed.

It is important to bear in mind that norms are expectations that exist in the minds of group members They provide guidelines about what group members should do, ought to do, are expected to do (Homans, 1950). They are not laws or formalized rules. Thus, if a team had a rule relating to curfew — "anyone missing curfew will not be on the roster for the next game" — it would not be considered a norm. Norms do emerge around rules and regulations, however. The norm, the expectation of the group, might be that the curfew is unimportant.

A comparable situation seems to exist in terms of the normative expectations which have emerged around the formal rules of sport. These formal rules proscribe specific behaviors in order to insure that the competition between teams is fair. There is considerable evidence, however, that shows that under certain circumstances it is not only legitimate for athletes to break these rules, it is expected. The "good foul" in basketball and soccer, the "good penalty" in hockey are some examples.

John Silva (1983) has suggested that the norms surrounding rule violations in sport — the necessity of committing the good foul in critical situations — have "become so important that participants in many sports must learn not only the written rules, but the unwritten or normative rules of their sport in order to be successful" p. 438). Some support for this suggestion is available from a study by McIntosh (reported in Silva, 1983). When he asked soccer players whether a player in a good position to score should be brought down unmercifully, 70% of the professionals and 54% of the amateurs agreed.

In his study, Silva presented male and female college students with seven slides depicting rule violating behavior (in baseball, basketball, hockey, and football). The subjects were required to rate the acceptability of the behavior on a four-point scale which varied from "totally unacceptable" to "totally acceptable". Silva's results showed that males rated rule violations as more acceptable than females (a mean of 21.4 points versus a mean of 15.2 points out of a possible 28.0). Also, the perception that rule violations are an acceptable part of the game was strongest in males who had the most sport experience,

Table 12.2 Illustrations of various group norms (Adapted from Mott, 1965)

Type of Norm	Example
Prescribed Norms: Reflect the pattern of behaviors considered appropriate	"When a kid comes to camp and sees what's expected of him ... he thinks, 'I've got no choice' It's a lot easier to assimilate someone into that than to start it from scratch" (Philadelphia Flyer captain Dave Poulin, quoted in Swift, 1987, p.99).
Proscribed Norms: Reflect the pattern of behaviors not considered appropriate	"I want our boys to look like the All-American boy ... the All-American boy is clean shaven and his hair is in order. That is how I expect them to look" (Former Tennessee basketball coach Ray Mears, quoted in Eitzen & Sage, 1982, p. 71).
Permissive Norms: Reflect the pattern of behaviors permitted but not expected	"We're always looking at an advantage-disadvantage situation ... Did the person do something illegal to create an advantage for himself or put his opponent at a disadvantage? If he did, then it's a foul. If not ... that's a foul we wouldn't call" (NBA official Darrell Garretson, quoted in Monteville, 1987, p. 68).
Preference Norms: Reflect the pattern of behaviors preferred but not expected	"I play without officials on the playground ... I never call a foul. You call a foul and then you have your 10 minutes of arguing and then maybe five minutes of fighting before you can start playing again. It's not worth it ... unless, of course, the score is 9-9 and the game is 10. Then you call everything and go ahead with the fight" (Detroit Piston player Isiah Thomas, quoted in Monteville, 1987, p. 69).

who were participating at the highest levels of competition, and who were involved in sports with the greatest amount of physical contact.

As Table 12.2 shows, there are also *permissive norms* — patterns of behavior that are permitted but not required. This type of norm is illustrated in Darrel Garretson's statement that the norm for officiating in the NBA evolves around the *principle of advantage*. Behaviors for which a foul might be called are ignored if no advantage is gained or if no disadvantage to an opponent results.

Another place where permissive norms exist is baseball. David Rainey and Janet Larsen (1988) demonstrated empirically that baseball umpires use a strike zone which differs from what is set out in the rule book. They had 16 high school/college level umpires describe the official rule-book definition of the strike zone The umpires were then required to reproduce the strike zone by drawing lines across a picture of a

batter's body. Finally, they were asked to draw two more lines showing the upper and lower boundaries of the strike zone they actually used.   A significant deviation was found between the top of the actual strike zone and the line umpires used. The umpires reduced the size of the strike zone by lowering the top boundary. The reasons given for not following the rule book fell into five general categories: (a) positioning problems (with a low stance behind the catcher, it is difficult to call the high pitch), (b) others' expectations (the coaches and players expect a lower strike zone), (c) major league influence (the high pitch is not called in the major leagues), (d) convenience (the letters on a player's jersey are a better reference), and (e) discretion (provide the batters with a better opportunity to hit).

The final type of norm presented in Table 12.2 is the *preference norm* — behaviors preferred but not required by group members. The quote by Isiah Thomas provides a good illustration. Fouls could be called constantly in a playground basketball game. But, players prefer not to call them because they disrupt the flow of the play. However, in a close game, a foul likely will be called if an advantage/disadvantage results.

Emergence of Norms

If a norm is a behavioral standard, how does it develop? One essential factor is *group interaction*. The contacts members have with each other help to clarify the standards that are acceptable for behavior. As Victor Vroom (1969) pointed out, the "interaction among persons tends to decrease the variance in their behavior, and, in the extreme, can produce highly standardized behavioral patterns" (p. 223).

A second essential factor is *reinforcement*. The behaviors that the vast majority of group members find acceptable are reinforced; unacceptable behaviors are discouraged. Consequently, each individual comes to understand the standards (norms) deemed appropriate. The role of interaction and reinforcement in the emergence of group norms is illustrated in a quote by Jacques Lamaire of the Montreal Canadiens:

> *Winning in team sports is a process. You don't just draft the best talent and leave it to their creativity. You have to build up a team identity and work ethic where every individual knows his role and what is expected of him.* (Goyens & Turowetz, 1986, p.388).

When a bridge club forms, for example, a wide range of differences are possible in issues such as punctuality, the amount of "coaching" permissible during the bidding, the amount of social conversation appropriate during the play, and even the type of food and beverages served. Through interaction and reinforcement, a general understanding develops within the group; the range of behaviors considered permissible by the group decreases. The general standards that develop help the group operate smoothly. Similarly, as a sport team develops, and team members interact frequently, differences in the amount of effort they expend at practices, the type of clothing they wear on road trips, and so on gradually decreases.

There are a number of factors which influence the level of adherence to the group norms. These are discussed in a subsequent section which deals with social norms.

The Function of Norms

By providing group members with general prescriptions for appropriate behavior and implicitly outlining the limits for permissible deviations from those prescriptions, group norms serve two functions within the group (Kiesler & Kiesler, 1969). One of these is *informational*. Norms help the individual gain insight into the group, they provide a standard against which a new member can validate his/her opinions, attitudes, and behavior. Norms also insure that the individual's opinions, attitudes, and behavior don't deviate dramatically from other group members. The informational function of group norms was illustrated in the quote by Dave Poulin which is presented in Table 12.2. Philadelphia Flyer rookies come to camp, see how the veterans are working, and see what is expected to be successful. This information helps to insure that their opinions, attitudes, and behaviors are consistent with what is expected on the Flyers.

The second, related function is *integration*. The individual who understands and accepts the group norm is drawn into the group, the individual who does not is rejected or removed from the group. When the group norms are accepted, the group goals can be successfully pursued and the continuation of the group is insured. The integrative function of a group norm was illustrated in both the quote used to introduce this chapter and the quote by Poulin in Table 12.2. Conformity to the group norms helps to contribute to the unity of the team. Deviance from the norms breaks down this unity.

The Stability of Norms

In a typical study on conformity to group standards, Jacobs and Campbell (1961) had groups of four subjects judge the distance a light moved. Initially, three of the four group members in each group were confederates of the experimenter; they all reported that the light had moved 15 to 16 inches. The naive subjects in the group correctly perceived (and reported) that the light had moved approximately 4 inches. However, after a series of trials in which the confederates continued to endorse an incorrect standard, the naive subjects also began to report that the light had moved 15 to 16 inches. When this incorrect norm was well established, the composition of the group was changed completely; old members were replaced by naive new members over a series of "generations".

The pattern outlined above was repeated in each generation. The new group member, the naive subject, reported that the light had travelled about 4 inches. The three established group members (who were no longer confederates of the experimenter) continued to report that the light had moved 15 to 16 inches. After a series of trials, the new naive group member adopted the group norm. Although each generation showed a tendency to move closer to the correct standard, it took four to five generations before this was accomplished (see Figure 12.1).

What this demonstrates of course is the stability of group norms. If a team develops negative norms such as abusive behavior toward officials or other team members, a poor work ethic, or an emphasis on individual rather than team goals, these can persist over a number of seasons — long after the individuals primarily responsible for their development have left the team. At the same time, positive norms are also transmitted to succeeding generations. This is the essence of any good team or organization, a point E.M. Swift (1987) continually emphasized in an article about the development of the Philadelphia Flyers over a 20-year period. Through a series of quotes, Swift illustrated the stability of a work ethic over three successive generations. (It helps to appreciate the transition from one generation to the next if it is understood that, initially, Bob Clarke was a rookie, then a team captain, and then the general manager.)

"Guys like Ashbee and Dornhoefer set a standard of performance that the young players had to match" says Pat Quinn ....

Says Clarke, "Those guys had played a long time in pro hockey and understood the commitment it takes to play this game. They understood the importance of playing as good as they could all the time" ...

Clarke set the standards at the team level," says Snider

....

The standards are higher in Philadelphia than anywhere in hockey this side of the Montreal Forum. "I talk to Davey Poulin all the time", says Clarke. "I've told him, by rights you shouldn't even have a bad practice, never mind a bad game. The one demand we can make of our players is that they work hard ....

Work hard, don't back down and win. That attitude has been assimilated from Ashbee's Flyers to Clarke's to Poulin's ... there has never been an extended period when the Flyers didn't play like the Flyers. (Swift, 1987, pp. 94-99)

It was pointed out previously that group norms develop slowly in a team. But when they are present, they are also changed slowly. It is irrelevant whether a group norm is positive or negative, correct or incorrect (as was the case in the Jacobs and Campbell study). Once it develops, it will take a number of generations before it is changed.

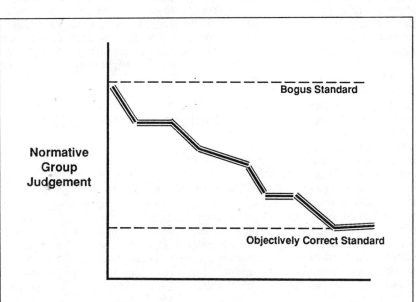

Normative Group Judgement

Bogus Standard

Objectively Correct Standard

Generations of New Groups

Figure 12.1 Schematic representation of the stability of norms over sucessive generations within a group (Based on research by Jacobs & Campbell, 1961)

Implications for the Effectiveness of Sport Groups

There are three basic points that should be made

before implications are drawn from the information on group norms. The first is that the emergence of norms is inevitable in a group. Norms are a fundamental component of any group's structure. In essence, they help to confirm the very existence of the group. Could ten independent strangers put pressure on one another to dress in a similar fashion, or to train at a particular intensity? Obviously not. But a group can. In short, the evolution from being independent athletes to being an interdependent, effective team is accompanied by the development of group expectations concerning what is appropriate.

Second, although the appearance of norms is inevitable, only a limited number develop. As Marvin Shaw (1981) pointed out, norms are value judgments and groups don't establish value judgments about every conceivable situation. Norms only develop around those areas that are most important to the group.

Third, norms have to develop from within the group in order for them to be accepted and adopted. Obviously, standards for behavior can be imposed on the group from outside. For example, the management of a team can set a curfew during training camp. Every team has similar rules and regulations. However, the group norm that develops around this rule might be to try to beat the curfew through any means possible. Imposed standards don't become norms until they are accepted by at least half the group (Shaw, 1981).

These three factors — norms are inevitable, only a limited number emerge, and they cannot be readily imposed on the group from outside — are important because they effect the impact that coaches and management can have on norm development. First, since norms are inevitable and only a limited number emerge, some effort must be made to insure that those that do exist are positive in nature. If a positive work ethic exists in the team, then individual athletes will put continual pressure on each other to maintain this standard. And, similarly, if beating the system by putting in as little effort as possible is the norm, then individual athletes will also put pressure on each other to maintain this standard. From a team perspective, the former is a norm which should be emphasized and promoted; the latter, a norm which should be discouraged and eliminated. But how is this done?

Because norms cannot be readily imposed on the group from outside, coaches and management will only have limited success in promoting a positive norm by themselves. Athlete involvement and participation are essential. A good work ethic on a team can't emerge solely from management. Acceptance and involvement by athletes in the critical leadership positions is essential.

What this suggests is that coaches or management should attempt to influence the one or two areas that are considered most critical to team success. These might be the work ethic in the group, the nutritional habits of the athletes, their lifestyle, or out-of-season training commitments. After the area of emphasis is identified, the individuals in critical leadership roles in the group must be recruited. They must be convinced of the wisdom of revising the current standards. In turn, these athletes also must be convinced to recruit other influential team members. This process of recruitment would have to continue until at least half of the team (including the most influential members) had accepted and internalized the norm.

In some instances, individuals in critical leadership roles cannot be convinced of the necessity of adopting a positive norm or eliminating a negative norm. For example, the most outstanding member of a team might consider positive norms related to proper nutrition and a good lifestyle as unnecessary. If it appears that other team members will be influenced by this position, some action must be taken. As indicated earlier, norms are stable — they can persist for generations in a group. If a dominant individual is largely responsible for the development of a negative norm within the group, it might be better to release, trade, remove him/her. Not only does an inappropriate norm have a negative impact on that specific team, it can continue to influence the behavior of teams in the future.

Conformity to Group Norms

Social Norms

The great majority of the research which has examined the factors influencing the development of group norms has been undertaken in laboratory research on conformity. For example, in one classic study Muzafer Sherif (1936) used an optical illusion to examine the impact of group standards on individual judgments. An illusion occurs when a stationary single light is shown in a darkened room. The light appears to move (sometimes erratically) because there are no reference points, no frame of reference within which to place it. When Sherif had subjects estimate the amount of movement of the light alone and in groups, he found that the presence of others made a considerable difference. Individuals who made judgments alone established their own idiosyncratic pattern in which the estimates of movement varied erratically from 1 to 10 inches. However, in group situations, a consensus was reached. The judgments of individual gradually converged. It was as if a funnelling effect had occurred — from divergence and discrepancy to convergence and consensus.

In another classic study, Solomon Asch (1951) had individuals in a group setting make judgments on the length of a line. A standard line was provided and then a judgement was made concerning which of three comparison lines was identical in length. In every instance, the correct choice was readily apparent. The subjects were tested in groups of seven but six of the individuals present were actually confederates of the experimenter. The only true subject responded sixth in the group. During the experiment, the confederates unanimously gave incorrect responses on 12 of the 18 trials. Asch found that 33 percent of the true subjects adopted the group norm (the incorrect judgement) on 50 percent or more of the incorrect trials. Only 25 percent consistently maintained an independent (correct) judgement.

In the research which followed these early classic studies, the focus was on identifying the conditions which influence conformity to social pressure and group norms. Essentially, two classes of conditions have been identified: *personal* factors and *situational* factors (Carron, 1980). An overview of these is presented in Table 12.3.

Two of the personal factors which are associated with conformity to the group's norms are *personal status* and *idiosyncrasy credit*. Individuals with greater status have a greater impact on the develop-

ment of group norms. The more influential team members — team leaders, the most competent athletes, individuals with the greatest status in the group — have a major role in setting and enforcing the standards adopted by the group (e.g., Hollander, 1961). There is also less pressure on them to conform strictly to these norms. Status and conformity to the group norms over an extended period of time contributes to the development of what has been referred to as *idiosyncrasy credit* (Hollander, 1971) — positive impressions of the individual by the group. High status individuals more readily build up idiosyn-

Table 12.3 Factors influencing conformity to group norms (Adapted from Carron, 1980)

Personal Factors

Category	Generalization
Personal Status	Individuals with higher relative status have a greater influence on the development and enforcement of group norms
Idiosyncrasy Credit	Individuals with higher relative status are permitted greater latitude to deviate from group norms
Style of Behavior	A minority that behaves in a consistent, coherent, and forceful manner can influence the group norm
Sex	There are no differences in conformity to group norms in men and women
Personality	The relationship of personality to conformity is weak. Authoritarian, less intelligent, conservative, extraverted individuals tend to exhibit greater conformity

Situational Factors

Category	Generalization
Size of the Opposition	Conformity to group norms increases with increases in group size
Number of Supportive Others	Conformity to group norms decreases with increases in the number of supportive others
Ambiguity of the Task	Conformity to group norms increases with increases as the ambiguity in the situation increases
Group Cohesiveness	Conformity to group norms increases as the cohesiveness in the group increases
Leadership Structure	Conformity to group norms is greater in groups with a decentralized leadership structure

crasy credit and are given more latitude in the degree to which the group requires them to conform to group norms. Thus, the team leaders may help to establish a norm in which the team weightlifts every day in the offseason. After this norm has been well established, the team leaders might miss occasionally. There would be less pressure exerted on them by the group if this occurred than if low status individuals missed occasionally.

A minority of group members can have a significant impact on the group norms if their *style of behavior* is consistent, coherent, and forceful (Moscovici, 1980). For example, a team might have a norm for dress for road trips which consists of team blazers and slacks. If a small minority began to dress in a more casual fashion, they could change the norm — providing they stayed united, dressed consistently trip after trip, and promoted their style aggressively.

The relationship between *sex* and conformity to group norms is unclear. Early studies contributed to the conclusion that females are more conforming than males. Nord (1969) summarized this early research very well when he concluded that "it has ... been well established, at least in our culture, that females supply greater amounts of conformity under almost all conditions than males" (p. 198). More recently, however, it has been suggested that these results might be due to the fact that the tasks used have favored the masculine sex role. Conformity is greatest in situations of high uncertainty, a situation which would exist if a female were performing a task more appropriate to the masculine sex role. When Sistrunk and McDavid (1971) included neutral, masculine-type, and feminine-type items, they found that conformity was greater by females in the masculine-type tasks, greater by males in the feminine-type tasks, and the same in the neutral tasks.

Although it seems intuitively obvious that certain *personality* characteristics will more naturally be associated with conformity to group norms than others, the relationship is very weak. Only slightly greater adherence to group norms is exhibited by individuals who are more authoritarian, less intelligent, more conservative, and more extraverted (Shaw, 1981).

One important situational factor associated with conformity to group norms is *group size* — both the number of individuals in opposition and the number of supportive others. When the number of supportive others increases, resistance to the group norm also increases. Individuals who want to behave in a way contrary to the group norm, more readily do so as the number of people supporting their position increases. The group is not able to exert as much pressure.

Similarly, when the number of people forming the opposition increases, there is a tendency for conformity to the group norm to increase. Studies on conformity behavior have shown, however, that there is a limit to the group's influence. At some critical point, further increases in the size of the opposition no longer have any social impact. This failure of increasingly larger groups to continue to exert influence on their members has been attributed to two related factors. First, a large opposition of 50 individuals could be perceived as a single unit, not 50 units. Second, a large number of opponents who are in agreement could be considered to be in collusion (Carron, 1980).

Not surprisingly, another situational factor which influences conformity is the *degree of ambiguity* present in the group norm (e.g., Nordholm, 1975). Consider for example, two regulations which might be established by management and eventually adopted as team norms: a curfew and an acceptable standard of dress for public appearances. If the curfew is established at midnight, there is no ambiguity, no uncertainty. Deviation from this standard can be assessed in minutes or hours. Conversely, it is more difficult to establish fixed standards concerning what is acceptable in the case of a dress code. A norm might develop in which a jacket, slacks and a tie are the team standards but considerable latitude could appear around these criteria.

The relationship between conformity to group norms and *group cohesion* is reciprocal (Widmeyer, Brawley, & Carron, 1984). More cohesive groups exert greater pressure on their members to adhere to the group norms. In turn, greater adherence to the group norms leads to a more cohesive group.

The final situational factor presented in Table 12.3 is the *leadership structure* of the group (Shaw, 1981). When the group leadership is centralized and resides almost exclusively in the hands of one individual, there is less conformity than when it is decentralized. When a number of individuals have leadership responsibilities, there are more individuals to exert pressure on other members to adhere to group standards.

Performance Norms

Not only do groups develop norms concerning social behavior, they also develop normative expectations for performance and productivity. These are referred to as norms for productivity. The development of this type of work norm is extremely prevalent in settings where the task is a major concern. Industry and sport are two good examples. A standard is established for performance and pressure is exerted on group members to adhere to this standard. An example of the norm for productivity and the group pressures associated with it are contained in an discussion by Roethlisberger and Dickson (1975) dealing with the concept of a fair day's work. Roethlisberger and Dickson carried out research at the Western Electric Company, a telephone assembly plant. Management had introduced an incentive scheme in an attempt to increase production. This incentive plan was the object of considerable discussion because it came into conflict with a norm for productivity which had emerged in the group over a long period of time. Roethlisberger and Dickson presented the following discussion between two workers:

> W4: (to W6) "How many are you going to turn in?"
> W6: "I've got to turn in 6,800."
> W4: "What's the matter — are you crazy? You work all week and turn in 6,600 for a full day, and now today you're away an hour and a quarter and you turn in more than you do the other days."
> W6: "I don't care. I'm going to finish these sets tomorrow."
> W4: "You're screwy."
> W6: "All right, I'll turn in 6,400."
>
> W4: "That's too much."
> W6: "That won't make any difference. I've got to do something with them."
> W4 "Well, give them to me."
> W6 did not answer. (p. 92)

Also, throughout this present chapter, the norm for productivity in sport situations has been illustrated in a series of quotes. The quote relating to the Montreal Canadiens which introduced the chapter was one of these. The quote by Dave Poulin in Table 12.2 was another. And, the quotation on the stability of a good work ethic in the Philadelphia Flyers was a third.

Adherence to productivity norms seems to depend on various group properties. The level of *cohesion* present in the group is one important consideration. For example, in an often-cited study by Schachter, Ellertson, McBride, and Gregory (1951), high- and low-cohesive groups were examined in a laboratory experiment on a task which involved cutting cardboard squares. It was observed that the high-cohesive groups conformed to the norm more than the low-cohesive groups independent of whether the norm was for high or low productivity. Subsequent research has supported these findings for industrial groups (Mikalachki, 1969), military crews (Berkowitz, 1956), and laboratory groups (Berkowitz, 1954).

The implications seem clear (see Table 12.4). If group cohesion is high and the norm for productivity is high, (Quadrant 1 of Table 12.4), performance will be high. If cohesion is high but the norm for productivity is low, performance will be poor (Quadrant 4). In both of these situations, the strong unity in the group would result in a great deal of pressure being exerted on members to adhere to the norm.

The two intermediate positions are represented by those situations where cohesion is low and the norm for productivity is either high (Quadrant 2) or low (Quadrant 3). The more desirable of these latter two situations would be Quadrant 2 — a high norm for productivity with low cohesion. A general expectation would be present in the group to maintain a good work ethic. Because of the low cohesiveness, however, less pressure could be placed on those individuals who deviated from the norm than would be the case in Quadrant 1.

Table 12.4 The interaction of cohesion and the group norm for productivity (From Carron, 1986. Used with permission of the publisher).

		Group Cohesion	
		High	Low
Norm for Production	High	Best Performance (1)	Intermediate Performance (2)
	Low	Worst Performance (4)	Intermediate Performance (3)

Implications for the Effectiveness of Sport Groups

The information contained in Table 12.3 serves to highlight a number of points made earlier in this chapter. First, high status individuals on a team play an important role in both the development and the level of adherence to group norms. Thus, their support for the rules and regulations which govern the conduct of the team in and out of competition is crucial. Also, conformity to group norms is dictated by the number of people who endorse the norm as well as the number of people who are supportive of behaviors which deviate from the norm. Third, the ambiguity of the norm influences conformity. Adherence is greatest to standards which are precise, detailed, and objective. And, fourth, group cohesion makes a difference. There is greater pressure on individual group members to adhere to group norms when the group is highly cohesive.

What if a negative norm exists? How can it be changed? What factors influence the ability of coaches, managers, and/or team captains to persuade the high status individuals and/or a majority of team members to change existing group norms? Essentially, a norm reflects the group attitude on appropriate standards of behavior. Thus, changing group norms involves changing attitudes. A considerable amount of research has been carried out in social psychology examining the factors influencing attitude change.

Steven Penrod (1986) has summarized these factors into three general categories: the source of the communication, the nature of the communication, and the nature of the target.

The Source of the Communication. The personal characteristics of the individuals attempting to change a team norm — the coach, team captains, team members — have an impact on their effectiveness. The characteristics emphasized by Penrod are presented in Table 12.5. Individuals who are more credible, better liked, similar, attractive, or powerful possess greater powers of persuasion. These characteristics might be expected because they are also associated with status. And, of course, individuals with high status play a significant role in norm development and maintenance.

On an organized sport team, the coaching staff or management might be interested in modifying existing norms. If a choice is available among different coaches, the best individual might not necessarily be the head coach (although he or she is certainly the most powerful). The coach who is perceived to be most credible by the athletes (in terms of trustworthiness and expertise on the specific issue), more similar, attractive, or better liked would be more effective.

Style of speech is another factor which has an impact on the degree to which a target group is influenced by a communicator. For example, the effectiveness of an argument increases if it is developed in the form of rhetorical questions — questions to which an answer is already known. Consider the following presentations to a team, for example:

> "We do want to become better as a team don't we? A tired athlete doesn't play as well, right? Don't you think it would be better if we established a minimum curfew for the nights before the game?"

versus

Table 12.5 Factors in the source of the communication which influence the degree to which persuasion is effective in changing attitudes and modifying group norms (Adapted from Penrod, 1986)

Factor	Rationale
Credibility	More credible sources -- individuals with greater expertise and/or trustworthiness -- possess greater powers of persuasion
Liking, Similarity, Attractiveness	Individuals who are liked, similar , or are considered attractive by the target possess greater powers of persuasion
Power	Individuals who have greater power over rewards and punishment have grearter powers of persuasion
Style of Speech	The use of rhetorical questions increases the effectiveness of persuasive arguments. A relatively rapid delivery (as opposed to a slow, deliberate approach) increases the effectiveness of persuasive arguments

If we are going to play better as a team, we have to be better rested. So a curfew has been established for the nights before a game.

The first argument appears to be a cooperative decision, the second represents a demand. The first is more persuasive than the second.

Another element in style of speech which influences persuasibility is speed. Individuals who communicate in a relatively rapid manner as opposed to a slow, more deliberate fashion are more effective. "People who speak rapidly, we seem to believe, must know what they're talking about. In spite of the stereotype of the fast-talking salesperson who is regarded with suspicion, MacLachlan (1979) found that audiences generally prefer communicators who speak rapidly, and apparently learn more from them in a given amount of time" (Penrod, 1986, p. 265).

The Nature of the Communication Itself. According to Penrod, a number of elements in the communication itself can also influence reception by the target audience (see Table 12.6). One of these is the amount of discrepancy between the viewpoint being advanced and the position held by the team. For example, the members of a team might generally believe that going out for drinks after games and practices was good for team unity and morale. If the coaching staff attempted to persuade the team that complete abstinence in season was better, the discrepancy between these two positions could produce considerable resistance.

Both the quality and quantity of the arguments advanced influence the effectiveness of the persuasion. Communications which are novel, have a number of points supporting a particular position, and present both sides of the issue are more effective. Thus, any attempt to persuade athletes to abstain from alcohol during the season might be more successful if a physiologist was brought in to present research evidence on both sides of the issue.

Persuasion is greater when the communicator comes to a conclusion and presents it to the target group. Consider the above example in which rhetorical questions were used to advance the case for a curfew. The third question, "Don't you think it would be better if we established a minimum curfew for the nights before the game?" is a conclusion. It's also essential to the case. If it is left out, the total argument is not persuasive.

The evidence on the effectiveness of fear as a persuader is mixed (Penrod, 1986). Sometimes messages which highlight the negative consequences of a behavior are effective. Advertisements on drinking and driving or the use of seat belts have used this approach to advantage. However, fear isn't consistently effective. For example, the destructive consequences of substance abuse (e.g., cocaine, anabolic steroids) have been repeatedly outlined. Yet, many professional athletes continue to be victims.

The Nature of the Target. Despite an effective communicator and communication, changes in norms still might not occur. The target group is the third factor in the equation. Penrod identified a number of characteristics of the target person or group which influence the degree to which a persuasive message

Table 12.6 Factors in the nature of the communication which influence the degree to which persuasion is effective in changing attitudes and modifying group norms (Adapted from Penrod, 1986)

Factor	Rationale
Communication Discrepancy	The discrepancy between the position advanced and the viewpoint of the target influences the effectiveness of persuasion
One- vs Two-sided Arguments	Communications which present both sides of the issue are more effective
Novelty vs Repetition	Novel communications are more effective than familiar communications
Fear	Communications based on fear are only effective in limited situations
Quantity	The greater the number of communications, the more powerful the persuasion
Drawing Conclusions	A communication is a more powerful persuader if the conclusion is stated explicitly for the target instead of permitting the target to arrive at it independently

is accepted (see Table 12.7).

The perception that there is freedom of choice is important. People who feel coerced into adopting an attitude show more resistance than those who feel they had a choice.

One factor which increases resistance to a new perspective is ego-involvement. It is more difficult to change the attitudes of targets who are more highly involved with an issue. If an athlete believes that weight training is harmful for highly skilled performance, for example, a general discussion on the benefits probably will have little impact. Also, it is possible for inoculation to occur if the initial argument is weak. This happens in much the same way that resistance to diseases develops. As a result of an inoculation with a weaker strain of bacteria, the body builds its resistance to stronger strains. Initially, if a weak argument is presented for weight training, the target could develop effective counter arguments. When a better case is presented later, these counter arguments are used to resist the persuasion.

Forewarning the target group that a new perspective will be presented is often effective. Again, however, it depends on the initial level of resistance in the target group. If resistance is high, forewarning may simply provide opportunities to prepare counter arguments against the new perspective.

There is also evidence that people who are resistant to a new viewpoint are selective in the information

Table 12.7 Factors in the nature of the target which influence the degree to which persuasion is effective in changing attitudes and modifying group norms (Adapted from Penrod, 1986)

Factor	Rationale
Commitment	Individuals who have made a small commitment (are minimally persuaded) to a new position can be more readily persuaded to make greater commitments
Selectivity	Communications which confirms a held belief are better retained than communications which contradict a belief
Inoculation	Targets who have received a weak form of an argument may develop counterarguments which they will use against stronger arguments
Forewarning	The value of forewarning a target about an impending argument depends on the commitment of the target and the status of the communicator
Ego-Involvement	It is more difficult to change attitudes of targets who are more ego-involved with an issue.
Freedom of Choice	Targets who feel coerced into adopting an attitude show more resistance than targets who feel that they had a choice

they pick out of a presentation. If both sides of argument were presented on weight training, for example, an individual who was strongly opposed would probably retain most of the negative content but little of the positive.

A final technique which is effective for establishing a high norm for productivity is to set up a *goal setting program* in which team goals are emphasized (Carron, 1984). Goals serve four functions (Locke, Shaw, Saari, & Latham, 1981). First, they direct the team's attention and actions to the components which are most relevant to team success. They also mobilize energy expenditure — goals act as a stimulant. Third, they contribute to prolonged effort. And, finally, they motivate the individual or team to develop strategies or plans-for-action to insure goal attainment.

13 Group Leadership

No discussion of group structure is complete without dealing with group leadership. It is probably the group role most closely associated with group effectiveness. In Chapter 10, two types of group roles were discussed: informal and formal. The informal roles are those which emerge as a result of the interactions and communications which take place among group members. The group acknowledges and is influenced in its actions by those individuals who are most dominant, assertive, competent. Because these individuals emerge from the group to occupy leadership roles, they are referred to as emergent leaders.

Here's what I know about managing a baseball team: if you get good players and they play well, you're a genius .... Once a manager gets good players, about 75 percent of his job is handling the pitching. The rest of it is to keep the players happy, keep the writers happy, and try to see that he's got the right players in the right situations during the game. Then he makes damned sure that the players hustle and play smart baseball, which makes the fans happy and keeps them coming back to the park, which makes the owner of the club happy. If everything goes right, his club will contend every year and win a pennant every four or five years, so he'll keep his job, which any manager will tell you is a lot more important than being a genius. (Herzog & Horrigan, 1987, pp. 2-3)

different behaviors. Nonetheless, they are also similar; there are parallels between them. The major source of that similarity lies in their fundamental responsibilities. Every formal leader in every type of group has two identical responsibilities.

The first is to insure that the demands of the organization are satisfied, that the group is effective in terms of the goals and objectives of the organization. Thus, for the general manager of a large corporation, effectiveness might mean increased production and greater sales. For the general manager of a professional sport team, effectiveness might mean increased attendance, a positive winning percentage, or both. Organizations have different goals and objectives and a leader must reach those to be considered effective.

Formal roles, on the other hand, are those which are specifically prescribed by the organization or group. Consequently, individuals who occupy formal leadership roles are referred to as *prescribed leaders*. Coaches and managers of professional sport teams are one example of prescribed group leaders — they are the occupants of a formal group role. They possess what John French and Bertram Raven (1959) referred to as legitimate power, expert power, coercive power, reward power, and sometimes, referent power (see Table 10.5 again). In this chapter, the focus is on the formal leadership role and prescribed leaders.

Leaders who occupy formal group roles in sport, in education, in industry, and in the military are quite dissimilar in the sense that they engage in a variety of very

The second responsibility of every leader is to insure that the needs and aspirations of group members/subordinates are satisfied. When team members are satisfied and the team is successful, the coach or manager of a sport team is considered to be an effective leader.

In the quote used to introduce this chapter, Whitey Herzoz, manager of the St. Louis Cardinals, effectively summarized these two essential aspects of leadership. He pointed out that all a manager

133

needs to do to be a genius is to keep the players happy, keep the fans happy, win enough games to be in contention every year, and win a pennant every four or five years. Both the organization's needs and the players needs would then be satisfied. This seems to be a simple prescription. Apparently it isn't because there are still more questions than answers about leadership. In fact, James McGregor Burns (1978) has observed that leadership is "one of the most observed and least understood phenomena on earth" (p. 2).

The Nature of Leadership

A Typology of Leadership Theories

Leadership has been approached from so many different perspectives that Behling and Schriesheim (1976) provided a typology to aid in the classification of leadership theories. This typology, which is presented in Table 13.1, contains four categories: universal trait theories, universal behavior theories, situational trait theories, and situational behavioral theories.

The *universal trait* approach is one of the oldest perspectives advanced about leadership. The predominant focus in this approach is on the personality traits of leaders. Did Winston Churchill, Ghandi, Martin Luther King, Vince Lombardi, and John Kennedy have similar personality characteristics? Are there some traits which naturally contribute to the emergence of leaders in a group? The search for a universal set of personality traits in leaders is the main objective of the universal trait approach.

In the *universal behavioral* approaches, interest shifts from the search for general traits to the identification of the general behaviors in leaders. Thus, for example, Churchill, Ghandi, King, Lombardi, and Kennedy might have been completely different in personality. But, they might have behaved in a very similar fashion when they were involved in leadership — directing, training, representing, facilitating, nurturing, and so on. In the universal behavioral approach, the focus is on the identification of general behaviors exhibited by all leaders.

In the *situational trait* approach, the focus is on both the traits of the person and the characteristics of the specific situation. History has shown that all of the individuals mentioned above — Churchill, Ghandi, King, etc. — were effective leaders. Assume for a moment that they were fundamentally different from each other in personality. And, also take it as a given that the situations in which they had to operate were also fundamentally different. Is it possible that each had a personality that was right for a specific situation? At other times or in other places, they might not have been as effective. In the situational trait approach, the focus is on identifying the characteristics of specific situations where specific personality traits will be most effective.

In the *situational behavioral* approach, interest shifts from the identification of specific traits which are effective in specific situations to the identification of specific behaviors which are effective in specific situations. When Winston Churchill and John Kennedy were in the process of exerting political leadership what did they do? When Vince Lombardi was coaching what did he do? In the situational behavioral approach, the focus is on identifying the specific behaviors characteristic

Table 13.1 A typology of leadership theories in sport situations (Adapted from Behling & Schriesheim, 1976).

	Traits	Behaviors
Universal	**Universal Traits** The Description of the Personality Traits of Coaches	**Universal Behaviors** The Coaching Behavior Assessment System
Situational	**Situational Traits** The Contingency Model of Leadership	**Situational Behaviors** The Multidimensional Model of Leadership

of different leaders in different situations.

In the sections which follow, each of these four approaches is discussed from the perspective of sport. This does represent a slight departure from the Behling and Schriesheim model. When they referred to a universal approach, they were referring to a broad spectrum of situations (e.g., sport, industry, the military, politics) and not simply a broad spectrum of sport situations.

Universal Leadership Traits for Sport

It was pointed out above that the universal trait approach is one of the oldest approaches to the study of leadership. It has sometimes been referred to as The Great Man Theory of Leadership because it was based on the assumption that human progress has been the result of the accomplishments of great men. A considerable amount of research was carried out in management science and industrial psychology in order to determine what common personality traits helped outstanding leaders become successful.

This research met with limited success. No consistent pattern of traits was found for successful leaders. In the late 1940s, on the basis of his review of 124 studies, Stogdill (1948) concluded that there was no support for the universal trait perspective, that there are no specific personalty traits associated with the assumption and performance of leadership. Following Stogdill's review, the search for the universal traits in leaders received less attention. Researchers began to concentrate on better understanding the traits of leaders in various specific situations such as sport, the military, and industry.

In sport, George Sage (1975) outlined the rationale for this approach when he noted that "the notion of occupational specific personality types is rather common. Thus, we have the "Mr. Peepers" stereotype of the male teacher, the "absent-minded" professor, and many more" (p. 408). Sage then quoted Jack Scott (1969) on the typical stereotype held for a coach:

> The typical ... coach is a soulless, back slapping, meticulously groomed team oriented efficiency expert — a jock's Robert MacNamara ... Most coaches have as much concern for the welfare of their athletes as a general has for the soldiers he sends into battle ... for most college coaches, the athlete is significant only to the extent that he can contribute to a team victory ... For every relaxed, understanding coach ... there are one hundred rigid, authoritarian coaches who have

so much ... character armor that they rattle. (p. 7)

A number of studies have tried to determine if Scott's stereotype is accurate for coaches. One test which received a considerable amount of use in this type of research was the Machiavellian Scale developed by Christie and Geis (1970). It's name is derived from infamous Prince Machiavelli, who believed that cunning duplicity, and bad faith were acceptable for manipulating the behavior of others. The research with coaches clearly showed that they are not any different than the average person in Machiavellianism (e.g., Sage, 1972; Walsh & Carron, 1977).

Testing of coaches has also been carried out using more general personality tests such as Cattell's 16 Personality Factor Questionnaire (e.g., Hendry, 1968). Again, however, no consistent pattern of traits has emerged that distinguishes either more and less successful coaches or coaches from society in general. The general conclusion which must be drawn from this research is that there is no general (universal) pattern of personality traits which is characteristic of coaches as leaders.

Universal Leadership Behaviors in Sport

A behavioral approach concentrates on what people do rather than on their responses to questionnaires and inventories. One comprehensive system for analyzing coaching behaviors was developed at the University of Washington by Ron Smith, Frank Smoll and their colleagues (Curtis, Smith & Smith, Smoll & Hunt, 1977; Smoll, Smith, Curtis and Hunt, 1978). As Table 13.2 shows, the Coaching Behavior Assessment System (CBAS) identifies 12 behaviors (B1 - B12) considered to be typical of coaches in athletic situations. Using the CBAS, an observer can record the ongoing behavior of a coach and assess the frequency of various types. The twelve behaviors included in the CBAS fall into two classes: reactive and spontaneous. Reactive behaviors are responses to something the athlete has done such as a good or bad performance. Spontaneous behaviors are initiated by the coach; they are not the result of prior activity by the athlete.

The reactive behaviors are further subdivided into three categories: reactions by the coach to desirable performances by the athlete, reactions by the coach to an athlete's mistakes or errors, and reactions by the coach to misbehaviors on the part of the athlete. When the athlete's performance is effective or desireable, it can be positively reinforced by the coach (B1) or ignored through nonreinforcement (B2). A mistake

Table 13.2 The Smith, Smoll, Curtis & Hunt *Coaching Behavior Assessment System*

Stimulus Event	Coaching Response	Description
Class 1. Reactive Behaviors		
Desireable Performance	B.1. Positive Reinforcement	Verbal or nonverbal reaction to an athlete's behavior
	B.2. Nonreinforcement	Failure to reinforce an athlete's behavior
Mistakes or Errors	B.3. Mistake-Contingent Encouragement	Encouragement following an athlete's mistake
	B.4. Mistake-Contingent Technical Instruction	Instruction to an athlete following a mistake
	B.5. Punishment	Verbal or nonverbal negative reactions to an athlete's mistake
	B.6. Punitive-Mistake Contingent Technical Instruction	Combination of negative reaction and instruction following a mistake
	B.7. Ignoring Mistakes	Failure to respond in any way to an athlete's mistake
Misbehaviors	B.8. Keeping Control	Responses designed to maintain order and control
Class 2. Spontaneous Behaviors		
Game Related	B.9. General Technical Instruction	Communications to the athlete on technical strategy
	B.10. General Encouragement	Spontaneous encouragement to the athlete
	B.11. Organization	Communication of an administrative nature
Game Irrelevant	B.12. General Communication	Interactions unrelated to the sport or game

The spontaneous behaviors of the coach are subdivided into two categories: game related and game unrelated. When a coach exhibits a spontaneous behavior during the game, it either involves providing instruction on techniques (B9), giving general encouragement (B10), or organizing and administering the team (B11). Finally, the spontaneous behaviors which are irrelevant to the game represent general communications on the part of the coach (B12).

Smoll and his colleagues (Smoll, Smith, & Curtis, 1978) used the CBAS to chart the behavior of 51 Little League coaches during the season. An average of 1,122 behaviors were recorded for each coach. Almost two thirds of these coaching behaviors were from three categories: positive reinforcement (B1), general technical instruction (B9), and general encouragement (B10). The behavior of the Little League baseball coaches was positive and directed toward instruction and teaching.

Interviews were also conducted with the athletes involved to assess their perceptions of their coaches's

or error by the athlete can be reacted to with encouragement (B3), with instruction about the correct technique (B4), with punishment (B5), with both punishment and instruction on the correct technique (B6), or the mistake can simply be ignored (B7). Finally, misbehaviors on the part of the athlete can lead to coaching behaviors associated with keeping control (B8).

behaviors. A total of 542 players were included which represented 83 percent of the athletes. Interestingly, the athletes overestimated the amount of time that their coaches had spent keeping control (B8). This behavior occurred very infrequently but it had such an impact on the athletes that they perceived that it occurred much more frequently. Maybe this is typical of all coach-athlete relationships — in amateur and professional. Coaches exert control and this produces a strong negative reaction in athletes. Consider, for example, an anecdote Reggie Jackson recalled about a confrontation with his manager, Earle Weaver, which occurred shortly after Jackson joined the Baltimore Orioles:

> Earl was sitting in the front of the plane, where managers sit. I think they passed that rule right after the Wright Brothers invented the airplane. He didn't make a big fuss. He just said, "If you don't put on a tie, you can't make the trip, Reggie". It's all the Big Game. It has always gone on between managers and players, especially managers and new players. Earl had wanted me desperately, but he was the boss and he had rules, and he had to show the rest of the team right away that those rules applied to the new kid. (p. 117)

Smoll and his colleagues also found that being negative while providing instruction after a mistake (B6) occurred only infrequently — 2.8 percent of all of the behaviors recorded. (An example of this behavior might be "you dummy, keep your head down".) Nonetheless, it also had a significant impact on the athletes in that they were very accurate in their perception of its frequency.

On the basis of this early research, Smith, Smoll, and Curtis (1979) then developed a set of behavioral guidelines for effective teaching and coaching. These guidelines were designed to emphasize positive behaviors and produce a better competitive environment for the young athlete. A group of 18 Little League coaches were then introduced to the guidelines and trained in the use of positive behaviors. Throughout the season feedback was also given on their actual coaching behaviors. Another set of 13 coaches who were not given the training program or exposed to the behavioral guidelines was used as a control group. The actual behaviors of the two groups were then observed throughout the season. In addition, the attitudes of the athletes playing for the trained and untrained coaches were compared.

The differences between the two groups of coaches are quite dramatic — particularly if it is remembered that the untrained coaches weren't poor coaches. They were probably typical of every coach involved in youth sports — fathers, older brothers, individuals interested in coaching young athletes. The group that was trained provided more reinforcement (B1). They were also perceived by their athletes as better, more knowledgeable coaches who provided more reinforcement, more encouragement, and more instruction. The untrained coaches were perceived as providing more punishment and being less sensitive to good performances.

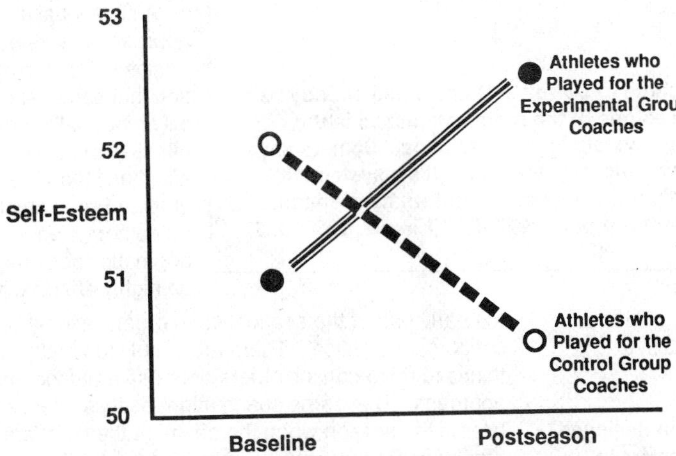

The athletes who played for the trained coaches were more satisfied with their experiences, felt that the team atmosphere was better, and had a greater desire to play for the same coach in the future. One of the most interesting findings was in the changes in self-esteem (see Figure 13.1). The athletes who played for the trained coaches had scored slightly lower in an early measure of self-esteem. However, when they were assessed following the season, they showed an increase. On the other hand, the athletes who played for the untrained coaches showed a decrease. Smith and his colleagues concluded that "training programs designed to assist coaches, teachers, and other adults occupying leadership roles in creating

Figure 13.1 Self esteem scores for Little League baseball players who played for trained or control group coaches (From Smith, Smoll, & Curtis, 1979. Reproduced with permission of the publisher)

Table 13.3 Illustrations of the dimensions of Fiedler's Contingency Theory of Leadership.

Type	Example
A. Leader's Style of Interacting	
Task Oriented Major satisfaction is derived from successful completion of the group task	"I'm not buddy-buddy with the players; if they need a buddy, let them buy a dog. I'm the manager, and I've got a job to do .... I'm flattered that players say they like to play for me. Luckily, everywhere I've been we've managed to win -- and winning does more than anything else to keep the players happy" (Herzog & Horrigan, pp. 16-17)
Person Oriented Major satisfaction is derived from the development of harmonious interpersonal relationships	"Stankey ... didn't appreciate Southworth's style. Southworth was a mild litle man who had won pennants with the wartime Cardinal teams of 1942, '43, and '44 by exercising a lot of patience and just letting the Cardinals play. He wanted evertbody to like him" (Dark & Underwood, 1950, p. 44)
B. Favorableness of the Situation	
Power Position of the Leader The degree of authority and control, the amount of organizational support	"A few weeks after the Christmas holidays, Bear Bryant resigned as Maryland football coach .... What had happened was the one thing he would not tolerate, not then, not ever, from anybody. Curly Byrd had stuck his nose into Bryant's football business. Twice" (Herkowitz, 1987, p.53)
Leader-Member Relations The quality of the personal relations between the leader and his subordinates	"Buddy [Ryan] was hard on his Bear players. That was his way of motivating them. And it worked. His players hated him at first, but they grew to love him" (Madden & Anderson, 1986, p. 210)
Task Structure The degree to which the task is structured, goals are clarified, and procedures are clear	"Before he came to Detroit ... Demers had already had a reputation as one of the premier coaches in the league ....'Our system is just discipline, ' Demers says. 'You know what tight-checking is? It's a system. It's hard work. It's not complicated, but we have specific things we want our players to do'" (Klonke, 1988, p. 8)

teachers, student-teacher interactions, and the behaviors of coaches (e.g., Anderson & Barrette, 1978; Cheffers & Mancini, 1978; Fishman & Tobey, 1978; Morgenegg, 1978; Rushall, 1977). The general conclusion to be drawn from this research — all of which has used the universal behavioral approach — is that it has provided highly useful information on how coaches and teachers actually behave. Behavioral analyses of what coaches and teachers *do* and the impact of this on the people that they *do it to* helps in the development of prescriptions for more effective leadership in sport groups.

The Situational Trait Approach to Leadership

A situational trait approach has its origins in the assumption that some personality types will be more effective in some situations than in others. For example, an authoritarian, dogmatic coach might be highly effective in

a positive and supportive environment can influence children's personality development in a positive manner" (p. 74).

A number of other inventories have been designed to observe and categorize leadership behaviors in sport groups. Some of these have been used to assess the general behavior of teachers in physical education classes, the type of feedback used by teachers, the communication patterns of students and

the early part of the season when organizational concerns are critical. There are simply too many things to do to consult others or to use a democratic approach. That same coach might be less effective later in the season when the affairs of the team are running more smoothly. Similarly, an authoritarian, dogmatic coach might be highly effective with less mature athletes in high school but relatively ineffective with more mature athletes in professional sport.

One of the best known situational trait approaches is the *contingency theory of leadership* which was developed by Fred Fiedler (e.g., Fiedler, 1967; Fiedler & Chemers, 1974). A contingency is something that depends on something else — if A, then B. This relationship is the cornerstone of Fiedler's theory. According to Fiedler, leadership effectiveness — defined as group performance and member satisfaction — depends equally (is contingent) upon the leader's style of interacting with the group and the favorableness of the situation.

Style of Interaction. A leader's style of interacting is considered by Fiedler to vary along a continuum from *task-oriented* to *person-oriented* (see Table 13.3). Task-oriented individuals derive their greatest satisfaction from the group's performance, productivity, and successful task completion. On the other hand, person-oriented individuals derive their greatest satisfaction from social contacts, affiliation, and successful interpersonal relationships.

These two interaction styles represent a hierarchy of preferences within the leader. Both orientations are present in every leader. That is, every leader is interested in both outcomes — people and productivity — but the importance attached to each varies. Essentially, a task-oriented leader says "if we can successfully carry out this task, we'll feel very good about one another". On the other hand, a person-oriented leader says "if we get along well, we'll be more effective on the job". The quote by Whitey Herzog In Table 13.3 helps to illustrate the priorities placed on task and person concerns. In Herzog's quotation, the task-oriented style is more dominant. But, from the quote, it is also evident that Herzog feels a successful team's performance will contribute to good interpersonal relationships.

The quote by Alvin Dark in Table 13.3 illustrates a situation in which a person-oriented style had the highest priority. In this quote, Dark discussed the reactions of Eddie Stankey to his manager, Billy Southworth. Although Southworth was person-oriented, this style also was associated with considerable performance success. As was pointed out above, the important point about the contingency theory is that either a person-oriented or a task-oriented leader can be effective depending upon the situation.

The Favorableness of the Situation. What makes a situation favorable for a leader? One of the elements is the *power position* of the leader. If the leader is clearly in control, has authority, and the support of the organization, he or she is in a powerful position to influence and direct the group. Conversely, if the group perceives that the leader's power position is not very strong, that the leader doesn't have the support of

management, it will be more difficult to lead.

The quote in Table 13.3 is concerned with the circumstances surrounding Paul (Bear) Bryant's decision to leave his coaching job at the University of Maryland. Dr. D.H. (Curly) Byrd, the president (and a former football coach) of the university had reinstated an athlete suspended by Bryant and had fired one of Bryant's assistant coaches. Without consulting Bryant. From a leadership perspective, Bryant's power position was so unacceptable he quit his job — his first head coach position — after only one year.

A second element that contributes to situational favorableness is *leader-member relations*. If the group likes the leader, it will more readily follow directions, work harder, and make sacrifices. And, because the situation is favorable, it's easier for the leader to carry out the responsibilities of leadership. The quote in Table 13.3 concerning Buddy Ryan's relationship with his athletes illustrates a case of good leader-member relations.

The third element in situational favorableness is the *task structure*. In some tasks, the goals and objectives are clear and the steps necessary to achieve those are readily apparent. This makes it easier for the leader because there is only a limited number of possibilities or options present. In general, sport tasks are relatively structured but there are subtle differences among different sports. For example, open team sports are sports in which the athlete must continually adjust to constantly changing conditions in the situation. Hockey, basketball, and soccer are some examples. On the other hand, closed individual sports are sports in which the athlete is faced with a relatively fixed and unchanging environment. Track, archery, and bowling are examples. Closed sports are somewhat more structured and, therefore, would be more favorable from a leadership perspective. In the quote in Table 13.3, the Detroit Red Wings coach, Jacques Demers, has pointed out how he likes to develop a highly structured situation for his athletes.

The Contingency Theory. The specific relationship proposed by Fiedler for the leader's style of interacting and the favorableness of the situation is illustrated in Figure 13.2. The favorableness of the situation can be rank-ordered into eight segments which vary from highly favorable on one end to highly unfavorable on the other. The most favorable situation for a leader is present when his/her power position is strong, the task is highly structured, and leader-member relations are high. In these types of situations, a task-oriented leader is more effective than a person-oriented leader. As Figure 13.2

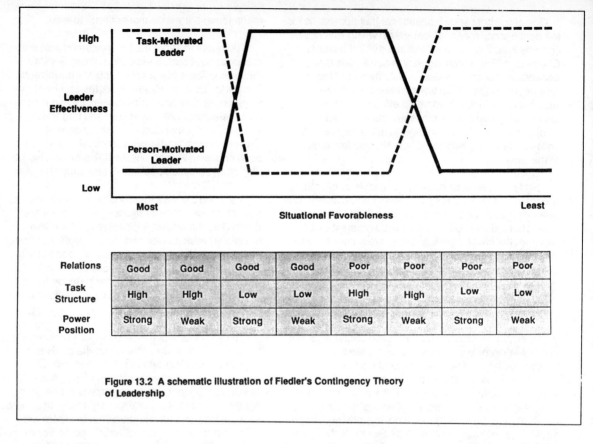

Relations	Good	Good	Good	Good	Poor	Poor	Poor	Poor
Task Structure	High	High	Low	Low	High	High	Low	Low
Power Position	Strong	Weak	Strong	Weak	Strong	Weak	Strong	Weak

Figure 13.2 A schematic illustration of Fiedler's Contingency Theory of Leadership

illustrates, a task-oriented leader is also more effective in the most unfavorable situations — when the leader's power position is poor, the task is unstructured, and leader-member relations are poor. According to Fiedler, a person-oriented leader is more effective in situations that are moderately favorable.

William Straub (1978) has used the case of Forest Gregg, a former coach of the Cleveland Browns, to illustrate some of the principles of the contingency theory. Gregg, who used a task oriented style of interacting, was the Associated Press NFL Coach of the Year in 1976. A year later, he was fired. Straub pointed out that after getting off to a good start in the season, the Browns began to lose. Gregg's relationship with the owner, Art Modell, and his players began to deteriorate. In short, his power position deteriorated and leader-member relations were poor. Since the task of football is relatively structured, the favorableness of the situation would be represented in the sixth column. And, consequently, a person-oriented style of interacting would be suggested within Fiedler's model. However, Gregg became even more forceful and autocratic in his style and the results were disastrous.

Much of Fiedler's initial work in developing his theory was conducted with basketball teams. Subsequently, a number of researchers have used the contingency theory to examine leadership on sport teams (e.g., Bird, 1977, Danielson, 1978; Inciong, 1974). Their results have provided only limited support for the model. But, it is difficult in sport situations to systematically vary the situational factors which are such an integral part of the model. And, "in the absence of differences in the situational parameters, Fiedler's model cannot be adequately tested" (Chelladurai & Carron, 1978, p. 29).

The Situational Behavior Approach to Leadership

In the situational behavior theories of leadership, it is assumed that particular coaching behaviors are more effective in specific situations. The Multidimensional Model of Leadership developed by P. Chelladurai of the University of Western Ontario uses this approach. A schematic representation of his model is presented in Figure 13.3. Chelladurai has pointed out that the two main consequences of a coach's behavior are athlete *satisfaction* and more effective *perform-ance.* Although there are other possible conse-quences of participation — for example, absenteeism and adherence — performance and satisfaction are considered to be the most important. Are the athletes satisfied with their experience? Are individual perform-ance and team performance as effective as they could be?

There are also a number of factors which contribute to team and individual effectiveness and athlete satisfaction. The coach's behavior is one of them. According to Chelladurai, coaching behavior can be viewed from three perspectives: the behavior that is *preferred* by the athlete, the behavior that is *prescribed* by the situation, and the *actual* behavior of the coach (Figure 13.3).

It is reasonable to assume that different athletes have different preferences for behavior on the part of the coach. A very young athlete, for example, might be much more sensitive to criticism than an older more experienced athlete. Or, older, more experienced

athletes might like more input into the development of their training programs than novices. It's also reason-able to assume that in some situations, specific coaching behavior are essential (i.e., are prescribed) if satisfaction and performance are to develop. For example, at the beginning of the season when 150 athletes are present, a democratic approach (where coaches and athletes jointly make decisions) isn't effective. Chaos results. Thus, an autocratic ap-proach by the coach is prescribed, is necessary. And, finally, the coach's actual behavior is of two general types: *adaptive* and *reactive*. Adaptive behaviors consist of the responses by the coach to the con-straints of the situation. Is the team young or old, large or small, experienced or inexperienced? Reac-tive behaviors consist of the discretionary responses of the coach to meet athletes' needs. Does the athlete respond best to praise and encouragement? Should the athlete be given some opportunity to make deci-sions?

The antecedents for each of these types of coach-ing behavior are also illustrated in Figure 13.3. As the

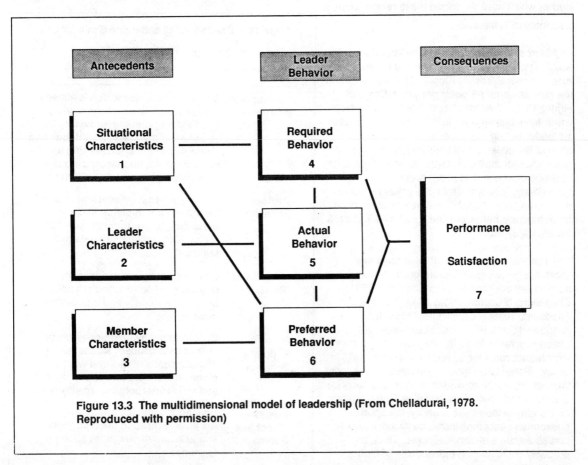

Figure 13.3 The multidimensional model of leadership (From Chelladurai, 1978. Reproduced with permission)

141

above discussion highlighted, the prescribed coaching behaviors are influenced by situational characteristics — size of the team, the purposes of the organization, and so on. The coach's attributes — personality, experience, age — also have an influence on his/her behavior. And, finally, an athlete's characterisitcs have an influence on the coaching behavior preferred from the coach.

The Leadership Scale for Sports (LSS) was developed by Chelladurai to assess five main behaviors considered to be characteristic of coaches-as-leaders (Chelladurai & Saleh, 1978; Chelladurai & Carron, 1981). These include the degree to which the coach provides *positive feedback,* gives *social support,* t*rains and instructs* the athletes in the skills of the sport, uses a *democratic* approach, and is *autocratic* (authoritarian). Table 13.4 provides a description of these five behaviors.

Chelladurai's model has been tested in a number of studies and the links between the various elements in the model have been examined. An overview of the studies which have examined these relationships is presented in Table 13.5).

Member Characteristics. One important link which has received attention has been between *member characteristics* (Box 3 of Figure 13.3) and the *type of leader behavior preferred* (Box 6 of Figure 13.3). Two member characteristics which which have been shown to influence preferences for leader behavior are the sex and the experience of the athlete. Male athletes have a greater preference for autocratic behavior, training and instruction behavior, and social support behavior. Conversely, female athletes like greater input into decision-making; they have a greater preference for democratic behavior (Erle, 1981; Chelladurai & Saleh, 1978).

The more experience athletes have in a sport, the greater is their preference for social support behavior from their coach (Erle, 1981; Chelladurai & Carron, 1982, 1983; Weiss & Friedrichs, 1986). Chelladurai (1984) has suggested that this is almost inevitable. As athletes increase in ability, they must pay increasingly higher costs for additional increments in ability. These costs include the need to give more time, effort, and energy to training and to sacrifice social contacts outside of athletics. Consequently, as the athlete increases in ability, the sport environment becomes increasingly more important as a source of social support. Thus, it's probably not surprising that athletes of higher

ability show higher preferences for more social support behavior from the coach.

Also, more experienced athletes have a greater preference for autocratic behavior (Chelladurai, 1978; Chelladurai & Carron, 1982; Chelladurai & Saleh, 1978). This is probably a result of social learning. Athletes come to learn that the athletic environment is essentially autocratic. With time and experience they also come to expect that the coach will make the majority of decisions. Eventually, the autocratic approach is preferred by the athlete.

Each athlete is different, however. Some athletes prefer more autocratic behavior than others. Horne and Carron (1985) found that the coach-athlete relationship was rated as incompatible by the athlete when the coach was perceived to be more autocratic than was preferred. This finding is not inconsistent with the studies that have shown that the preference for autocratic behavior increases systematically as athletes gain in experience. In the Horne and Carron study, the important point was not that the athletes didn't want autocratic behavior; only that the amount

Table 13.4 Chelladura's Leadership Scale for Sport	
Behavior	Description
Training and Instruction	Coaching behavior which is aimed at improving athlete performance by emphasizing training, providing instruction in the skills, techniques and strategies of the sport, setting up team systems, and structuring and coordinating member's activities
Democratic Behavior	Coaching behavior which provides for athlete participation in decisions pertaining to group goals, practice techniques, and game strategies and tactics
Autocratic Behavior	Coaching behavior which involves independent action, and stresses personal authority and independent decisions
Social Support Behavior	Coaching behavior which is characterized by a concern for the welfare of individual athletes and which emphasizes a positive group climate and warm interpersonal relationships
Positive Feedback Behavior	Coaching behavior which rewards the athlete through the recognition and acknowledgement of good performance

Table 13.5. Relationship of coaching behavior to athlete satisfaction

Authors	Sample	Results
Chelladurai & Saleh (1978)	College athletes from a variety of sports	Male athletes had a high preference for more autocratic and social support behavior from their coaches
Erle (1981)	Intercollegiate & Intramural ice hockey players	Male athletes had a high preference for more training, autocratic, and social support behavior from their coaches. Female athletes had a high preference for more democratic behavior from their coaches. Intercollegiate athletes had a high preference for more social support, training, and reward behavior
Chelladurai & Carron (1982)	College athletes from a variety of sports	Athletes high in cognitive structure had a high preference for more training. Athletes high in impulsivity had a high preference for more social support
Chelladurai & Carron (1983)	Mideget, junior, & senior high school and college basketball players	Older and more experienced athletes had a high preference for more social support. Athlete preference for training decreased to university age then increased
Chelladurai (1984)	College athletes from wrestling, basketball, & track	As the coach's training and positive feedback increased relative to the athlete's preferences, athlete satisfaction increased
Horne & Carron (1982)	Female athletes from a variety of sports	Coach-athlete relationships were poor when the coach was perceived to provide less positive feedback and more autocratic behavior than was preferred
Weiss & Friedrichs (1986)	College athletes & coaches from basketball teams	Athlete satisfaction was associated with high positive feedback, social support, and democratic behavior

given was higher than they preferred.

Situational Characteristics. The situation also has an influence on the preferences that athletes have for different leader behaviors (the link between Boxes 1 and 7 in Figure 13.3). A comprehensive study which examined this issue was reported by Maureen Weiss and Warren Friedrichs (1986). The athletes and coaches from 23 basketball teams participating in the National Association of Intercollegiate Athletics were tested. Weiss and Friedrichs assessed the size of the school, the percentage of the coach's workload devoted to basketball, the size of the team's budget, the amount of scholarship money available, and the tradition of success in the school. The only situational variable found to be important was institutional size — athletes from larger institutions expressed greater overall satisfaction than athletes from smaller institutions.

Other situational variables that influence the athlete's preference for leader behaviors include the type of organization and the nature of the sport. In intramural sports, where the primary emphasis is on participation and enjoyment, athletes don't want as much training and instruction, social support, or positive feedback as athletes on intercollegiate sport teams (Erle, 1981). And, athletes in team sports such as basketball prefer more training and instruction than athletes in individual sports such as track and wrestling (Chelladurai & Carron, 1982).

Coaching Characteristics. In their study, Weiss and Friedrichs also included a number of coaching characteristics including the coach's playing experience, coaching experience, age when hired, and prior win/loss record as a head coach (these are variables in Box 2 of Figure 13.3). Then Weiss and Friedrichs had the athletes evaluate their coach's perceived behavior (Box 5) and indicate their satisfaction with supervision, playing conditions, teammates, amount of work, kind of work, and school identification (Box 7).

The coaches who had less playing experience, had a better prior record, and were hired at a younger age had athletes who were more satisfied. Also, those coaches who more frequently provided positive feedback, provided more social support, and used a more democratic style had the most satisfied athletes.

Implications for the Effectiveness of Sport Groups

One implication which emerges from the discussion on leadership is that the *nature of the situation* is an extremely important consideration insofar as understanding leader effectiveness is concerned. There are two reasons for making this claim. First, individual behavior is a joint product of the personality of the individual and the nature of the situational demands. Research which has focused on the universal trait approach to leadership has clearly shown that there is no single "coaching type". Coaches are different, not identical in their personalities. In a quote presented earlier, Jack Scott (1969) claimed that coaches are authoritarian and uninterested in the welfare of their athletes.

If it can be assumed for the moment that coaches have behaved in a manner similar to Scott's stereotypical description, then the reasons for this must lie largely in the situation, not in the coaches' personalities. What is it about the athletic situation which causes a large number of individuals who are different in personality to behave in a relatively similar manner? Some factors which have been identified include the size of the group, the type of group task, the nature of the organization, and the age and maturity of the group. But, the picture is certainly not clear.

The work of Fiedler is a second reason for suggesting that the situation is an important consideration in leadership. He has pointed out that leader effectiveness is jointly determined by the leader's style of interacting and the favorableness of the situation. From a situational perspective, it's easier to lead if you are in a position of power, if you have a good relationship with your subordinates, and the task is highly structured.

A second implication which arises from the discussion on leadership is that *a positive coaching approach* not only is preferred by athletes, it leads to positive changes in social psychological factors such as self esteem. The importance of a positive approach is so important that Smoll and Smith (1979) have suggested that coaches should:

Be liberal with reward. Look for positive

things, reward them ... praise the little things that others might not notice ... Have realistic expectations and consistently reward players when they succeed in meeting them. Reward positive things as soon as they occur (pp. 6-7).

Care must be taken, however, to insure that a wide variety of verbal rewarding behaviors are used. In a study undertaken with an experienced 32 year-old male swimming coach, Brent Rushall and Kenneth Smith (1979) found that the coach had a very limited repertoire of rewarding words — "good" tended to be the predominant word used. After Rushall and Smith introduced a training session, however, both the quality and the quantity of the coach's verbal reinforcer's were increased substantially. It is likely that the most experienced coaches habitually use the same words or phrases — thereby diminishing their effectiveness.

Although positive reinforcement is preferable, there does appear to be some instances where a negative approach can be effective. Daniel Kirschenbaum and Robert Smith (1983) pointed out that there are sound reasons for interpolating some negative feedback along with positive feedback:

> Conformity research has shown that when opinions are expressed in a highly consistent (rather than variable) fashion, the individual's social influence decreases;
>
> Research on interpersonal attraction has shown that individuals who provide only positive feedback are not as well liked as individuals who change the sequence of their feedback from negative to positive; and,
>
> Research on interpersonal influence has shown that both a positive-negative and a negative-positive sequencing of feedback are effective. If a positive approach is used initially, it can decrease defensiveness to later negative feedback. And, if a negative approach is used initially, it can increase the impact of later positive feedback.

Kirschenbaum and Smith had college students take basketball free throws in two blocks of trials under the supervision of an experimenter who served as a coach. The feedback within each block was either positive-positive, negative-negative, positive-negative, or negative-positive. Continuous positive and continuous negative feedback produced the same result — a linear decrement in performance from the initial baseline measure. Similarly, the groups experiencing a positive-negative and a negative-positive sequencing of feedback also had the same result — a linear positive improvement from the initial baseline measure.

Kirschenbaum and Smith emphasized that these results should not be interpreted to mean "that coaches should abandon the regular use of positive feedback. These findings merely suggest that *continuous* positive feedback, in the absence of any critical comments, may, under some conditions, produce some of the same adverse effects as continuous negative feedback. Clearly, the use of incessant criticism seems much more definitely ill-advised" (p. 340).

An approach which might be best involves the frequent use of positive reinforcement coupled with the use of feedback on correct performance. The former is behavior described as Positive Reinforcement (verbal or nonverbal positive reaction to the athlete's behavior) in the Coaching Behavior Assessment System (see B-1 in Table 13.2). The latter would be the behavior described as Mistake-Contingent Instruction (B-4, technical instruction to the athlete after a mistake). The combination of these two would represent the positive and negative feedback necessary.

Leadership and Decision Making

The Nature of Decision Styles

One important aspect of leadership is decision-making. Leaders must continually process information, weigh the alternatives, and then come to a decision. What offensive and defensive systems should be used? What training schedules are best? What athletes work best together? What time should practice start? How long should it last? Although the list of examples where decisions have to be made in sport seems endless, the process of decision-making

Table 13.6 Illustrations of decision styles in the process of leadership.

Type	Example
Autocratic The leader comes to the decision alone	"In `discussing [owner] Charlie Finely, 'master' is precisely the right word. If he's your boss, he has to own you, from the first warm up of the spring to the last putout of the fall. Every minute, every day." (Dark & Underwood, 1980, p. 6)
Consultive The leader comes to the final decision after consulting one or more subordinates	"He and the coaches would ... review the first half and make decisions about the second ... The coaches' pow-wows consisted, more often than not, of Knight's analysis of the first half ... The coaches listened. Often they agreed with Knight's assessments" (Feinstein, 1987, p. 100)
Delegative The leader delegates the decision to one or more subordinates	"The first time I met [owner Gussie Busch] ... he cut through a lot of bullshit, gave me a three-year contract to manage his team, and told me he didn't care what it took, just bring him a winner ... The smartest people are those who hire good people and then just get the hell out of the way" (Herzog & Horrigan, 1987, p. 11-12).
Participative The group and the leader0 jointly make the decision	"'We don't all agree with what the union stands for', says [Dallas Cowboy player represenative Doug] Cosbie. "but we believe in the collective bargaining process. Collectively, we can improve working conditions'" (Lieber, 1987, p. 42)

involves four basic approaches; Table 13.6 provides a summary of these. The major difference among them is in the relative amount of involvement or influence by the leader and his/her subordinates.

When an *autocratic* decision style is used, the leader makes the decision alone. Consequently, this approach involves the greatest amount of independence by the leader. The example in Table 13.6 helps to illustrate this point. Alvin Dark portrayed Charlie Finley, the owner of the Oakland Athletics, as a man completely in control.

A *consultive* decision style is similar to the autocratic approach in that the leader makes the decision alone. A difference between them, however, is that the leader initially consults with subordinates to obtain their input. This input may or may not be used when the decision is made but subordinates do have some involvement. The example in Table 13.6 describes the half-time consultations between Coach Bobby Knight of the Indiana Hoosiers and his assistant coaches.

A *delegative* decision style is also similar to the autocratic approach in that the leader again makes the decision. But, this time, however, the decision consists of handing over the responsibility to subordinates or to the group who then make the decision independently. The quotation which appears in Table 13.6 is a good illustration of this process. The owner of the St. Louis Cardinals, August A. Busch, delegated the responsibility of running the team to his subordinate, Whitey Herzog, the manager. In turn, Herzog made the decisions pertaining to the day-to-day management of the team.

The *participative* or *democratic* approach involves the greatest amount of involvement by the group in the decision-making process. The group (which could include the leader) jointly comes to a decision with the leader having no more influence than any other group member. When the National Football League players went on strike in 1987, it was a decision that was arrived at through the democratic approach. The example in Table 13.6 presents the viewpoint of one of the player representatives, Doug Cosbie. Essentially, Cosbie pointed out that while not everyone agreed with the action taken, the strike represented a collective decision.

An analysis of the decision styles preferred by athletes and/or used by coaches was undertaken by Chelladurai and Arnott with male and female basketball players and Gordon (1988) with male soccer players. Their findings are summarized in Table 13.7. It is apparent that both coaches and athletes view the athletic situation as autocratic in nature. On the average, the coaches were perceived to make decisions using an autocratic approach 82.9% of the time. In some instances, this was done after consultation (38%) but in the majority of cases, the decisions were totally autocratic (44.9%). The participative style was used very infrequently (15.5%) whereas the delegative style was almost nonexistent (1.6%).

The major discrepancy between what coach's do and what players prefer lies in the use of a participative decision style. Male athletes prefer almost twice as much participation (29.5%) and female athletes three times as much participation (46.9%) as coaches provide. The delegative style was not only used

Table 13. 7 Percentage distribution of decision style choices (Adapted from Chelladurai, 1986 based on data from Chelladurai & Arnott,1985 and Gordon, 1988)

Group	Decision Styles			
	Autocratic	Consultive	Participative	Delegative
Coach's Decision Styles				
Coach's Choice	46.3	33.3	18.5	1.9
Coach's Perception of Other Coaches' Choice	45.5	41.2	12.5	0.8
Player's Perception of Coach's Choice	43.0	39.6	15.4	2.0
Average	44.9	38.0	15.5	1.6
Male Athlete's Preferences for Coach's Decision Styles				
Soccer Players	31.2	41.9	24.9	2.0
Basketball Players	38.9	25.8	34.1	1.2
Average	35.1	33.8	29.5	1.6
Female Athlete's Preferences for Coach's Decision Styles				
Basketball Players	33.0	18.1	46.9	2.0

infrequently, it was not wanted by either male or female athletes.

Chelladurai and Arnott (1985) have provided one interesting way of looking at the amount of involvement and influence by coaches and team members in the various decision styles. This is illustrated in Figure 13.4. They suggested that the coach's influence falls along a continuum which ranges from 100% when the autocratic approach is used to 0% when the delegative approach is used. As would be expected, with the participative approach, the coach's influence is in between at a moderate level. Chelladurai and Arnott also suggested that the influence of team members is maximal when a participative approach is used. However, both the autocratic and the delegative approaches exclude them from participating in the decision.

At the management level, the delegative approach can be effective when it is clearly understood who is in command. An athletic director, general manager, or owner who hires a coach and then constantly interferes in the day-to-day leadership of the team reduces the coach's effectiveness. The sentiments expressed by Whitey Herzog in the quote presented in Table 13.6 are typical of the view held by most coaches —" The smartest people are those who hire good people and then just get the hell out of the way" (Herzog & Horrigan, 1987, p 12). The delegative approach is ineffec-

tive when it is unclear who is in command. One example, of this occurred in the 1988 National Basketball Association season. The Sacramento Kings hired former coach and player, Bill Russell, to coach the team. But after only nine months on the job:

> the Kings finally acknowledged that Russell, though a legendary player, is no longer capable of being a successful NBA coach .... "I'd say the effort was adequate," said [King's president and general manager Joe] Axelson. "Bill delegated a lot of authority, but he was always there". The fact remains: The Sacramento system, in which Russell acted as an "executive" head coach who gave many of the everyday coaching duties to assistants Willis Reed ... and Jerry Reynolds ... only left the players confused. "It was obvious that there was no direction on that team," said an assistant coach of a Western Conference team. (McCallum, 1988, p. 15)

Normative Model of Decision Making

A question which often arises is which of the four decision styles — autocratic, consultive, participative, or delegative — is most effective. The answer is that it depends. In some situations, an autocratic decision style is most effective, in others one of the other three is most effective. In an attempt to provide some general guidelines for leaders, Vroom and his associates (Vroom & Yetton, 1973; Vroom & Jago, 1974) developed a normative model of decision making. Subsequently, Chelladurai and Haggerty (1978) adapted this model for coaching situations.

It was pointed out in Chapter 12 that a norm is a standard, a standard which provides the individual with guidelines for behavior in specific situations. This is what the normative model does for leaders in decision-making situations (see Figure 13.5). According to Chelladurai and Haggerty, seven situational factors have an influence on what type of decision style is best. The first is time pressure. The amount of time available to deliberate, weigh alternatives, and consult with other people varies from one situation to another. In turn, this has a direct influence on the type of decision style which is most appropriate.

A second situational factor is quality

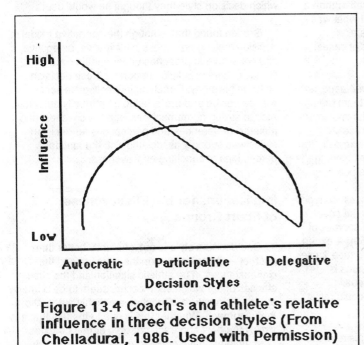

Figure 13.4 Coach's and athlete's relative influence in three decision styles (From Chelladurai, 1986. Used with Permission)

requirement. In some instances, the coach may be satisfied with any one from a number of equally good alternatives. Thus, the quality requirement in that situation is low. The decision concerning which individual to select as team captain is an example. It's not an unimportant issue but if the coach is satisfied that all the potential candidates are acceptable, the quality requirement in the situation is low. On the other hand, the coach may feel that the selection of the final two or three players on the roster is important to assure maximum flexibility. An optimal decision must be made so the quality requirement of this decision is high.

A third situational factor is *information location.* In the introduction to this section, it was pointed out that decision making involves the processing of information and the weighing of alternatives. Thus, it makes good sense that those individuals who possess the best information on an issue should be involved in the decision.

Problems are *complex* if they involve a series of interconnected steps — where one decision has an influence on every subsequent decision. Picking the athletes for an Olympic basketball team is one example. A coach who has picked her best five might be faced with the dilemma of choosing a poor defensive player who is an outstanding 3-point shooter versus a versatile athletes who can play more than one position. Or selecting an offensive specialist rather than a defensive specialist. This is an example of what was referred to in Chapter 2 (see Table 2.3) as a noneureka disjunctive task. In these types of cases, the judgement of a single individual is best.

The fourth situational factor, *group acceptance,* is an acknowledgement that acceptance by team members is sometimes critical for the successful implementation of a decision. A coach might autocratically decide to introduce a full-court press in basketball. If the athletes were convinced that they didn't have the ability to make it work, their effort might be poor.

Another situational factor which influences the type of decision style which is most effective is the *coach's power.* When coaches possesses the five sources of power outlined by French and Raven (1959) — expert, coercive, reference, legitimate, and reward (see Table 10.5 again) — compliance with their decisions is virtually assured. On the other hand, if a coach doesn't possess expert power, the group could resist the decision.

The final factor is *group integration.* This refers to the level of task and social cohesiveness present. Thus, for example, a participative decision style could be used effectively with a highly cohesive team. It wouldn't be as effective with a noncohesive group.

Sandy Gordon (1988) tested the normative model of decision making with intercollegiate soccer players and their coaches. A decision style questionnaire was developed that consisted of 15 cases (situations) which were characterized by the presence or absence of the seven situational attributes included in the Chelladurai and Haggerty model (see Figure 13.5). One typical case — which includes the attributes of *restrictive time pressure* and *high relevant information* — is as follows:

Case one Early in the second half of an important game a key mid-field player is injured. The players on the bench have been with you for a few seasons, so you know them and their capabilities very well. You have to choose between them to substitute for the injured player who is unable to continue. How is the decision made? (pp. 59 -60)

The options presented to the soccer players and their coaches were autocratic, participative, delegative, and consultive. The coaches were asked to indicate which decision style they would use in the situation and which decision style they thought other coaches would use. The athletes were asked to indicate which decision style they would prefer their coach to use and which decision style they thought he would use.

Gordon found that although the normative model of decision making prescribes participative, delegative, and consultive approaches under certain circumstances, there was little support for these decision styles in his study. Coaching intercollegiate soccer was perceived and preferred to be primarily autocratic. Also, a strong agreement between the coaches' and athletes' preferences and perceptions for decision styles was strongly associated with the athletes' perceptions of coaching effectiveness.

Implications for the Effectiveness of Sport Groups

One decision style is not inherently better than another — it depends upon the situation and the circumstances. The athletic situation and the circumstances under which sport occurs seem to be primarily autocratic in nature. Coaches are highly autocratic in their approach. Whether this is due to the fact that it is simply the best approach possible or that coaches (and athletes) have come to expect this approach through a process of social learning isn't clear. There is a strong preference by male and female athletes for

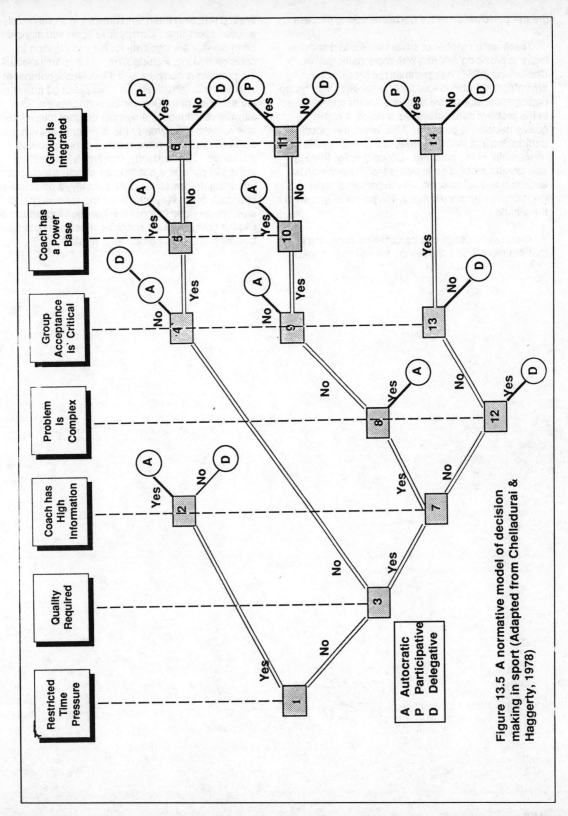

Figure 13.5 A normative model of decision making in sport (Adapted from Chelladurai & Haggerty, 1978)

A Autocratic P Participative D Delegative

greater participation in the decision-making process.

There are a number of advantages and disadvantages in providing athletes with more participation. Chelladurai (1986) has summarized these. One advantage is that in discussions associated with group participation, alternative solutions and/or approaches to the problem can surface. As a result, a higher quality decision is possible. Also, when the group participates in a decision, there is a greater sense of "ownership" in the outcome. Consequently, there is also greater motivation to insure that the decision is accepted and acted upon. Third, participation in decision making contributes to the personal growth of the athlete.

One disadvantage of a participative approach is that it is more time consuming. Introducing alternatives, discussing them, and arriving at a compromise solution takes time. Competitive sport situations don't often provide enough time for full participation in decision making. Participation also has limitations if the problem is complex — if it involves a number of interrelated alternatives. An example used earlier was the selection of an Olympic basketball team. One alternative influences a number of other interrelated alternatives. The greater the number of individuals involved, the greater the number of perspectives advanced. Consequently, one highly competent individual such as a coach is as effective as a group operating democratically. And, finally, a participative approach is not very effective if the team is not cohesive. Rivalry and competition between individuals or cliques could produce solutions which are not in the best interests of the group as a whole.

5 Group Cohesiveness

At the airport, the discrepancies in their lifestyle would disappear; they became an entity. They dressed similarly, in slacks and well-tailored sports jackets, or well-cut suits ....Even their baggage was alike .... the sense of pack that characterized them in airplanes was not confined to the road. The team was the nucleus of their lives. The rest of the world spun around it -- trainers, coaches, agents, writers, and at the very outside, fans -- was extrinsic. Even their families sometimes seemed less important to them than their playmates. After a trip of several days, during which they had traveled, eaten, dressed, drunk, played hockey, and roomed with one another, they were liable on their return to foresake their women and children and congregate in one of theEdmonton watering holes they favoured. Friendships were between the player and the team as a whole, rather than between individuals. (Gzowski, 1981, pp. 14-16)

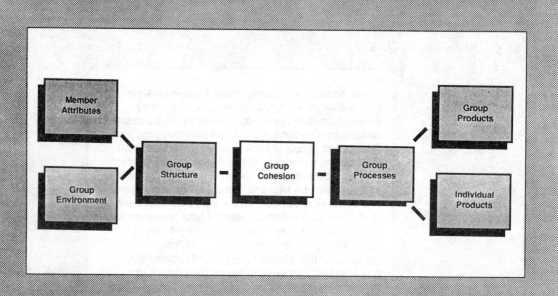

14 The Nature of Group Cohesion

The term *cohesion* is derived from the Latin word *cohaesus* which means to cleave or stick together. Not surprisingly, the term cohesion has been used by social psychologists to describe the tendency of groups to stick together and remain united. Groups are social units composed of two or more individuals. Cohesion reflects the strength of the bond among the members within the group. Cohesiveness is so fundamental to groups that it has been suggested that "there can be no such thing as a non-cohesive group; it is a contradiction in terms. If a group exists it is to some extent cohesive" (Donnelly, Carron, & Chelladurai, 1978, p. 7). But, obviously, different groups can vary in their level of cohesiveness — in the strength of bond which is present.

In the quote which introduced this section, Peter Gzowski (1981) described the presence of a very strong bond in the Edmonton Oilers hockey team. According to Gzowski, the team was the primary focus of the players' lives. The team as a whole became the basis for friendships. Team members dressed similarly. They looked and acted as an entity and outsiders which included trainers, coaches, agents, fans, writers, and even family were excluded.

On the other hand, in the quote which introduced this chapter, Steve Wulf (1988) provided a description of the Cincinnati Reds baseball team which illustrated a low level of group cohesiveness. According to Wulf, team members had adopted an individual perspective rather than a team perspective. And, when friction arose between the manager, Pete Rose, and a player, Dave

Where did the Cincinnati Reds and manager Pete Rose go wrong last year? Basically, too many players were thinking of themselves and not of the team ... Dave Parker is gone — to Oakland for nothing much — and while the Reds might miss his power, they won't miss his presence. He and Rose clashed, and the players took sides. If Cincinnati can rise above last year's pettiness, it will be a very formidable team. (Wulf, 1988, pp.93).

Parker, it divided the team into two camps. The strength of the bond in the group was weak and the team's effectiveness suffered.

In order to make sense out of group cohesiveness and understand its impact on team effectiveness, it is necessary first to examine the nature of cohesiveness. This is the focus in this chapter. In the next chapter, the correlates of cohesiveness — the factors associated with its presence and absence — are examined. Much of which is discussed in these two chapters has also been presented elsewhere (e.g., Carron, 1980, 1982, 1984, 1986; Carron and Chelladurai, 1981; Carron, Widmeyer, & Brawley, 1985; Widmeyer, Carron, & Brawley, 1985).

The Concept of Group Cohesion

Cohesion has been defined by a number of authors in slightly different ways. These definitional differences reflect the different perspectives on this complex construct. For example, Festinger, Schachter, and Back (1963) defined it as the total field of forces causing members to remain in the group. They also proposed that that there are two general types of forces: the attractiveness of the group (which essentially represents the social and affiliative aspects of a group) and means control (which essentially represents the task, performance, and productive aspects of a group).

The Festinger et al. viewpoint concentrates on the impetus underlying participation and involvement with the group — the primary reason why individuals join a group. This is illustrated in Figure 14.1a. If a large number of forces draw individuals to a team and each of these forces is strong — good friends, good coaching, good trips, a chance to win a championship — the attractiveness of the group is high. Consequently, the level of cohesiveness would be high.

Gross and Martin (1952) felt that it makes more sense to define cohesion as the resistance of the group to disruptive forces. This perspective is illustrated in Figure 14b. Thus, if a fraternity basketball team is highly cohesive, it can tolerate a great deal of negative pressure — losing games, one or two players dominating the shooting, criticisms by senior players, and so on. The cohesiveness which binds the group into an entity also helps it resist all the pressures which can tear it apart. And, of course, if the team is not highly cohesive, minimal disruptive factors can cause members to begin leaving the team.

In order to understand cohesiveness — the factors which draw members to the group and/or help the group to resist disruptive forces — it is necessary to understand the group's goals and objectives. Every group has reasons for existing and these are interwoven into its development and maintenance. For example, social clubs, work crews, delinquent gangs, fraternity basketball teams, counselling groups, army platoons, and professional sport teams are all differ-

ent. But, they are also all similar in the sense that they exhibit cohesiveness. The members of these different groups stick together because they all endorse some underlying common purposes. An outsider who was unaware of those specific purposes would be unable to comprehend the bases for the cohesiveness. Similarly, an insider (a group member) who was either unaware, unappreciative, or unaccepting of the bases for cohesiveness would either choose or be forced to discontinue involvement with the group. From this perspective, cohesion can be viewed as a dynamic process which is reflected in the tendency for a group to stick together and remain united in the pursuit of its goals and objectives.

The Measurement of Cohesion in Social and Work Groups

Another way of understanding the nature of cohesion is to examine the approaches taken to measure it — the *operational definitions*. Measurement helps to give precise meaning to theoretical constructs by showing how they are manifested in everyday situations. If cohesion is defined as the binding substance in groups, for example, this might seem reasonable. But, if cohesion is then measured by assessing the amount of time athletes spent together in the locker room after a game, this might seem unreasonable. Factors such as the number of shower heads, the availability of transportation, the length of the coach's postgame analysis, and so on would contribute to the length of time athletes spend in the locker room. And, these factors are unrelated to friendships and affiliative needs (i.e., social cohesion), or to commitment to the team goals and objectives (i.e., task cohesion), or to contractual obligations (i.e., normative cohesion).

Four general approaches have been taken to operationally define cohe-

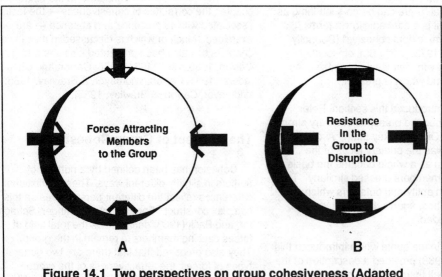

Figure 14.1 Two perspectives on group cohesiveness (Adapted from Carron, 1980)

A — Forces Attracting Members to the Group

B — Resistance In the Group to Disruption

siveness in social and work groups. These are summarized in Table 14.1. Possibly the most frequent approach has been to assess the degree of interpersonal attraction in the group. The underlying assumption for this approach is that if the group contains a large number of individuals who are good friends, it will stick together and strongly resist disruption.

A second approach has been to assess the level of attraction members feel for the group. For example, Bovard (1951) asked students to indicate how much they liked their class as a whole. The underlying assumption in this approach is that if a large number of groups members view the group as attractive (prestigious, enjoyable, successful), there will be a greater degree of cohesiveness present.

The operational measurement of cohesiveness through the use of some measure of attraction has been the subject of some criticism (Escovar & Sim, 1974). One of the reasons for this is that attraction underrepresents the concept of cohesiveness. Friendships, for example, are a measure of interpersonal attraction. But the number of friendships in a work group, social group, or sport team is never the sole basis for individuals sticking together and remaining united in the pursuit of their groups' goals and objectives. A second, related criticism is that measures of attraction don't explain why groups stick together when there is extreme conflict, tension, or disagreements.

Table 14.1 Approaches taken for the assessment of cohesion in social and work groups

General Category	Examples	Reference
Interpersonal Attraction	The presence of friends	Dimock (1941
	The absence of cliques	Lenk (1969)
	The numer of reciprocal sociometric choices	Deep et al (1967)
Individual Attractions to the Group	Attactions to the group as a whole	Bovard (1951)
	Sense of belonging to the group	Indik (1965)
	Value of having membership in the group	Schachter (1951)
	Social activities of the group	Horsfall & Anderson (1949)
Commitment to the Group	Desire to maintain the group	Schachter (1951)
	Resistance to moving to other groups	Seashore (1954)
	Ratio of within to out group choices	Dimock (1941)
Similarity to Other Members	Similarity of intrerpersonal perceptions	Fiedler et al (1952)
	Similarity of interests in the group task	Smith (1968)

A third criticism is that attraction — either interpersonal attraction or attraction to the group as a whole — is not necessary for group formation and development. Ten strangers could sign up for intramural volleyball, be assigned to the same team, and attend practices and games regularly. The team might lose every game. Possibly friendships would not develop. And, the team might not be distinguishable from any other team in terms of value of membership and prestige. Yet, those ten people might continue to stick together. Measures of attraction would have a difficult time accounting for this behavior.

A fourth criticism is statistical in nature. The correlations between various measures of attraction are quite low. Research supports the view that cohesion is multidimensional and attraction is only one of the forces binding members to the group (e.g., Rumuz-

Nienhuis & Van Bergen, 1960).

As Table 14.1 shows, the third approach to the measurement of cohesiveness involves the assessment of the group members' commitment to the group. The question Schachter (1951) used with a group of factory workers is one example — if enough members decide not to stay so that it seems this group might disband, would you like the chance to persuade others to stay? If no cohesiveness was present, very few members would express an interest in persuading others to stay in the group. Conversely, if a high degree of cohesiveness was present, a large number of members would be interested in keeping the group together.

The fourth general approach used to operationally measure the level of cohesiveness present in work and social groups has been to assess the level of similarity in sociopersonal characteristics. This approach is based on the assumption that if a large number of group members see themselves as similar in attitudes, personalities, and beliefs, they will stick together and resist disruption from outside pressures.

The Measurement of Cohesion in Sport Groups

The Sport Cohesiveness Questionnaire (SCQ)

The operational measurements of cohesiveness that were used with work and social groups served as a basis for the development of inventories for sport groups. Table 14.2 provides a overview of these. The Sport Cohesiveness Questionnaire (SCQ), which was the first to be developed, served as the impetus for a considerable amount of research over a 15-year period (Martens, Landers, & Loy, 1972). This research is discussed in Chapter 15.

The SCQ consists of seven individual items considered to represent various aspects of cohesiveness in sport groups. These are friendship, power and influence, value of membership, sense of belonging, enjoyment, closeness, and teamwork. The friendship and power items measure *individual-to-individual attraction* — each team member's perceptions of his/her relationship with every other group member. The assumption is that if there are good individual-to-individual relationships among a large number of team members, high cohesiveness is present.

The questions which deal with value of membership, sense of belonging, and enjoyment assess *individual-to-group relationships.* With these questions, the individual evaluates his/her personal relationship and involvement with the group as a unit. It is assumed that if a large number of group members possess a strong sense of belonging to the group, value their membership in the group, and enjoy their involvement, the level of group cohesion is high.

The final two questions, teamwork and closeness, involve an assessment of the *group-as-a-whole.* Each individual team member is required to step back and answer, "What are we like as a team (in terms of teamwork, in terms of closeness)". If the overall ratings are high, the team is considered to be cohesive.

Despite its utility and the important role it has played in stimulating research into cohesiveness in sport teams, the Sport Cohesiveness Questionnaire suffers from one major limitation. Its *psychometric properties* have never been established. In order to place confidence in the results of a questionnaire, it is necessary to know that all of the items are measuring the same thing (which is referred to as internal consistency), that the questionnaire produces similar results with repeated testing (which is referred to as reliability), and that the test is a valid measure of the concept. These psychometric properties provide a form of consumer protection — the good housekeeping seal of approval. Without these, the utility of the test is diminished.

In an attempt to overcome the limitations in the Sport Cohesiveness Questionnaire and provide psychometrically sound instruments, David Yukelson and his colleagues as well as a research team in which I am a member carried out comprehensive research programs to develop sport cohesion inventories

Table 14.2 Approaches taken for the assessment of cohesion in sport groups

Inventory	General Description	Reference
Sport Cohesiveness Questionnaire (SCQ)	Seven items which measure friendship, power, value of membership, enjoyment, sense of belonging, closeness, and teamwork	Martens, Landers, & Loy (1972)
Multidimensional Sport Cohesion Instrument (MSCI)	Twenty-two items which measure four factors: attraction to the group, unity of purpose, quality of teamwork, and valued roles.	Yukelson, Weinberg, & Jackson (1984)
Group Environment Questionnaire (GEQ)	Eighteeen items which measure four factors: individual attractions to the group task, individual attractions to the group social, group integration task and group integration social	Carron, Brawley, & Widmeyer (1985)

(Yukelson, Weinberg, and Jackson (1984), Brawley, et al. 1987; Carron et al. 1985; Widmeyer et al. 1985). There are two major protocols used in developing any instrument or inventory: a data driven and a theory driven approach. With the data driven approach, a large number of items are collected that are thought to reflect situations in which the concept is manifested. This battery of items is given to a sample of subjects and the results are analyzed. Those items which fall together in meaningful patterns (clusters, factors) are retained and a suitable label is attached. The remaining items are discarded. The results from the statistical analyses are then used to help identify the concept. This was the protocol used by Yukelson and his colleagues to develop the Multidimensional Sport Cohesion Instrument.

With the theory driven protocol, a conceptual model of the concept is developed initially. This conceptual model then provides the basis for the subsequent development of an initial battery of items. Statistical analyses are then used to determine whether the battery of items adequately reflects the conceptual model. This was the general strategy used by my colleagues and me to develop the Group Environment Questionnaire.

The Multidimensional Sport Cohesion Instrument (MSCI)

The MSCI (see Table 14.2 again) evolved from the belief that cohesion in sport teams reflects "factors associated with the goals and objectives the group is striving to achieve, as well as factors associated with the development and maintenance of positive interpersonal relationships (Yukelson et al., p. 106). Initially, 41 task and social items were generated (a) from other cohesion instruments, (b) from definitions proposed by theoreticians, (c) from pertinent research in industrial and organizational psychology, and (d) by interviewing coaches and social scientists. This original questionnaire was then administered to 16 male and female basketball teams and the results were analyzed. Twenty-two items measuring four categories (factors) of cohesion were identified.

One of the factors, Quality of Teamwork, is a measure of how well teammates work together to achieve group success. The second factor, Attraction to the Group, represents the degree to which individuals are attracted to and satisfied with group membership. The third factor, Unity of Purpose, is composed of items which assess commitment to the group's norms, rules, and goals. The last factor, Valued Roles, is a measure of the degree to which there is identification with group membership.

The Group Environment Questionnaire (GEQ)

The conceptual model which forms the basis for the GEQ was developed from research and writing in the group dynamics literature which has focused on the nature of the group and the nature of group cohesiveness. This literature can be categorized into two general areas: the individual and group perspective of group involvement and the task and social aspects of cohesiveness.

The Individual and Group Perspective of Group Involvement. In Chapter 1, the need to distinguish between the individual and the group was discussed. This has been a frequent theme in group dynamics research. For example, Cattell (1948, 1953) pointed out that a group can be described at three different levels. At the first level, which Cattell referred to as the *population level,* the focus is on the individual group members — their personalities, aspirations, motives, attributes, and so on. The research which was discussed in Chapter 6 is an example of this approach. What is the personality of team versus individual sport athletes? What is the predominant motives (orientations) of athletes on intramural basketball teams? In order to answer these questions, it is necessary to evaluate the characteristics of individual team members.

At the second or *structural level,* the focus is on the member-to-member interactions. The research which was discussed in Chapter 8 illustrates this orientation. What are the factors contributing to coach-athlete compatibility? This question can only be answered by examining the specific interactions and relationship between the coach and the athlete.

The third level was referred to by Cattell as *syntality.* In this approach, the focus is on the group as a whole. What are the team goals for the Detroit Pistons in 1987-88? Individual team members may have personal goals for themselves but the group also establishes goals and objectives for the team as a totality.

Not surprisingly, the need to distinguish between the individual and the group has also been emphasized by a number of authors in the area of group cohesion. Table 14.3 provides an overview. The distinction made by Van Bergen and Koekebakker (1959) between individual attraction to the group (ATG) and cohesion is typical. Cohesion was the label

Table 14.3 The labels used to describe individual and group levels of cohesiveness

Individual Level Terminology	Group Level Terminology	Reference
Individual Attraction to the Group	Cohesion	Van Bergen & Koekebakker (1959)
Individual Attraction to the Group	Cohesion	Evans & Jarvis (1980)
Attraction to the Group Valued Roles	Quality of Teamwork Unity of Purpose	Yukelson, Weinberg, & Jackson (1984)
Individual-to-Group Cohesion	Group-as-a-Unit Cohesion	Carron, & Chelladurai (1981)
Individual Attraction to the Group	Group Integration	Carron, Brawley, & Widmeyer (1985)

Table 14.4 The labels used to describe the task and social aspects of cohesion (Adapted from Iso-Ahola & Hatfield, 1986)

Social Cohesion Terminology	Task Cohesion Terminology	Reference
Attraction to the Group	Means Control	Festinger, Schachter, & Back (1963)
Intrinsic Attraction	Instrumental Attraction	Enoch & McLemore (1967)
Social Cohesion	Task Cohesion	Mikalachki (1969)
Attraction to the Group	Unity of Purpose Quality of Teamwork Valued Roles	Yukelson, Weinberg, & Jackson (1984)
Social Cohesion	Task Cohesion	Gill (1977)
Social Cohesion	Task Cohesion	Nixon (1977)
Social Cohesion	Task Cohesion	Carron, Brawley, & Widmeyer (1985)
Social Cohesion	Task Cohesion	Widmeyer & Martens (1978)

used for the group property that Cattell referred to as the syntality level. ATG was the label used for the individual property that Cattell described as the population level.

Task and Social Aspects of Cohesiveness. There is no single primary goal or objective for social groups, delinquent gangs, fraternity basketball teams, army platoons, and so on. Not only are there differences across the broad categories of groups (i.e., social groups versus work crews), there are also differences in the goals and objectives of groups within the same category. For example, not every fraternity basketball team has the same reasons for forming and staying together. In one case, the opportunity to meet weekly and socialize may be predominant; in another, winning the university intramural championship may be most important.

In the study of groups in general, it has usually been assumed that there are two classes of goals and objectives which dominate the activities of all groups. The first is represented by the activities associated with the development and maintenance of social relationships; the second, by activities associated with task accomplishment, productivity, and performance (Fiedler, 1967; Hersey & Blanchard, 1977). Historically, cohesion has also been considered to be composed of these two elements — although the specific terminology used has varied from one author to another (see Table 14.4).

For example, it was pointed out above that Festinger et al. assumed that two major fields of forces cause members to remain in the group: attraction-to-the-group and means control. The former is social in nature, the latter, task. Also, Enoch and McLemore (1967) viewed cohesiveness as attraction to the group which, in turn, was assumed to be composed of an intrinsic (social) dimension and an instrumental (task) dimension. And, finally, Mikalachki (1969 advocated that cohesion be subdivided into two components — social cohesion and task cohesion.

A Conceptual Model for Cohesion in Sport Teams. On the basis of the views of the group and of cohesiveness — the distinctions made between task and social dimensions and individual and group orientations — Carron, Widmeyer, and Brawley (1985) proposed a conceptual model for cohesion in sport teams. It is illustrated in Figure 14.2.

In the model, cohesion is divided into two major categories. One of these, which is called *group integration,* represents a member's perceptions of the group as a totality. The focus is on the total group — Cattell's syntality level. How close is the group as a whole? Does the team stick together? Is the group unified?

The second category, which is called *individual attractions to the group,* represents a member's personal attractions to the group. The focus is on the individual's involvement in the group — similar but not identical to Cattell's structural level. How well do I fit in with the group? Is the group an attractive place for me personally? Both of these perceptions help bind members to the group.

The member's perceptions of the group as a unit and their perceptions of the group's attractions are centered around two concerns. One of these is the group *task.* On sport teams, members are concerned with group performance, productivity, achievement. Shared concerns about the task help to bind the team together into a cohesive unit. A second element is the *social* aspects of the group. Mutual friendships and shared feelings of togetherness, closeness, and affiliation also help to bind the team together into a cohesive unit.

As Figure 14.2 illustrates, the categories of group integration and individual attractions to group in combination with task and social concerns result in four manifestations of cohesion in sport teams: group integration-task, group integration-social, individual attractions to the group-task, and individual attractions to the group-social. Although other aspects of cohesiveness have been discussed in the literature (e.g., normative cohesion), the four presented in Figure 14.2 are thought to account for the greatest variability in cohesion among sport groups.

Implications for the Effectiveness of Sport Groups

Cohesion as a construct which is used to describe the group has a number of direct parallels with personality as a construct which is used to describe the individual. First, both are integral to understanding behavior. Personality is the foundation for individual behavior; cohesion is the foundation for group behavior. Any attempt to describe, explain, predict, and possibly exert control over individual behavior, must begin with personality as a foundation. Similarly, the description, explanation, prediction, and control of group behavior in sport must evolve from an understanding of the group's cohesiveness.

A second parallel is that both terms are used in general everyday conversations in a manner that seems to suggest that they are simple, single-dimensional constructs. An example of this is the statements, "He has a nice personality" and "They are a cohesive group". In both cases, there is the suggestion that a single, global pleasant, positive quality is present. Neither personality nor cohesiveness

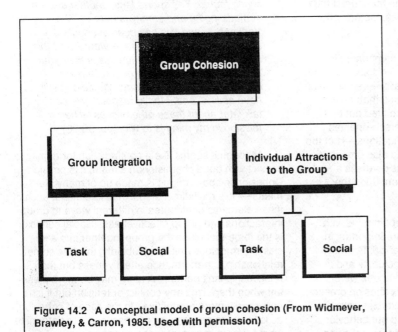

Figure 14.2 A conceptual model of group cohesion (From Widmeyer, Brawley, & Carron, 1985. Used with permission)

are simple, single constructs.

A third, related parallel is that, inevitably, numerous conceptual perspectives have emerged to explain personality and cohesion. This is more easily highlighted in the case of personality because it has been a dominant issue in psychology almost from its origins as a science. Personality has been explained in a number of markedly different ways including psychodynamic theories, phenomenological theories, social learning theories, trait theories, and body type theories. It has also been measured by a wide variety of techniques such as rating scales, projective tests (e.g., Rorschach Test, Thematic Apperception Test), and paper and pencil questionnaires. Also, the numerous paper and pencil questionnaires developed to measure personality vary considerably in their purpose. Some measure personality disorders (e.g., Minnesota Multiphasic Personality Inventory); others, a number of general personality traits (e.g., California Psychological Inventory, Cattell Sixteen Personality Factor Questionnaire); others, one or two general traits (e.g., Manifest Anxiety Scale, Machiavellian Scale); and others, a situationally-specific trait (e.g., Sport Competition Anxiety Scale).

Conceptual complexity is also evident in the case of cohesion. It has been the subject of different theoretical explanations and different operational definitions in work groups, social groups, and sport groups. Also, the tests that have been developed to measure it have contained a number of different scales, factors, and constructs.

A fourth parallel is that not every component is equally important in every situation. This seems to be well accepted in the case of personality — some traits are more important in certain situations than others. For example, in Chapter 13, it was pointed out that Fiedler emphasized the task- and person-oriented behaviors of leaders in leadership situations — not the leader's general personality. And, he also proposed that the relative effectiveness of a task- versus a person oriented approach is contingent upon the favorableness of the situation.

A similar orientation should be kept in mind with group cohesion. Different aspects are important in different situations. For example, Carron, Brawley, and Widmeyer (1988) found that punctuality and absenteeism in summer recreation leagues were strongly related to the level of social cohesion present; task cohesion was not a factor. In exercise classes and elite sport groups, however, drop out behavior was strongly related to the degree of task cohesion present. In another study, Brawley, Carron, and Widmeyer (1988) found that the perceptions of individual group members regarding the ability of their group to resist disruptions was strongly related to group cohesion. But the type of cohesion which was most important varied in exercise classes, recreational sport groups, and elite sport groups.

An example which illustrates that not all of the components of cohesion are equally important in every situation is provided from professional baseball. At the beginning of the 1988 baseball season, conflict arose between George Steinbrenner, the owner of the New York Yankees baseball team, and one of his players, Dave Winfield. The situation was described by E.M. Swift (1988) as follows:

> Ah, baseball. In the Bronx. It's comforting to know that some things in this crazy world never change. As the New York Yankees wrapped up dress rehearsals and took their sideshow north for the opening of the 1988 campaign, all your favorite characters were already in midseason form. At center stage was the Boss, George Steinbrenner, and his $1.9 million nemesis, Dave Winfield. [Player] Willie Randolph was thrust reluctantly into the spotlight, too. [Manager] Billy Martin chirped in with a brief lecture about ethics in literature, and [player] Don Mattingly joined the chorus, crying foul .... Yes sports fans, another season of mudslinging and enmity is here .... The Yankees — and this has been overlooked amid all the lovely verbiage — went 22-10 this spring and are confident that this is their year ... "What irks me is we've got really good chemistry on this team," says Winfield. I still have ability. And, I think, respect. We can talk later about these other issues. The mission in my mind is to win. (pp. 36-38)

Although it seems like a contradiction for enmity to coexist with good chemistry on a team, it is possible. Cohesion in sport groups is made up of many elements — it is multidimensional in nature. And, each of these elements contributes in different ways to group interactions and group effectiveness. Social cohesion is the force that binds the group together into a socially, harmonious unit. Undoubtedly, this has some relationship to performance effectiveness but the relationship isn't perfect. A team may be more pleasant when there isn't any conflict or tension but it isn't necessarily more productive. In the case of cohesion, as is the case personality, it is necessary to determine what factor is important in the specific situations.

15 The Antecedents and Consequences of Group Cohesion

A popular assumption in sport groups has been that cohesiveness in its many forms — togetherness, team spirit, closeness, teamwork, team unity — is a direct **cause** of team effectiveness. A quote by Alvin Zander (1974) helps to illustrate this perspective:

> *In spite of the individual athletes who make headlines when they strike off for themselves, team spirit is the rule rather than the exception in sports. In fact, both amateurs and professionals generally feel that a team can't become a winner without it.* (p. 65)

Another belief, however, is that togetherness, team spirit, and closeness are more of a *consequence* of team success than a cause. This is the view advanced by John Madden, a former coach of the Oakland Raiders football team:

> *The more the Raiders won, the closer the team got. In any sport, success breeds togetherness. But don't be fooled, togetherness doesn't breed success. If a bad team tries to develop togetherness, that's nice; but it's still a bad team. Take the Pittsburgh Pirates. When they won the 1979 World Series, they were "family", they were a good team. But when the Pirates dropped out of contention after that, they weren't family anymore. They were a bad team — that's why they weren't a family.* (Madden and Anderson, 1986, p. 212)

A third perception, one contained in the quote which introduced this chapter, is that the value of being cohesiveness (being close-knit) is *dependent on the*

> **I knew that there was something like a country club atmosphere around the Leafs that had to be changed. They were a close-knit group ... If they'd been contenders, being close-knit would have been great. But they were a solid ninth-place team. (Imlach & Young, 1982, p. 135)**

level of team performance. Punch Imlach suggested that if the team had been a contender, the cohesiveness present would have been beneficial. Because it wasn't, he felt that the togetherness was detrimental.

And, finally, there is even support for the suggestion that cohesiveness, closeness, and togetherness might be *irrelevant* in some instances. The essence of this perspective is that some teams with unity, closeness, and togetherness are successful, others are not. In contrast, some teams that are characterized by friction and tension are successful, others are not. In his description of the German rowing eights, Hans Lenk (1969) portrayed a team that was riddled with friction and tension and yet was a world champion:

> *Several times conflict almost led to the destruction of the team ... no performance detriment as a result of the tensions within the group was noticeable. But there should have occurred a performance decrement in comparison with the initial situation ... At best there could have been only a small performance increase. Actually, the performance did increase and paralleled the sharpness of the conflict during the two years in which the eight existed ... The team became unbeaten Olympic champions.*

It should be obvious that the relationship of cohesiveness to group effectiveness in sport groups is highly complex. It may be a benefit, a detriment, dependent on performance, or irrelevant. In order to better understand the complexity of cohesiveness and discuss its causes and consequences in a systematic manner in this chapter, an overall frame-of-reference is used. It is presented in Figure 15.1.

This frame-of-reference begins with the premise that a large number of factors contribute to the development of group cohesiveness (Carron, 1982). Some of these exist in the situation, others the individual brings to the group, others are a product of the leadership, and still others build within the group as a unit. Another premise of this conceptual frame-of-reference is that there are two general categories of consequences of group cohesiveness. One of these is related to the impact of cohesiveness on group's products and the the second is related to the impact of cohesiveness on individual products.

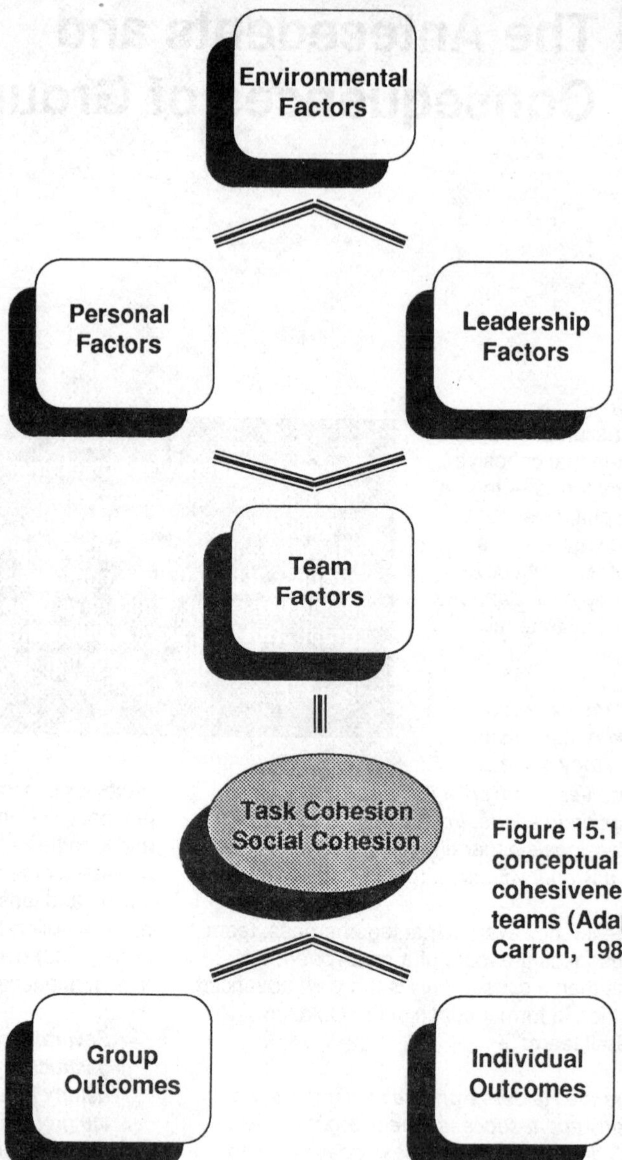

Antecedents of Cohesiveness

Situational Factors

The most general category of factors which contribute to cohesiveness are environmental — they exist in the situation itself (see Table 15.1). One of these, *contractual responsibilities*, consists of eligibility and/or transfer rules, geographical restrictions, and the contractual obligations which exist in professional and amateur sport. Contractual responsibilities are one major difference between a social group and a sport team. Members can leave social groups if they wish; they cannot do so in most sport situations if they wish to continue participating.

There are also *normative pressures* associated with cohesiveness. These are a product of our society's low regard for "quitters". Quitters are considered irrespon-

Figure 15.1 A general conceptual system for cohesiveness in sport teams (Adapted from Carron, 1982)

sible and undependable. Consequently, once an individual joins a group, there are pressures on him/her to maintain involvement.

A third situational factor which contributes to the development of cohesiveness is the *organization's orientation*. Organizations differ in their goals, strategies for achieving those goals, and the age, sex, and maturity of their members. Little League and professional baseball are good examples of two types of organizations which differ in organizational orientation. It could be predicted that there would be differences in the amount of task and social cohesion present between teams at these two levels.

Geographical factors such as physical and functional proximity also contribute to group cohesiveness. When team members are physically close to one another in playing position or locker location, for example, they become closer. This is due to the increased opportunities to interact and communicate about task and social issues. The classic study which is often used to illustrate this point was reported by Festinger, Schachter, & Back (1950, 1963). In the late 1940s, they studied the social patterns of married students attending MIT and living in the communities of Westgate and Westgate West. Their measure of cohesiveness was the question "What three people in Westgate or Westgate West do you see most of socially? (Festinger et al. 1950/1963, p. 37). By considering the courts and buildings within the community as individual groups, Festinger and his colleagues were able to compare the proportion of in-group to out-group choices. Physical proximity was found to be the major contributor to the development of friendships within the communities.

The *size of the group* also influences the development of group cohesion. Larger groups can be an advantage. They have more members available with the expertise, skills, and/or motivation necessary to complete the group's task. On the other hand, in large groups it is more difficult to communicate with all group members, coordinate the team's activities, and insure that everyone has an equal chance to compete. Thus, there is an optimal group size for the development of task cohesion, social cohesion, and team performance.

A study by Widmeyer, Brawley, & Carron (1988) illustrated this point. Recreational basketball players were matched on ability and then put into teams of 3 members, 6 members, or 9 members. The groups practiced for two weeks prior to competing in a 3-on-3 basketball league. Measurements of cohesion prior to the season showed that task cohesive was greatest in the 3-person groups and least in the 9-person groups. There were no differences in the amount of social cohesion. During the 7-week season which followed, the teams played 2 games each week. Measurements taken at the end of the season showed the same pattern for task cohesion. However, the 6-person teams were the most socially cohesive followed by the 3-person and then the 9-person groups. This same

Table 15.1 Environmental (situational) factors contributing to the development of group cohesion

Factor	Reference
Contractual responsibilities including geographical restrictions, eligibility rules, legal contracts, transfer rules	Carron (1982)
Social pressures against quitting, droping out, letting the team down	Carron (1982)
Organizational orientation including goals and strategies, age and sex, and maturity of the members	Carron (1982)
Size of the group	Hare (1952) Widmeyer et al (1988)
Geographical factors including physical and functional proximity	Festinger et al (1950) Kipnis (1957)

curvilinear relationship was found for performance with the 6-person groups being the most successful, then the 3-person, and then the 9-person (see Figure 3.3).

What these result show is that it's easiest to obtain consensus on the groups goals, objectives, and strategies for play in smaller groups. Consequently, task cohesion is stronger. When it comes to performance, however, the smallest groups don't have enough resources to compete successfully against moderately sized groups. And, the groups that are too large are not overly successful because it's difficult to coordinate the talents of all members and use them effectively. So moderately sized groups are best. Moderately sized groups are also best for group cohesion from a social perspective. It was pointed out in Chapter 3 that one advantage of larger groups is that they provide greater opportunities to meet attractive and interesting others. But, if the group becomes too large, strong social relationships can develop within subsets of individuals rather than within the group as a whole.

Personal Factors

As Figure 15.1 illustrates, a second category of factors which contributes to the development of group cohesion is the characteristics of the group members. A summary is presented in Table 15.2. One general factor is similarity in *personal attributes* of the individuals — attributes such as personality, social background, and the sex of the group members. Cohesiveness is enhanced when group members are similar in personality (Preston et al. 1952), and social background (Eitzen, 1975). As Stanley Eitzen pointed out, "the more alike the members of a group, the more positive the bond among the members .... This is usually explained by the assumption that internal differentiation on some salient characteristic such as religion, race, and socioeconomic status leads to greater likelihood of clique formation" (p. 41).

Another similar personal factor listed in Table 15.2 is the presence of *shared perceptions* including similarity in attitudes, beliefs, and motives. The relationship of similarity to cohesion was emphasized by Alvin Zander (1982) who observed that "birds of feather flock together, and create a more distinct entity when they do ... Persons whose beliefs do not fit together well have a hard time forming a strong group" (p. 3).

Attitude similarity seems to also operate in a reciprocal fashion with group cohesiveness. An initial similarity in attitudes increases the likelihood that individuals will come together and develop group cohesiveness. And, over time, the group's work, experiences together, and cohesiveness increase the degree to which individual members adopt similar attitudes (Terborg, Castore, & DeNinno, 1976).

The *sex* of the participant is another personal attribute sometimes considered to be associated with the development of cohesiveness. The basic orientation of males and females toward competitive sport is different. Males most strongly endorse competition,

winning, and beating one's opponent whereas females most strongly endorse participating in the game, interacting with teammates and opponents, and socializing (Reis and Jelsma, 1978). Thus, males are expected to be higher in task cohesiveness, females in social cohesiveness. However, research has not borne this out. Widmeyer and Martens (1978) failed to find any sex differences in cohesiveness while Widmeyer et al. (1985) found that male team-sport athletes were higher in social cohesiveness than female team-sport athletes.

Finally, individual *satisfaction* with the task and social aspects of the group also contributes to cohesiveness. Rainer Martens and James Peterson (1971) proposed that cohesion, satisfaction, and performance are related to each other in a circular fashion. That is, the presence of cohesiveness contributes to team performance and, ultimately, to team success. In turn, success produces satisfaction in the individual athlete which leads to the development of a greater sense of cohesiveness. When Jean Williams and Colleen Hacker (1982) tested the cause-effect relationships among performance, cohesion, and satisfaction in women's intercollegiate field hockey teams, they did find support for the Martens and Peterson proposal.

Leadership Factors

The third major influence on the development of group cohesion is *leadership* — leader behavior, the decision style used, and coach-athlete compatibility (see Table 15.3). The interrelationship between the leader, subordinates, cohesiveness, and group performance is complex. For example, a group in mutiny or rebellion could be highly cohesive but would also be strongly oriented to perform poorly or contrary to the organization's goals. The leader is excluded from the group (Schachter, Ellertson, McBride & Gregory, 1951). This can occur in sport — at least in professional sport. Punch Imlach, a former coach and general manager in the National Hockey league commented that

Any group of players on any pro team — hockey, basketball, whatever — can get together and undermine the coach or manager to the point that he's fired. But it is mainly teams that are going nowhere anyway who have the time and inclination to do that. The winners work at their game, their profession, instead of shafting

---

Table 15.2 Member characteristics (personal) factors contributing to the development of group cohesion

Factor	Reference
Shared personal attributes including personality, social background, and sex	Preston et al (1952) Eitzen (1975) Widmeyer et al (1985)
Shared perceptions including including similarity in attitudes and motives	Terborg et al (1976) Carron (1982)
Individual satisfaction with the task and social aspects of the group and feelings of acceptance	Grand & Carron (1982) Martens & Peterson (1971) Dittes (1959)

Table 15.3 Leadership factors contributing to the development of group cohesion

Factor	Reference
Use of appropriate task-oriented behaviors by the leader including the clarifying of group goals and member roles	Anderson (1975) Schriesheim (1980) Raven & Reitsema (1957)
Leader communication including the appropriate provision of feedback for performance, appreciation of individual contributions, and the equitable use of rewards	Carron (1986) Biondo & Pirritano (1985) Phillips & D'Amico (1956)
Provision for involvement in decision making	Carron & Chelladurai (1981) Bovard (1951)

management. (Imlach & Young, 1982, p. 164)

One general aspect of leadership which is related to the development of group cohesion is the leader's *behavior*. In work groups which are by nature task-oriented, leader behaviors directed toward the completion of the task are most important. Clarifying the group goals and developing strategies that will be used to achieve these helps to produce a cohesive unit. So does insuring that there is role clarity in the group — that every group member clearly understands his/her role (e.g. Anderson, 1975; Raven & Rietsema, 1975).

Another related aspect of leadership that contributes to group relationship between cohesion and *communication* — communication increases cohesiveness and, in turn, the amount of communication relating to task and social issues increases as the group becomes more cohesive. In Chapter 13, the importance of communications from the leader relating to performance (feedback) and the establishment of a supportive environment (reward) were discussed. Recognition enhances athlete satisfaction. It's not surprising, given the links between satisfaction and cohesion, that the use of reward and feedback are also associated with the development of group cohesion (Biondo & Pirritano, 1985; Phillips & D'Amico, 1956).

The level of group cohesion present influences the specific type of leader behavior which is most effective. (Schriesheim, 1980). In groups that are low in cohesiveness, task-oriented behaviors produce better performance, greater role clarity, and higher individual satisfaction. In groups that are high in cohesiveness, person-oriented behaviors are better.

A third element in leadership that contributes to group cohesion is *decision style* (Bovard, 1951, Carron and Chelladurai, 1981). Specifically, a democratic (participative) decision style produces greater group cohesion than autocratic, consultive, or delegative approaches. Collective input into a decision provides group members with greater "ownership" of the decision and the group. A feeling develops that it "was our decision for our group".

Team Factors

The team factors associated with the development of group cohesiveness are summarized in Table 15.4. One of the more important is chronic (long term) team

Table 15.4 Team factors contributing to the development of group cohesion

Factor	Reference
Performance success over an extended period of time	Carron & Ball (1977) Salminen (1987)
Shared negative experiences including failure, frustration, and the perception of threat from an outside force	Kennedy & Stephen (1977) Pepitone & Kleiner (1957) Turner et al (1984)
Immediate competition success	Ruder & Gill (1982)
Group task	Carron & Chelladurai (1981)
Team stability	Carron (1980)
Communication	Plutchik (1981)
Group structure including high status consensus, role differentiation, satisfaction, and conformity to the group norms	Plutchik (1981) Schriesheim (1980) Shelley (1960)

success. This is consistent with the opinion offered by John Madden which was presented earlier in this chapter — "in any sport, success breeds togetherness (Madden and Anderson, 1986, p. 212). Madden also went on to say, however, that "togetherness doesn't breed success (p. 212). Most group dynamicists wouldn't agree with this either-or position. They would accept the suggestion, however, that there is a stronger tendency for performance success leading to cohesion than for cohesion leading to performance success.

A research strategy which has been used to examine this issue involves the use of a *cross-lagged correlational design* (see Figure 15.2). Repeated measures are obtained for cohesion and performance throughout a season. Correlations are then computed between the various measures and compared. Thus, if the correlation r1 is greater than the correlation r2, it could be concluded that there is a stronger tendency for performance to lead to cohesion, not the reverse. As Table 15.5 shows, the vast majority of work with sport groups has supported this conclusion.

Although it is easy to appreciate that success can produce feelings of togetherness, it's less obvious how failure or some other *shared negative experience* can also do so. But this is the case (e.g., Kennedy & Stephan, 1977). Certainly, not every negative experience leads to increased cohesiveness. But, there are many instances where adversity, failure, threats from outside, and frustration serve to draw groups closer together. England after the Battle of Dunkirk and

during the Battle of Britain is one example. The entire population drew together for a common purpose. They shared a common highly emotional experience and developed a stronger sense of "we/us" clearly distinct from "they/them".

Turner, Hogg, Turner, and Smith (1984) have offered an explanation for this phenomena which evolves from the research on social categorization and forced compliance. *Social categorization* involves attaching labels to people or putting them into categories. Research has shown that simply being defined as a group member (prior to any contact or involvement) is sufficient for an individual to feel attracted to a group. Recruits who have never attended a practice or played a game with a team will begin to feel that they have the same interests, characteristics, and values as team members. When those recruits eventually join the team (and their claim to the label or social categorization becomes even stronger), their commitment to the group also increases. When commitment is extremely high, a negative experience can serve as a catalyst to enhance cohesiveness (e.g., England during the Battle of Britain).

In *forced compliance situations,* the individual must behave in accordance with some standard or rule. Research has shown that when this happens, there is a tendency to adopt private attitudes that are consistent with the public behavior. When there is a feeling of personal responsibility and the resulting behavior leads to negative consequences, there is an even greater tendency to shift personal attitudes in line with the behavior. What all of this means is that when individuals hold a strong perception (attitude) that they are members of a group — they perceive themselves in the category "group member" and are willingly acting on its behalf. — and the costs of their actions are high, their sense of commitment to that group is enhanced. To draw on the Battle of Britain example again, the population was forced to use food stamps and ration what they used. Hardships resulted. This didn't lead to riots and protests but, rather, to an attitude that the deprivation was appropriate given the nature of the times.

Turner et al. have offered another example which helps to illustrate this mechanism:

> If one is a Christian in the Roman empire, knows that a likely outcome is being thrown to the lions, chooses to continue being a Christian, and that outcome eventuates, then at least before being eaten one should tend to

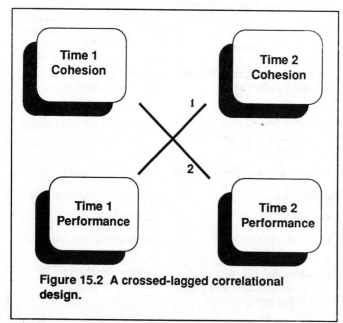

Figure 15.2 A crossed-lagged correlational design.

Time 1 Cohesion

Time 2 Cohesion

1

2

Time 1 Performance

Time 2 Performance

justify and
explain one's
actions in
terms of one's
definition of
oneself as a
Christian
(which should
be enhanced
as a result).
(p. 98)

Table 15.5 Summary of the studies comparing the strength of relationship betwee cohesion leading to performance versus performance leading to cohesion			
Reference	Sample	Results	Important Variables
Carron & Ball (1977)	Ice hockey players	A stronger relationship was present for performance leading to cohesion	Enjoyment, influence, value of membership, sense of belonging
Salminen (1987)	Ice hockey players	A stronger relationship was present for performance leading to cohesion	A composite index of the Sport Cohesiveness Questionnaire
Landers et al (1982)	Basketball players	A stronger relationship was present for cohesion leading to performance	Friendship
Williams & Hacker (1982)	Field hockey players	A stronger relationship was present for performance leading to cohesion	Teamwork, closeness
Shangi & Carron (1987)	Basketball players	A stronger relationship was present for performance leading to cohesion	Task cohesion and social cohesion

A similar process can occur in sport teams when an unexpected, divestating defeat occurs. The media and fans are critical and often look for scapegoats. Psychologically, the team then "circles the wagons" to withstand the threats, criticisms, and pressures directed against it. An example of this occurred in the 1988 Stanley Cup playoffs. After leading the league in the regular season, the Calgary Flames were defeated in four straight games in a quarter final series. A newspaper account at the time commented that:

Some disgruntled fans may already be calling them the Shames, but the Calgary Flames aren't ashamed of anything.... "We have nothing to be ashamed of," Coach Terry Crisp reminded his players ... "It was a four-game sweep, but we were in every game .... There will be a lot of analyzing why the league's top regular-season team came to such a sour end just nine games into the playoffs. Fingers will be pointed at [the] forwards ... who failed to score the way they had all season. More fingers will point at a power play that went from the league's best to pitifully anemic and at [the] goaltender ... who never came up with a really big save when his team needed it most. But those fingers, said team leader Lanny McDonald, will be pointed only by people outside Calgary's dressing room. "It's a team effort out there. You all take credit when you win and you all take the blame when you lose". (London Free Press, 1988, p. C-1)

Turner et al., in two laboratory studies, tested their proposition that perceptions of commitment and perceived responsibility help to account for increased cohesiveness after a defeat. In one study, they manipulated the degree of choice individuals had about doing a group task as well as the success and failure experienced. A second study was similar except that individual commitment to the group was manipulated. It was found that the failures produced greater cohesion than the successes when group members had a high degree of choice about their behavior or a high commitment to their membership in the group. On the other hand, lower cohesiveness was produced when choice and commitment were low.

It should be reemphasized that not every defeat serves to increase the level of group cohesion in sport groups. In the introduction to this section, it was pointed out that teams that experience consistent success over the course of a regular season are stronger in cohesion than teams that experience consistent failure. A gradual change occurs over time. The *immediate outcome* can also influence cohesiveness. Unless the competition is particularly critical, however, game-to-game fluctuations because of winning and losing are generally minimal — particularly if the team is stable and well established.

This was illustrated in a study by Karen Ruder and

Diane Gill (1982) which examined the immediate effects of winning and losing in intramural and intercollegiate volleyball teams. In the intercollegiate teams, no differences were found in cohesiveness from pregame to postgame as a result of winning versus losing. Ruder and Gill pointed out that "more stable teams (such as the intercollegiate teams) are more likely to have an established level of cohesion and thus are less susceptible to the influence of a single game win or loss" (p. 233).

Ruder and Gill did find that the outcome had an influence on the cohesiveness of intramural teams, however. Cohesiveness was assessed with a number of different measures; the ones showing the greatest effect were closeness, teamwork and a direct measure ("how would you rate the cohesion of your team?"). The winners increased their ratings for teamwork, closeness, and cohesion. On the other hand, the losers decreased their ratings of teamwork and cohesion but showed an increase in closeness (the increase was less than that shown by the winners). It was pointed out by way of explanation that "spontaneously formed teams, which most intramural teams are, consist of players who participate voluntarily, meet occasionally, and have socially oriented goals, all contributing to less stability of structure" (p. 233).

Ruder and Gill's findings for the intramural teams are not inconsistent with the propositions (and results) of Turner et al. Following a loss, players might reasonably perceive that their teamwork and coordination was poor and yet reaffirm their group membership by increasing their ratings of closeness. (To borrow the Turner et al. analogy, two Christians who faced two lions might rate their teamwork and coordination lower after the match. On the other hand, they might feel closer for having gone through the experience together!)

The *group task* is another team factor which influences the development of (or even the necessity for) cohesion (see Table 15.4 again). Cohesion is fundamentally "togetherness" — either in a social or task sense. Consequently, it can be argued that togetherness is more important in sports where cooperation is essential for effective group coordination. This point was discussed in detail in Chapter 2 (see Figure 2.2 again). After conducting an analysis of research concerned with task structure and cooperation versus competition, Miller and Hamblin (1963) concluded that performance is most effective with intragroup cooperation when high task interdependence is required. Volleyball, basketball, soccer — in fact most team sports — are characterized by high task interdependence. Miller and Hamblin also concluded that performance with intragroup competi-

tion was most effective in situations where high task independence is required. Wrestling, bowling, archery are characterized by high task independence.

The results from a study concerned with cohesion in bowling teams are consistent with this perspective (Landers and Lueschen, 1974). The most effective teams in terms of success had the lowest levels of group cohesion. Possibly if members become too concerned with the welfare or the feelings of other group members in sports where task independence is required, it detracts from their own performance. Rivalry may produce the best performance.

It is generally assumed that *team stability* — longevity and the duration of time that members have spent together — is another team factor that contributes to group cohesiveness. Although there is no direct evidence for this assumption, it does seem reasonable. For example, being in close physical proximity contributes to increased cohesiveness. Increased opportunities to communicate lead to increased cohesiveness. More involvement in task and social interactions results in greater cohesiveness. Feelings of acceptance by the group and sharing similar beliefs and attitudes are associated with greater cohesiveness. In short, a large number of variables which increase or improve with time are directly related to the increases in cohesiveness. Therefore, the greater the stability of the team, the stronger will be the feelings of togetherness.

One of the leader factors contributing to cohesiveness was *communication* (see Table 15.3). It is also one of the group or team factors which helps to draw group members together (Plutchik, 1981). Through communication and the the exchange of ideas, group members come to possess similar beliefs, hold similar attitudes and increase the pressures on conformity to the group norms.

A group's *permeability* — the degree to which it is open to other groups — has an influence on cohesiveness. Groups that become socially and physically isolated (less permeable) draw upon their own membership to fulfill important psychological needs. Communication and interaction occur predominantly or exclusively within the group. Consequently, the group becomes more cohesive

The final team factor listed in Table 15.4 is *group structure*. When individuals first come together to form a group, little or nor structure exists. Gradually through interaction and communication, differences emerge as various positions are filled, a status hierarchy evolves, members adopt or are assigned different roles, and group norms develop concerning expectations for behavior. The development of this group structure is closely allied to the development of group cohesiveness. Not surprisingly, when there is consensus on group status, cohesiveness is improved (e.g., Shelley, 1960). Similarly, groups with high role differentiation (i.e., individual members have different specialized functions), more readily develop group cohesiveness (Plutchik, 1981). Thus, a volleyball team in which each member carries out equally the role of setter and spiker is not likely to be as cohesive as a team in which these roles are differentiated and filled by different individuals.

Implications for the Effectiveness of Sport Groups

Cohesion is a group property — a dynamic, evolving property that helps to account for the fact that groups stick together and remain united in the pursuit of their goals and objectives. The discussion in this chapter serves to highlight the fact that there are a wide variety of factors associated with the development of group cohesiveness. These were categorized under four headings: situational, personal, leadership, and team factors. It should be pointed out that these categories were used because they made it easier to discuss this complex topic. They were not intended to represent fixed, permanent groupings. For example, group size and geographical factors, two elements discussed within the category of situational factors could just as easily have been included under the category of team factors because they influence the development of cohesion in the total group.

It should also be pointed out that these four categories should not be viewed as independent or unrelated. For example, leadership behavior and individual satisfaction are both associated with the development of group cohesion. They also have an influence on each other. So, while they were presented separately, in performing groups they are interwoven. In short, the situational factors, personal factors, leadership factors, and team factors combine in a complex fashion to produced a more cohesive group.

Table 15.6 Techniques for team building (Adapted from Zander, 1982)

Category	Elements
Team Identity	Situate individuals in close proximity Physically separate the team from other teams Provide the team with unique identifiers such as logos, songs, flags, & uniforms Emphasize the unique history and traditions of the team Rcognize the importance of pride in the team and develop its sources
Team Structure	Develop a team structure in which there is a clear differentiation in team roles Clarify role expectations for members Establish consensus on status differences in the team Provide for team involvement in the selection of team leaders
Team Goals	Set clear and realistic goals Emphasize team rather than individual goals Clarify how adherence to team standards facilitates team effectiveness Establish pride in the team by assessing and providing feedback on the achievement of team goals Promote cooperation, discourage individual rivalry
Team Motives	Help individuals identify personal needs and goals and clarify how these can be satisfied in a team context Encourage significant team members to make sacrifices for the team Instill in each team member a sense of responsibility for the team's success

In business and industry, it has been recognized (a) that cohesion is complex, (b) that it has an impact on group productivity and employee morale, and (c) that it doesn't necessarily develop maximally without direct intervention. As a result, over the past 20 years, programs have emerged which have as their specific purpose, the improvement of the organization's effectiveness. These programs are included under the broad umbrella term of organizational development (OD). One OD program which has been used successfully is referred to as *team building*. A summary of the major strategies used in team building is presented in Table 15.6. In his book, **Making groups effective,**

Alvin Zander (1982) has presented a number of specific intervention strategies which can be used to develop a stronger, more cohesive team. These are also summarized in Table 15.6.

One of the most fundamental strategies is to develop a sense of *team identity*. As Table 15.6 shows, there are many different approaches which can be used to achieve this objective. Some represent geographical considerations such as situating individuals in close proximity to each other and/or physically separating the team from other teams. Others involve focusing on or developing team uniqueness — through uniforms, songs, history and tradition and so on. A wide variety of strategies are possible. What they possess in common is an attempt to highlight the distinctiveness of the group and to foster a sense of "we".

Not surprisingly, clarifying the *group's structure* also serves to enhance the cohesiveness of the group. It was pointed out in Section 4 that the four elements of structure are position, status, roles, and norms. The examples presented in Table 15.6 all relate to the development of one of these four elements.

Another set of strategies outlined in Table 15.6 pertains to *team goals*. Work groups and teams are task-oriented groups. Goal setting has proved to be an effective motivator for task-oriented groups. The activities listed in Table 15.6 which are related to the setting of clear, realistic team goals are also associated with the development of a stronger group.

Team communication also enhances group cohesion. Some of the approaches which can be used to improve communication include encouraging members to contribute their ideas for improving team functioning, insuring that team members know each other's roles, duties, and responsibilities, and providing a practice and dressing room environment that's conducive to open communication.

The final consideration presented in Table 15.6 is *team motivation*. Individual team members are motivated personally. What also must be developed and continually reinforced is a motivation for the team to do well. Approaches which center on the importance of the team and its success also help to enhance cohesiveness.

Consequences of Cohesiveness

Group Outcomes

When cohesiveness is present in groups, it contributes to some important group outcomes. An overview of these is provided in Table 15.7. One of the factors which might seem surprising given the earlier discussions is *performance success*. It was pointed out in the section on the antecedents of cohesiveness that there is a stronger relationship for performance contributing to cohesiveness than the reverse. This is the case. When groups are highly successful, their members feel very close to one another. But, there is also a relationship between cohesion and performance. Cohesive groups work harder toward the achievement of the group's goal; they are more successful.

Table 15.8 presents a summary of research carried out with sport teams. There are studies in which no effect was found and other studies in which low cohesion was associated with better performance. Nonetheless, the overall pattern of results does support a conclusion that when groups are more cohesive, they are more effective.

Sport and physical activity groups that are more cohesive are also more *stable* and this stability is manifested in a variety of ways.. One measure which represents stability is drop out behavior. Highly cohesive groups retain members better than groups that are low in cohesion. Even in exercise classes —

Table 15.7 Group outcomes associated with the presence of cohesion	
Factor	**Reference**
Improved performance including greater effort toward the achievement of group goals	**Widmeyer & Gossett (1981) Ball & Carron (1976) Shaw (1981)**
Team stability including increased adherence and reduced absenteeism and resistance to group disruption	**Carron et al (1986) Robinson & Carron (1982) Brawley et al (1988)**
Improved interaction and communication	**Lott & Lott (1961)**
Increased self-deception including the overevaluation of within team processes and products and the underevaluation of processes and products from outside	**Ross & Sicoly (1979) Sherif & Sherif (1969)**

where the sense of being in a group generally is not heavily promoted — there are less drop outs in more cohesive groups. In a study which examined this issue, Carron, Widmeyer, & Brawley (1988) compared the perceptions of cohesiveness in adherers and nonadherers in exercise classes and elite sport teams. The drop outs in both situations rated their groups much lower in both task and social cohesiveness than the individuals who maintained involvement.

Two other measures of team stability are absenteeism and punctuality. In a second study, Carron et al. explored the relationship between individual perceptions of cohesiveness and absenteeism and lateness in summer recreation sport league. The perception of cohesiveness had an influence on the group's stability. But, in this instance, however, social cohesion was the most important. The participants who tended to either arrive late or not show up for practices and games had a substantially lower perception of their team's social cohesion than participants who were never absent or late.

A third measure of team stability is the group's ability to resist the negative impact of disruptive events. Cohesive groups can tolerate a great deal of adversity and still maintain a strong bond. On the other hand, groups that are low in cohesiveness, begin to lose members when they are faced with negative circumstances. With very weak groups, the adversity could even be minimal but still be sufficient to cause a breakup.

Resistance to disruption is a difficult phenomena to test in a scientific way. First of all, it occurs very infrequently. And, it's not possible (for ethical reasons) to cause disruptions in laboratory or natural groups.

Table 15.8 An overview of studies examining the cohesion-performance relationship in sport groups

Authors	Sample	Important Variables
Studies Showing Higher Cohesion Leads to Better Performance		
Arnold & Straub (1972)	College Basketball	Teamwork closeness
Carron & Ball (1976)	College ice hockey	Teamwork, closeness, enjoyment
Carron & Chelladurai (1981)	High school basketball	Sense of belonging, value of membership, enjoyment
Carron & Chelladurai (1981)	High school wrestling	Sense of belonging, value of membership, enjoyment
Landers, Wilkinsopn, Hatfield, & Barber (1982)	Intramural basketball	Friendship
Shangi & Carron (1987)	High school basketball	Task cohesion, social cohesion
Williams & Hacker (1982)	College field hockey	Teamwork, closeness, enjoyment, belonging, value of membership
Studies Showing No Relationship Between Cohesion and Performance		
Williams & Hacker (1982)	College field hockey	
Melnick & Chemers (1974)	Intramural basketball	
Studies Showing that Lower Cohesion Leads to Better Performance		
Landers & Lueschen (1974)	Intramural bowling	Attraction
Lenk (1969)	International rowers	Attraction
McGrath (1962)	Rifle shooting	Attraction

Finally, a disruptive force for one group may not be a disruption for another. One possible solution used by Brawley, Carron, and Widmeyer (1988) was to assess the impact of *hypothetical* as opposed to *real* disruptive forces. Participants on sport teams provided a list of events/actions that they believed would disrupt their team *if they were to happen*. The participants were then asked to rate how severe each of those disruptions would be for the group. Finally, the participants were required to rate the degree of resistance their group would put up if any of the negative events actually occurred.

Over 2/3 of the potential disruptions were associated with some aspect of the task (e.g., losing all the time); the remainder were social in nature (e.g., team members don't get along). The group members' perceptions of their group's ability to resist the adverse factors were directly associated with their perceptions of cohesiveness. Group members who were high in task and social cohesiveness were more confident that their group was capable of overcoming the disruptions.

Another outcome of cohesiveness which is listed in Table 15.7 is increased *interaction and communication*. This factor was also discussed in the previous section as an antecedent of group cohesion. Increased opportunities to interact and communicate serve to bind the group closer together. At the same time, when groups become more cohesive, their members also tend to interact and communicate more — the relationship is cyclical.

The basis for the cohesion is an important consideration in order for the interaction and communication to contribute to group effectiveness. If social cohesion is predominant, the interactions and communication will reflect this; if task cohesion predominates, the interactions and communication will reflect this also.

In a study which illustrates this point, Back (1951) used experimental manipulations to create six groups — three high in cohesion and three low in cohesion. The cohesiveness was either based on interpersonal attraction, attraction to the task, or the prestige of the group. Members of the low cohesive groups generally worked alone while members of the high cohesive groups worked together on the task. However, the prevalent interactions and communications in the three high cohesive groups were quite different. When cohesion was based on interpersonal attraction, the group members tended to converse about things not associated with the task. In those groups where cohesion was based on attraction to the task, the group members tended to work quickly and efficiently. And, finally, in groups where the cohesion was based on the group's prestige, the chief concerns were on maintaining that prestige.

The *perception of the group* also becomes distorted when cohesiveness is high. There is a tendency toward self-deception. Group members, their accomplishments, behaviors, and performances are overvalued while those of opponents are undervalued or underestimated. The tendency to look inward and engage in self deception could produce difficulties for a newly appointed leader of a cohesive team (Jewell & Reitz, 1981). If the former coach was an integral part of that cohesive group, the new coach might be considered inferior in ability or personality. And any proposed changes to established team customs or practices could be met with resistance.

Individual Outcomes

Not only does group cohesion have an influence on the group as a whole, it also has an impact on individual members. Humans are social by nature and being with "my group" is psychologically reassuring. Research has shown that cohesion can have a positive impact on various *psychological states* including self esteem, feelings of trust, and security, and openness to change. Group cohesion also contributes to reduced anxiety (see Table 15.9). Consider the following story told by Bobby Bragan, a member of the Brooklyn Dodgers, during the period that Jackie Robinson broke baseball's color line:

> Those early days were awfully tough on Jackie. I remember times on the train when nobody would sit with him or talk with him. Pee Wee [Reese] always seemed to be the first to break the tension. He kidded Jackie before anyone else did and made him a part of the team. He was probably the first Dodger to have a meal with him off the field. Pee Wee was a real leader on our club, and when he started being friendly with Jackie everybody started being friendly. In the beginning Jackie was alone at the dinning table. By the middle of the year you couldn't get a seat at the dining table with him, there were so many guys. (Bobby Bragan, quoted in Allen, 1987, pp. 102-103)

The positive psychological outcomes resulting from the presence of supportive teammates can be readily appreciated simply by imagining, from Jackie Robinson's perspective, the differences on the Dodgers from early to late in the season. The prejudice and bigotry Jackie faced from other teams didn't simply disappear. But the feeling of being totally alone even on his own team was substantially reduced which made it easier for him to withstand the outside pressures.

One of the antecedents for cohesion discussed earlier was *group structure* — when the structure of a team becomes more formalized, it helps to bring group members together into a closer unit. Improved group structure is also a by-product of cohesion. role clarity, role acceptance, and role performance are improved as the team's cohesion becomes stronger (Grand & Carron, 1982). There is also greater conformity to the group norms. More cohesive groups are able to exert greater pressure on individual members to adhere to the group standards (Schachter, Ellertson, McBride, & Gregory, 1951).

Another by product of group cohesion is *individual satisfaction*. Individuals on cohesive teams find the experience more satisfying than individuals who participate on less cohesive teams (Williams & Hacker, 1982).

Finally, groups, like individuals, attempt to make sense out of events that effect them. Two relatively persistent patterns have emerged when the attributions used in problem-solving groups have been analyzed. First, members of successful groups have a greater tendency to assume more absolute responsibility for the group's performance than do members of unsuccessful groups. Second, members of successful groups perceive that their relative contribution is greater than the "average" group member whereas members of unsuccessful groups perceive that their relative contribution is less than average (Carron, 1980). An egocentric pattern of attributions is prevalent— "it's not my fault if we lose; I deserve considerable credit if we win"

The *attributions* group members make for themselves and for the group are influenced by group cohesion — particularly in failure situations. If the group is low in cohesiveness, the same egocentric pattern emerges; individuals attribute a large portion of the responsibility for the group's lack of success to other members. On the other hand, if the group is high in cohesiveness, group members strive to be fair. Consequently, they accept the fact that they are as responsible as the average group member for the group's shortcomings (Brawley et al., 1987). This topic is discussed in greater depth in Chapter 17 (see Table 17.6).

Implications for the Effectiveness of Sport Groups

Group cohesiveness represents the unity and togetherness which exist in teams. There seems to be little doubt that in any endeavors which require a concerted effort from a collection of individuals, cohesiveness is a positive force. A group becomes more effective if there is consensus among its members about what it is trying to accomplish and about how it can best do so. This notion is embedded in the very definition of cohesion — a dynamic process which is reflected in the tendency for a group to stick together and remain united in the pursuit of its goals and objectives.

But as Marvin Shaw (1981) has pointed out "despite the apparently obvious nature of this conclusion about cohesiveness and productivity, a considerable amount of research has been devoted to determining whether it is valid" (p. 222). Shaw also pointed out "the problem often is that groups do not set the same goals for themselves that outside agencies ... set for them. Hence a cohesive group may achieve its own goals but be relatively unproductive with regard to the goals [set by outside agencies]" (pp. 222-223).

The challenge in sport groups is to obtain an accurate reading on the predominant goals and objectives of the group. If the group's goals and objectives are not considered to be consistent with those of the larger organization (which are usually associated with productivity, achievement, success), a change of focus is necessary. How can this be brought about?

Table 15.9 **Individual outcomes associated with the presence of group cohesiveness**

Factor	Reference
Improved personal states including increased self esteem, trust, feelings of security, openness to change, and reduced anxiety	Julian et al (1966) Pepitone & Reichling (1955) Braver (1975) Cartwright (1982)
Increased role clarity, role acceptance, and role performance	Grand & Carron (1982)
Increased group goal acceptance and conformity	Schachter et al (1951)
Increased satisfaction	Williams & Hacker (1982)
Increased tendency to share equally in the attribution of responsibility for unfavorable outcomes	Schlenker & Miller (1977) Brawley et al (1987)

Donelson Forsyth (1983), in a discussion on the dynamics of group change, recounted the results of research carried out by Kurt Lewin (1943) during World War II. Because of the shortages in beef, Lewin was asked by the National Research Council to develop a strategy for changing food preferences in the general population. A brief period of time was provided in which to convince volunteer homemakers to serve readily available but less desirable products to their families. Lewin set up an experimental situation in which two different approaches were tried. In the first, an attempt was made to change individual attitudes and behaviors. Groups of homemakers listened to a lecture that incorporated appeals to patriotism, information on the nutritional benefits of the alternate foods, and possible recipes. There was no interaction among the homemakers. In the second approach, an attempt was made to change the attitudes and behaviors of a group. Situations for group interaction were introduced in which the same information used in the lecture was discussed by groups of homemakers. The groups were then urged to reach consensus on an issue.

In a subsequent follow-up, Lewin found that 3% of the homemakers who had heard the lecture (the individual approach) had served the less desirable food products to their families. On the other hand, 32% of homemakers who had been involved in the group discussions, who worked to develop a consensual opinion (the group approach), had served at least one dish. Later, Lewin and his colleagues followed this work up with a number of other similar studies and found the same pattern of results. In summary, he concluded that "it's easier to change individuals formed into a group than to change them separately" (Lewin, 1951, p. 228, quoted in Forsyth, 1983).

An examination of the consequences of group cohesion clearly shows that it is an important group property worth developing. Although a number of strategies can be used with individual team members to persuade them of the significance and worth of the group, a group-centered approach is most effective.

6 Group Processes

There was one time when [Bobby] Orr and Phil Esposito were running neck-and-neck for the scoring championship. Time and again Bobby would find himself in excellent scoring position but instead of firing the puck he would look around for someone to pass to and often it was Phil. So, finally, I asked my defenseman Carol Vadnais what was going on with Bobby and why he was squandering potential points. "Don't you know?", he said. "He's trying not to get too far ahead of Phil for the scoring title". He risked the Art Ross Trophy [for the most scoring points] in order to make the team play better. (Cherry & Fischler, 1982, p. 163)

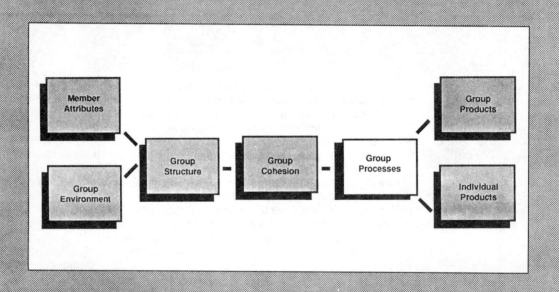

16 Group Motivation

Motivation is the term used to represent the reasons why certain actions are chosen over others, carried out with energy and enthusiasm, and adhered to with a high level of commitment. In short, motivation is the term used to account for the *selectivity*, the *intensity*, and the *persistence* in behavior (Carron, 1984). Surprisingly, despite its seemingly obvious importance, there is a great deal still unknown about when to use motivation in sport groups. For example, it is sometimes assumed that all athletes are motivated and that the coach doesn't have to be concerned with this issue. When Coach Jacques Martin was fired in 1988 by the St. Louis Blues, one of the reasons advanced was that he had not done an adequate job in motivating the team. One of his players, Doug Gilmour, countered, however, that "I don't think a coach has to do that all the time" (London Free Press, 1988, p. C1). Similarly, a former coach of the Toronto Maple Leafs, Mike Nykoluk, felt that it wasn't his responsibility to try to motivate his team — that his athletes were professionals and capable of motivating themselves.

There are other coaches and athletes who hold the opposite viewpoint, of course. In the quote used to introduce this chapter, Mychal Thompson of the Los Angeles Lakers emphasized the importance of goals and motivation for team success. He also stated that his coach, Pat Riley, had not only set out goals (as a motivator) for the current year but also for the next one as well. And, Punch Imlach, a former coach and general manager in the National Hockey League commenting on the Mike Nykoluk perspective suggested that:

Mike Nykoluk's idea that he didn't have to bother

> You need goals and motivation as a player. [Coach Pat Riley] set up this year's, and we're going after it ... we already have a goal set for next season. (Los Angeles Lakers player Mychal Thompson quoted by Jack McCallum, 1988, p. 57)

motivating players is wrong, terribly wrong .... The most important job of any coach is to motivate his players. If I'd been general manager when the ... Nykoluk quote was published I would have called Nykoluk in and asked if he had said what he was quoted as saying. If he answered yes, I would ask "Do you believe that? Or were you just talking for some guy to write a story about?" If he said he believed it, I would fire him. (Imlach & Young, 1982, pp. 206-207)

Another issue which sometimes surfaces is associated with differences between individual and group motivation. Alvin Zander (1982), in his book **Making groups effective**, noted that "persons who study group behavior commonly assume that a member's major interest is the benefits he personally will receive from belonging to his organization. Thus, he is more likely to join a group and remain there only if it provides outcomes he values for himself and if he believes that success by the group will increase these personal rewards" (p. 119).

Is group motivation some simple summation of the motives, needs, and aspirations of individual team members? The answer is "not necessarily". Alvin Zander also pointed out, there are many instances where individuals forgo or postpone personal rewards and accomplishments for the sake of their group. Individual members not only have personal goals, they also have goals for the group (see Figure 16.1). The parents of a large

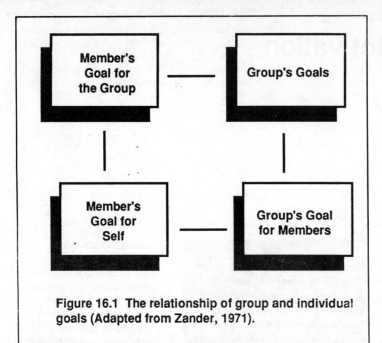

Member's Goal for the Group	Group's Goals
Member's Goal for Self	Group's Goal for Members

Figure 16.1 The relationship of group and individual goals (Adapted from Zander, 1971).

also conscious of avoiding open competition with each other in order to work toward team success (team goal), the overall benefits for the team would be even greater.

Individual Motivation

What are the factors that contribute to group motivation? Table 16.1 presents some of the more important ones. Not surprisingly, *individual motivation* tops the list. When each individual team member is highly motivated, the collective effort of the team is enhanced. Consequently, the factors that influence individual motivation will also have a spillover effect and enhance group motivation. A basketball team with 12 highly motivated individuals will be more effective *as a group* than another team with 12 poorly motivated individuals.

In an earlier book (Carron, 1984), I have discussed the factors that can influence individual motivation. There is little value (and insufficient space) to reproduce that whole discussion on individual motivation in this book. Instead, the focus here is on those factors which have been emphasized insofar as the *group* is concerned.

family are one example. Their concern for the welfare of their family can override any personal considerations. Placing the welfare of the group over personal concerns also happens frequently in sport. In the quote used to introduce this section, Don Cherry, a former coach of the Boston Bruins, recalled a period when Bobby Orr and Phil Esposito were in contention for the league scoring championship. Cherry suggested that Orr passed up good scoring opportunities because he felt that it would be detrimental for the overall good of the team if he got too far ahead in the scoring championship. Orr's motivation was not centered primarily or exclusively on personal rewards.

According to Zander, each group member has the choice of working for (1) a personal benefit, (2) the benefit of the team as a whole, (3) a personal benefit as well as a benefit for the group, and (4) none of these. He also pointed out that Options 1 and 2 (working for personal benefits, working for group benefits) could be directed toward similar goals. Consequently, if both were in operation at the same time, their combined effects would result in a stronger source of motivation than if either was present alone. In the anecdote told by Don Cherry, the motivation of Orr and Esposito to win the scoring championship represented their individual personal goal. If both athletes were

Table 16.1 Factors contributing to the development of group motivation

Factor	Reference
Individual motivation	Carron (1984)
Group desire to achieve group success and avoid group failure	Zander (1971) Zander (1985)
Group size (social loafing increases with increases in group size)	Kerr (1983) Latane' et al (1979)
Group goals	Locke & Latham (1984) Schnake & Cochan (1984)
Collective efficacy	Bandura (1982)
Intragroup interaction and communication	Emerson (1966)

Desire to Achieve Group Success and Avoid Group Failure

A conceptual model was developed by Alvin Zander (1971) in order to better understand the achievement motivation which develops in groups. An overview of the main elements is presented in Table 16.2. Zander proposed that when groups are in achievement situations, individual group members develop a *tendency to try for group success (Tgs)*.

As an example, in a cross-country meet, all the members of a school team have a personal motive to do well. But because team scores and placements are also recorded, individual members also develop an interest in the standing of the team. In some schools, this interest will be strong leading to a strong tendency to work hard for team goals while in others, it will be weaker. According to Zander, three factors have an influence on the strength of the tendency to try for group success: the desire for group success, the probability for group success, and the incentive value of group success. This can be expressed as a formula: Tgs = Dgs X Pgs X Igs.

The *desire for group success (Dgs)* represents the individual's concern for the group's welfare, the disposition to experience pride and satisfaction if the group is successful in accomplishing its goals and objectives. Zander (1985) emphasized that this is not a group-oriented motive, it's a desire for the group as a whole to do well. This desire for group success influences individual motivation and behavior. Team members are not only motivated to finish as high as possible for personal reasons, they are also concerned about doing well in order to contribute to the group's success.

The *perceived probability of group success (Pgs)* represents the likelihood that the group will achieve its goals and objectives. The members of the cross-country team may have a strong desire to win the team championship but also recognize that because of the caliber of the other teams present this is highly unlikely.

Some group goals and objectives are more important than others. The outcome of a regional meet, for example, has less prestige and importance attached to it than a national championship. Thus, the tendency to strive for group success is also influenced by the *incentive value of group success (Igs)*. The incentive and the probability are inversely related to each other; as one increases, the other decreases. The outcome of a regional meet has less incentive value but there is a higher probability of success than is the case in a national championship. Conversely, a national championship has a lower probability of success but greater incentive value.

Table 16.2 The bases for group-oriented achievement behavior (Adapted from Zander, 1971)

Factor	Description
Desire for Group Success (Dgs)	Members' concern for the group's welfare, the disposition to experience pride and satisfaction if the group is successful
Perceived Probability of Group Success (Pgs)	The subjective estimate by members that the group will achieve its goals and objectives
Incentive Value of Group Success (Igs)	The anticipation by members for the level of pride and satisfaction that will be experienced if the group is successful
Tendency to try for Group Success (Tgs)	The overall tendency for individual members to strive for the goals and objectives of the group
Desire to Avoid Group Failure (Dagf)	Members' disposition to experience shame and dissatisfaction if the group is unsuccessful
Perceived Probability of Group Failure (Pgf)	The subjective estimate by members that the group will not achieve its goals and objectives
Incentive value of group Failure (Igf)	The anticipation by members for the level of shame and dissatisfaction that will be experienced if the group is unsuccessful
Tendency to Avoid Group Failure (Tagf)	The overall tendency for members to resist engaging in activities because they could lead to failure

Table 16.3. Characteristic behaviors of group members in situations where the tendency to avoid group failure is predominant (Adapted from Zander, 1985)

Behavior	Example
Members engage in behaviors designed to avoid the embarrassment associated with group failure	"I'll have to miss practice again so it's going to be difficult for us to prepare adequately"
Goals chosen for the group are impossibly difficult so no shame results from not reaching them	"Although last year was a poor one, our goal this year is the state championship"
Members misrecall the group's performance so that it is evaluated more positively	"I'm not sure of the score. I think it was about 7-2"
Members attribute causes of performance ego-centrically and deny personal responsibility for failure	The team is doing poorly but I'm playing well personally".
Attributions for responsibility are made to factors external to the group; members conclude that the group's performance was acceptable "under the circumstances"	"We don't get as much practice time as other teams in the league"
Members remove or replace the group goals thereby eliminating or changing the criteria for success	"This is a party team. We may not play well but we have a good time"

Groups can also fail. And that failure can be embarrassing and dissatisfying. In fact, some groups may be so afraid of failing that they avoid certain situations; the potential embarrassment associated with failing is too great. A cross-country team that has a winning streak, for example, might avoid a particularly strong meet in order to keep its streak intact. In short, all achievement situations lead to the development of a *tendency to avoid group failure (Tagf)*. It is also the product of three factors: the *desire to avoid group failure (Dagf)*, the *probability of group failure (Pgf)*, and the *incentive value of group failure (Igf)*. The equation is similar to the one presented above: $Tagf = Dagf \times Pgf \times Igf$.

Since both the tendency to try for group success

and the tendency to avoid group failure are present in every situation, the group's resulting actions depend upon the relative strengths of the two $(Tgs - Tagf)$. On the one hand, if the tendency toward success is stronger, the members will work positively toward the achievement of group success and the resulting pride and satisfaction it will bring. On the other hand, if the tendency to avoid group failure is predominant, the members become preoccupied with avoiding the shame and dissatisfaction associated with group failure.

The behaviors and actions of group members in these two contrasting situations are dramatically different. Some of the characteristic behaviors which appear when groups fail and/or their members become preoccupied with avoiding failure are listed in Table 16.3.

For example, in a highly unsuccessful sport team, members may engage in behaviors which are designed to reduce the embarrassment associated with their involvement. One way this can be done is to physically or psychologically withdraw from the team. This can be achieved by quitting, missing and/or coming late to practices, over-emphasizing the severity of an injury to avoid practicing and competing, or performing with minimal motivation. In this way, the athlete becomes less a part of the team, and less responsible for the team's performance. Another way is to adopt unreasonably difficult goals for the team. There is minimal embarrassment when the team fails at an impossible task. A third approach involves the deliberate distortion or poor retention and recall of an outcome. These two actions are quite different. Deliberate distortion is practiced by a team member who is sufficiently involved with the team to feel embarrassment from the outcome. Poor retention and recall result when the member begins to lose interest in the group's performance.

The attributions for responsibility are also quite different in unsuccessful teams. This is clearly illustrated in a discussion by Punch Imlach about a highly unsuccessful season experienced by the Buffalo Sabres:

Being able to put your finger on what is wrong, and being able to do some-

thing about it, are two different things. I had private conversations with each player after the season ended. I didn't let them get into their views on the coach. Mostly, what I heard was what you hear from everyone when things go bad on a hockey team. "I did my job, but the other guys didn't do theirs". The old refrain. It made me remember one time years earlier when I had a lot of bitching on a team and I went into the dressing room and told each of the players to look at the guy on his right and say, "You're a bleep-bleep lousy hockey player!" Then do the same to the guy on his left. Then I told them that in case they were too stupid to realize it, every man in the room had someone who thought he was a bleep-bleep lousy hockey player. That was the Buffalo Sabres, by then, every one blaming everyone else. (Imlach & Young, 1982, p. 112).

In low-cohesive, unsuccessful teams, individual team members can become ego-centric in their perceptions of who is responsible (e.g., Iso-Ahola, 1977). Blame is either attributed to the poor performance of other team members — which was the case in Imlach's discussion of the Buffalo Sabres — or to some external factor which can't be controlled. Some examples of the latter would include poor equipment, inadequate practice facilities, a difficult travel schedule, poor coaching, and so on.

In the final example listed in Table 16.3, members either remove or replace the team's goals; the criteria for success are either ignored or changed. As a result, minimal shame and embarrassment are experienced. A highly unsuccessful team that develops the reputation for partying is an example. Winning and losing can't be ignored in sport. But by developing a reputation for having a good time, the team removes some of the embarrassment for performing poorly. The fact that winning seems to be unimportant serves as an alternative to the explanation that the team is inept.

Group Size

In Chapter 3, it was pointed out that group size has an impact on the motivation of the members — as size increases, individual motivation decreases. Four different explanations were advanced to account for this effect (e.g., Latane', Williams, & Harkins, 1979; Orbell & Dawes, 1981). These were presented in Table 3.3 The *allocational strategy* is based on the premise that individual group members save their best efforts for those times when they perform alone or when their performance is evaluated directly. The *minimizing strategy* is based on the belief that individual group members are motivated to get by with the least amount of effort possible. When they work in a situation where identifiability and accountability are low, personal motivation is diminished. The basic premise of the *free-rider strategy* is that when individual group members conclude that someone else is better qualified and more capable of doing the job, they reduce their own efforts and go along for the ride. The final explanation, the *sucker effect,* begins with the assumption that individual members don't want to "play the sucker" and provide a free ride for less productive group members. Consequently, they reduce their personal efforts in a group endeavor.

The motivation losses resulting from increased group size can be reduced if (1) the contributions of individual group members can be clearly differentiated and identified, (2) individual group members perceive that their involvement is essential to the group, and (3) their contributions are perceived to be appropriate relative to the contributions of other members. The clear identification of individual effort not only insures that all team members are personally accountable for their personal performance but that each receives the personal credit (or blame) which is due. Also, although the role of each team member is not equal in importance for the group's success, every group member must feel that he or she has a significant part to play. And, that contribution must be appropriate relative to what is expected from other group members.

Group Goals

Benefits of Goal Setting. As Table 16.1 indicates, goal setting is another highly effective technique for improving group motivation. Edwin Locke and Gary Latham (1984) in their book **Goal setting: A motivational technique** that works have pointed out that goal setting is effective because it produces:

- increased productivity,
- improved work quality,
- reduced boredom,
- increased clarity of expectations,
- increased liking for the task,
- increased satisfaction with performance,
- greater recognition from peers and supervisors,
- enhanced self-confidence,
- greater feelings of pride in achievement, and
- increased willingness to accept future challenges

Locke and his colleagues (Locke, Shaw, Saari, & Latham, 1981) have suggested that there are four principle motivational mechanisms which contribute to the effectiveness of goal setting. Goals serve to (a) *direct attention and action,* (b) *mobilize energy expenditure,* (c) *prolong energy expenditure,* and (d) *motivate strategy development.* Thus, for example, one basketball coach could set out team defensive objectives for rebounds and steals while a second coach might have team defensive objectives relating to the number of shots attempted and points allowed. Through their different goal setting programs, these two coaches would have highlighted (i.e., directed their athletes' attention to) two different aspects of defensive team play. The goals set would also serve as a challenge and a focus for the team's efforts every game (i.e., mobilize energy expenditure). Also, the athletes would continue to work toward achieving the goals until they were successful (i.e., prolong energy expenditure). And, if the team goals were sufficiently difficult and challenging, the athletes would probably have to devise collective and individual strategies in order to insure that the team was successful.

A good goal setting program can also help to reduce intrateam conflict. This was illustrated in a study conducted by Mel Schnake and Daniel Cochran with 8,938 employees of a large utility company. Schnake and Cochran assessed *goal clarity* and *goal difficulty* by having the employees provide a rating of the extent to which (1) clear specific performance goals were established for their job and (2) the goals set out were challenging and difficult. A third factor, the level of individual *work motivation* present, was measured by three questions (e.g., I feel bad and unhappy when I discover that I have performed poorly on this job). A fourth variable, the amount of *intrinsic job satisfaction,* was assessed by having the employees rate how satisfied they were with various aspects of their job (e.g., the chance to accomplish something worthwhile on the job). The final factor, *intradepartmental conflict*, was assessed with four questions in which the employees rated the extent to which their department was free from disagreements and the team was working toward the same goal.

It was found that higher levels of goal difficulty and goal clarity were associated with lower levels of intradepartmental conflict. Those employees who felt that they had goals that were challenging and clear also perceived that their work group was lower in conflict. And lower intradepartmental conflict was also associated with higher work motivation and intrinsic job satisfaction. Schnake and Cochran concluded that when a team is performing poorly because of low motivation and/or low satisfaction, the team leader should attempt to determine if a high level of conflict is the source of the problem. If high intrateam conflict is present, the team leader should then establish whether the team goals are too easy or unclear. In short, Schnake and Cochran felt that by introducing clear, challenging goals, team leaders can help to insure that motivation and satisfaction stay high and intrateam conflict stays low.

Individual Goal Setting. On the basis of a comprehensive review of research evidence, Locke and his colleagues outlined a number of generalizations about the effectiveness of goal setting for *individual performance.* (The word "individual" should be emphasized because not all of the generalizations about goal setting for individuals apply without qualification to goal setting for groups and organizations.) One of the generalizations is that goals should be set out in specific and measurable terms. Vague, general, imprecise goals do not serve to direct the individual's attention to the important elements in the situation. A second generalization is that a goal should be as hard and as challenging as possible — with the qualifier that the individual must accept it and have the ability necessary to attain or closely approximate it. A hard but attainable goal motivates the individual to action much better than moderate or easy goals, do-your-best goals, or no goals. Locke and Latham (1984) commented that "specific, challenging goals consistently lead to better performance than the goal of 'doing one's best' ... because paradoxically, people do not do their best when they are trying to do their best! 'Doing your best' is a vague goal because the meaning of 'best' is not specified. The way to get individuals to truly do their best is to set a challenging, quantitative goal that demands the maximum use of skills and abilities" (p. 23).

What if the goal is too difficult, too challenging? Will the athlete simply give up? As Figure 16.2 illustrates, this can occur. Generally, this tends to happen when the individual lacks self confidence or when partial successes are either impossible or meaningless (Locke & Latham, 1984). For example, an athlete might be able to bench press 150 lbs. If he is assigned a goal of lifting 350 lbs. within six months in order to make a team, he might simply give up because of a lack of confidence. Or, his confidence might be high but he might only show gains of 5 to 10 lbs. every month. These would be virtually meaningless in terms of ultimately achieving his final goal and making the team. Consequently, the goal of 350 lbs. could be seen as impossible, the partial successes of 5 to 10 lbs. every month would not be very rewarding, and the goal would lose its

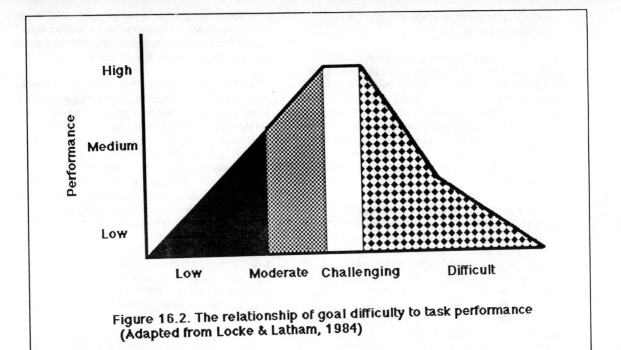

Figure 16.2. The relationship of goal difficulty to task performance (Adapted from Locke & Latham, 1984)

motivational properties.

A third generalization advanced by Locke et al is that intermediate goals or subgoals should be used as links to long term goals. A fourth is that feedback is necessary if goals are to have maximum effectiveness as a motivator. Also, supportiveness from the leader is an important positive factor in the success of a goal setting program. And, a sixth generalization is that token rewards are useful for increasing commitment toward a specific goal. These last four generalizations highlight the importance of providing both support and some information about progress. Feedback allows the individual to compare a current performance with a long-term objective. Subgoals increase the likelihood that periodic successes will be achieved. Token rewards are tangible evidence that some progress has been made. And, support is a form of positive reinforcement. When the individual has knowledge about progress made and/or has had partial successes through the attainment of intermediate goals, motivation is better sustained.

A seventh generalization advanced by Locke et al. for individual goal setting is that competition among individuals for goal achievement produces greater commitment and better performance. When individuals compete against each other in a goal setting program, there are two sources of motivation, two types of goals — achieving the task objective and beating the other person.

Group Goal Setting. The seventh generalization highlights some problems in the use of individual goal setting in a team context. Individual goals can detract from team goals. The quote used to introduce this section serves to illustrate this point. If Orr and Esposito had goals for individual scoring and were also competing with one another for the attainment of these goals, their competition might have caused the team to break up into two camps. Or, as another example, a team could have a goal setting program consisting of individual goals for offensive performance (e.g., points scored, number of assists) and team goals for defensive performance (e.g., reducing the number of shots attempted or points scored). In pursuing the individual goals, it is possible for the team goals to suffer.

In their discussion of team versus individual goals, Edwin Locke and Gary Latham (1984) pointed out that:

The late Rensis Likert, a psychologist at the University of Michigan, argued that group goal setting fosters a higher degree of cooperation and communication than individual goal setting, and thus is preferable ... When the tasks to be accomplished are highly interdependent, group goals are indeed appropriate. But this is unlikely to be the case where the jobs are not interdependent. (p. 37)

In short, Locke and Latham proposed that team goals are better than individual goals in sports such as basketball, soccer, ice hockey, field hockey — sports where a high degree of task cooperation and coordination are necessary. On the other hand, they also felt that individual goals are more effective than team goals in sports such as track and field, wrestling, archery — sports where a team score can be obtained but where cooperation and coordination are not essential.

There is some research evidence, however, that group goals are also better even in the latter type of situation. This was the conclusion from a study in which Tamao Matsui, Takashi Kakuyama, and Mary Lou Uy Onglatco (1987) compared the effects of three goal setting conditions on performance in a additive problem solving task (see Table 2.3 again for a discussion of task-types). In one of the conditions, the subjects set a personal goal and were then tested alone. In another condition, the subjects set both a personal goal and a goal for their group. Again, the individuals were tested alone. This

condition is comparable to the situation which exists when a team score is obtained in a wrestling meet. The athletes compete independently but their results are combined to obtain a team score.)

As Figure 16.3 shows, there were no differences in the level of the individual goals set by individuals working independently or in groups. The subjects set the same personal target for performance whether they were working independently or with a partner. However, the goal set for the group was significantly higher than the summation of the two personal goals. Individual performance in the group situations was also significantly better. Matsui et al. suggested that group goal setting is superior to individual goal setting because (1) the collective goals that individuals set are higher than the goals they set individually and (2) goal acceptance is better in groups. When individuals set a personal goal, they just work to the minimum level necessary to achieve that goal. When they set a group goal, however, they work to achieve and then surpass that goal.

In a follow-up study, Matsui et al. also found that when group goals are used, it is important to evalu-

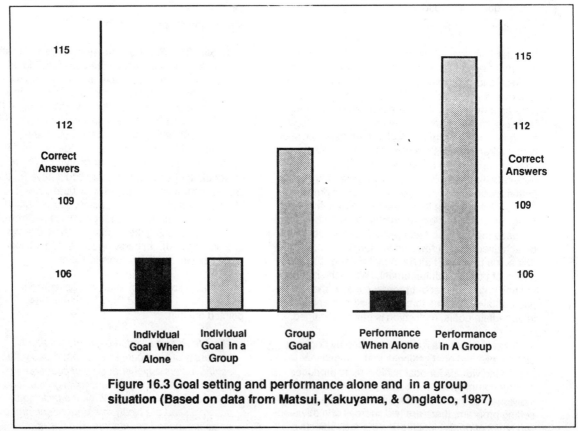

Figure 16.3 Goal setting and performance alone and in a group situation (Based on data from Matsui, Kakuyama, & Onglatco, 1987)

184

ate the individual contributions to the group effort. Otherwise, performance is not as effective. This is consistent with what has been discussed earlier in relation to social loafing. Individuals working in a group reduce their output if their contributions can't be readily identifiable and distinguished from the contributions of others.

It is also possible in most team sports to set up team goals and still have individual goals for offensive and defensive parameters. In a run-and-gun offense, for example, a team goal could be set for the number of shots taken each half in order to generate as much offense as possible. At the same time, it would also be possible to have individual goals for different team members that were compatible with this team goal. The best shooter could have personal goals for points scored, the playmaker for assists obtained, the rebounder for defensive and offensive rebounds, and so on.

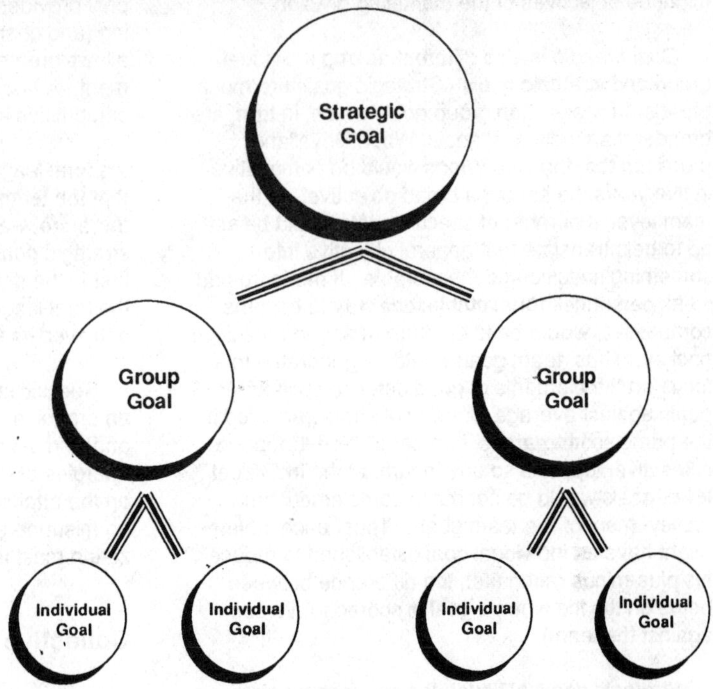

Figure 16.4. Strategic, group, and individual goals.

Strategic (Organizational) Goals

The concept of strategic goals was introduced by Locke and Latham (1984) to represent the standards, objectives, or goals of the whole organization or a significant aspect of it. Strategic goals represent the general objectives of an organization and provide the basis for setting group (unit) goals, which in turn form the basis for setting individual goals (see Figure 16.4). An example of a strategic goal is illustrated in the following quote concerning Jim Devellano, the vice president and general manager of the Detroit Red Wings hockey team:

> Devallano answered owner Mike Illitch's call to rebuild the once proud Detroit franchaise. On the day he was introduced to the local media, Devallano promised fans a competitive team within five years and a Stanley Cup contender by the end of the 1980s. (p. 4)

Detroit's strategic goal of first becoming competitive and then being a contender influenced the organization's decision to hire a coach and actively try to sign free agents. These decisions eventually also influenced the style of play of the team, the team's objectives, and ultimately the goals for individual players.

Strategic goals are different from both individual goals and group goals in multiplicity, breadth, complexity, duration, and specificity. Consequently, not all of the generalizations that apply to individual goal setting are equally applicable to strategic goals.

Goal multiplicity refers to the fact that it is possible for an individual athlete to have only one primary explicit goal but an organization usually has multiple strategic goals. For example, a coach may set one goal for her playmaking guard such as "reduce the number of turnovers". Obviously, other aspects of the athlete's performance are also important. But turnovers could be the single element that the coach would want her athlete to emphasize. On the other hand, an organization develops different goals for its different departments or units. In the case of the Detroit Red Wings, for example, improving the team's standing might the objective for the team; increasing attendance, profitability, and the number of support personnel in the organization might be objectives of the marketing division.

Goal breadth is also different among individual, group and strategic goals. Strategic goals are much broader in scope than group goals which, in turn, are broader than individual goals. When Devallano promised that the Red Wings would be competitive in five years, he set out a broad objective. At the team level, a number of specific goals would be set up to help translate that general objective into something specific and measurable. If the team had weak personnel, for example, one way to become competitive would be to emphasize sound defensive hockey. Thus, team goals could be generated to focus on the elements of good defense such as goals against average, number of shots permitted in the prime scoring areas, number of 2-on-1 opportunities given up, and so on. In turn, at the individual level, goals would be set out to complement the achievement of the team goals. Thus, each athlete might have an individual goal established to reduce his plus-minus rating (i.e., the difference between being on the ice when a goal is scored for versus against the team).

Strategic goals although they appear simple are more *complex* than group or individual goals. This should be evident from the examples used above to illustrate goal breadth. Any organization that has the strategic goal of improvement in performance, in attendance, and in the number of personnel, must also identify the actions that are important to achieve each. At each level the focus of the actions become narrower. What must be done at the management level? At the team level? At the individual level? Unless the strategic goals are well thought out, appropriate group and individual goals cannot be established.

A fourth difference among individual, group and strategic goals lies in their *duration*. The Detroit Red Wings example serves to illustrate this as well. In terms of the duration of time involved, the strategic goal of being competitive within five years would take the longest to accomplish. Group and individual goals would be set out for each year, segments of the year, and/or each game.

A final difference is in the degree of *specificity versus generality* present. Group and individual goals are usually presented in very specific terms. And, they're more effective because of it. There is some question whether strategic goals should be general or specific. Locke and Latham pointed out that there are advantages and disadvantages with each course of action. A strategic goal that is general in nature — "becoming competitive" — not

only provides greater flexibility in terms of establishing (and changing) possible courses of action, it allows greater flexibility in interpreting goal achievement. A last place team might become more competitive in its division by increasing its standing two or three places to become the sixth best team in the total league. It could be argued quite reasonably that the team had achieved its strategic goal and, therefore, was successful. On the other hand, if the strategic goal was phrased specifically — "end up first in the division and among the top four teams in the total league" — it could be argued that it had not achieved its strategic goal and was unsuccessful.

Specific strategic goals are an advantage when an organization is suffering from a lack of direction and/or must change its focus. Then, all of the energies of the organization can be clearly focused on the attainment of that specific goal and there is no misunderstanding about the direction the organization must take.

Collective Efficacy

As Table 16.1 shows, collective efficacy is another source of group motivation. Self-efficacy represents the strength of an individual's belief that he or she can successfully carry out a task or handle the responsibilities necessary to produce a desired outcome. It is similar to self confidence except that self confidence is considered to be a global trait (i.e., an individual with high self confidence has high expectations for success in any subject in school, in a wide variety of social situations, in a wide cross section of sport situations, and so on). On the other hand, self-efficacy is a situationally specific form of self confidence. An individual could have high perceptions of self-efficacy in mathematics but not physics, in a debating class but not at parties, in basketball but not wrestling.

Self-efficacy has a direct influence on motivation — on the activities people select, on the intensity with which they carry them out, and on the degree to which they persist in the face of adversity. Albert Bandura (1982), a psychologist who has been the primary catalyst for research on this topic, has elaborated on why this is the case:

In their daily lives people continuously make decisions about what courses of action to pursue and how long to continue those they have undertaken. Because acting on misjudgments of personal efficacy can produce adverse consequences, accurate appraisal of one's own capabilities has considerable functional value. Self-efficacy judgements, whether accurate or faulty, influence choice of activities and environmental settings. People avoid activities that they believe exceed their coping capabilities, but they undertake and perform assuredly those that they judge themselves capable of managing (Bandura, 1977). Judgements of self-efficacy also determine how much effort people will expend and how long they will persist in the face of obstacles or aversive experiences. When beset with difficulties people who entertain serious doubts about their capabilities slacken their efforts or give up altogether, whereas those who have a strong sense of efficacy exert greater effort to master the challenge. (p. 123)

Feelings of efficacy — whether they develop in an individual or a group — are based on four principal sources of information: prior performance, vicarious experiences, verbal persuasion, and physiological arousal (Bandura, 1977). Prior performance has the most powerful impact on feelings of efficacy. When an individual or group has been successful, a perception of efficacy develops which is accompanied by an expectation for future successes in similar situations (McAuley, 1985). Not surprisingly, the expectation for subsequent success.

Perceptions of efficacy can also develop from vicarious experiences — seeing others perform. When others who are highly similar in competence, ability, or some other important characteristic are successful, it contributes to the development of feelings of efficacy (McCullagh, 1987). Conversely, expectations for personal success are lowered when similar others are observed to fail despite high effort.

Verbal persuasion can also increase self efficacy (Chambliss & Murray, 1979). However, it has the weakest impact. Individuals or groups who lack the confidence to successfully carry out a task, are not easily convinced otherwise. A "win it for the Gipper" peptalk may always produce results in the movies; its success rate is much lower in real life.

And, finally, people use information relating to their own state of physiological arousal as an index of efficacy. High arousal including an elevated heart beat, increased respiratory rate, sweating, and so on, are associated with lower feelings of efficacy (Bandura, 1977). Conversely, low arousal is associated with feelings of mastery and expectations for success. When individuals are not overly anxious, they feel more confident.

Although Bandura's original discussions were centered around personal or individual self-efficacy, he also pointed out that "people do not live their lives as social isolates. Many of the challenges and difficulties they face reflect group problems requiring sustained collective effort to produce any significant change" (Bandura, 1982, p. 143). Groups vary in their perceptions of collective competency and expectations for success. These differences in perceptions and expectations were referred to by Bandura as collective efficacy. Collective efficacy influences the selection of group activities, the effort directed by the group toward those activities, and the persistence exhibited in the face of adversity.

A unpublished study by Forward and Zander which was reported by Zander (1971) serves to illustrate the impact of collective efficacy on group performance (see Figure 16.5). (Although Forward and Zander were interested in evaluating the desire for group success, the experimental manipulations they used produced a condition conceptually identical to collective efficacy.) A total of 148 high school boys were tested in groups of three on a hand dynamometer task. When the subjects arrived at the laboratory, each was required to fill out a questionnaire and was given two trials on a hand grip dynamometer (to obtained a baseline measure of strength). The subjects were then told that they would be involved in an experiment to evaluate team muscle control and coordination. It was stated that the results from the questionnaire (which had actually measured nothing and was not used for any purpose in the study) had revealed "how much each of you is inclined toward working for group goals" (Zander, 1971, p. 148). After reporting that the maximum score on the test was 50 and that the average team in the school had scored 28, one half of the groups were informed that their team score was 42. The other half were informed that their team score was 14. Consequently, prior to the actual testing, half of the groups held the perception that their members were strongly inclined to work toward group goals (high collective efficacy) while half held the perception that their members were poorly inclined (low collective efficacy).

In the test, the groups of three subjects were required to squeeze a hand dynamometer in unison in two tasks of varying difficulty to produce a single strength score. As Figure 16.5 shows, groups that had a high collective efficacy consistently performed better than the low collective efficacy groups on the difficult, medium, and easy tasks.

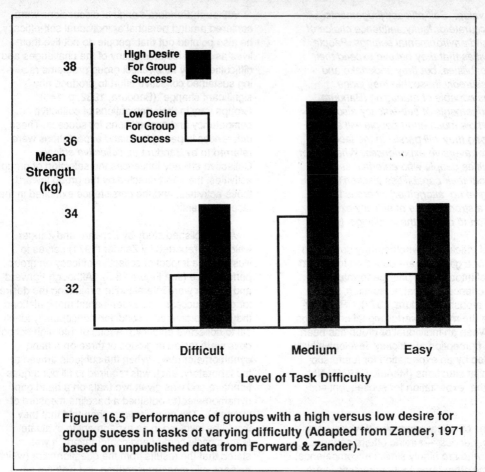

Figure 16.5 Performance of groups with a high versus low desire for group sucess in tasks of varying difficulty (Adapted from Zander, 1971 based on unpublished data from Forward & Zander).

Intragroup Interaction and Communication

Interaction and communication among members of task-oriented groups also serves to facilitate group motivation (see Table 16.1 again). This was demonstrated through an analysis of the group dynamics in a mountain climbing team which was conducted by Richard Emerson (1966) during the 1963 American expedition to Mount Everest. The team consisted of Western mountaineers and a support group of Nepalese-Tibetan Sherpas. When the climb was initially planned, the objective was to ascend Everest by a route known as the South Col. However, subsequently, as the team began its initial approach, some members put pressure on the group to attempt the climb by way of a more difficult and uncertain route known as the West Ridge. This interest in the West Ridge route developed into what Emerson referred to as a "pathological motivation" (p. 219). In order to resolve the increasing conflict over the group's route (goal), it was agreed to subdivide the expedition into two primary objectives:

the South Col route and the West Ridge route. Three separate units then evolved: a South Col team with 5 subjects, a West Ridge team with 5 subjects (one was killed in an ice-avalanche early in the climb), and a Peripheral South Col team in various roles marginal to the actual climb.

Emerson collected data over a period of 92 days, the duration of time it took the West Ridge team to reach the summit. The South Col team completed their phase of the expedition and reached the summit after 70 days. Data collection had to be as unobtrusive as possible, so Emerson used four approaches. One approach consisted of providing each subject with a *diary* for personal and research use.Prepared questions were woven into the diary for the regular recording of cognitions and feelings. Some questions appeared daily (e.g., "Tomorrow I (should, will, would like to ...."), others every second, fourth, or eighth day. Another approach was to use stimulus statements. Emerson, as a partici- pant observer, introduced *stimulus statements* into his natural discussion with subjects and then re- corded whether the feedback he received was optimistic or pessimistic in nature. Using a tape recorder, Emerson also *recorded group discussions* including planning sessions, bull sessions, and reconnaissance meetings. Finally, all inter-camp *radio communications* were automatically recorded on tape.

Emerson felt that *uncertainty about goal outcome* is the crucial variable in maintaining goal-directed behavior (i.e., goal striving). Consequently, he proposed that the primary function of communication in task-oriented groups is to sustain uncertainty in order to maintain group motivation at a high level. There was considerable support for this proposal. In all task communications, there was an overwhelming tendency for the reply to both negative and positive stimulus statements to be pessimistic in nature. This is summarized in Table 16.4. Thus, for example, a positive suggestion such as "the weather is ideal for making good progress" would be reacted to with a negative reply such as "but we haven't capitalized on it very well". Conversely, a negative suggestion such as "the weather hasn't been very good for making progress" would be reacted to with a negative reply such as "and it will probably get worse". In both cases, the negative reply practical purpose — sustaining uncertainty in the group and helping it maintain high motivation in reference to its goal.

As Table 16.4 shows, there was one exception to this pattern of generally negative feedback — when the South Col team communicated about the West Ridge team. The South Col team had very little motivation for the West Ridge objective and they perceived that this aspect of the expedition was likely to fail. When members of the South Col team were presented with pessimistic stimulus statements about the West Ridge goal, there was a overwhelming tendency to respond positively. It was suggested by Emerson that the general tendency to respond negatively in order to sustain uncertainty and motivation occurs when individuals are involved in collaborative problem-solving requiring coordination and cooperation. The West Ridge goal was seen as a threat to the South Col goal — the original objec-

tive which remained the principal goal for the expedition-as-a-whole. Members of both the West Ridge team and the South Col team considered the South Col goal important and attempted to sustain high motivation for it by responding pessimistically. Similarly, the West Ridge team considered the West Ridge goal important and attempted to sustain high motivation for it by responding pessimistically. But, the South Col team was not supportive of the West Ridge goal and, therefore, responded in a manner not designed to sustain high motivation.

Implications for the Effectiveness of Sport Groups

As Figure 16.1 shows, individual group members can work primarily for themselves, for the benefit of the team, for both the team and self, or none of these. Zander has suggested that the third option is the best — working for personal and team benefits. Former goaltender Ken Dryden (1983) has illustrated how this option can operate in a team sport in his discussion of teammate, Bob Gainey:

He is the consummate team player. An often misunderstood phrase, it does not mean that Gainey is without the selfish interests the rest of us have. It means that without the team's tangible rewards, without the wins and the Stanley Cups, there are few tangible rewards for him. For Gainey's skills are a team's skills, ones that work best and show best when a team does well; ones that seem less important when it doesn't. While other players, in their roles, constantly battle the tension between team and self (it is surely good for [defenseman] Larry Robinson to score a goal; if the team is ahead and the score is close, it may not be good for the team that he try), simply put, what's good for Bob Gainey is good for the team; and vice versa. In many ways he is like former basketball star Bill Bradley. Without virtuoso individual skills, team play becomes both virtue and necessity, and what others understand as unselfishness is really cold-eyed realism — he

Table 16.4 Communication feedback to optimistic and pessimistic stimulus statements about goals under varyingconditions of uncertainty and motivation (Adapted from Emerson, 1966)

| Group | Goal | Prevailing Conditions | | | Negative Feedback (%) |
		Outcome	Motivation	Stimulus	
West Ridge	West Ridge	Outcome Uncertain	Very High	Optimistic Pessimistic	84.2 81.6
West Ridge	South Col	Success Likely	High	Optimistic Pessimistic	75.0 57.9
South Col	South Col	Success Likely	Very High	Optimistic Pessimistic	83.3 62.5
South Col	West Ridge	Failure Likely	Low	Optimistic Pessimistic	84.6 27.3

simply knows what works best for the team and for him (p. 85).

The individual motivation present in athletes can't be replaced entirely by a motivation for the team. But, individual motivation can be used as a foundation which can be combined with an interest in the welfare of the team to produce a higher overall motivation. One way to achieve this is suggested by the Dryden quote — highlight for each individual member how he or she will profit if the group does well. This same point was made by Alvin Zander (1985) when he noted that the desire for group success can be enhanced by "privately indicating to members how membership in this group is helpful to them as individuals so that each person will view the group as an attractive entity worthy of membership" (pp. 120-121).

Zander provided a number of other proposals for increasing the desire for group success which have relevance for sport groups: (a) emphasize the reasons for having pride in the group and its accomplishments, (b) ensure that individual members understand their role in the group's functions, (c) point out the interdependence of various roles within the group and their relevance for the successful achievement of the group's goals, (d) emphasize team unity, team effort, team performance, (e) build a sense of responsibility to the team by showing the link between individual accomplishments and team success, (f) give individual members assignments that suit their skills and temperament, (g) arrange group goals, work plans, and procedures to insure some group success because success increases the desire for future successes, (h) set clear, challenging group goals so members have a focus for the group's activities and a method of evaluating progress.

Goal setting where group performance rather than individual performance is the principal focus has been used successfully to enhance motivation. Edwin Locke and Gary Latham (1984) have listed five sequential stages which should be followed in setting out group goals. The first is to *specify the general objectives* of the tasks of the group. Does the group leader want to reduce absenteeism and increase adherence? Increase offensive production? Build a better defense? Build character? In establishing group goals ore than one objective or critical group requirement might be listed.

In the next stage, it becomes necessary to

specify how behavior or performance will be measured. Some objectives are readily measured by commonly used indices such as time, points, kilograms, inches, and so on. Others are more difficult. Determining a way to assess whether character is present, for example, would be a difficult assignment. A common strategy is to use behaviors which can be measured and are thought to represent the concept. Determining how performance will be assessed is a crucial stage because the goal-setting program can't proceed until it's competed.

The third stage is to *specify the standard or target to be reached.* Once the method of measurement has been established in the second stage, the degree of projected improvement is determined and set out as a goal or objective. Thus, a decision might be made to measure adherence in a fitness group using the percentage of members who are absent, leave early, or arrive late. In an attempt to increase adherence, a standard (goal) could be set for the group.

In the fourth stage, the group leader must *specify the time span* for the program. Either a deadline is set out for achieving the goal or a time span is established for the goal setting program to run its course. In the above example, the time span for the adherence goal could be established for the week and/or the year.

Because most groups have multiple goals, it becomes necessary to *prioritize goals.* Each goal is a target for the group but proportionately more action and attention are directed toward the higher priority goals. In the fitness class example, the instructor might assign the highest priority to reducing absenteeism followed by late arrivals and then early departures.

In the final stage, the group leader must *determine coordination requirements.* Adherence in a fitness class may be beyond personal control if the students are experiencing timetable difficulties, for example. A goal setting program set up to reduce absenteeisms, late arrivals, and early departures might be destined to fail if the students can't work out coordination problems inherent in the timetable. Similarly, a group goal for defense on a basketball team might be in conflict with some offensive goals set out for individual members. Until these coordination problems are resolved, the goal setting programs can't be initiated.

17 Group Interaction and Communication

The scenario represented in the quotation used to introduce this chapter is familiar to anyone who has ever been involved in a group activity. Group members interact and communicate frequently, examine previous accomplishments, resolve areas of actual or potential concern, plan strategies for upcoming activities, and develop closer bonds among members. Decisions are arrived at which represent a group perspective. Interaction and communication are essential in order for the group to come to an understanding about itself and where it is going. A collection of individuals with different needs, attitudes, personalities, interests, and motives becomes a stronger, more effective group through interaction, communication, and the achievement of consensus on important issues. For this reason, these processes are fundamental to the development and maintenance of group structure. They also influences other group processes including goal setting, cooperation and competition, and the development of member harmony and group morale. In short, interaction, communication and group decision making are important, primary group processes.

> When things were not going well, we were frank with one another. Doug Harvey would call a team meeting and we would all show up early at some local bar to have it out. Sometimes we deliberated for hours during the long train rides between cities. (Ralph Backstrom quoted in Goyens & Turowetz, 1986, p. 113)

Group Communication

The Nature of Communication in Groups

Communication in groups is influenced by variability in the personal characteristics of group members. The nature and extent of that influence depends on the characteristics in which the group members are similar or different. Individuals in a group can be heterogene-ous in two important dimensions (Burgoon, Heston, & McCroskey, 1974). One of these is represented by nonchangeable or slowly changing ("static") characteristics such as age, sex, religion, language, culture, and educational attainment. The second dimension is represented by more changeable, ("dynamic") characteristics such as attitudes, knowledge, and beliefs.

A group is heterogeneous to the degree that differences in these static and dynamic characteristics are present. Thus, for example, a sport team which contains individuals from different cultural backgrounds who speak different languages and practice different religions would be highly heterogeneous.

There are three principles of group communication which are related to the concepts of homogeneity and heterogeneity (Burgoon, Heston, & McCroskey, 1974). The first is that *communication patterns are normally homogeneous* — individuals tend to communicate with others who are similar to them in attitudes and characteristics. Members of a university basketball team tend to communicate most frequently and easily with other team members, gymnasts with other gymnasts, and so on.

The second principle is that *communication is more effective among people who are homogeneous.* The more that individuals are alike as team members, the greater is the likelihood that they will share common meanings in language, common motives, common values. It is evident that individuals who share a common culture share idiosyncrasies in speech. The use of "eh" by Canadians, "mate" by Australians, and "you all" by Americans from the southern United States helps to illustrate this point. How difficult would it be for Sherlock Holmes to establish the country of origin for the three individuals in this conversation?

> A: "It's sure nice to see you all again."
>
> B: "And, what a great day, eh?"
>
> C: "She'll be right mate!"

The third principle is that *effective communication, in turn, leads to increased homogeneity in dynamic characteristics* — attitudes, knowledge, and beliefs. This reflects the cyclical relationship of communication and homogeneity. Homogeneity increases the likelihood that communication will occur and that that communication will be effective. In turn, communication increases the likelihood that the individuals involved will adopt similar attitudes and beliefs and share common perceptions. (Burgoon, Heston, & McCroskey, 1974). Birds of a feather really do flock together insofar as communication is concerned.

A note of caution is also necessary. As Donelson Forsyth (1983) noted, "the ability to communicate with others is a mixed blessing" (p.161). Communication also can be used by the sender to exchange information or create misunderstandings, to reduce conflicts or accelerate the growth of problems, to test new ideas or produce conformity. There are also a number of problems which arise in the processing of information by the receiver (Campbell, 1958; quoted in Forsyth, 1983). These include *levelling* whereby a communication is reduced and simplified, *ordering* in which the beginning and the end of a communication are better retained than the middle portion, *sharpening* in which a communication is reinterpreted by emphasizing some components and deemphasizing others, and *assimilating* in which the meaning of a communication is shifted so that it matches a previous important message.

Although the three principles of communication are undoubtedly in operation and have relevance in sport teams, it is not clear how team effectiveness is influenced. There is no empirical evidence available and the anecdotal accounts are varied. The complexity of the homogeneity-group effectiveness relationship was highlighted in the quote by Ken Dryden which was used to introduce Section 3. Dryden, a former goaltender, pointed out that the Montreal Canadiens, like most sport teams, were heterogeneous in static and

dynamic characteristics. That is, differences were present among team members in culture and language, age, religion, ability, educational attainment, and personality. According to Dryden, at first glance, these differences weren't evident; the Canadiens seemed perfectly compatible personally and professionally. He pointed out , however, that a second glance showed that heterogeneity was present along Anglophone versus Francophone lines and it influenced communication. And, finally, Dryden stated that a third glance showed that no divisions existed because the differences that were present were unconscious, unintended, unnoticed, and irrelevant to the team.

Other sport teams have not been as fortunate; the heterogeneity that was present in static and dynamic characteristics became significant. Dave Meggyesy (1971), in his book, **Out of their league** recalled how racial tensions on the 1967 St. Louis Cardinals eventually destroyed the fabric of the group:

> *In 1967, the racial tension that I'd seen simmering for years on the Cardinals finally reached the boiling point. What I saw around the locker room made me expect a race war at any moment.*
>
> *I was first introduced to racism on the team ... in my rookie year, 1962; room assignments, wings of the dormitory, and the dining room were all segregated. In the half hour between the end of practice and dinner, all the white ball players would head up to the town's only bar, the Lantern. I never saw a black football player in the Lantern at any time during my first five years with the team ....*
>
> *Racism was not a matter of individual quirks in the St. Louis organization; it was part of the institution .... Near the end of the 1967 season, these tensions had become so intense that there was almost no communication between black and white ball players. It was a miracle we weren't forced to field two separate teams. (pp. 167-171)*

The members of the Canadiens were able to overcome, ignore, or work around their differences; the members of the Cardinals were not. The Canadiens were remarkably successful, as the six Stanley Cup Championships won while Dryden was their goaltender clearly show. The Cardinals were highly unsuccessful. What isn't clear is what came first, the attitude that the heterogeneity that was present in the group wasn't important or the team's success. Did increased communication contribute to a reduction in the importance attached to the heterogeneity among members and, subsequently, to team success? Or, did team success contribute to a reduction in the importance attached to the heterogeneity among members which, in turn, led to increased communication? Probably both causal relationships were in operation but there has not been any direct test of this supposition.

Implications for the Effectiveness of Sport Groups

The composition of almost all sport teams is generally heterogeneous in terms of race, religion, culture — what has been referred to as the static characteristics. It is also heterogeneous in terms of member's ability and skill, their attitudes and beliefs, and their involvement and contributions to the team — what has been referred to as the dynamic characteristics. Frequent communication among team members obviously can't produce homogeneity in static characteristics such as race and culture. Also, over the short term, frequent communication won't have much impact on all of the dynamic characteristics. It does seem to have an impact over the long term, however. Slavin and Madden (1979), using data collected by Educational Testing Services, found that participation on sport teams was one of the few practices that produced strong positive effects on the racial attitudes and behaviors of blacks and whites.

Sport groups have performance as their primary focus. Thus, one important objective of communication within the sport group is to obtain consensus — homogeneity in attitudes, beliefs, and behaviors — on the group goals and objectives and the methods of achieving them.

Alvin Zander (1982) has offered a number of practical solutions on how to improve communication among team members. One is to insure that team members know each other's duties and responsibilities. Providing opportunities to socialize also helps team members become comfortable with each other. The physical environment is important. Consequently, the practice and dressing room areas should be made conducive to easy interchange by insuring physical proximity. Each team member should be shown that his/her contributions are valuable to the team. If team members are friendly, any differences of opinion should be made evident in order to promote discussion and communication. Team members should be actively encouraged to modify their ideas and compromise if differences have caused conflict. Finally, cooperation should be promoted and rivalry reduced by emphasizing the group and deemphasizing personal goals and objectives.

Group Decision Making

Group polarization is the term used to represent the shift that occurs in the attitude of individual members following group interactions and communication. This shift leads to a riskier position if the initial tendency was toward moderate risk or to a more conservative position if the initial tendency was toward caution. Thus, for example, two noon-hour joggers privately might be mildly tempted to enter a marathon. If they sat down together to discuss the pros and cons, it is likely that group polarization would occur and that they would decide to enter the marathon.

Much of the early research in the area of group polarization centered around an attempt to understand the *risky shift phenomenon* -- the tendency for groups to adopt riskier positions than individuals. Part of the impetus for this research came from Nathan Kogan and Michael Wallach who developed the *Choice Dilemma Inventory*. (Kogan & Wallach, 1964). This inventory consists of 12 real-life dilemmas in which a central character is confronted with a choice between two alternatives. One is risky, the other more conservative. The decision that a subject (or group) must come to is what advice to give this central character. One of the dilemmas which deals with a sport situation is as follows:

> *Mr. D. is the captain of College X's football team. College X is playing its traditional rival, College Y, in the final game of the season. The game is in its final seconds, and Mr. D's team, College X, is behind in the score. College X has time to run one more play. Mr. D., the captain, must decide whether it would be best to settle for a tie score with a play which would be almost certain to work or, on the other hand, should he try a more complicated and risky play which could bring victory if it succeeded, but defeat if not.*
>
> *Imagine that you are advising Mr. D. Listed below are several probabilities or odds that the risky play will work.*
>
> *Please check the lowest probability that you would consider acceptable for the risky play to be attempted.* (Kogan & Wallach, 1964, p. 257)

The experimental subject in the role of an advisor is required to select the minimum probable level for success which would lead him or her to advise the central character to take the riskier but more attractive alternative. In the Choice Dilemma Inventory, the options are presented on a scale varying from 1 chance in 10 of being successful to 10 chances in 10 of being successful. In order to examine the impact of the group influence on decision making, subjects initially respond to the 12 problems while alone. After this, the subjects are put into a group situation where the issues are discussed and then a group decision is reached.

How realistic are the dilemmas and the decisions? Interestingly, on New Year's Day in 1988, life imitated science. In the Sugar Bowl, the Auburn Tigers, trailing 16-13, had the ball on the Syracuse Orangemen's 13 yard-line with four seconds left in the game. Auburn's coach, Pat Dye, was faced the same dilemma as Mr. D, the Kogan and Wallach character — kick a field goal for a tie or run a play from scrimmage in an attempt to win. Dye chose to kick. And, it was successful. Sportswriter Douglas Looney described the situation following the game as follows:

> Stoney-faced and sullen, Auburn coach Pat Dye tried to defend his nonsporting decision to play for a tie against undefeated Syracuse in the Sugar Bowl: "My decision was not to get beat". Not to get beat? No coach worth his whistle ought to think like this ...
>
> "Our guys were not real happy" said [Kicker Win] Lyle. "They really didn't like it when I went out there. They were screaming that they wanted to go for the touchdown ...
>
> Afterward, the more Syracuse coach Dick MacPherson thought about what had happened, the madder he got. "Why didn't Dye ask his players what they wanted to do?" he said, fuming. Obviously, coaches don't ask their players to make such decisions, but MacPherson was angry beyond logic. (Looney, 1988, p.22)

From the accounts presented, it seems apparent that the Auburn players endorsed the riskier alternative. If they had been questioned *as a group*, they probably would have advocated trying for the touchdown and a win. However, what would their response have been if they had been questioned *in private*? How would each player have advised Dye if he had talked to his coach in a one-on-one situation?

When Wallach, Kogan, and Bem (1962) examined these questions in an experimental situation, they found that individuals are much more prepared to take chances when they are in a group than when they are alone. As Table 17.1 shows, the group score for risk for males and females is 9.4% greater than the average individual response. Thus, (a) if Pat Dye had discussed the issues with his coaching staff and/or his players, (b) if he and they had been slightly inclined to gamble, and (c) the ultimate decision had been voted on by the total group, then the chances of Auburn taking a gamble would have increased by 9.4%. Wallach and his colleagues also found that when the individual judgements are collected after the group discussion, males show a 10.4% increase in endorsement for risk; females, a 8.2%. So there's a even greater chance that Dye would have taken the gamble following a discussion even if he had made the decision alone. Finally, As Table 17.1 shows, when individual judgements (in the case of males only) are delayed and collected from two to six weeks later, the tendency toward risk increases even more. It's probably of little value to know that if the issues had been discussed and then Pat Dye had had six weeks to make a decision, there's a 12.3% greater chance that he would not have kicked.

It was pointed out earlier that group discussions increase the likelihood of a risky shift *if the members in the group are initially predisposed toward some risk*. During the 1960s, 1970s, and 1980s literally hundreds of studies on attitudes, values, judgements, cognitions, and perceptions have shown that this is the case (e.g., Myers, 1982). At the same time, however, numerous studies have also shown that there were instances when the opposite process occurred. That is, if the members in a group are initially predisposed toward caution, a *cautious shift* occurs. If Dye and his coaching staff had privately believed that the conservative option of kicking was the best, then any discussion

---

Table 17.1 Shifts in the level of risk perceived to be acceptable alone versus in a group situation (Adapted from Wallach, Kogan, & Bem, 1962)

Comparisons	Shift Toward Greater Risk (%)	
	Males	Females
Individual Pretest vs. Group Decision	9.4	9.4
Individual Pretest vs. Individual Postest	10.4	8.2
Individual Pretest vs. Individual Delayed Postest	12.3	······

that followed would have simply strengthened that belief. In short, group discussions seem to produce group polarization
— the tendency to adopt a more extreme
position (either risky or cautious) than the
one held by the individual members. The
direction of movement toward either
extreme depends upon what point-of-view
was initially dominant.

Explanations for
Group Polarization

A number of overlapping explanations
have been advanced to account for group
polarization effects (Pruitt, 1971). These
can be summarized into four general
theoretical categories: diffusion of responsibility theory, leadership theories, information theories, and value theories (see
Table 17.2).

The basis for the *diffusion of responsibility theory* is the fact that in groups
responsibility for a decision can be
shared. When individuals operate alone,
it cannot. All people have some anxiety about the
potential negative consequences of an unfavorable
outcome from a decision. When an individual arrives at
a decision alone, he or she must assume full responsibility for the consequences. But, when a decision is
made in concert with others, the responsibilities are
diffused among all of the members of the group.

A number of *leadership theories* have also
emerged in which the qualities of the dominant individuals in the group discussion are highlighted. In
these explanations, it is proposed that group leaders,
either because of their personal traits (e.g., need for
risk), more extreme views, greater confidence, or
assertiveness, are more influential and persuasive in
the group.

In the *value theories* it is assumed that the energy
behind the shift is the presence of some commonly
held human values (Pruitt, 1971). Thus, if the majority
of group members privately endorse (value) a risky alternative, that perspective will be intensified within the
group discussions. Conversely, if a cautious position
is privately valued by the majority, group discussions
will serve to increase the attractiveness of this perspective.

The basis for the *information theories* is the belief
that individuals try to process information in a logical,
rational fashion. They compare their views with the

Table 17.2 Explanations advanced to account for the group polarization effects in decision making (Adapted from Pruitt, 1971)

Explanation	Description
Diffusion of Responsibility Theories	The repsonsibility for negative con- sequences can be diffused among all of the members of the group
Leadership Theories	Dominant individuals because of their personal traits, more extreme views, confidence, or assertiveness are more influential and persuasive in the group
Information Theories	The group discussion produces relevant arguments about the utility or merits of a position
Value Theories	The group discussion brings out the dominant values in the group. Individu- als compare themselves against that standard and adopt a position which is at least as risky or as cautious

views of other group members, they weigh the evidence, and go with the best option (Isenberg, 1987).
In a group discussion, the majority of good arguments
are generally advanced in favor of the dominant
position — which might be for caution or for risk.
Group members judge this information and shift
toward greater endorsement of that position.

Although there has been some level of support for
all of these explanations in different experiments, it is
now thought that the latter two approaches — the
social comparison approach (which is a value theory)
and the persuasive arguments approach (which is an
information processing theory) — offer the best
explanation for group polarization effects. The *social
comparison approach* begins with the assumption that
all people have a desire to present themselves and to
be perceived in a socially desirable way. As a consequence, when an individual is faced with a decision, he
or she attempts to determine what view others might
hold. After this comparison is made between the
position held by others and by the self, the individual
further endorses his/her initial decision. This endorsement is the same or slightly more extreme (for either
risk or for caution depending upon the problem) than is
considered to be typical of other individuals in the
group. In the group discussion which follows, direct
social comparison occurs. When it becomes apparent
through the discussion that others also hold similar
views, there is a shift in the direction represented by

the greater social value.

According to the *persuasive arguments approach,* "the dominant value or values in a decision problem elicit persuasive arguments in group discussion that convince group members to move further in the direction of these values" (Pruitt, 1971, p. 354). Thus, a coach faced with a difficult decision will draw on past experiences and weigh the pros and cons of both options. The number and the persuasiveness of these arguments will contribute to an initial impression. Then, when the issue is discussed in a group setting with the team or other coaches, persuasive arguments in favor of the initial impression cause a further shift.

The impact of polarization on group decisions is apparent if the outcomes from jury deliberations are examined (see Table 17.3). After hearing the evidence in the courtroom, each juror forms an initial opinion on the basis of the number and persuasiveness of the arguments. The vote on the first ballot is a reflection of this opinion. The subsequent group discussion then provides the jurors with an opportunity to highlight different aspects of the evidence. When there is a majority (for guilty or not guilty) on the first ballot, this judgement becomes the jury's verdict 81.4% of the time. As Table 17.3 shows, the other outcomes are rare. The majority seldom shifts its initial opinion to the minority perspective (3.9%). Also, consistent with other research on group influence and conformity, there are very few instances (8.3%) where the minority withstands the pressures from the majority. And finally, consistent with what might be predicted from other research on group polarization, when a jury is evenly divided on the initial ballot (i.e., where there is no initially dominant position), it very infrequently (6.4%) arrives at a verdict.

Group Polarization and Groupthink

In a classic book called **Victims of groupthink** which was published in 1972, social psychologist Irving Janis introduced the term groupthink to represent "a mode of thinking that people engage in when they are deeply involved in a cohesive-ingroup, when members' strivings for unanimity override their motivation to realistically appraise alternative courses of action" (p. 8). The catalyst for Janis' work was an interest in exploring the reasons behind some well-known, disastrous group decisions — the Bay of Pigs invasion, the inadequate defense of Pearl Harbor prior to World War II, the escalation of the Vietnam War. There are some close parallels between the process of group polarization and the process of groupthink. In

Table 17.3 Jury outcomes as a function of the initial ballot (Adapted from Penrod & Hastie, 1980)

Jury Outcomes	No. of Juries	Percentage
Position Favored by the Majority Becomes the Jury's Decision	127	81.4
Position Favored by the Minority Becomes the Jury Decision	6	3.9
Position Favored by the Minority Leads to a "Hung" Jury	13	8.3
Jury is Split 6-6 on the First Ballot and Reaches a Decision	10	6.4

groupthink, as in group polarization, "members show interest in facts and opinions that support their initially preferred policy and take up time in their meetings to discuss them, but they ignore facts and opinions that do not support their initially preferred policy" (Janis, 1972, p. 10).

Janis identified six symptoms of groupthink. These are presented in Table 17.4. This table also contains an example to show how this phenomenon might occur in sport situations. The sport example used, the 1972 hockey series between Canada and Russia was mentioned previously in Chapter 9 (see Table 9.2 again). This series represented the first meeting between North American professionals and European amateurs and the anticipation and excitement were high. The USSR had assumed international dominance in Olympic and World Cup competitions in a sport which most Canadians viewed chauvinistically. Generally, the prevailing mood prior to the series was that now that Canada was able to use her best players she would be able to demonstrate quite clearly who was superior. Subsequent events proved otherwise. Jack Ludwig (1972), in his book **Hockey night in Moscow,** clearly shows how the process of groupthink developed on a national level.

An *illusion of invulnerability* was created when preliminary reports confirmed the generally held expectation that the NHL was decidedly superior. Although some evidence was available that the Russian team was talented, this was discounted or ignored — as Janis would say, there was a *collective*

Table 17.4 The symptoms of groupthink (The list of symptoms are from Janis, 1972. The quotations are from Ludwig, 1972)

Symptom	Description	Example
Illusion of Invulnerability	A highly optimistic picture is presented to the group	"[Scouts] brought back only good news, nothing calculated to get Team Canada stampeding into midnight practice sessions. Only one player on the USSR could make the NHL" (p.230).
Collective Efforts to Rationalize	Alternate opinions and warnings are ignored	"I myself, watching the practices, saw everything ...[but] discounted what I saw...my blindness to what was before my eyes made me ignore what was, later, so painfully obvious" (p. 23)
Unquestioned Belief in the Group's Inherent Morality	The group is assumed to possess an inherent superiority over the opposition	"I wouldn't have bet on the Russians if somebody had offered odds of 100-1. I would have assumed, as I think most Canadians did, that people who don't speak the Queen's English can hardly be expected to keep up with those that do" (p. 24)
Stereotyped Views of the Opposition	The opposition is characterized in stereotypical terms	"Their defensemen were slow, their pass patterns slower, their attack telegraphed and easily broken up by the NHL players who, unlike athletes in an unfree society like the USSR, are taught to think for themselves" (p. 23)
Direct Pressures to Conform	Pressures are brought to bear against members who present alternate views	"Isn't it time the media laid off the NHL who, through the cooperation of the US clubs, made it possible to have the greatest hockey team ever assembled represent Canada" Conn Smythe, quoted by Ludwig, p. 16)
Self Censorship of Deviations	Members censor themselves in order to produce a unanimous group position	"Experts, like ex-hockey star ... Aggie Kukulowicz, made sharp observations about how the Russians might handle Team Canada, and then, like a scientist refusing to believe the results of an experiment because the results don't fit in with his hypotheses, scrapped his observations and came out for Team Canada 'in eight straight'" (p. 24).
Shared Illusion of Unanimity	Members believe that the group position is universally shared	"We concluded what we *had* to conclude and remain faithful to Foster Hewitt, and the icy nights under a street light in Hockeyland, Canada, that the *drill* was on the Russian side, the *talent* with Team Canada" (p. 26)
Emergence of Self-Appointed Mindguards	Members protect the group from adverse information	"Any player good enough to make the NHL ... was NHL stuff, and that, like beauty being truth and truth being beauty, was all there was to know, and all one need to know" (pp. 26-27)

effort to rationalize. The Ludwig quotation used in Table 17.4 which illustrate an *unquestioned belief in the group's inherent morality* was obviously written tongue-in-cheek but it does reflect the prevailing sentiment at that time. An important aspect of groupthink is the implicit belief that "goodness is on our side". Consistent with this perspective is the use of *stereotyped views to characterize the opposition.* The presence of these stereotypes contributes to an expectation that the opposition's responses can be readily predicted and countered.

These initial four symptoms are generally related to the development of a positive appraisal of the relative strengths and merits of the group with respect to its opposition. The group also works toward the achievement of consensus among its membership, a process associated with the next four symptoms.

Alternate perspectives are discouraged as the

group applies *direct pressures to conform* on its members. At the same time, members engage in *self-censorship* in order to produce a unanimous group perspective. Ultimately, opposition to the group's decision is virtually eliminated and there is a *shared illusion of unanimity.* Although individual members may have private misgivings, public proclamations suggest otherwise. And, finally, there is *emergence of self-appointed mindguards* — group members who suppress any dissenting views in order to preserve group solidarity.

Implications for the Effectiveness of Sport Groups

Earlier in the chapter in the account of the Auburn-Syracuse game, coach Dick MacPherson of Syracuse is quoted by Douglas Looney as asking why the Auburn players weren't consulted in the decision. Looney then went on to answer the question — "obviously, coaches don't ask their players to make such decisions" (p. 22). Looney is right of course. The sport environment is largely characterized by an autocratic approach to decision making. This is unfortunate for at least two functional reasons. First, there are a number of positive outcomes associated with group participation in decision making (Chelladurai, 1986). Group discussion increases the likelihood that alternate solutions and/or approaches will surface. Also, the group has greater "ownership" in the decision and works harder for its success. And, a democratic approach contributes to the development of responsibility and self-determination — the bases for intrinsic motivation.

A second reason is that the dominant position in the group — whether it's for a cautious or risky, conservative or liberal positions — will in all probability be even more strongly endorsed after the group discussion. Group discussions produce a polarization in attitudes, beliefs, motives, and judgements. Thus, if the prevailing mood was for more rigid training or a stricter curfew, for example, group discussions would enhance the group's commitment to these positions. In short, if a particular position or judgement is significantly important to a majority of the group, group discussions can serve to strengthen the level of commitment.

Groupthink, a phenomenon which has some of the same characteristics as group polarization, doesn't always occur. Janis has suggested that groupthink is more likely when groups are (a) highly cohesive and there are strong pressures toward conformity, (b) relatively isolated from outside influences, and (c) influenced by leaders with a closed style of leadership

(see Figure 17.1). With an open style, leaders withhold their personal opinion, solicit input on the pros and cons of alternate positions, encourage meetings when they are absent, and welcome healthy criticism.

Some of the strategies which have been advanced to prevent groupthink are evident in Figure 17.1. Initially, a large *number of alternatives* should be solicited and then listed. The group has greater flexibility when more options are available. When the list of alternatives is completed, one or two will be obviously preferable to the group, others will be rejected almost immediately. The *preferred alternatives should be reconsidered,* examined for defects, discussed in terms of the strategies necessary for implementation and possible problems associated with that implementation. At the same time, the *rejected alternatives should be reconsidered* and examined for any advantages that might have been overlooked previously. Peter Drucker (1966), in a discussion of the decision process, recounted that Alfred P. Sloan, the chairman of General Motors, had stated at a meeting:

> *Gentleman, I take it we are all in complete agreement on the decision here .... Then I propose we postpone further discussion of this matter until our next meeting to give ourselves time to develop disagreement and perhaps gain some understanding of what the decision is all about.* (Drucker, 1966, p. 148)

Cohesive groups value consistency, conformity, consensus. Consequently, another technique to prevent groupthink is to solicit the *input of experts* outside the group. They bring a different perspective and are not committed to the need for group solidarity. *New information* -- facts, strategies, alternatives — may arise when the group is well along in its deliberations. Nonetheless, the desire for closure should be resisted and the new information scrutinized completely. Finally, *contingency plans* should be developed for all of the possible outcomes of the decision. If a sport group decides after considerable discussion to introduce compulsory drug testing for everyone in the organization, it must also establish contingency plans (i.e., "if this .... then this") for all the possibilities. What if athletes, coaches or administrative personnel refuse to be tested? What if an athlete, coach, or administrator tests positive? An attempt to develop contingencies also serves as a protection against groupthink.

Group Attributions

Individuals within groups also repeatedly come to

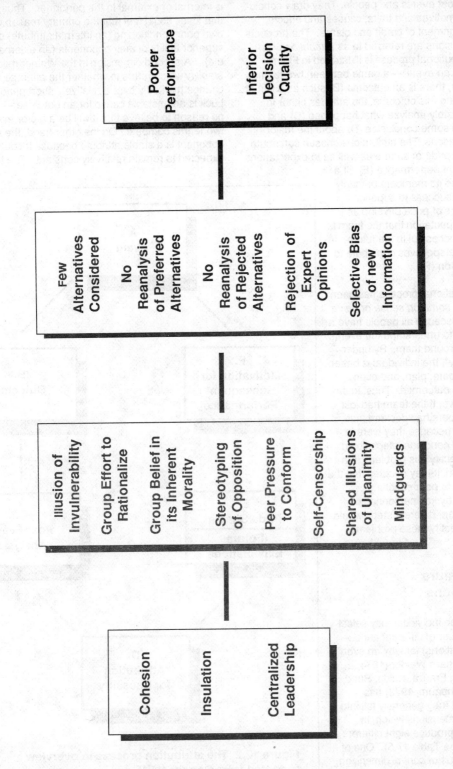

Figure 17.1 A model for groupthink (Adapted from Janis 1972)

Cohesion

Insulation

Centralized
Leadership

Illusion of Invulnerability

Group Effort to Rationalize

Group Belief in
its Inherent Morality

Stereotyping
of Opposition

Peer Pressure
to Conform

Self-Censorship

Shared Illusions
of Unanimity

Mindguards

Few
Alternatives Considered

No
Reanalysis
of Preferred
Alternatives

No
Reanalysis
of Rejected
Alternatives

Rejection of Expert
Opinions

Selective Bias
of new
Information

Poorer
Performance

Inferior
Decision
Quality

decisions about events and people. They draw conclusions about motives and traits, causes and effects, and the assignment of credit and blame. The products of these decisions are referred to as *attributions*. A general attributional process is illustrated in Figure 17.2. When an event — a game between two teams — occurs (A), there is an outcome (B) such as a win or loss. Following this outcome, the athletes either in public or privately analyze what happened (C) and then come to some conclusion (D) about the major causes or reasons. The attributions chosen contribute to feelings of pride or shame as well as to expectations for subsequent performance (E). If a team wins and its members primarily attribute that success to superior talent, feelings of pride develop as well as an expectation that the team is likely to be successful in the future. In turn, these perspectives contribute to team motivation (F).

The attributional process has been described as *common sense or naive psychology* because all people have a natural need to understand the events and people around them. By understanding "why", the individual is better able to anticipate, plan, and even control future outcomes. Thus, in the example above, if the team had lost and it's members had decided that this occurred because they were in poor physical condition, steps could be taken to rectify this problem. On the other hand, if they decided that the loss was due to poor coaching, absenteeism by key personnel, or poor motivation, different steps would be taken to rectify these problems.

General Nature of Attributions

Although an individual may select any of a number of different attributions (explanations) for why an event occurred, Bernard Weiner (1974, 1979; Weiner, Freeze, Kukla, Reed, Rest, & Rosenbaum, 1972) has proposed that they generally fall into three main dimensions which, in combination, produce eight different categories (see Table 17.5). One of these, the *locus of control* dimension, refers to whether the perceived cause

is internal or external to the performer. Thus, a team that loses could feel that the primary reason was their own poor conditioning (an internal attribute) or the superior ability of their opponents (an external attribute). A second dimension in the Weiner model is *stability* which refers to whether the attribute is likely to change markedly over a relatively short period of time. Luck is an unstable cause for an outcome — there's no reason to believe that it will be a factor every time two teams compete. On the other hand, the skill of an opponent is a stable attribute because it could be expected to remain relatively constant. The third

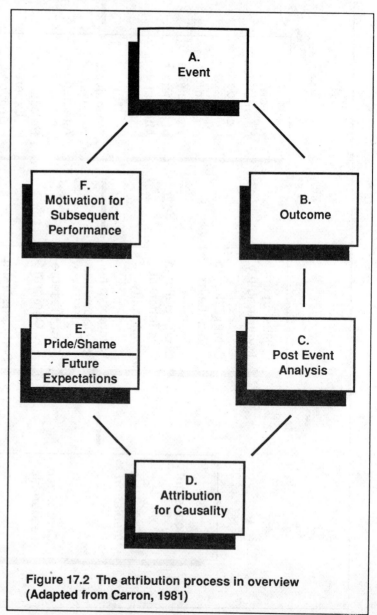

Figure 17.2 The attribution process in overview (Adapted from Carron, 1981)

Table 17.5 Weiner's classsification scheme for causal attributions.

		Internal	External
Uncontrollable	Stable		
	Unstable		
Controllable	Stable		
	Unstable		

dimension is *controllability*. Some causes are under the direct control of the team or its opponents whereas others are not under anyone's control. Effort (of a team or its opponent), for example, can be controlled; the weather cannot.

It was pointed out above (see Figure 17.1 again) that when a particular cause for an outcome is established, it also leads to feelings of pride or shame and to the development of expectations for subsequent performance. The locus of control dimension, for example, has a major impact on feelings of pride/shame. If a team feels that personal factors such as hustle, effort, and hard work were the major reasons for a victory, it experiences pride and satisfaction. On the other hand, if it feels that a lack of hustle, effort, and hard work were the major reasons for a loss, it feels shame and dissatisfaction. The stability dimension has an influence on expectations for future performance. Similar outcomes are expected from causes that are stable (i.e., an opponent is highly competent) whereas a different outcome is expected from causes that are unstable (i.e., an opponent was extremely lucky). Finally, the controllability dimension is associated with reactions to others. Praise, rewards, and approval are expected for controllable successes; punishment, criticism, disapproval are expected for failures that are controllable.

Attributions in Achievement Situations

The research which has examined causal attributions in achievement situations has produced some reasonably consistent generalizations. One of these is that when individuals are working *independently on a laboratory task,* they have a tendency to take personal credit for success. And, when failure is experienced, they have a tendency to deemphasize the importance of internal factors and to shift the blame to external conditions (e.g., Gill & Gross, 1979; Roberts, 1978). In short, individuals working alone in laboratory situations adopt self serving explanations for successes and failures.

A second generalization is that in *sport situations,* when athletes make attributions which are restricted to their degree of *personal (individual) responsibility* for their own performance, there is a tendency to take personal credit for successes and to deemphasize personal responsibility for failures (e.g., Iso-Ahola, 1977, Scanlan & Passer, 1980; Spink, 1978). Thus, athletes are also self serving when they explain their own performances.

A third generalization is that when individuals are working *collectively on a laboratory task,* there is a greater tendency for members of successful groups to assume responsibility for the group's performance than members of unsuccessful groups (e.g., Forsyth & Schlenker, 1977). Also, members of successful groups tend to view their contribution as greater than that of the average group member while members of unsuccessful groups tend to view their contribution as less than that of the average group member (e.g., Wolosin, Sherman, & Till, 1973). In short, individuals working in groups in laboratory situations adopt self serving explanations for group successes and failures.

One instance where a self serving pattern isn't the norm is in *sport situations.* A fourth generalization from research is that when athletes explain *team outcomes,* there is a tendency for members of successful teams to either share equally or give a disproportionate amount of credit to their teammates. Similarly, members of unsuccessful teams either share equally or take a disproportionate amount of the blame (e.g., Gill, 1980, Taylor & Doria, 1981). This pattern of causal attribution represents a team enhancing rather than a self enhancing perspective.

Team Enhancing Attributional Strategies

The differences between self enhancing and team enhancing strategies are summarized in Table 17.6. In the case of the latter, the team is emphasized and protected. With success, care is taken to insure that the credit is distributed equally among all of the team members and that the individual's personal role is deemphasized. With failure, scapegoating is avoided — responsibility is either distributed equally among all team members or each individual assumes a disproportionate amount of blame. Diane Gill (1980) has suggested that this occurs because a *team norm* is in operation in sport, a norm which leads members to place the group's welfare first. Protecting teammates and the team after a failure and crediting them after a victory helps to insure the team unity is maintained.

Three factors have a moderating influence on the degree to which a team enhancing versus a self enhancing strategy is used in the assignment of the responsibility for team outcomes. One is *team cohesiveness*. When low cohesive groups fail, a self serving pattern of attributions is not unusual. Members feel minimal association with the group and, therefore, protect their own interests by attributing the majority of the blame for the loss to their teammates. When high cohesive groups fail, however, members protect the solidarity of the group by adopting a team enhancing pattern of attributions. They assume a responsibility for failure which is at least equal to the average group member. This pattern has been demonstrated both with ad hoc laboratory groups (e.g., Schlenker & Miller, 1977b) and with intact sport teams (Brawley, Carron, Widmeyer, 1987; Bird, Foster, & Maruyama, 1980)

A second factor is the *amount of interaction and communication*. Individuals who are not in groups but are working in highly cooperative situations involving considerable face-to-face interaction reduce the extent to which they use a self serving strategy and increase the extent to which they use a team enhancing strat-

egy (Gill, 1980; Schlenker, Soraci, & McCarthy, 1976). Close associations and interactions lead to the development of a group perspective. Consequently, an attributional pattern emerges that is also similar to that of a group rather than of an independent individual.

The individual's *role* in the group also has a moderating influence on the degree to which self enhancing strategies are used. This was demonstrated in a study reported by Bruce Caine and Barry Schlenker (1979). ROTC cadets participated in 3-man groups on a problem solving task. The written instructions provided prior to the experiment contributed to the subjects' expectations that they were either a group leader, a follower, or an equal. Bogus feedback was then provided after the problem-solving which led the groups to perceive that they had either been successful or unsuccessful. Followers and equals in the groups showed a self serving pattern in their attributional analysis. They assumed a high level of personal responsibility if the group was successful but a very reduced level if the group was unsuccessful. The group leaders, on the other hand, assumed a high level of personal responsibility after both success and failure. The attributional analysis used after the success was self enhancing but the one after the failure was team enhancing.

Cognitive and Motivational Bases for Attributions

When it became obvious that different patterns were present in the types of attributions that were used following success and failure, attempts were made to understand why. One proposal advanced has been referred to as a *motivational or functional model* (Kelley, 1967). This approach is based on the assumption that individuals are motivated by a desire to maintain or enhance their self-esteem. Thus, when success is attributed to personal factors, a self-enhancing strategy is in operation; when failure is attributed to external factors, a self-protecting strategy is in operation.

A second explanation advanced has been referred to as a *cognitive model* because it focuses on the logical, rational basis for assigning responsibility (Miller & Ross, 1975). The cognitive model is based on the assumption that individuals logically search, analyze, and draw inferences

Table 17.6 Team enhancing versus self enhancing attributional strategies for team outcomes

	Team Success	Team Failure
Team Enhancing Strategies	The role of the team is emphasized. Credit is distributed among other team members	The role of the team or of the self is emphasized. Responsibility is shared equally or the individual assumes disproportionately greater personal blame.
Self Enhancing Strategies	The role of the self is emphasized. Greater personal credit is assumed for the outcome	The role of others is emphasized. Greater responsibility is assigned to teammates

from past experiences to arrive at the reason(s) why an outcome occurred. Thus, an athlete who has consistently been outstanding in sport all her life might be expected logically to attribute winning to personal factors (ability, effort) rather than to external factors (easy opponent).

An experiment was conducted by Schlenker and Miller (1977a) in order to directly compare the motivational and cognitive models. They had individuals work in groups of four on a problem solving task. Three of the people in the group were confederates of the experimenters, the fourth was the only true subject. The experimental situation was manipulated so that the solution offered by the subject was used by the group the majority of the time. Following the problem solving phase, one half of the subjects were informed that their group had been successful on the task; the other half, that their group had not done very well. The subjects were then asked to evaluate their own absolute responsibility as well as their responsibility relative to other members of the group. The subjects who were in groups that had been successful quite accurately assumed the majority of responsibility. They had had the greatest input into the group's decisions and they assigned the greatest amount of credit to themselves. Subjects who were in groups that had been unsuccessful, however, displayed a self serving bias. They rated their input into the group's decisions and their responsibility as equal to that of the other members of the group. Although individuals may process information and make attributions in a logical fashion in some instances, there is also a strong motivation to maintain self esteem.

Implications for the Effectiveness of Sport Groups

Attributions for causality are products of personal perceptions. But personal perceptions are not always accurate. Like the perception of beauty, the perception of causality is often in the eye of the beholder. As a consequence when self enhancing and team enhancing strategies are used to explain team outcomes, they can present a problem for group effectiveness.

The use of self enhancing explanations contribute to the reduction of team cohesiveness and, eventually, to disruption in the group. This is particularly so when the self enhancing strategy is also associated with scapegoating — attaching the majority of blame to one or two group members. This was illustrated in a study conducted by Shaw & Breed (1970). Confederates of the researchers were included on the rosters of teams that were in competition. These confederates then singled out an actual subject who was blamed for the team's failure. Relative to subjects who were not blamed, the scapegoats were less satisfied with their team, held a lower perception of their teammates' abilities, and showed a stronger preference to work with another group in the future.

Forsyth, Berger, and Mitchell (1981) also found that the use of a self enhancing strategy leads to a reduction in the level of interpersonal attraction on a team. Subjects working on a simulated survival exercise were provided with feedback which indicated that their group had either been successful or unsuccessful. After rating their own and other members' level of responsibility for the outcome, the subjects were required to evaluate individuals they were led to believe had assumed either a low, moderate, or high level of responsibility. The least liked group members were those individuals who adopted a self enhancing strategy in victory (high responsibility claimed) and defeat (low responsibility claimed). The best liked were those individuals who adopted a team enhancing strategy in victory (low or moderate responsibility claimed) and defeat (high or equal responsibility claimed).

While a team enhancing strategy is obviously better for maintaining group cohesiveness, it shouldn't interfere with an accurate appraisal of the actual causes of the outcome. The team may be successful primarily because the defense played well. Credit should be shared among the total team without losing sight of the need to pay special attention to the offense. Conversely, a team may be unsuccessful primarily because the offense played poorly. In order to retain the solidarity of the group, the responsibility must be shared equally. Then, the offense can be given special attention.

Another implication of the attribution process which has been discussed elsewhere (cf. Carron, 1984) concerns the use of internal (personal) explanations for an outcome versus external (situational) explanations. After a loss, the greatest dissatisfaction results when an internal attribution is adopted; e.g., poor ability, inadequate conditioning, low effort. As a consequence, external attributions are often adopted after teams lose. Thus, for example, a defeat may be attributed to poor officiating, bad luck, or unfair play by an opponent. Because these causes cannot be controlled personally, the athlete's shame and dissatisfaction are reduced. And, he or she also can reasonably conclude that no changes are necessary for subsequent competitions — external factors are outside personal control. This conclusion may be completely inconsistent with the facts and contribute to a false sense of optimism.

The reverse of this scenario is also a problem. After a victory, the greatest satisfaction results when an internal attribution is adopted; superior effort, high ability, smarter play selection. Internal attributions which might be quite inappropriate could be adopted after a success. If the opponent is markedly inferior, strategies and approaches which are inadequate could be maintained. An objective evaluation of team performance against realistic goals and objectives should help to reduce the impact of both of these attributional biases.

18 Cooperation & Competition in Groups

In this opening quote, former professional basketball player, Bill Bradley (1976), discussed his intense competition with teammate Cazzie Russell when they were members of the New York Knicks. Bradley found that the constant, intense competition left him drained of emotional energy. He was unable to relax even at practices; he experienced tension the moment he stepped onto the court. The competition also affected his interpersonal relations with Russell in situations away from basketball because "even off the court, the anger and aggressive drive spilled over and prevented closeness" (Bradley, 1976, p. 108).

The intragroup competition between Russell and Bradley also influenced their relationship with others — other teams, the fans, and media. In his description of this latter aspect, Bradley stated:

> We divided the basketball fans in New York into warring camps. The press and public emphasized our dissimilarities. Cab drivers would tell me Cazzie should start. Cab drivers would tell me I should start. People at courtside would do the same. If Cazzie or I missed several shots during warm-ups, someone would invariably yell that the other one of us should be starting. (pp. 107-108)

From the perspective of a scientist, the Bradley and Russell situation could be looked at in three ways — from an individual perspective, from a within group perspective, and from a between group perspective. In other words, it is possible to look at this situation by

I came to view our competition as a sad but necessary aspect of professional basketball. Playing time is like food for a player; without it he cannot survive. However much Cazzie [Russell] and I respected each other, since neither of us was prepared to accept twenty minutes of playing time as sufficient, every game and every practice became a battle to show [Coach Red] Holzman that one of us was better than the other. (Bradley, 1976, p. 108)

trying to determine what Bradley or Russell was like in terms of their personal aspirations, motivations, and frustrations. It is also possible to look at this situation by trying to better understand the pattern of interactions between Bradley and Russell and/or within the Knicks as a team. And finally, it is possible to look at the impact of this situation in terms of the Knicks' relationships with other groups — how it affected their success, the choice of their opponent's offensive and defensive strategies, and so on. The kind of insight obtained from each approach would be different. Social scientists Muzafer Sherif and Carolyn Sherif (1979) emphasized this point when they pointed out that "we cannot legitimately extrapolate from the individual's motivational urges and frustrations to his experiences and behaviors in group situations as if the interaction processes and reciprocities within a group were a play of shadows. It is equally erroneous to extrapolate from the properties of relations *within* a group to explain relations *between* groups, as though the area of interaction between groups consisted of a vacuum" (p. 9).

The study of intragroup and intergroup processes has intrigued a wide spectrum of social scientists because the issues involved have such universal importance. For example, gaining an understanding of team dynamics in sport, stereotyping and social discrimination in society, the functioning of action groups in politics, and the causes and consequences of aggression at a national and international level are based on an understanding of intragroup and intergroup processes. It's not surprising then that numerous books have been devoted to research and theory on the topic; e.g., **Making groups effective** (Zander, 1982), **The social psychology of intergroup relations** (Austin & Worchel, 1979), **Group conflict and cooperation** (Sherif, 1966). And, the present book is concerned with intragroup and intergroup processes in sport teams. In this chapter, the dynamics of cooperation and competition and their influence on intra- and intergroup relations are discussed.

Nature of Cooperation and Competition

Cooperation and competition have been viewed in a number of different but related ways. For example, Morton Deutsch (1949a) emphasized the distribution of rewards when he defined a *cooperative social situation* as one in which the gains by one individual contribute to a gain by all individuals. Rewards are shared equally, independent of the amount of relative personal contribution by various group members. This is the case in professional sport when a team wins a championship. The league awards a bonus and this money is then distributed equally among team members. In a *competitive social situation,* the gains by one individual reduce the potential for gains by other individuals. Rewards are provided on the basis of relative contribution and, therefore, are shared unequally. The prize money awarded in professional golf is a good example.

Competition has also been referred to as a *zero-sum condition* because the rewards to a winner (+) are balanced off against the absence of rewards to the loser (-). Cooperation represents a *nonzero-sum condition* because rewards are available for all participants.

From a slightly different perspective, Marvin Shaw (1981) has considered cooperation and competition in terms of the heterogeneity and homogeneity of the group goals. A characteristic of cooperative situations is that group members hold the same (homogeneous) perception of the group goal and are committed to achieving it. In competitive situations on the other hand, members either have different (heterogeneous) perceptions of the group goal or they have personal goals which interfere with the achievement of the group goal.

It is possible to have cooperation and competition both *within* groups and *between* groups. Figure 18.1 contains examples of four possible combinations of intra- and intergroup processes. In the top example,

there is cooperation within each group and they are competing against each other — a situation which exists in most team sport situations. The second example contains intragroup and intergroup cooperation. This is rare in sport but it does exist — when the teams in a conference get together to establish rules and regulations which govern eligibility, the rules of play and so on. The third example, competition within and between groups, is characteristic of the situation which exists in college golf teams. A team score is important but each golfer in the competition also strives to have the lowest personal score. The final example is contained in the Bradley and Russell situation. They were competing with each other and, at the same time, competition was present between the Kicks and their opponents.

The Robbers Cave Experiment

In 1954, the classic experiment which became known as the *Robbers Cave Experiment* was initiated by a research team led by Muzafer and Carolyn Sherif (Sherif, Harvey, White, Hood, & Sherif, 1961). The main purpose of this study was to examine intragroup and intergroup relations within a natural environment. To achieve this objective, a boys' camp was set up in an isolated setting in Robbers Cave State Park in Oklahoma. In the original selection of the 22 11-year old boys and their eventual assignment to one of the two groups, care was taken to insure that there were no idiosyncratic characteristics which could have contributed to alternate explanations for the results. Thus, the boys selected were homogeneous in age, race, religion, and socioeconomic status and relatively similar in appearance. No previous friendships were present and the assignments to each of the two groups were made so that each group was matched for ability and size.

The two groups were brought to the camp separately and in the initial phase (which lasted for a week), they were kept segregated. This strategy provided the researchers with an opportunity to chart the development of group structure in the two settings — the emergence of status hierarchies, leadership roles, group norms, and so on. The researchers were also able to observe the appearance of various intragroup processes such as cohesiveness, goal setting, cooperation, and competition. Near the end of the initial phase, the groups became aware of each other. Gradually, the boys interests became more and more centered on the presence of the other group. In their conversations, the distinction between "we" and "they" was prevalent, and interest was expressed in holding some competitions between the group.

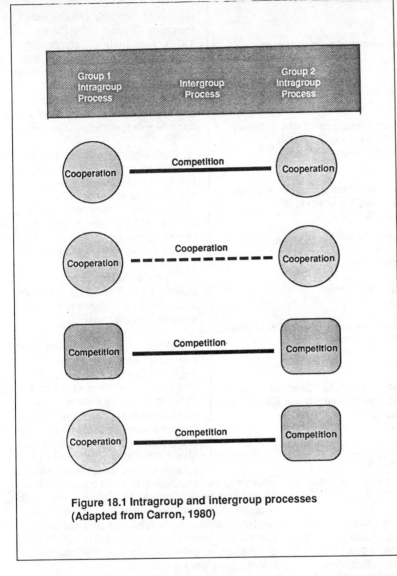

In an attempt to reduce the hostility, the researchers brought the boys together during the third phase in a variety of different noncompetitive situations. They ate together, watched films, played games. When this failed to reduce the hostility, a series of crises were staged which required a cooperative effort from both groups. In this fourth phase, the boys worked together to locate the disruption to their water supply, pull a broken truck, rent movies, and prepare meals. The Sherifs and their colleagues referred to these as *superordinate goals* — goals which required the combined resources of the total group for success. During this fourth phase, intergroup hostility and group polarization were reduced and intergroup contact, friendships, and cooperation were increased.

Figure 18.1 Intragroup and intergroup processes (Adapted from Carron, 1980)

Behavioral Consequences

A number of studies in addition to the work of the Sherifs and their colleagues have shown that the combination of intragroup cooperation and intergroup competition is associated with some relatively consistent behavioral patterns. An overview of these is presented in Table 18.1. Some of these behavioral patterns are interrelated in the sense that they represent a growing tendency by the ingroup to differentiate itself from outgroups.

When these were arranged and initiated, it marked the beginning of the second stage of the study. During this period, the researchers were able to chart the development of intergroup cooperation and competition. Initially, there was some intergroup tension resulting from the competition but it was minimal (e.g., teasing, mild insults). Eventually, however, open hostilities resulted when one group (the Eagles) burned the other group's (the Rattlers) flag after losing a tug-of-war. This marked the beginning of a period of escalating intergroup tension and hostility. At various times, the boys had to be physically restrained from fighting each other. Eventually, the researchers took the two groups to different parts of the camp.

This is the case when social categories are used. When a group forms, *social categorization* helps it establish a sense of identity and serves to differentiate it and its members from others. "The mere perception of belonging to two distinct groups — that is, social categorization per se — is sufficient to trigger intergroup discrimination favoring the in-group. In other words, the mere awareness of the presence of an outgroup is sufficient to provoke intergroup competitive or discriminatory responses on the part of the in-group" (Tajfel & Turner, 1979, p. 38). "We" versus "they" is a simple form of social categorization. But, with the

Table 18.1 Behavioral consequences of cooperation and competition

Factor	Consequences	Reference
Social Categorization	Outgroup members are categorized into restrictive perceptual categories and stereotyping occurs	Tajfel & Turner (1979)
Evaluative Bias	An evaluative bias develops which favors the group's members and its products	Dustin & Davis (1970)
Outgroup Rejection	Ratings of interpersonal attraction favor ingroup members. Friendship choices are predominantly ingroup. Ingroup similarities and outgroup differences are exaggerated	Brewer (1979) Coser (1956)
Group Cohesiveness	Group cohesion is increased but it is influenced by success. Wining teams show increases, losing teams show decreases	Sherif et al (1961)
Leadership Style	An autocratic decision style is increasingly used and favored over a democratic style	Sherif et al (1961) Blake & Mouton (1961)

introduction of competition, the categorizations used by ingroup members become more stereotypical.

Groups that are in competition also show a strong *evaluative bias* in favor of the ingroup (Table 18.1). In relation to the perceptions held for other groups and their members, there is a tendency to overestimate ingroup successes and strengths — the group's product is considered more favorably (e.g., Dustin & Davis, 1970; Janssens & Nuttin, 1976). There is also a tendency to misjudge the motives and intentions of other groups. For example, Doise (1978) found that ingroup members attributed more cooperative motives to themselves and fellow group members than to the outgroup.

Another consequence of intergroup competition is that there is increased *outgroup rejection* (see Table 18.1 again). This is strongly related to the evaluative bias mentioned above. When cooperative groups are competing with other groups, ratings of interpersonal attraction favor the ingroup and there is a greater

number of friendship choices within the group (Brewer, 1979; Coser, 1956). Also, groups in competition have a tendency to emphasize their differences rather than their similarities. Communalities between the groups are downplayed or ignored and any minor differences which exist become exaggerated (Coser, 1956).

The belief that outgroup rejection is a natural consequence of competition isn't universally endorsed. After reviewing the evidence on this issue, Marilyn Brewer (1979) proposed that rejection of the outgroup depends upon the presence of four situational factors: (1) similarity versus dissimilarity of ingroup and outgroup members, (2) the likelihood of future interactions, (c) the type of reward structure present, and (d) the nature of the evaluation being made.

Intragroup cooperation with intergroup competition also influences the development of *group cohesion*, a consequence which is evident in the Robbers Cave Experiment. A clearly defined group structure emerged and cohesiveness was present within the two groups of boys during the initial phase of the study. Then, when competition was initiated, the two groups became even more closely knit and cohesive. The Sherifs and their colleagues also found, however, that success and failure had an influence on the relative level of cohesion — a result which also has been observed in sport teams (Carron & Ball, 1977). With group success, cohesiveness was strengthened, with failure, it was weakened.

Kenneth Dion (1979) has suggested that there are four possible interpretations for the increases in ingroup cohesiveness during competition. One is based on Heider's (1958) *balance theory* and the premise that individuals seek out perceptual consistency. This consistency is achieved by balancing positive perceptions (+) with negative perceptions (-). When ingroup membership is perceived in a positive way, the outgroup is perceived in a negative way and balance and consistency are achieved. A *reinforcement* explanation is based on the fact that the group can serve as a vehicle for the achievement of extrinsic rewards. Competition provides an opportunity to secure rewards such as social approval, trophies, and so on. The ingroup is perceived more favorably because it is the vehicle through which the individual can receive rewards. This explanation also helps to account for the decrease in cohesiveness in failure groups — they are not providing the reinforcement necessary to maintain committed group membership. Competition also poses a *threat to goal attainment,* prestige, and self-evaluation. When groups are threatened from outside, they tend to draw closer together. The final explanation, is associated with a *self enhancement hypothesis.* The ingroup is perceived to be superior to the outgroup by its members in order to protect and enhance their self esteem.

The *style of leadership* used by leaders and endorsed by subordinates is also influenced by cooperation and competition (Table 18.1). Cooperative groups inherently are more prone to a participative decision style. With the introduction of competition, however, there is a shift to a more autocratic style and this is acceptable to the group as a whole. Blake and Mouton (1979) have referred to this as *leadership consolidation.* Those group members who are slightly more dominant, exercise greater initiative, and provide more and better input during the cooperative phase, assume a greater proportion of the leadership responsibility during competition. In their research with industrial work groups, Blake and Mouton also observed that leadership replacement occurs in groups that fail. Group members who take a leadership role lose status and influence when the group is unsuccessful. Consequently, they are replaced by other group members.

Performance Consequences

It was pointed out above that in a cooperative situations, the gains by one individual contribute to a gain by all. This is the case in relay events where an exceptional time by one individual benefits the whole team. In a competitive situation, on the other hand, the gains by one individual reduce the potential for gains by other individuals. This is the situation which exists in individual sprint events. There is only one first place finisher, one second place, one third, and so on. Although these are the two predominant possibilities in sport, a third is available in educational settings — individualism. With an individualistic situation, each person is rewarded on the basis of personal merit. As a consequence, any number of people can reach the highest category and be appropriately rewarded. During elementary school track and field days, this is what often occurs. A first place ribbon is awarded to every child who surpasses a baseline (threshold) time in the track events or achieves a set distance (or height) in the field events.

What are the merits of competition versus cooperation versus individualism for performance? Proponents of competition have cited the advantages of working independently, not having to share the credit or blame, accepting the challenges of social comparison. Individualism offers many of the same advantages with one other — the individual's goal is to achieve success in the task and not to beat another person. The proponents of cooperation, on the other hand, point to the social benefits of working with others (e.g., increased interaction, communication, trust, tolerance) as well as to the greater opportunities provided for learning from others.

In 1981, Johnson, Maruyama, Johnson, Nelson, & Skon (1981) drew together 122 studies published since the 1920s and carried out a meta-analysis — a statistical procedure which is used for combining the results from a number of studies. With a meta-analysis, it is possible to statistically search for reliable, consistent trends (and their relative magnitude) in a large number of individual studies (Glass, 1977). On the basis of their analysis, Johnson and his colleagues concluded that:

1. Cooperation is superior to competition for achievement and productivity.

2. Cooperation is superior to individualism for achievement and productivity.

3. Cooperation without intergroup competition is superior to cooperation with intergroup competition for achievement and productivity.

4. There is no difference between competition and individualism for achievement and productivity.

Furthermore, it was stated that these four relationships were present for virtually every subject area including language arts, reading, math, science, social studies, psychology, and physical education. The only situations in which cooperation was not superior to individualism and competition were rote learning and correcting tasks.

The Johnson et al. conclusions were subsequently

criticized for being too simplistic and for not taking into account some of the factors which have been shown to modify the impact of cooperation and competition (e.g., Cotton & Cook, 1982; McGlynn, 1982). Some of these modifying variables which were highlighted by John Cotton and Michael Cook (1982) are task interdependence, task complexity, and group size. A summary of the impact of these factors on the relative effectiveness of cooperation and competition is presented in Table 18.2.

Cooperation is more effective for performance in *interdependent tasks* — those tasks characteristic of team sports such as basketball. Task interaction is required among members of the group for team success. Conversely, competition is better for performance in independent tasks such as archery. No task interaction among members of the team is required. It can be argued that if Cazzie Russell and Bill Bradley had approached practices and games with a cooperative orientation, both would have become better basketball players and the Knicks would have become an even better team.

Another aspect of the task which has an impact on the effectiveness of cooperation and competition is its *complexity*. Tasks such as basketball, badminton, judo, and volleyball are very complex, and, therefore, are learned and performed better under cooperative situations. Tasks such as simple RT in the laboratory are not complex; competition is better for their successful achievement.

Group size is also a mediating variable. Cooperation is superior in large groups while competition is superior in smaller groups (fewer than six members). In large groups, coordinating the group's resources and ensuring that individual members have opportunities for interaction and communication are important considerations. These are more easily accomplished with a cooperative orientation.

Another meta-analysis which was concerned with identifying what *group-oriented approach* in education is most effective for promoting student learning was carried out by Robert Slavin (1983). Table 18.3 presents an overview of the six possible techniques. As this summary shows, Slavin distinguished between tasks in which a division of labor is either possible or not (and therefore, specialization by group members is also possible or not). He also made a distinction among three reward systems: (1) where the group is rewarded because of the summed contributions of individual members (e.g., bowling teams, tennis teams); (2) where the group is rewarded for a single group product (e.g., rowing teams, volleyball teams); and, (3) where each person is rewarded on the basis of personal accomplishment (e.g., individuals train together and then compete independently at a competition).

Slavin found that group rewards are essential in order for group-oriented approaches to be successful. When individuals work together in a group and then are rewarded on the basis of their individual performance (the last column in Table 18.3), there are no advantages over working alone. In order for the group to be effective — for cooperation to occur — a group payoff is necessary.

Social loafing can also occur in education (as any person who has ever worked within a group to produce a one term paper can testify). Thus, individual accountability is an important consideration in group work. When individual contributions can be readily identified (the first column as well as the lower cell in the middle column of Table 18.3), group work is superior to working alone.

In Table 18.3, sport examples are

Table 18.2 Performance consequences of cooperation and competition (Adapted from Johnson et al, 1981 and Cotton & Cook, 1982)

Factor	Condition	Consequences
Task Inter-dependence	High	When task interdependence is high, cooperation is superior to competition
	Low	When task interdependence is low, competition is superior to cooperation
Task Complexity	High	When tasks are highly complex, cooperation is superior to competition
	Low	When tasks are simple, competition is superior to cooperation
Group Size	Large	When groups are large (greater than six), cooperation is superior to competition
	Small	When groups are small (fewer than six), competition is superior or no different than cooperation

Table 18.3 Group oriented approaches to the enhancement of individual learning in educational settings (Adapted from Slavin, 1983)

Task Structure	Group Rewards for Individual Learning	Group Rewqards for a Group Product	Individual Rewards Following Group Involvement
No Division of Labor is Possible in the Group Task	Each person carries out the same task in the group and individual scores are summed to produce a group score, e.g., team bowling	Each person carries out the same task in the group. A single group product is produced, e.g., rowing teams	Each person carries out the same task in the group and individual scores are based on individual achievement, e.g., a group of wrestlers in the same weight class training for the Olympics
A Division of Labor is Possible in the Group Task	Each person becomes an expert in one component of the task and individual scores are summed to produce a group score, e.g., college tennis	Each person becomes an expert in one component of the task. A single group product is produced, e.g., volleyball teams	Each person becomes an expert in one component of the task. Each person's score is based on personal achievement, e.g., members of a track team training for the Olympics

used for illustrative purposes. Nonetheless, there is some question about how relevant Slavin's conclusions are for sport and physical activity. The transfer of generalizations across different situations is difficult and this is particularly so in this instance. Ultimately, in education, *individual outcomes* and *performances* are of primary importance. Group activities are simply used as a means toward this end. In many team sport and physical activity situations, however, *group* outcomes are of primary importance. Individual activities are a means toward this end.

Implications for the Effectiveness of Sport Groups

Behavior. Henri Tajfel and John Turner (1979) have found that cohesiveness, social categorization, evaluative bias, and outgroup rejection — perceiving the situation in terms of "we" versus "they" — occurs even in what they refer to as *minimal groups.* These are ad hoc categories of individuals which are formed on the basis of some trivial criteria. In the Tajfel and Turner research, the individual members are unfamiliar with each other, there is no face-to-face social interaction, and there is no opportunity to gain from favoring ingroup individuals. Nonetheless, a bias becomes evident almost immediately; individuals show favoritism toward the ingroup and discrimination against the outgroup.

Tajfel and Turner have suggested that one of the reasons why individuals respond in this way is that they have a strong need to protect and enhance their self esteem. When they enter into a group, a social bond forms with other group members. One significant contributor to individual self esteem is social identity which results from membership in groups. Other groups in which the individual is not a member provide a reference for comparison. When the comparison yields a positive evaluation, it also provides prestige. But, when the comparison yields a negative evaluation, prestige suffers.

If increased cohesiveness, social categorization, evaluative bias, and outgroup rejection can occur in ad hoc groups, it can be expected that they are also present in sport groups — cooperating teams that are engaged in intergroup competition. The negative behavioral consequences listed in Table 18.1 are inevitable. In professional sport, these behaviors might be considered desirable and there might even be merit in encouraging their development. But in amateur and youth sport, an attempt should be made to reduce their influence as much as possible. Steven Worchel (1979), in a review dealing with the reduction of intergroup conflict in society, has presented four strategies that have been used with varying success: increasing intergroup contact, utilizing group representatives, finding a common enemy and, promoting intergroup cooperation.

Intergroup contact can be used in youth sport. Encouraging interaction, and communication and insuring physical proximity help to reduce stereotyping and discrimination and break down the barriers between groups. Worchel pointed out, however, that there are mixed opinions on the effectiveness of this general strategy for reducing conflict between societies or racial groups. On the one hand, some research has shown that increased familiarity through contact does draw individuals from different groups together. On the other hand, there is also evidence that increased contact has either had no impact or has increased intergroup hostility.

Another strategy which has been used — particularly if the groups are very large — is to have leaders or *group representatives* meet together and then report back to their groups. This approach is not very successful for reducing intergroup conflict, however. Only the group representatives are strongly influenced. Attitudes and beliefs held by individual group members remain unaffected. It is doubtful that this approach would produce beneficial effects in amateur sport situations.

A third strategy which has been used is to establish a *common enemy*. The assumption here is that a threat which is mutually perceived will draw the two groups closer together. Drawing on the work of the Sherifs (Sherif & Sherif, 1969), Worchel argued against this approach. Facing a common threat doesn't break down the barriers between groups, it simply serves to set up new barriers. And, when the common threat has been dealt with, the hostilities between the two groups flare up again.

An effective approach is to promote *intergroup cooperation*. This was the strategy used by the Sherifs and their colleagues in the Robbers Cave experiment when they developed superordinate goals for the two groups. "When groups in a state of friction are brought into contact under conditions embodying superordinate goals whose attainment is compellingly desired by each group, but which cannot be achieved by the efforts of one group alone, they will tend to cooperate toward the common goal (Sherif, 1979, p. 260). When a goal is developed which becomes the focus for the two groups, there is an increase in interaction and communication, negotiations, and so on. In this way, the principals involved establish a sense of "we" and the distinctions between "we" and "they" become blurred.

Performance. Traditionally, it has been believed that competition is a fundamental aspect of sport and physical activity. And, traditionally it has also been held that competition is more effective for the learning and performance of sport skills. This isn't necessarily the case. A strong case can be made for cooperation from a performance perspective. As Table 18.2 shows, high task interdependence, high task complexity, and large groups favor the use of a cooperative rather than a competitive approach. Task interdependence is a characteristic of many sports — basketball, soccer, ice and field hockey, volleyball, and so on. Similarly, every sport is complex for a young athlete who is trying to master a new skill. And, finally, there are very few sport groups consisting of less than six members. There are situations where competition may be more effective but these should be identified before it is automatically assumed that competition is always superior.

Finally, the work of Robert Slavin contributes to the conclusion that the product of group activities should be group rewards rather than individual rewards. There is little advantage in promoting group cooperation and then providing rewards based on individual accomplishments. The individual bonus systems which are prevalent in professional sport are one example of this practice. The team would be better served if it set up an group incentive system based on group goals.

7 Concluding Observations

Our brain trust, which was Shoat Cooper and Burt Danby, tried to rebuild the dynasty. The record shows how good a job they did. Through our portals swaggered the grandest collection of scum ever perpetrated on a squad room. When we didn't welcome a sullen, millionaire rookie who wouldn't learn his plays and traveled with a busines manager, we inherited a malcontent who'd been with five other clubs and came to us with a nickname like dump, Point Spread, or Bail-out. It seemed like the harder I played, the more games we lost. Shake had a good football mind. I asked him one evening in a tavern what he thought our biggest problems were. He looked off from his cocktail for a minute, then turned back to me with a sigh. "Billy C., I'd rather try to tell somebody what an oyster tastes like". (Billy Clyde Puckett, quoted in Jenkins, 1984, p. 29)

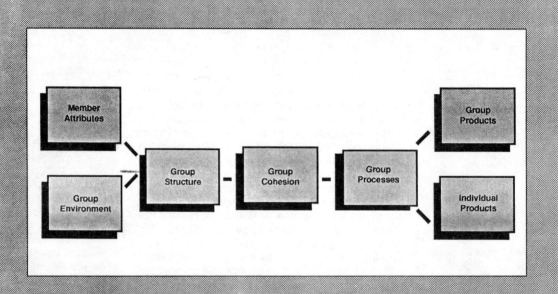

19 Issues in Group Dynamics in Sport Groups

In 1978, Christian Buys wrote what he described as a part tongue-in-cheek, part serious article entitled "Humans Would Do Better Without Groups" (Buys, 1978a 1978b). In this article, Buys presented a rather large list of negative, destructive consequences which are associated with group involvement. His fundamental point was that these negative consequences clearly show that otherwise rational, logical individuals often behave quite the opposite when they are in group situations. As a result of his analyses, Buys concluded that "humans would do better without most forms of groups" (Buys, 1978a, p. 123).

Inevitably, Buys' article produced a number of responses in which his conclusion was criticized and alternate perspectives offered (Anderson, 1978; Green & Mack, 1978; Kravitz, Cohen, Martin, Sweeney, McCarty, Elliott, & Goldstein, 1978; Shaffer, 1978). Essentially four major points were made in these rebuttals. One was that it isn't groups that are responsible for destructive behaviors, it is individuals. Consequently, if the behavior of individuals could be improved, groups would not be a problem. A second was that many of the phenomena listed by Buys are characteristic of the collective behavior of individuals in crowds, not groups. A third was that many of the consequences listed by Buys can be either negative or positive depending on the context. A social movement, for example, would be negative if it contributed to facism and led to the elimination of civil liberties; it would be positive if it contributed

> Any player who was known to talk to me automatically became *persona non grata* in the dressing room. Carl Brewer laid that out clearly in a court case three years later when he was claiming that his pay cheques had been short about $8000 in the first three weeks he spent with the Leafs. The judge asked him why he had not gone to me immediately to get it straightened out. Brewer replied, under oath, that to talk to me at all would have destroyed his chances of acceptance by the other players in the dressing room and on the ice. (Imlach & Young, 1982, pp. 136-137)

to the enhancement of human dignity. And, finally, it was pointed out that Buys ignored many of the positive functions served by groups — the pursuit of civil liberties by action groups, the charitable work done by humanitarian organizations, the effectiveness of the family unit in raising children, and so on. In short, groups can be highly positive and should not be considered soley from the perspective of their potentially negative, destructive consequences.

The main point that Buys brought out, however, and that should be kept in mind is that group involvement can be associated with some negative consequences. And these negative consequences can have an impact on individual behavior and group effectiveness in social groups, work groups, and sport teams.

Some Potential Limitations of Groups

One negative aspect of group involvement is *social loafing* -- the reduction in individual effort which occurs when people are involved in group activities. The reasons for this phenomenon (see Chapter 16) seem to be that individuals either (1) save their best effort for those instances when they perform alone (allocation strategy), (2) try to get by with as little effort as possible and the group provides them with a good opportunity to coast (minimizing strategy), (3) reduce their personal efforts in order not to be taken advantage of in a group (sucker effect), or (4) assume that others in the group are better qualified, and therefore, let them do the bulk of the work (free rider strategy).

The losses associated with social loafing can be reduced substantially by insuring that individual contributions are identifiable. It is also beneficial when the individual understands that his or her contributions are necessary for group success. And, finally, social loafing is also reduced when all group members see that their respective contributions are relatively appropriate.

A second negative aspect of groups is the tendency toward *self-deception*. There is a tendency for ingroup members to overvalue ingroup members, ingroup processes and ingroup products and to undervalue those from the outgroup. The process of self-deception begins almost as soon as groups form. Social categorization which produces a "we" verus "they" is an important element in group formation. With intragroup cooperation and increasing cohesiveness (see Chapters 15 and 18), an evaluative bias becomes established and there is an increase in outgroup rejection. Intergroup competition further contributes to this pattern.

Some of the strategies which have been advanced to reduce self-deception ((Worchel, 1979) include increasing the amount of contact between groups, having group represenatives meet to explore common interests and resolve common concerns, establishing a common enemy to bring the groups together in a cooperative way, and setting out superordinate goals that require a collaborative effort on the part of both groups (see Chapter 18).

When an individual behaves in accordance with group norms because of the social pressures brought to bear by a group, it is referred to as *conformity*. It can be a negative aspect of group membership. Conformity can be represented in either compliance (the individual carries out the behavior but doesn't approve of it internally) or internal acceptance (the individual carries out the behavior and agrees with it internally). The quotation by Punch Imlach which was used to introduce this chapter helps to illustrate the pressures of conformity. A Toronto Maple Leaf hockey player, Carl Brewer, was unwilling to meet with his general manager to rectify a major salary issue because of concerns about how this might be perceived by other players.

Conformity is also considered to be a positive

feature of group membership. In order for any group to be effective and operate in a cohesive fashion, its membership must ascribe to common standards and hold similar perceptions on what is acceptable and unacceptable. Consequently, social pressures are inevitably put on all members to conform to the group's norms. If the group norm is negative or destructive, it has to be changed. In Chapter 12, a variety of approaches for accomplishing this purpose were outlined (see Table 12.5).

A fourth negative correlate of group involvement is *groupthink*. The choice of the term groupthink was influenced by George Orwell's book **1984**. It is a mode of thinking that people in highly cohesive groups engage in when they are so deeply involved in maintaining unanimity that critical thinking is suspended or rendered ineffective (Janis, 1972). The group develops a closeness, an *esprit de corps*. As a consequence, a strong, common motivation to maintain group harmony and solidarity develops and pressure is exerted on all group members to insure that this occurs. In group interactions, a set of nonconscious shared illusions emerges and is accepted by all members without any serious dissent. The result is unanimity but an imperfect, flawed decision (see Table 17.4 again).

The eight characteristics of groupthink that were identified by Janis are (1) a perception that the group is invulnerable, (2) a collective effort to rationalize and discount negative information, (3) an unquestioned belief in the group's moral superiority, (4) stereotypical views of the opposition, (5) active group pressures toward unanimity, (6) self-censorship of opinions which deviate from the group's consensual position (7) a shared illusion that unanimity is present, and (8) the emergence of mindguards that protect the group against dissenting viewpoints. When these conditions are present, the group becomes preoccupied with solidarity and the quality of the decision suffers.

The coach of a highly successful team preparing for an opponent considered to be quite inferior is faced with the problem of groupthink. High cohesiveness is likely to be present because the team is successful. This, coupled with the eight characteristics listed by Janis could produce a condition of groupthink. As a result, the team could be unprepared either physically or mentally for its opponent.

Merrill Melnick (1982) has suggested that one way to combat groupthink in sport groups is to actively work to maintain goal uncertainty. This uncertainty might be achieved by emphasizing the strengths of selected individuals on the opposition, the opponent's strategies, previous upsets, or some other factor. As

Melnick pointed out, this was the approach adopted by the mountain climbing team studied by Richard Emerson (1963) during its ascent of Mount Everest (see Table 16.4). Any positive and negative suggestions to the climbers about the goal and the team's progress were countered with responses that seemed to have the purpose of sustaining uncertainty about the group goal and maintaining high group motivation. Thus, for example, a suggestion that the climb was going well would be countered with the observation that the weather couldn't be expected to stay as favorable. Or a comment that a difficult aspect of the climb was imminent would be countered with the observation that the team would have to be at its best to be successful. In both instances, the communications served to maintain a state of goal uncertainty.

A fifth negative aspect of group involvement is *deindividuation* -- the loss of personal identity, self-awareness, and inner restraints that can occur when the individual becomes submerged in the group. When Festinger, Pepitone, and Newcomb (1952) first introduced this term, they characterized it as follows: "individuals are not seen or paid attention to as individuals. The members do not feel that they stand out as individuals. Others are not singling a person out for attention nor is the person singling out others" (p. 382). Essentially, the individual loses his/her sense of personal identity and becomes an indistinquishable part of a group. As a result of deindividuation, individuals in groups behave in ways that are atypical of them when they are alone.

In Chapter 17, the 1972 USSR-Canada hockey series was discussed. In Moscow, during the closely contested final game, a tying goal was scored by a Canadian player midway through the third period. However, the goal judge was slow in flashing the red light. Jack Ludwig (1972) described what happened next:

The goal judge seemed to be clearing it with Brezhnez. And in the stands, Alan Eagleson, seeing that the light hadn't gone on, thought it had been disallowed and blew up, and was launching himself toward the scorer's bench when two policemen grabbed him. He hollered and Pete Mahovlich, not having much to do while the hassling was going on, happened to be counting the house. Who should he see but his old agent, Alan Eagleson, dangling from the cops' arms like a New Year's baby from a stork's bill! ... Big Pete, 6'8" in his naked steel skates, charged the boards, vaulted up, and over, his shoulder pads four cops wide, his stick ready, offering to trade peace for Eagleson! In two seconds twenty other Team Canada players

were out there ... Eagleson [who was] reclaimed ... who cried out against injustice, was the great hero, though Eagleson, to free himself from the encumbrance of unnecessary adulation, looked back at the cops and the enemy and flashed first a one-finger salute, and, perhaps thinking himself stingy, unselfishly gave the cops his whole arm. (pp. 175-176)

Phillip Zimbardo (1969) has described the process of deindividuation and it bears close resemblance to the behaviors described by Ludwig (see Figure 19.1). At least four of the five predisposing conditions for deindividuation were present in the Moscow situation. The situation was novel since the series was being played for the first time. There was high arousal because of the closeness of the game and the series. The group (of which Eagleson was a member) was closely knit. The team as a whole had been the object of extensive criticism so a sense of shared responsibility was present. Finally, since the Canadian team was in Russia for the first time, it is likely that a feeling of anonymity was also present.

The actions of Eagleson and Team Canada when the goal judge failed to signal the goal were also consistent with what would be expected of individuals in a state of deindividuation. A loss of self-regulation occurred and to use Zimbardo's terms, there was reduced self-monitoring, a lack of sensitivity to relevant norms, an increased reliance on the group for reinforcement and approval of behavior, and a lack of sensitivity to the long range consequences of the behavior. Finally, as a consequence, the behavior shown was typical of deindividuation — impulsive, intense, irrational, nonnormative, and emotional,

Although deindividuation is considered to be primarily a negative consequence of group involvement, it can also have positive results (Zimbard, 1975). The sense of belonging that is associated with group cohesiveness is heightened. Strong feelings of love, trust, commitment, and affiliation emerge. And, members readily achieve consensus on and become committed to a general group purpose. The result is a stronger group. Despite these advantages from a group perspective, most authors suggest that a balance must be achieved between recognition of individual and group accomplishments (e.g., Forsyth, 1983; Gill, 1984; Yukelson, 1984). For example, Donelson Forsyth (1983) has suggested that many of the negative events thought to be caused by deindividuation such as rioting and violence, for example, can also be reinterpreted as identity-seeking behaviors. Individuals who are members of a large homogeneous group engage in these atypical behaviors in order to stand out from others. In sport situations,

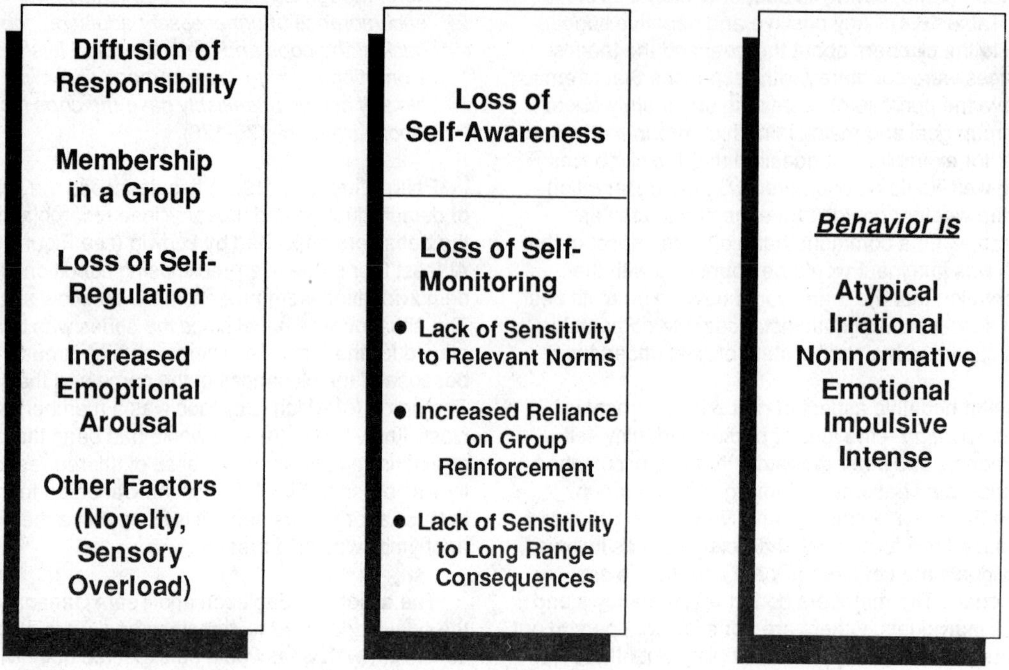

Figure 19.1 The deindividuation process (Adapted from Zimbardo, 1969)

The boxes in the figure contain:

Box 1:
Diffusion of Responsibility

Membership in a Group

Loss of Self-Regulation

Increased Emotional Arousal

Other Factors (Novelty, Sensory Overload)

Box 2:
Loss of Self-Awareness

Loss of Self-Monitoring
- Lack of Sensitivity to Relevant Norms
- Increased Reliance on Group Reinforcement
- Lack of Sensitivity to Long Range Consequences

Box 3:
Behavior is

Atypical
Irrational
Nonnormative
Emotional
Impulsive
Intense

Diane Gill (1984) has recommended that coaches work toward identifying the individual behaviors that contribute to the group's product and then providing encouragement, feedback, and reinforcement for them. It is her belief that coaches who specifically recognize individual contributions will have more success than coaches who only reward group efforts.

The debate set off by the Buys' article is informative and anyone interested in the study of group dynamics should read this series of articles. They leave no doubt concerning the question of whether groups can or should be eliminated in society. As Buys, himself, pointed out, "clearly, many forms of groups are beneficial, if not essential to humans. Indeed, it seems nonsensical to search for alternatives to human groups" (Buys, 1978b, p. 568). Groups are a necessary, integral part of society.

Quo Vadis: Some Thoughts

Psychology, social psychology, and sociology textbooks — not to mention those in management science, political science, and cultural anthropology — include references to groups in society. Social clubs, sport teams, families, religious organizations, work committees, and so on play a major role in our daily lives. In fact, Mills (1967) has suggested that the average person belongs to five or six groups at one time. In these groups, we have an impact on other members and, in turn, they have an impact on us. Because they are so prominent in our lives, numerous authors have emphasized the importance of gaining a better understanding of how groups work. For example, Cartwright and Zander (1968) have stated that:

Whether one wishes to understand or to improve human behavior, it is necessary to know a great deal about the nature of groups. Neither a coherent view of man nor an advanced social technology is possible without dependable answers to a host of questions concerning the operation of groups, how individuals relate to groups, and how groups relate to larger society. (p. 4)

This conclusion on the importance of understanding

groups can be very readily extended to sport and physical activity. To paraphrase Cartwright and Zander, if we wish to understand behavior in sport and physical activity, it is necessary to know a great deal about the nature of sport groups. Sport and physical activity are largely organized on the basis of groups — clubs, teams, organizations, social pairings, instructional classes. This social structure has both a direct and an indirect influence upon individual behavior. Given the obvious importance of group dynamics in sport and physical activity, it might be expected that this general area would be the object of extensive research. The evidence indicates otherwise.

One barometer of the scholarly interest in an area is the number of articles published in scientific journals. In sport psychology, the **Journal of Sport and Exercise Psychology (JESP)** has been a premier journal for scholars to publish their research. Landers, Boutcher, and Wang (1986) reported that over its seven-year history, only 8% of the articles published in **JSEP** were concerned with group dynamics. Further, the majority of these articles either focused on leadership or group cohesion.

Another barometer of scholarly interest is the number of reports presented at professional conferences. In sport psychology, The North American Society for the Psychology of Sport and Physical Activity has been a premier association for scholars to present and discuss their research. An identical pattern has emerged; less than 10% of the papers presented over the past five years have focused on group dynamics topics. And, again, the majority of these have been concerned with either leadership or group cohesion.

What this means is that it is very difficult to answer the question "How do we produce an effective sport team?" When the Dan Jenkins character, Shake Tiller, was asked this question by Billy Clyde Puckett (in the quote used to introduce this final section of the book), he answered " I'd rather try to tell somebody what an oyster tastes like" (Jenkins, 1984, p. 29). Shake Tiller might be right. Certainly, at the present time we know very little about the how, why, and what of effective sport groups. On the basis of common sense, intuition, and research available from other fields of study, some reasonable suggestions can be offered. This was the approach taken in the present book. It was pointed out in earlier chapters that the nature of member resources is important. Also, environmental factors including the group's task and the group's size must be taken into consideration. Similarly, structural factors within the group — roles, norms, leadership, status, position — provide a foundation that influences group processes and, therefore, they must be better

understood. Cohesion is also important. The terms "group" and "cohesion" are tautological (i.e., redundant). If a collection of people is a group, it is also cohesive. Since "cohesion" is a construct that only has relevance in a group context, the study of cohesiveness is also essential for understanding group dynamics in sport groups. And, finally, group processes are the basis of group dynamics and the primary reason why scholars are interested in the study of groups.

Despite the presence of sufficient content to fill eighteen chapters in this book, it is safe to say that we know very little about sport groups. There are still more questions than answers. So, at the risk of being presumptuous, I would like to close by addressing the quo vadis issue — the question of where we might go from here. One suggestion that seems fundamental is that research in sport psychology must try to take into account the impact of group factors — even when the group is not the primary focus of the research. It was pointed out earlier that Muzafer Sherif and Carolyn Sherif (1979) noted that intergroup conflict could be looked at from three levels of interaction — from an individual perspective, from an intragroup perspective, and from an intergroup perspective. They emphasized that it is a mistake to try to extrapolate from the individual's motivations, frustrations, and attitudes and make assumptions about the relations which exist within the group. They also emphasized that it would be equally erroneous to extrapolate from the pattern of interactions which occur within a group to make assumptions about the relations between groups. Research has shown that the nature of motivation, goal setting, and attributional explanations to name but a few are different for individuals and for groups. Thus, one essential first step in gaining a better understanding of behavior and performance in sport and physical activity is to increase the amount of attention paid to the group.

Second, the focus of research in sport group dynamics topics must be expanded. It was pointed out above, that the questions pursued to date have largely been concerned with leadership or cohesion. These are important topics, as indicated by the fact that they are also among the most extensively examined in the general group dynamics literature. Nonetheless, they are not sufficient by themselves to account for the dynamics of effective sport groups. It is necessary to improve our understanding of the impact of member resources, environmental factors, structural parameters, and group processes.

A third concern is related to the focus of group research. Performance outcome is an important issue in sport. But group dynamics researchers in other fields have identified a host of equally meaningful outcomes of group involvement — adherence, conflict, aggression, satisfaction, conformity, and self-deception, for example. Any science or area of science which restricts itself to an interest in only one outcome has only limited utility.

Fourth, care must be taken in sport research to examine group dynamics problems in a wide cross-section of research settings — field studies, field experiments, laboratory experiments, and real life situations. Daniel Landers (1983) was particularly persuasive on this point in an article in which he argued for the need for theory testing in sport psychology. Landers noted that field studies are useful in the initial stages when very little is known about a phenomenon. Research with intact, natural groups can help to identify more important variables for further analysis. Then the relationships among these variables can be examined in field experiments and laboratory experiments where greater control is possible. Theories can be refined in this context and then validated in real-life situations.

A fifth, related point is that research in sport on group dynamics must go beyond simple description — a suggestion that can be directed toward much of the research in sport psychology generally. According to Zanna and Fazio (1982), there are three generations of research questions. The first is descriptive in nature; it addresses the question *what is it?* The concern here is with issues such as "What is the relationship of x to y?" What are the characteristics of x?" The second generation of research question focuses on the question *when does it?*. The concern here is with issues such as "When does x influence y?" In the third generation, the researcher attempts to answer the question *why?*. Thus, for example, it might be interesting to know that groups composed of female athletes score higher on task cohesion than groups composed of males (Widmeyer, Brawley, & Carron, 1985). But why is this the case?

Sport psychology is still an infant science. And group dynamics is one of the youngest members in the family. In order for it to grow and make a meaningful contribution to the psychology of sport and physical activity, it needs a large number of researchers pursuing a wide variety of topics with a broad cross section of methodologies. Otherwise it might remain an easier task to describe how an oyster tastes than to outline the group dynamics that are characteristic of effective sport groups.

References

Aamodt, M.G. (1981) Criteria used by fans in All-Star Game selections. Journal of Sport Psychology, 3, 355-357.

Abdul-Jabbar, K. & Knobler, P. (1983) Giant steps: The autobiography of Kareem Abdul-Jabbar. Toronto, Ont.: Bantam House.

Adams, R.S. & Biddle, B.J. (1970) Realities of teaching: Explorations with video tape. New York: Holt, Rinehart, & Winston.

Albinson, J.G. & Bull, S.J. (1988) The mental game plan: A training program for all sports. London, Ont.: Spodym Publishers.

Alderman, R.B. & Wood, N.L. (1976) An analysis of incentive motivation in young Canadian athletes. Canadian Journal of Applied Sport Sciences, 1, 169-176.

Allen, M. (1987) Jackie Robinson: A life remembered. New York: Franklin Watts.

Allport, F.H. (1924) Social psychology. Boston, MA: Houghton Mifflin.

Alsop, J. (1982) FDR: A centenary remembrance. New York: Viking Press.

Altman, I. (1975) The environment and social behavior. Monterey, CA: Brooks/Cole.

Anderson, A. (1975) Combined effects of interpersonal attraction and goal-path clarity on the cohesiveness of task-oriented groups. Journal of Personality and Social Psychology, 31, 68-75.

Anderson, L.R. (1978) Groups would do better without humans. Personality and Social Psychology Bulletin, 4, 557-558.

Anderson, W.G., & Barrette, G.T. (1978) Teacher behavior. In W.G. Anderson & G.T. Barrette (Eds), What's going on in gym: Descriptive studies of physical education classes, Monograph 1, Motor Skills: Theory into Practice.

Anthrop, J. & Allison, M.T. (1983) Role conflict and the high school female athlete. Research Quarterly for Exercise and Sport, 54, 104-111.

Argyle, M. (1969) Social interactions. London: Methuen & Co.

Arkin, R.M., Gleason, J.M. & & Johnston, S. (1976) Effect of perceived choice, expected outcome, and observed outcome of an action on the causal attributions of actors. Journal of Experimental Social Psychology, 12, 151-158.

Arnold, G.E. & Straub, W.F. (1972) Personality and group cohesiveness as determinants of success among interscholastic nbasketball teams. In I.D. Williams & L.M. Wankel (Eds.), Proceedings of the Fourth Canadian Symposium on Psycho-Motor Learning and Sport Psychology. Ottawa: Fitness and Amateur Sport Directorate, Department of National Health and Welfare.

Asch, S. (1955) Opinions and social pressures. Scientific American, 193, 31-35.

Austin, W.G. & Worchel, S. (1979) The social psychology of intergroup relations. Belmont, CA: Wadsworth.

Baker, P. (1981) The division of labor: Interdependence, isolation, and cohesion in small groups. Small Group Behavior, 12, 93-106.

Baker, P.M. (1981) Social coalitions. American Behavioral Scientist, 24, 633-647.

Bales, R.F. (1966) Task roles and social roles in problem solving groups. In B.J. Biddle & E.J. Thomas (Eds.), Role theory: Concepts and research. New York: John Wiley.

Bales, R.F. (1980) SYMLOG case study kit. New York: Free Press.

Bales, R.F., Cohen, S.P. & Williamson, S. A. (1979) SYMLOG: A system for the multiple level observation of groups. New York: Free press.

Ball, J.R. & Carron, A.V. (1976) The influence of team cohesion and participation motivation upon performance success in intercollegiate ice hockey. Canadian Journal of Applied Sport Sciences, 1, 271-275.

Bandura, A. (1977) Self-efficacy: Toward a unifying theory of behavioral change. Psychological Review, 84, 191-215.

Bandura, A. (1982) Self-efficacy mechanism in human agency. American Psychologist, 37, 122-147.

Bass, B.M. (1960) Leadership, psychology, and organizational behavior. New York: Harper.

Bass, B.M. (1962) The orientation inventory. Palo Alto, CA: Consulting Psychologists Press.

Bass. B.M. (1980) Team productivity amd individual member competence. Small Group Behavior, 11, 431-504.

Bass, B.M., Dunteman, G., Frye, R., Vidulich, R. & Wambach, H. (1963) Self, interaction, and task orientation inventory scores associated with overt behavior and personal factors. Educational and Psychological Measurement, 23, 101-116

Baum, A. & Valins, S. (1977) Architecture and social behavior: Psychological studies of social density. Hillsdale, NJ: Erlbaum.

Baumeister, R.F. (1985) The championship choke. Psychology Today, 19, 48-52.

Baumeister, R.F. & Steinhilber, A. (1984) Paradoxical effects of supportive audiences on performance under pressure: The home field disadvantage in sports championships. Journal of Personality and Social Psychology, 47, 85-93.

Behling, O. & Schriesheim, C. (1976) Organizational behavior: Theory, research and application. Boston, MA: Allyn & Bacon.

Berger, J., Fisek, M.H., Norman, R.Z. & Zelditch, M. (1977) Status characteristics and social interaction. New York: Elsevier.

Berkowitz, L. (1954) Group standards, cohesiveness, and productivity. Human Relations, 7, 509-514.

Berkowitz, L. (1956) Group norms among bomber crews: Patterns of perceived crew attitudes, "active" crew attitudes, and crew liking related to air crew effectiveness in Far Eastern combat. Sociometry, 19, 141-153.

Biondo, R. & Pirritano, M. (1985) The effects of sport practice upon the psycho-social integration of the team. International Journal of Sport Psychology, 16, 28-36.

Bird, A.M. (1977) Team structure and success as related to cohesiveness and leadership. Journal of Social Psychology, 103, 217-223.

Bird, A.M. (1977) Development of a model for predicting team performance. Research Quarterly, 48, 24-32.

Bird, A.M., Foster, C.D., & Maruyama, G. (1980) convergent and incremental effects of cohesion on attributions for self and team. Journal of Sport Psychology, 2, 181-194.

Blake, R.R., Shepard, H.A., & Mouton, J.S. (1964) Managing intergroup conflict in industry. Houston, TX:Gulf.

Bovard, E.W. (1951) Group structure and perception. Journal of Abmormal and Social Psychology, 46, 389-405.

Bradley, B. (1976) Life on the run. New York: Bantam Books.

Braver, S. (1975) Reciprocity, cohesiveness, and co-operation in two-person games. Psychological Reports, 37, 371-378.

Brawley, L.R., Carron, A.V., & Widmeyer, W.N. (1987) Assessing the cohesion of teams: Validity of the Group Environment Questionnaire. Journal of Sport Psychology, 9,275-294.

Brawley, L.R., Carron, A.V., & Widmeyer, W.N. (1988) Exploring the relationship between cohesion and group resistance to disruption. Journal of Sport and Exercise Psychology, 10, 199-213.

Bray, R.M., Kerr, N.L., & R.S. Aitken (1978) Effects of group size, problem difficulty, and sex on group performance and member reactions. Journal of Personality and Social Psychology, 36, 1224-1240.

Breglio, J. (1976) Formal structure and the recruitment of umpires in baseball organizations. Paper presented at the American Sociological Association Annual Meeting, New York, NY.

Brewer, M.B. (1979) The role of ethnocentricism in intergroup conflict. In W.G. Austin & S. Worchel (Eds.), The social psychology of intergroup relations. Belmont, CA: Wadsworth.

Bryant, P.W. & Underwood, J. (1974) Bear: The hard life and good times of Alabama's Coach Bryant. Boston, MA: Little Brown.

Budge, S. (1981) Group cohesiveness revisited. Group, 5, 10-18.

Burgoon, M. Heston, J.K., & McCroskey, J. (1974) Small group communication: A functional approach. New York: Holt, Rinehart and Winston.

Burns, J.M. (1978) Leadership. New York: Harper.

Buys, C.J. (1978) Humans would do better without groups. Personality and Social Psychology Bulletin, 4, 123-125. (a)

Buys, C.J. (1978) On groups would do better without groups: A final note. Personality and Social Psychology Bulletin, 4, 568. (b)

Caccese, T.M. & Mayerberg, C.K. (1984) Gender differences in perceived burnout of college coaches. Journal of Sport Psychology, 6, 279-288.

Caine, B.T. & Schlenker, B.R. (1979) Role position andgroup performance as determinants of egotistical perceptions in cooperative groups. Journal of Psychology, 101, 149-156.

Capel, S.A., Sisley, B.L., & Desertrain, G.S. (1987) The relationship of role conflict and role ambiguity to burnout in high school basketball coaches. Journal of Sport Psychology, 9, 106-117.

Caplow, T. (1964) Principles of organization. New York: Harcourt, Brace & World.

Carron, A.V. (1978) Role behavior and coach-athlete interaction. International Review of Sport Sociology, 13, 51-65.

Carron, A.V. (1980) Social psychology of sport. Ithaca, NY: Mouvement.

Carron, A.V. (1981) Processes of group interaction in sport teams. Quest, 33, 245-270.

Carron, A.V. (1981) Social psychology of sport: An experiential approach. Ithaca, NY: Mouvement.

Carron, A.V. (1982) Cohesiveness in sport groups: interpretations and considerations. Journal of Sport Psychology, 4, 123-138.

Carron, A.V. (1984a) Motivation: Implications for coaching and teaching. London, Ont.: Sports Dynamics.

Carron, A.V. (1984b) Cohesion in sport teams. In J.M. Silva III & R.S. Weinberg (Eds.), Psychological foundations of sport. Champaign, IL.: Human Kinetics.

Carron, A.V. (1986) The sport team as an effective group. In J.M. Williams (Ed.), Applied sport psychology: Personal growth to peak performance. Palo Alto, CA: Mayfield.

Carron, A.V. & Ball, J.R. (1977) Cause-effect characteristics of cohesiveness and participation motivation in intercollegiate hockey. International Review of Sport Sociology, 12 49-60.

Carron, A.V., Ball, J.R., & Chelladurai, P. (1977) Motivation for participation, success in performance and their relationship to individual and group satisfaction. Perceptual and Motor Skills, 45, 835-841.

Carron, A.V. & Bennett, B.B. (1977) Compatibility in the coach-athlete dyad. Research Quarterly, 48, 671-679.

Carron, A.V., Brawley, L.R.. & Widmeyer, W.N. (1988) Group size and adherence in fitness classes. Psychology of Motor Behavior and Sport: Abstracts 1988. Knoxville, TN: North American Society for the Psychology of Sport and Physical Activity.

Carron, A.V. & Chelladurai, P. (1978) Psychologicalfactors and athletic success: An analysis of coach-athlete interpersonal behavior. Canadian Journal of Applied Sport Sciences, 3, 43-50.

Carron, A.V. & Chelladurai, P. (1979) Cohesiveness as a factor in sport performance. International Review of Sport Sociology, 16, 21-41.

Carron, A.V. & Chelladurai, P. (1981) The dynamics of group cohesion in sport. Journal of Sport Psychology, 3, 123-139.

Carron, A.V. & Chelladurai, P. (1981) Cohesion as a factor in sport performance. International Review of Sport Sociology, 16, 21-41.

Carron, A.V. & Garvie, G.T. (1978) Compatibility and successful performance. Perceptual and Motor Performance, 46, 1121-1122.

Carron, A.V., Widmeyer, L.R. & Brawley, L.R. (1985) The development of an instrument to assess cohesion in sport teams: The group environment questionnaire. Journal of Sport Psychology, 7, 244-266.

Carron, A.V., Widmeyer, W.N. & Brawley, L.R. (1988) Group cohesion and individual adherence to physical activity. Journal of Sport and Exercise Psychology, 10, 119-126.

Cartwright, D.C. (1968) The nature of group cohesiveness. In D. Cartwright & A. Zander (Eds.), Group dynamics: Research and theory (3rd ed.). New York: Harper & Row.

Cartwright, D. & Zander, A. (1968) Group dynamics: Research and theory. New York: Harper & Row.

Cattell, R.B. (1948) Concepts and methods in the measurement of group syntality. Psychological Review, 55, 48-63.

Cattell, R.B. (1953) New concepts for measuring leadership in terms of group syntality. In D.C. Cartwright & A. Zander, (Eds.), Group dynamics: Research and theory. New York: Row & Peterson.

Chambliss, C.A. & Murray, E.J. (1979) Cognitive procedures for smoking reduction: Symptom attribution versus efficacy attribution. Cognitive Therapy and Research, 3, 91-96.

Cheffers, J.T.F., & Mancini, V.H. (1978) Teacher-student interaction. In W.G. Anderson & G.T. Barrette (Eds), What's going on in gym: Descriptive studies of physical education classes, Monograph 1, Motor Skills: Theory into Practice.

Chelladurai, P. (1978) A contingency model of leadership in athletics. Unpublished doctoral dissertation, University of Waterloo, Waterloo, Ontario.

Chelladurai, P. (1984) Discrepancy between preferences and perceptions of leadership behavior and satisfaction of athletes in varying sports. Journal of Sport Psychology, 6, 27-41.

Chelladurai, P. (1984) Leadership in sports. In J.M. Silva III & R.S. Weinberg (Eds.), Psychological foundations of sport. Champaign, IL.: Human Kinetics.

Chelladurai, P. (1986) Styles of decision making in coaching. In J.M. Williams (Ed.), Applied sport psychology: Personal growth to peak performance. Palo Alto, CA: Mayfield.

Chelladurai, P. & Arnott, M. (1985) Decision styles in coaching: Preferences of basketball players. Research Quarterly for Exercise and Sport, 56, 15-24.

Chelladurai, P. & Carron, A.V. (1977) A reanalysis of formal structure in sport. Canadian Journal of Applied Sport Sciences, 2, 9-14.

Chelladurai, P. & Carron, A.V. (1978) Leadership. Ottawa, Ont: CAHPER Sociology of Sport Monograph Series.

Chelladurai, P. & Carron, A.V. (1981) Applicability to youth sports of the Leadership Scale for Sport. Perceptual and Motor Skills, 53, 361-362.

Chelladurai, P. & Carron, A.V. (1982) Task characteristics and individual differences and their relationship to preferred leadeership in sports. Psychology of motor behavior and sport - 1982: Abstracts. North American Society for the Psychology of Sport and Physical Activity.

Chelladurai, P. & Carron, A.V. (1983) Athletic maturity and preferred leadership. Journal of Sport Psychology, 5, 371-380.

Chelladurai, P. & Haggerty, T.R. (1978) A normative model of decision styles in coaching. Athletic Administrator, 13, 6-9.

Chelladurai, P. & Saleh, S.D. (1978) Preferred leadership in sports. Canadian Journal of Applied Sport Sciences, 3, 85-92.

Chelladurai, P. & Saleh, S.D. (1980) Dimensions of leadership behavior in sport: Development of a leadership scale. Journal of Sport Psychology, 2, 34-45.

Cherniss, C. (1980) Staff burnout: Job stress in the human services. Beverly Hills, CA: Sage.

Cherry, D. & Fischler, S. (1982) Grapes: A vintage view of hockey. Englewood Cliffs, NJ: Prentice-Hall.

Christie, R. & Geis, F.L. (1970) Studies in Machiavellianism. New York: Academic Press.

Cikler, J. (1967) The rise, the development and the extinction of a soccer team of boys. International Review of Sport Sociology, 2, 33-46.

Coleman, J.S. (1961) The adolescent society. New York: Free Press.

Comrey, A.L. (1953) Group performance in a manual dexterity task. Journal of Applied Psychology, 37, 207-210.

Comrey, A.L. & Deskin, G. (1954a) Further results on group manaul dexterity in men. Journal of Applied Psychology, 38, 116-118.

Comrey, A.L. & Deskin, G. (1954b) Group manual dexterity in women. Journal of Applied Psychology, 38, 178-180.

Cooper, R. & Payne, R. (1972) Personality orientations and performance in soccer teams. British Journal of Social and Clinical Psychology, 11, 2-9. Note difference in table

Cooper, R. & Payne, R. (1967) Personality orientations and performance in football teams: Leaders and subordinates' orientations related to team success. Organizational Psychology Group Report No. 1, January, 1967.

Cotton, J.L. & Cook, M.S. (1982) Meta-analysis and the effects of various reward systems: Some different conclusions from Johnson et al. Psychological Bulletin, 92, 176-183.

Cratty, B.J. (1983) Psychology in contemporary sport: Guidelines for coaches and athletes (2nd. ed.). Englewood Cliffs, NJ: Prentice-Hall.

Crosbie, P.V. (1975) The social order. In P.V. Crosbie (Ed.), Interaction in small groups. New York: Macmillan.

Curtis, B., Smith, R.E., & Smoll, F.L. (1979) Scrutinizing the skipper: A study of leadership behaviors in the dugout. Journal of Applied Psychology, 64, 391-400.

Danielson, R.R. (1978) Contingency model of leadership effectiveness: An empirical investigation of its application in sport. In F. Landry & W.A.R. Orban (Eds.), Motor learning, sport psychology, pedagogy, and didactic of physical activity, Book 7. Miami, FL: Symposia Specialists.

Dark, A. & Underwood, J. (1980) When in doubt, fire the manager. New York: Dutton.

Deep, S.D., Bass, B.M., & Vaughn, J.A. (1967) Some effects on business gaming of previous quasi-t group situations. Journal of Applied Psychology, 51, 426-431.

DeFrank, F. (1988) Jim Devallano: Vice president/general manager. Goal: Detroit Red Wings, 25(9). New York: Professional Sports Publications.

Deutsch, M. & Krauss, R.M. (1960) The effect of threat upon interpersonal bargaining. Journal of Abnormal and Social Psychology, 61, 181-189.

Dimock, H. (1941) Rediscovering the adolescent. New York: Association Press.

Dion, K. L. (1979) Intergroup conflict and intergroup cohesiveness. In W.G. Austin & S. Worchel (Eds.), The social psychology of intergroup relations. Belmont, CA: Wadsworth.

Ditka, M. & Pierson, D. (1986) Ditka: An autobiography. Chicago, IL: Bonus Books.

Dittes, J. (1959) Attractiveness of group as a function of self-esteem and acceptance by group. Journal of Abnormal and Social Psychology, 59, 77-82.

Doise, W. (1978) Intergroup relationsand polarization ofindividual and collective judgements. Journal of Personality and Social Psychology, 12, 136-143.

Donnelly, P. (1975) An analysis of the relationship between organizational half-life and organizational effectiveness. Paper presented at the advanced topics course, Department of Sport Studies, University of Massachusetts, Amherst.

Donnelly, P., Carron, A.V. & Chelladurai, P. (1978) Group cohesion and sport. Ottawa: CAHPER Sociology of Sport Monograph Series.

Drucker, P.F. (1966) The effective executive. New York: Harper & Row.

Dryden, K. (1983) The game: A thoughtful and provacative look at a life in hockey. Toronto, Ont: Macmillan.

Dryden, K. & Mulvoy, M. (1973) Face-off at the summit. Toronto, Ont: Little, Brown & Co.

Dunnette, M.D., Campbell, J. & Jaastad, K. (1963) The effect of group participation on brainstorming effectiveness for two industrial samples. Journal of Applied Psychology, 47, 30-37.

Dunteman, G. & and Bass, B.M. (1963) Supervisory and engineering success associated with self, interaction and task orientation scores. Personnell Psychology, 16, 16-22

Durand, D.E. (1977) Powere as a function of office space and physiognomy: Two studies of influence. Psychological Reports, 40, 755-760.

Dustin, D.W. & Davis, H.P. (1970) Evaluative bias in group and individual competition. Journal of Social Psychology 80, 103-108.

Edney, J.J., & Grundmann, M.J. (1979) Friendship, group size, and boundary size: Small group spaces. Small Group Behavior, 10, 124-135.

Edney, J.J. & Jordan-Edney, N.L. (1974) Territorial spacing on a beach. Sociometry, 37, 92-104.

Edney, J.J. & Uhlig, S.R. (1977) Individual and small group territories. Small Group Behavior, 8, 457-468.

Edwards, J. (1979) The home field advantage. In J.H. Goldstein (Ed.), Sports, games, and play: Social and

psychological viewpoints. Hillsdale, NJ: Erlbaum.

Eitzen, D.S. (1975) Group structure and group performance. In D.M. Landers, D.V. Harris, & R.W. Christina (Eds.), Psychology of sport and motor behavior, University Park, PA: College of HPER, Pennsylvania State University.

Eitzen, D.S. (1976) Sport and social status in American public secondary education. Review of Sport and Liesure, 1, 139-155.

Eitzen, D.S. & Sage, G.H. (1982) Sociology of American sport (2nd ed.). Dubuque, IA: W.C. Brown.

Eitzen, D.S. & Yetman, N.R. (1972) Managerial change, longevity, and organizational effectiveness. Administrative Science Quarterly, 17, 110-116.

Emerson, R. (1966) Mount Everest: A case study of communication feedback and sustained group goal-striving. Sociometry, 29, 213-227.

Enoch, J.R. & McLemore, S.D. (1967) On the meaning of group cohesion. Southwestern Social Science Quarterly, 48, 174-182.

Erle, F.J. (1981) Leadership in competitive and recreational sport. Unpublished master's thesis, University of Western Ontario.

Escovar, L.A. & Sim, F.M. (1974) The cohesion of groups: Alternative conceptions. Paper presented the meeting of the Canadian Sociology and Anthropology Association, Toronto, Ont.

Evan, W.M. (1963) Peer-group interaction and organizational socialization: A study of employee turnover. American Sociological Review, 28,436-440.

Evans, N.J. & Jarvis,P.A. (1980) Group cohesion: A review and reevaluation. Small group behavior, 11, 359-370.

Feinstein, J. (1987) A season on the brink: A year with Bobby Knight and the Indiana Hoosiers. New York, NY: Simon & Schuster.

Feld, N.D. (1959) Information and authority: The structure of military organization. American Sociological Review, 24, 15-22.

Festinger, L., Pepitone, A. & Newcomb, T. (1952) some consequences of deindividuation in a group. Journal of Abnormal and Social Psychology, 47, 382-389.

Festinger, L., Schachter, S., Back, K. (1963) Social pressures in informal groups. Stanford, CA: Stanford University Press. (Originally published in 1950)

Fiedler, F.E. (1967) A theory of leadership effectiveness. New York: McGraw-Hill.

Fiedler, F.E. & Chemers, M.M. (1974) Leadership and

effective management. Glenview, IL: Scott, Foresman & Co.

Fiedler, F.E., Hartmann, W., Rudin, S. (1952) The relationship of interpersonal perception to effectiveness in basketball teams. (Suppl. Tech. Rep. No. 3, contract N60T1-07135), Urbana, IL: Bureau of Records and Services, University of Illinois.

Fisher, A.C., Mancini, V.H., Hirsch, R.L., Proulx, T.J., & Staurowsky, E.J. (1982) Coach-athlete interactions and team climate. Journal of Sport Psychology, 4, 388-404.

Fishman, S. & Tobey, C. (1978) Augmented feedback. In W.G. Anderson & G.T. Barrette (Eds), What's going on in gym: Descriptive studies of physical education classes, Monograph 1, Motor Skills: Theory into Practice.

Forsyth, D.R. (1983) An introduction to group dynamics. Belmont, CA: Wadsworth.

Forsyth, D.R., Berger, R. & Mitchell, T. (1981) The effects of self-serving vs. other-serving claims of responsibility on attraction and attribution in groups. Social Psychological Quarterly, 44 49-64.

Forsyth, D.R. & Schlenker, B.R. (1977) Attributing the causes of group performance: Effects of performance quality, task importance, and furure testing. Journal of Personality, 45, 220-236.

Frank, F. & Anderson, L.R. (1971) Effects of task and group size upon group productivity and member satisfaction. Sociometry, 34, 135-149.

French, J.R.P. & Raven, B. (1959) The bases of social power. In D. Cartwright (Ed.), Studies in social power. Ann Arbor, MI: Institute for Social research.

Fromme, D.K. & Close, S.R. (1976) Group compatibility and the modification of affective verbalizations. British Journal of Social and Clinical Psychology, 15, 189-197.

Gamson, W.A. & Scotch, N.A. (1964) Scapegoating in baseball. American Journal of Sociology, 70, 69-72.

Garland, J., Kolodny, R., & Jones, H. (1965) A model for stages of developoment in social work groups. In S. Bernstein (Ed.), Exploration in group work. Boston, MA: Milford House.

Garvie, G.T. (1981) Adjusting your motivator intrinsically. In N.L. Wood (Ed.), Coaching science update: 1980/81 edition. Ottawa: Coaching Association of Canada.

Gayton, W.F., Matthews, G.R. & Nickless, C.J. (1987) The home field disadvantage in sports championships: Does it exist in hockey?. Journal of Sports Psychology, 9, 183-185.

Gill, D. L. (1977) Cohesiveness and performance in sport groups. In R.S. Hutton (Ed.), Exercise and sport science reviews (Vol 5). Santa Barbara, CA: Journal Publishing

Affiliates.

Gill, D. L. (1979) The prediction of group motor performance from individual member ability. Journal of Sport Psychology, 11, 113-122.

Gill, D.L. (1980) Success-failure attributions in competitive groups: an exception to egocentricism. Journal of Sport Psychology, 2, 106-114.

Gill, D.L. & Gross, J.B. (1979) The influence of group success-failure on selected interpersonal variables. In G.C. Roberts & K.M. Newell (Eds.) Psychology of motor behavior and sport - 1980. Champaign, IL: Human Kinetics.

Glass, G.V. (1977) Integrating findings: The meta-analysis of research. Review of Research in Education, 5, 351-379.

Goldman, F.W. & Goldman, M. (1981) The effects of dyadic group experience in subsequent individual performance. Journal of Social Psychology, 115, 83-88.

Gordon, S. (1988) Decision-making styles and coaching effectiveness in university soccer. Canadian Journal of Sport Sciences, 13, 56-65.

Gossett, D. & Widmeyer, W.N. (1981) Improving cohesion's prediction of performance outcome in sport. Paper presented at the Annual Meeting of the North American Society for the Psychology of Sport and Physical Activity, Monterey, CA.

Goyens, C. & Turowetz, A. Lions in winter. Scarborough, Ont: Prentice-Hall.

Grand, R.R. & Carron, A.V. (1982) Development of a team climate questionnaire. In L.M. Wankel & R.B. Wilberg (Eds.), Psychology of sport and motor behavior: Research and practice. Edmonton, Alta: Department of Recreation and Liesure Studies, University of Alberta.

Green, R.B. & Mack, J. (1978) Would groups do better without social psychologists? A response to Buys. Personality and Social Psychology Bulletin, 4, 561-563. (b)

Greenfield, J. (1976) The world's greatest team: A portrait of the Boston Celtics 1957-1969. New York: Random House.

Greenstein, T.N. & Knottnerus, J.D. (1980) The effects of differential evaluations on status generalization. Social Psychology Quarterly, 43, 147-154.

Gross, N. & Martin, W. (1952) On group cohesiveness. American Journal of Sociology, 57, 533-546.

Grusky, O. (1963a) Managerial succession and organizational effectiveness. American Journal of Sociology, 69, 21-31.

Grusky, O. (1963b) The effects of formal structure on managerial recruitment: A study of baseball organization.

Sociometry, 26, 345-353.

Gzowski, P. (1981) The game of our lives. Toronto, ONT: McClelland & Stewart.

Hackman, J.R. & Oldham,G.R. (1980) Work redesign. Reading, Mass., Addison-Wesley.

Halliwell, W.R. Intrinsic motivation in sport. In W.F. Straub (Ed.), Sport psychology: An analysis of athlete behavior. Ithaca, N.Y.: Mouvement.

Hardman, K. (1973) A dual approach to the study of personality and performance in sport. In H.T.A. Whiting, K. Hardman, L.B. Hendry, &M.G. Jones (Eds.), Personality and performance in physical education and sport. London: Henry Kimpton.

Hardy, C.J. & Latane', B. (1988) Social loafing in cheerleaders: Effects of team membership and competition. Journal of Sport & Exercise Psychology, 10, 109-114.

Hare, A. P. (1952) A study of interaction and consensus in different sized groups. American Sociological Review, 17, 261-267.

Hare, A. P. (1981) Group size. American Behavioral Scientist, 24, 695-708.

Hare, A.P. & Bales, R.F. (1963) Seating position aqnd small group interaction. Sociometry, 26, 480-486.

Harkins, S.G., Latane', B. & Williams, K. (1980) Social loafing: Allocating effort or taking it easy. Journal of Experimental Social Psychology, 16, 457-465.

Haythorn, W.W. (1968) The composition of groups: A review of the literature. Acta Psychologica, 28, 97-128.

Heider, F. (1958) The psychology of interpersonal relations. New York: Wiley.

Hendry, L.B. (1968) Assessment of personality traits in the coach-athlete relationship. research Quarterly, 39, 543-551.

Hersey, P. & Blanchard, K.H. (1977) Management and organizational behavior (3rd ed.). Englewood Cliff, NJ: Prentice-Hall.

Herzog, W. & Horrigan, K. (1987) White rat: A life in baseball. New York: Harper & Row.

Heslin, R. (1964) Predicting group task effectiveness from member characteristics. Psychological Bulletin, 62, 248-256.

Highlen, P.S. & Bennett, B.B. (1979) Psychological characteristics of successful and nonsuccessful elite wrestlers: An exploratory study. Journal of Sport Psychology, 1, 123-137.

Highlen, P.S. & Bennett, B.B. (1983) Elite divers and wrestlers: A comparison between open- and closed-skill athletes. Journal of Sport Psychology, 5, 390-409.

Hill, W.F. & Gruner, L. (1973) A study of development in open and closed groups. Small Group Behavior, 4, 365-381.

Hollander, E.P. (1961) Some effects of perceived status on responses to innovative behavior. Journal of Abnormal and Social Psychology, 63, 247-250.

Hollander, E.P. (1971) Principles and methods of social psychology, 2nd ed. New York: Oxford University Press.

Homans, G.C. (1950) The human group. New York: Harcourt Brace Jovanovich

Hopkins, T.K. (1964) The silent language. New York: Doubleday.

Horne, T. & Carron, A.V. (1985) Compatibility in coach-athlete relationships. Journal of Sport Psychology, 7, 137-149.

Horsfall, A.B. & Anderson, E.M. (1949) Team work and productivity in a shoe factory. Human Organization, 8, 13-26.

Huddleston, S., Doody, S.G., & Ruder, M.K. (1985) The effect of prior knowledge of the social loafing phenomenon on performance in a group. International Journal of Sport Psychology, 16, 176-182.

Imlach, P. & Young, S. (1982) Heavene and hell in the NHL. Toronto, Ont: McClelland & Stewart.

Inciong, P. (1974) Leadership style and team success. Unpublished doctoral dissertation, University of Utah.

Indik, B. (1965) Organization size and member participation: Some experimental tests of alternative explanations. Human Relations, 18, 339-350.

Ingham, A..G., Levinger, G., Graves, J., & Peckham, V. (1974) The Ringlemann Effect: Studies of group size andgroup performance. Journal of Experimental Social Psychology, 10, 371-384.

Isenberg, D.J. (1986) Group polarization: A critical review and meta-analysis. Journal of Personality and Social Psychology, 50, 1141-1151.

Iso-Ahola, S. (1977) Immediate attributional effects of success andfailure in the field: Testing some laboratory hypotheses. European Journal of Social Psychology, 7, 275-296.

Iso-Ahola, S. (1977) Effects of team outcome on children's self-perceptions: Little League baseball. Scandinavian Journal of Psychology, 18, 38-42.

Jackson, S.A. & Marsh, H.W. (1986) Athletic or antisocial? The female sport experience. Journal of Sport Psychology, 8, 198-211.

Jacobs, R.C. & Campbell, D.T. (1961) The perpetuation of an arbitrary tradition through several generations of a laboratory microculture. Journal of Abnormal and Social Psychology, 62, 649-658>

Janis, I.J. (1972) Victims of groupthink. Boston, MA: Houghton-Miffin.

Janssens, L. & Nuttin, J.R. (1976) Frequency perception of individual and group successes as a function of competition, coaction, and isolation. Journal of Personality and Social Psychology, 80, 103-108.

Jenkins, D. (1984) Life its ownself: The semi-tougher adventures ofBilly Clyde Puckett & them. Scarborough, ON: New American Library of Canada.

Jewell, L.N. & Reitz, H.J. (1981) Group effectiveness in organizations. Glenview,IL: Scott foresman & Co.

Johnson, D.W., Maruyama, G., Johnson, R., Nelson, D., & Skon, L. (1981) The effects of cooperative, competitive, and individualistic goal structures on achievement: A meta analysis. Psychological Bulletin, 89, 47-62.

Jones, M.B. (1974) Regressing group on individual effectiveness. Organizational Behavior and Human Performance, 11, 426-451.

Julian, J., Bishop, D., & Fiedler, F.E. (1966) Quasi-therapeutic effects of intergroup competition. Journal of Personality and Social Psychology, 3, 321-327.

Kahn, R. (1971) The boys of summer. New York: Harper & Row.

Kelley, H.H. (1967) Attribution theory in social psychology. In D. Levine (Ed.), Nebraska Symposium on Motivation (Vol 15). Lincoln, NE: University of Nebraska Press.

Kennedy, J. & Stephan, W. (1977) The effects of cooperation andcompetition on in-group-outgroup bias. Journal of Applied Social Psychology, 7, 115-130.

Kernaghan, J. (1987) The best brings out the best. The London Free Press, London, Ontario, September 15.

Kernaghan, J. (1988) Coach is always to blame. London Free Press, London, Ontario, January 27.

Kerr, N.L. (1983) Motivation losses in small groups: A social dilemma analysis. Journal of Personality and Social Psychology, 45, 819-828.

Kerr, N.L. & Bruun, S.E. Ringlemann revisited: Alternative explanations for the social loafing effect. Personality and Social Psychology Bulletin, 7, 224-231.

Khrushchev, N. (1970) Khrushchev remembers. Toronto: Little, Brown & Co.

Kiesler, C.A. & Kiesler,S.B. (1969) Conformity. Reading, MA: Addison-Wesley.

Kinal, S. & Carron, A.V. (1987) Effects of game outcome on cohesion in male and female intercollegiate teams. Canadian Journal of Sport Sciences, 12, 12p

Kipnis, D. (1957) Interaction between members of bomber crews as a determinant of sociometric choice. Human Relations, 10, 263-270.

Kirkpatrick, C. (1987) In an orbit all his own. Sports Illustrated, 67, November 9, pp. 82-99.

Kirschenbaum, D.S. & Smith, R.J. (1983) A preliminary study of sequence effects in simulated coach feedback. Journal of Sport Psychology, 5, 332-342.

Klein, M. & Christiansen, G. (1969) Group composition, group structure and group effectiveness of basketball teams. In J.W. Loy & G.S. Kenyon (Eds.), Sport, culture and scoiety. New York: Macnillan.

Klonke, C. (1988) Jacques Demers: Head coach. Goal: Detroit Red Wings, 25(9). New York: Professional Sports Publications.

Klonsky, B. (1975) The effects of formal structure and role skills on coaching recruitment and longevity: A study of professional basketball teams. Unpublished paper, Department of Psychology, Fordham University. Cited in Loy, J.W., McPherson, B.D., & Kenyon, G. (1978) Sport and social systems: A guide to the analysis, problems, and literature. Reading, MA: Addison-Wesley.

Kluckhohn, C. & Murrary, H.A. (1949) Personality in nature, society and culture. New York:Knopf.

Knight, H. (1987) Mark of excellence. The Philadelphia Flyer, 4, October 18, pp. 2-4.

Kogan, N. & Wallach, M.A. (1964) Risk taking: A study of cognition and personality. New York: Holt, Rinehart, & Winston.

Kramer, J. & Schaap, D. (1985) Distant replay. New York: G.P. Putnam's Sons.

Kravitz, D.A., Cohen, J.L., Martin, B., Sweeney, J., McCarty, J., Elliott, E., & Goldstein, P. (1978) Humans would do better without other humans. Personality and Social Psychology Bulletin, 4, 559-560.

Kravitz, D.A. & Martin, B. (1986) Fingelmann rediscovered: The original article. Journal of Personality and Social Psychology, 50, 936-941.

Kroll, W. (1967) Sixteen Personality Factor profiles of collegiate wrestlers. Research Quarterly, 38, 49-57.

Kroll, W. & Carlson, B.R. (1967) Discriminant function and hierarchical grouping analysis of karate participants. Research Quarterly, 38, 405-411.

Landers, D.M. (1983) Whatever happened to theory testing in sport psychology? Journal of Sport Psychology, 5, 135-151.

Landers, D.M., Boutcher, S.H., & Wang, M.Q. (1986) The history and status of the Journal of Sport Psychology: 1979-1985. Journal of Sport Psychology, 8, 149-163.

Landers, D.M. & Crum, T. (1971) The effects of team success and formal structure on interpersonal relations andcohesiveness on baseball teams. International Journal of Sport Psychology, 2, 88-96.

Landers, D.M. & Lueschen, G. (1974) Team performance outcome andcohesiveness of competitive co-acting groups. International Review of Sport Sociology, 9, 57-69.

Landers, D.M., Wilkinson, M.O., Hatfield, B.D. & Barber, H. (1982) Causality and the cohesion-performance relationship. Journal of Sport Psychology, 4, 170-183.

Lasnier, F. (1979) Group evolution: The life and growth of a team. Coaching Review, 2, 19-20.

Lasorda, T. & Fisher, D. (1985) The artful Dodger. New York: Arbor House.

Latane', B. (1981) The psychology of social impact. American Psychologist, 36, 343-356.

Latane', B. Williams, K. & Harkins, S. (1979) Many hands make light the work: The causes and consequences of social loafing. Journal of Personality and Social Psychology, 37, 822-832.

Lenk, H. (1969) Top performance despite internal conflict: An antithesis to a functional proposition. In J. Loy & G. Kenyon (Eds.), Sport, culture and society: A reader on the sociology of sport. Toronto, Ont: MacMillan.

Lewin, K. (1943) Forces behind food habits and methods of change. Bulletin of the National Research Council, 108, 35-65.

Lewin, K. (1951) Field theory in social science. New York: Harper.

Lewis, G.H. (1972) Role differentiation. American Sociological Review, 37, 424-434.

Liddell W.W. & Slocum, J.W. (1976) The effects of individual-role compatibility upon group performance: An extension ofSchutz's FIRO theory. Academy of Management Journal, 19, 413-426.

Lieber, J. (1987) A test of unity and loyalty. Sports Illustrated, 67, October 5, pp. 41-43.

Lieber, J. (1987) I will be ostracized. Sports Illustrated, 67, October 26, p. 61.

Locke, E.A. & Latham, G.P. (1984) Goal setting: A motivational technique that works. Englewood Cliffs, NJ: Prentice-Hall.

Locke, E.A. Shaw, K.N., Saari, L.M., & Latham, G.P. (1981) Goal setting and task performance: 1969-1980. Psychological Bulletin, 90, 125-152.

London Free Press (1988) Gillick talks to Bell, agent about DH role. London, Ontario, Friday, March 4th.

London Free Press (1988) Flames not hiding heads. London, Ontario, Wednesday, April 27.

London Free Press (1988) Martin latest coach to join unemployed. London, Ontario, Wednesday, May 18.

Looney, D.S. (1988) Why, oh why did Pat stand pat? Sport Illustrated, 68, January 11, pp. 22-23.

Lott, A.J. & Lott, B.E. (1961) Group cohesiveness, communication level, and conformity. Journal of Abnormal and Social Psychology, 62, 408-412.

Loy, J.W. (1970) Where the action is: A consideration of centrality in sport situations. Paper presented at the Second Canadian Psychomotor Learning and Sport Psychology Symposium, Windsor, Ontario.

Loy, J.W., McPherson, B.D. & Kenyon, G. (1978) Sport and social systems: A guide to the analysis, problems, and literature. Reading, Mass: Addison-Wesley.

Loy, J.W. & Sage, J.N. (1968) The effects of formal structure on organizational leadership: An investigation of interscholastic baseball teams. Paper presented at the 2nd International Congress of Sport Psychology, Washington, D.C.

Loy, J.W., Theberge, N., Kjeldsen, E. & Donnelly, P. (1975) An examination of hypothesized correlates of replacement processes in sport organizations. Paper prepared for presentation at the International Seminar for the Sociology of Sport, University of Heidelberg.

Ludwig, J. (1972) Hockey night in Moscow. Toronto, ON: McClelland & Stewart.

Mabry, E.A. & Barnes, R.E. (1980) The dynamics of small group communication. Englewood Cliffs, NJ: Prentice-Hall.

MacLachlan, J. (1979) What people really think of fast talkers. Psychology Today, 13, 113-117.

Madden, J. & Anderson, D. (1986) One knee equals two feet: (And everything else you need to know about football). New York: Jove Books.

Mahoney, M.J., & Avener, M. (1977) Psychology of the elite athlete: An exploratory study. Cognitive Therapy and Research, 1, 135-142.

Mann, R.D. (1959) A review of the relationship between personality and performance in small groups. Psychological Bulletin, 56, 241-270.

Martens, R. (1970) Influence of participation motivation on success and satisfaction in team performance. Research Quarterly, 41, 510-518.

Martens, R., Landers, D.M., & Loy, J.W. (1972) Sport cohesiveness questionnaire. Washington, DC: AAHPERD Publications.

Martens, R. & Peterson, J. (1971) Group cohesiveness as a determinant of success and member satisfaction in team performance. International Review of Sport Sociology, 6, 49-71

.   Martin, B. & Pepe, P. (1987) Billyball. Garden City, NY: Doubleday & Co.

Maslach, C. (1976) Burned out. Human Behavior, 5, 16-22.

Maslach, C. (1982) Understanding burnout: Definitional issues in analyzing a complex phenomenon. In W.S. Paine (Ed.), Job stress and burnout: Research, theory and intervention perspectives. Beverly Hills, CA: Sage.

Maslach, C. & Jackson, S.E. (1981a) Maslach Burnout Inventory Manual. Palo Alto, CA: Consulting Psychologist-Press.

Maslach, C. & Jackson, S.E. (1981b) The measurement of experienced burnout. Journal of Occupational Behaviour, 2, 99-113.

Maslach, C. & Pines, A. (1977) The burnout syndrome. Child Care Quarterly, 6, 100-114.

Massengale, J. & Farrington, S. (1977) The influence of playing position centrality on the careers of college football coaches. Review of Sport and Liesure, 2, 107-115.

Matsui, T., Kakuyama, T. & Uy Onglatco, M.L. Effects of goals and feedback on performance in groups. Journal of Applied Psychology, 72, 407-415.

McAuley, E. (1985) Modeling and self-efficacy: A test of Bandura's model. Journal of Sport Psychology, 7, 283-295.

McCallum, D.M., Harring, K., & Gilmore, R. (1985) Competition and cooperation between groups and between individuals. Journal of Experimental Social Psychology, 21, 301-320.

McCallum, J. (1982) Faith, hope, and Tony C. Sports Illustrated, 57, July 5, pp. 58-72.

McCallum, J. (1988) King for a year. Sports Illustrated, 68, March 21, p. 15.

McCallum, J. (1988) The dread R word. Sports Illustrated, 68, April 18, pp. 51-57.

McCallum, J. (1988) Air Jordan, air Bulls. Sports Illustrated, 68, May 16, pp. 32-39.

McCallum, J. (1988) All the Pistons were firing. Sports Illustrated, 68, May 23, pp. 22-23.

McCullagh, P. (1987) Modeling similarity effects on motor performance. Journal of Sport Psychology, 9, 249-260.

McGlynn, R.P. (1982) A comment on the meta-analysis of goal structures. Psychological Bulletin, 92, 184-185.

McGrath, J. E. (1962) The influence of positive interpersonal relations on adjustment and effectiveness in rifle teams. Journal of Abnormal and Social Psychology, 65,365-375.

McGrath,J.E. (1964) Social psychology: A brief introduction. New York: Holt, Rinehart & Winston.

McGrath, J.E. & Altman, I. (1966) Small group research. New York: Holt, Rinehart & Winston.

McGuire, A. (1987) Introduction. In J. Feinstein, A season on the brink: A year with Bobby Knight andthe Indiana Hoosiers. New York: Simon & Sshuster.

McIntosh, P. (1979) Fair play: The players' view. In P. McIntosh (Ed.), Fair play. London: Heinemann.

McPherson, B.D. (1976) Involuntary turnover and organizational effectiveness in the National Hockey League. In R.S. Gruneau & J.G. Albinson (Eds.), Canadian sport: Sociological perspectives. Don Mills, Ont.: Addison-Wesley.

Meggyesy, D. (1971) Out of their league. New York, Paperback Library.

Melnick, M.J. (1982) Six obstacles to effective team performance: Small group considerations. Journal of Sport Behavior, 5, 114-123.

Melnick, M. & Chemers, M. (1974) Effects of group social structure on the success of basketball teams. Research Quarterly, 45, 1-8.

Merton, R.K. (1957) Social theory and social structure (rev. ed.). New York: The Free Press.

Meyers, A.W., Cooke, C.J., Cullen, J., & Liles, L. (1979) Psycholgical aspects of athletic competitors: A replication across sports. Cognitive Therapy and Research, 3, 361-366.

Mikalachki, A. (1969) Group cohesion reconsidered. London, Ontario: School of Business Administration, University of Western Ontario.

Milgram, S. (1963) Behavioral study of obedience.

Journal of Abnormal and Social Psychology, 67, 371-378.

123-130.

Miller, D.T. & Ross, M. (1975) Self-serving biases in the attribution of causality: Fact or fiction? Psychological Bulletin, 82, 213-225.

Miller, L.K. & Hamblin, R.L. (1963) Interdependance, differential rewarding, and productivity. American Sociological Review, 28, 768-777.

Mills, T.M. (1967) The sociology of small groups. Englewood Cliffs, NJ: Prentice-Hall.

Mills, T.M. (1984) The sociology of small groups, (2nd ed.). Englewood Cliffs, NJ, Prentice-Hall.

Mitchener, J.A. (1976) Sports in America. New York: Random House.

Montville, L. (1987) Where fouls are fair. Sports Illustrated, 67, September 9, pp.66-69.

Morgan, W.P. (1979) Prediction of performance in athletes. In P. Klavora & J.V. Daniel (Eds.). Coach, athlete and the sport psychologist. Champaign, Il.: Human Kinetics.

Morgenegg, B. (1978) Pedagogical moves. In W.G. Anderson & G.T. Barrette (Eds), What's going on in gym: Descriptive studies of physical education classes, Monograph 1, Motor Skills: Theory into Practice.

Mott, P.E. (1965) The organization of society. Englewood Cliffs, NJ: Prentice-Hall.

Muscovici, S. (1980) Toward a theory of conversion behavior. In L. Berkowitz (Ed.), Advances in experimental social psychology,13, 365-379.

Murphy, A. (1988) Red Wing on a roll. Sports Illustrated, 68, 66-69, February 8.

Myers, D.G. (1982) Polarizing effects of social interaction. In H. Brandstatter, J.H. Davis, & G. Stocker-Kreichgauer (Eds.), Group decision making. New York: Academic Press.

Newcomb, T.M. (1951) Social psychological theory. In J.H. Rohrer & M. Sherif (Eds.), Social Psychology at the crossroads. New York, Harper.

Newman, B. (1987) Let's get physical. Sports Illustrated, 67, November 9, pp. 46-65.

Nixon, H.L. (1977) Cohesiveness and team success: A theoretical reformulation. Review of sport and liesure, 2, 36-57.

Nord, W.R. (1969) Social exchange theory: An integrative approach to social conformity. Psychological Bulletin, 71, 174-208.

Nordholm, L.A. (1975) Effects of group size andstimulus ambiguity on conformity. Journal of Social Psychology,97,

Orbell, J. & Dawes, R. (1981) Social dilemma. In G. Stephenson & J.H. Davis (Eds.), Progress in applied social psychology (Vol 1). Chichester, England: Wiley.

Pease, D.A., Locke, L.F., & Burlingame, M. (1971) Athletic exclusion: A complex phenomenon. Quest, 16, 42-46.

Penrod, S. (1986) Social psychology (2nd ed.). Englewood Cliffs, NJ: Prentice-Hall.

Penrod, S. & Hastie, R. (1980) A computer simulation of jury decision making. Psychological Review, 87, 133-159.

Pepitone, A. & Kleiner, R. (1957) The effects of threat and frustration on cohesiveness. Journal of Abnormal and Social Psychology, 54, 192-199.

Pepitone, A. & Reichling, G. (1955) Group cohesiveness and the expression of hostility. Human Relations, 8, 327-337.

Peterson, D.R. (1986) Learning through observation: The dancer's technique. In D. Peterson, G. Lapenskie, & A.W. Taylor (Eds.), The medical aspects of dance. London, Ontario: Spodym Publishers.

Petty, R.E., Harkins, S.G., & Williams, K.D. (1980) The effects of group diffusion ofcognitive effort on attitudes: An information processing view. Journal of Personality and Social Psychology, 38, 81-92.

Phillips, B. & D'Amico, L. (1956) Effects of cooperation and competition on the cohesiveness of small 65-70.

Plimpton, G. (1978) 'Lord, No more than five'. Sports Illustrated, 48, 32-38.

Plunkett, J. & Newhouse, D. (1981) The Jim Plunkett Story: The saga of a man who cameback. New York: Arbor House.

Plutchik, R. (1981) Group cohesion in a psychoevolutionary context. In H. Kellerman (Ed.), Group cohesion: Theoretical and clinical perspectives. New York: Grune & Stratton.

Preston, M. Peltz, W., Mudd, E., & Froscher, T.H. (1952) Impressions of personality as afunction of marital conflict. Journal of Abnormal and Social Psychology, 47, 326-336.

Pruitt, D.G. (1971) Choice shifts in group discussion: An introductory review. Journal of Personality and Social Psychology, 20, 339-360.

Rail, G. (1987) Perveived role characteristics and executive satisfaction in voluntary sport associations. Journal of Sport Psychology, 9, 376-384.

Rainey, D.W. & Larsen, J.D. (1988) Balls, strikes, and

norms: Rule violation and normative rules among baseball umpires. Journal of Sport & Exercise Psychology, 10, 75-80.

Raven, B.H. & Rietsema, J. (1957) The effect of varied clarity of group goal and group path upon the individual and hisrelation to the group. Human Relations, 10, 29-48.

Rees, C.R. & Segal, M.W. (1984) Role differentiation in groups: The relationship between instrumental and expressive leadership. Small Group Behavior, 15, 109-123.

Reilly, R. (1987) Staying away in flocks. Sports Illustrated, 67, November 9, pp. 38-43.

Reis, H.T. & Jelsma, B. (1978) A social psychology of sex differences in sport. In W.F. Straub (ed.), Sport psychology: An analysis of athlete behavior (2nd ed.). Ithaca, NY: Mouvement.

Roberts, G.C. (1978) Children's assignment of responsibility for winning and losing. In F. Smoll & R. Smith (Eds.), Psychological perspectives of youth sports. Washington, DC: Hemisphere.

Robinson, T.T. & Carron, A.V. (1982) Personal and situational factors associated with dropping out versus maintaining participation in competitive sport. Journal of Sport Psychology, 4, 364-378.

Rodin, J., Solomon, S.K. & Metcalf, J. (1978) Role of control in mediating perceptions of density. Journal of Personality and Social Psychology, 36, 988-999.

Roethlisberger, R.J. & Dickson, W.J. (1975) A fair day's work. In P.V. Crosbie (Ed.), Interaction in small groups. New York: Macmillan.

Roland, P. (1977) Ascription and position: A comparitive analysis of the influence ofplaying position on the careers of professional football coaches. Unpublished paper, Department of Sport Studies, University of Massachusetts. Cited in Loy, J.W., McPherson, B.D., & Kenyon, G. (1978) Sport and social systems: A guide to the analysis, problems, and literature. Reading, MA: Addison-Wesley.

Ross, M. & Sicoly, F. (1979) Egocentric biases in availability and attribution. Journal of Personality and Social Psychology, 37, 322-336.

Ruder, M.K. & Gill, D.L. (1982) Immediate effects of win-loss on perceptions of cohesion in intramural and intercollegiate volleyball teams. Journal of Sport Psychology, 4, 227-234.

Rumuz-Nienhuis, W. & Van Bergen, A. (1960) Relations between some components of attraction-to-group. Human Relations, 13, 271-277.

Rushall, B.S. (1977) Two observation schedules for sporting and physical education environments. Canadian Journal of Applied Sport Sciences, 2, 15-21.

Rushall, B.S. & Smith, K.C. (1979) The modification of the quality and quantity of behavior categories in a swimming coach. Journal of Sport Psychology, 1, 138-150.

Sage, G.H. (1972) Machiavellianism among high school and college coaches. In C.E. Mueller (Ed.), Proceedings of the Annual Meeting of the National College of Physical Education for Men. Minneapolis, MN: University of Minnesota.

Sage, G.H.. (1974) The effects of formal structure on organizational leadership: An investigation of collegiate football teams. Paper presented at the Annual Meeting of the American Association for Health, Physical Education, & Recreation, Anaheim, CA.

Sage, G.H. (1975) An occupational analysis of the college coach. In D.W. Ball & J.W. Loy (Eds.), Sport and social order: Contributions to the sociology of sport. Reading, MA: Addison-Wesley.

Sage, G.H. & Loudermilk, S. (1979) The female athlete and role conflict. Research Quarterly, 50, 88-103.

Sage, G.H., Loy, J.W. & Ingham, A.G. (1970) The effects of formal structure on organizational leadership: An investigation of collegiate baseball teams. Paper presented at the Annual Meetings of the American Association for Health, Physical Education, and Recreation, Seattle, WA.

Salminen, S. (1987) Relationships between cohesion and success in ice hockey teams. Scandinavian Journal of Sports Science, 9, 25-32.

Salminen, S. & Luhtanen, P. (1987) Do individual reactions predict group reactions. Perceptual and Motor Skills, 64, 217-218.

Scanlan, T.K. & Passer, M. W. (1980) Self-serving biases in the competitive sport setting: An attributional dilemma. Journal of Sport Psychology, 2, 124-136.

Schachter, S. (1951) Deviation, rejection, and communication. Journal of Abnormal and Social Psychology, 46, 190-207.

Schachter, S., Ellertson, N., McBride, D., & Gregory, D. (1951) An experimental study ofcohesiveness and productivity. Human Relations, 4, 229-238.

Schlenker, B.R. & Miller, R.S. (1977) Egocentricism in groups: Self-serving bias or logical infromation processing. Journal of Personality and Social Psychology, 35, 755-764. (a)

Schlenker, B.R. & Miller, R.S. (1977) Group cohesiveness as a determinant of egocentric perceptions in cooperative groups. Human Relations, 30, 1039-1055. (b)

Schlenker, B.R., Soraci, S. & McCarthy, B. (1976) Self-esteem and group performance as determinants of egocentric perceptions in cooperative groups. Human Relations, 35,

755-764.

Schnake, M.E. & Cochran, D.S. (1985) Effect of two goal setting dimensions on perceived intraorganizational conflict. Group & Organizational Studies, 10, 168-183.

Schriesheim, J.F. (1980) The social context of leader-subordinate relations: An investigation of the effects of group cohesiveness. Journal of Applied Psychology, 65, 183-194.

Schurr, K.T., Ashley, M.A., & Joy, K.L. (1977) A multivariate analysis of male athlete characteristics: Sport type and success. Multivariate Experimental Clinical Research, 3, 53-68.

Schutz, W.C. (1958) FIRO: A three-dimensional theory of interpersonal behavior. New York, Holt, Rinehart, & Winston.

Schutz, W.C. (1966) The interpersonal underworld, 5th ed. Palo Alto, Calif., Science and Behavior Books.

Schwartz, B. & Bursky, S. F. (1977) The home advantage. Social forces, 55, 641-661.

Scott, J. (1969) Athletics for athletes. Hayward, CA: Quality Printing Services.

Seashore, S.E. (1954) Group cohesiveness in the industrial work group. Ann Arbor, MI: Survey Research Group, University of Michigan.

Shaffer, L.S. (1978) On the current confusion of group-related behavior and collective behavior: A reaction to Buys. Personality and Social Psychology Bulletin, 4, 564-567.

Shangi, G. & Carron, A.V. (1987) Group Cohesion and its relationship with performance and satisfaction among high school basketball players. Canadian Journal of Sport Sciences, 12, 20p.

Shaw, M.E. (1981) Group dynamics: The psychology of small group behavior (3rd ed.). New York, McGraw-Hill.

Shaw, M.E. & Breed, G.R. (1970) Effects of attributions of responsibility for negative events on behavior in small groups. Sociometry, 33, 382-393.

Shaw, M.E. & Harkey, B. (1976) Some effects of congruency of member characteristics and group structure upon group behavior. Journal of Personality and Social Psychology, 34, 412-418.

Shelley, H. (1960) Status concensus, leadership, and satisfaction with the group. Journal of Social Psychology, 51, 157-164.

Shelley, M.W. (1964) The mathematical representation of the individual in models of organizational problems. In W.W. Cooper, H.J. Leavitt, & M.W. Shelley II (Eds.), New perspectives in organizational research. New York: Wiley.

Sherif, M. (1936) The psychology of social norms. New York: Harper & Row.

Sherif, M. (1966) Group conflict and cooperation: Their social psychology. London: Routledge and Kegan Paul.

Sherif, M. (1979) Superordinate goals in the reduction of intergroup conflict: An experimental evaluation. In W.G. Austin & S. Worchel (Eds.), The social psychology of intergroup relations. Belmont, CA: Wadsworth.

Sherif, M., Harvey, O.J., White, B.J., Hood, W.R., & Sherif, C.W. (1961) Intergroup cooperation and conflict: The Robbers Cavew Experiment. Norman, OK: Institute ofGroup Relations.

Sherif, M. & Sherif, C. (1969) Social psychology (Rev. ed.). New York: Harper & Row.

Sherif, M. & Sherif, C. (1979) Research on intergroup relations. In W.G. Austin & S. Worchel (Eds.), The social psychology of intergroup relations. Belmont, CA: Wadsworth.

Silva, J.M. III (1983) The perceived legitimacy of rule violating behavior in sport. Journal of Sport Psychology, 5, 438-448.

Silverman, I.W. & Stone, J.M. (1972) Modifying cognitive functioning through participation in a problem solving group. Journal of Educational Psychology, 63, 603-608.

Sistrunk, F. & McDavid, J.W. (1971) Sex variable in conforming behavior. Journal of Personality and Social Psychology, 17, 200-207.

Slavin, R.E. (1983) When does cooperative learning increase student achievement? Psychological Bulletin, 94, 429-445.

Slavin, R.E. & Madden, N.E. (1979) School practices that improve race relations. American Educational Research Journal, 16, 169-180.

Slusher, A., Van Dyke, J., & Rose, G. (1972) Technical competence of group leaders, managerial role, and productivity in engineering design groups. Academy of Management Journal, 15, 197-204.

Smith, G. (1968) An analysis of the concept of group cohesion in a simulated athletic setting. Unpublished masters thesis, University of Western Ontario, Lonon, Ontario.

Smith, M.D. (1978) Hockey violence: Interring some myths. In W.F. Straub (Ed.), Sport psychology: An analysis of athlete behavior. Ithaca, NY: Mouvement.

Smith, R.E., Smoll. F.L. & Curtis, B. (1979) Coaching behaviors in Little League Baseball. In F.L. Smoll & R.E. Smith (Eds.), Psychological perspectives in youth sports. Washington, DC: Hemisphere.

Smith. R.E., Smoll, F.L., & Curtis, B. (1979) Coach effectiveness training: A cognitive-behavioral approach to enhancing relationship skills in youth sport coaches. Journal of Sports Psychology, 1, 59-75.

Smith. R.E., Smoll, F.L., & Hunt, E. (1977) A system for the behavioral assessment of athletic coaches. Research Quarterly, 48, 401-407.

Smoll, F.L. & Smith, R.E. & (1979) Improving relationship skills in youth sport coaches. East Lansing, MI: Institute for the Study of Youth Sports.

Sommer, R. (1961) Leadership and group geography. Sociometry, 24, 100-110.

Sommer, R. (1969) Personal space. Englewood Cliffs, NJ: Prentice-Hall.

Spink, K.S. (1978) Win-loss causal attributions in high school basketball players. Canadian Journal of Applied Sport Sciences, 3, 195-201.

Stabler, K. & Stainback, B. (1986) Snake. Garden City, NY: Doubleday.

Steiner, I.D. (1972) Group processes and group productivity. New York, Academic Press.

Steinzor, B. (1955) The spatial factor in fgace-to-face discussion groups. In A.P. Hare, E.f. Borgatta, & R.F. Bales (Eds.), Small groups: Studies in social interaction. New York: Alfred A. Knopf.

Stogdill, R.M. (1948) Personal factors associated with leadership: Survey of literature. Journal of Psychology, 25, 35-71.

Stogdill, R.M. (1963) Team achievement under high motivation. Columbus, Ohio: The Bureau of Business Research, College of Commerce and Administration, Ohio State University.

Straub, W.F. (1978) How to be an effectivce leader. In W.F. Straub (Ed.), Sport psychology; An analysis of athlete behavior. Ithaca, NY: Mouvement.

Strodtbeck, F.L., & Hook, L.H. (1961) The social dimension of a twelve-man jury table. Sociometry, 24, 397-415.

Swift, E.M. (1987) The Flyers forever. Sports Illustrated, 67, October 12, pp. 90-99.

Swift, E.M. (1988) Yanked about by the boss. Sport Illustrated, 36, April 11.

Tajfel, H. & Turner, J. (1979) An integrative theory of intergroup conflict. In W.G. Austin & S. Worchel (Eds.), The social psychology of intergroup relations. Belmont, CA: Wadsworth.

Tannenbaum, A.J. (1960) Adolescents' attitudes toward academic brilliance. Unpublished Ph.D dissertation, New York University, New York. Cited in Coleman, J.S. (1961) The adolescent society. New York: Free Press.

Taylor, D.M. & Doria, J.R. (1981) Self-serving and group-serving bias in attribution. Journal of Social Psychology, 113, 201-211.

Terborg, J., Castore, C., & DeNinno, J. (1976) A Longitudinal field investigation of the impact of group composition on group performance and cohesion. Journal of Personality and Social Psychology, 6, 782-790.

Theberge, N. & Loy, J.W. (1976) Replacement processes in sport organizations: the case of professional baseball. International Review of Sport Sociology, 11, 73-93.

Thelen, H.A. (1949) Group dynamics in instruction: The principle of least group size. School Review, 57, 139-148.

Thirer, J. & Rampey, M.S. (1979) Effects of abusive aspectators' behavior on performance of home and visiting intercollegiate basketball teams. Perceptual and Motor Skills, 48, 1047-1053.

Thompson, J.D. (1967) Organization in action. New York: McGraw-Hill.

Tretiak, V. (1987) Tretiak: the legend. Edmonton, Alta: Plains Publishing.

Tropp, K.J. & Landers, D.M. (1979) Team interaction and the emergence of leadership and inerpersonal attraction in field hockey. Journal of Sport Psychology, 3, 228-240.

Tuckman, B.W. (1965) Developmental sequences in small groups. Psychological Bulletin, 63, 384-399.

Tuckman, B.W. & Jensen, M.A.C. (1977) Stages of small group development revisited. Group and Organizational Studies, 2, 419-427.

Turner, J., Hogg, M., Turner, P., & Smith, P. (1984) Failure and defeat as determinants of group cohesiveness. British Journal of Social Psychology, 23, 97-111.

Tutko, T.A. & Richards, J.W. (1977) Psychology of coaching. Boston, Allyn and Bacon.

Van Bergen, A. & Koekebakker, J. (1959) "Group cohesiveness" in laboratory experiments. Acta Psychologica, 16, 81-98.

Vander Velden, L. (1971) Relationships among member, team, and situational variables and basketball team success: A social psychological inquiry. Unpublished doctoral dissertation, University of Wisconsin.

Varca, P.E. (1980) An analysis of home and away game performance of male college basketball teams. Journal of Sport Psychology, 2, 245-257.

Volp, A. & Keil, U. (1987) Therelationship between performance, intention to drop out, and interpersonal conflict in swimmers. Journal of Sport Psychology, 9, 358-375.

Vroom, V.H. (1969) Industrial social psychology. In G. Lindzey & E. Aronson (Eds.), The handbook of social psychology Vol. 5. Reading MA: Addison-Wesley.

Vroom, V.H. & Jago, A.G. (1974) On the validity of the Vroom-Yetton model. Journal of Applied Psychology, 63, 151-162.

Vroom. V.H. & Yetton, R.N. (1973) Leadership and decision making. Pittsburgh, PA: Univerity of Pittsburgh Press.

Wallach, M.A., Kogan, N., & Bem, D.J. (1962) Group influence on individual risk taking. Journal of Abnormal and Social Psychology, 65, 75-86.

Walsh, J.M. & Carron, A.V. (1977) Attributes of volunteer coaches. Paper presented at the Annual Meeting of the Canadian Association of Sport Sciences, Winnipeg, Manitoba.

Webster' New Collegiate Dictionary (1987). Toronto, Ont: Thomas Allen & Son.

Weiner, B. (1974) Achievement motivation and attribution theory. Morrristown, NJ: General Learning Press.

Weiner, B. (1979) A theory of motivation for some classroom experiences. Journal of Educational Psychology, 71, 3-25.

Weiner, B., Freeze, I., Kukla, A., Reed, L.. Rest, S. & Rosenbaum, R.M. (1972) Perceiving the causes of success and failure. In E.E. Jones, D.E. Kanhouse, H.H. Kelley, R.E. Nisbett, S. Valins, & B. Weiner (Eds.), Attribution: Perceiving the causes of behavior. Morristown, NJ: General Learning Press.

Weiss, M.R. & Friedrichs, W.D. (1986) The influence of leader behaviors, coach attributes, and institutional variables on performance and satisfaction of collegiate basketball teams. Journal of Sport Psychology, 8, 332-346.

Widmeyer, W.N. (1981) The size of sport groups with special implications for the triad. Unpublished paper. University of Illinois, Champaign, Il.

Widmeyer, W.N. (1977) When cohesiveness predicts performance outcome in sport. Unpublished doctoral dissertation, University of Illinois, Champaign, Il.

Widmeyer, W.N., Brawley, L.R., & Carron, A.V. (1985) The measurement of cohesion in sport teams: The Group Environment Questionnaire. London, Ont.: Sports Dynamics.

Widmeyer, W.N., Brawley, L.R., & Carron, A.V. (1988) How many should I carry on my team? Consequences of group size. Psychology of Motor Behavior and Sport:

Abnstracts 1988. Knoxville, TN: North American Society for the Psychology of Sport and Physical Activity.

Widmeyer, W.N. & Gossett, D.M. (1978) The relative contributions of ability and cohesion to team performance outcome in intramural basketball. Paper presented at the Annual Meeting of the North American Society for the Psychology of Sport and Physical Activity, Tallahassee, FL.

Widmeyer, W.N. & Loy, J.W. (1981) Dynamic duos: An analysis of the relationship between group composition and group performance in women's doubles tennis. Paper presented at The Conference on The Content of Culture: Constants and Variants, Claremont California.

Widmeyer, W.N. & Loy, J.W.,& Roberts, J. (1980) The relative contribution of action styles and ability to the performance outcomes of doubles tennis teams. In C. Nadeau, W. Halliwell, K. Newell, & G. Roberts (Eds.), Psychology of Motor Behavior and Sport-1979. Champaign, Il.: Human Kinteics.

Widmeyer, W.N. & Martens, R. (1978) When cohesion predicts performance outcome in sport. Research Quarterly, 49, 372-380.

Wiley, R. (1988) The puck stops here. Sports Illustrated, 68, January 11, pp. 58-68.

Williams, J.M. & Hacker, C.M. (1982) Causal relationships among cohesion, satisfaction and performance in women's intercollegiate field hockey teams. Journal of Sport Psychology, 4, 324-337.

Williams, K., Harkins, S., & Latane', B. (1981) Identifiability as a deterrent to social loafing: Two cheering experiments. Journal of Personality and Social Psychology 40, 303-311.

Wilson, V. & Bird, E. (1984) Teacher-coach burnout. Paper presented at the Annual Convention of theNorthwest District Association for Health, Physical Education, Recreation, and Dance. Eugene, OR.

Wolosin, R.J., Sherman, S.J. & Till, A. (1973) Effects of cooperation andcompetition on responsibility attributions after success and failure. Journal of Experimental and Social Psychology, 9, 220-235.

Worchel, S. (1979) Cooperation and the reduction of intergroup conflict: Some determining factors. In W.G. Austin & S. Worchel (Eds.), The social psychology of intergroup relations. Belmont, CA: Wadsworth.

Wrong, D.H. (1979) Power. New York: Harper.

Wulf, S. (1988) Scouting reports. Sports Illustrated, 68, April 4, pp. 84 - 90.

Yukelson, D. Weinberg, R. & Jackson, A. (1984) A multidimensional group cohesion instrument for intercollegiate basketball. Hournal of Sport Psychology, 6, 103-117.

Zander, A. (1971) Motives and goals in groups. New York: Academic Press.

Zander, A. (1974) Team spirt vs. the individual achiever. Psychology Today, 8(6), 64-68.

Zander, A. (1976) The psychology of removing group members and recruiting new ones. Human Relations, 10, 969-987.

Zander, A. (1977) Groups at work. San Francisco, CA: Jossey-Bass.

Zander, A. (1982) Making groups effective. San Francisco: Jossey-Bass.

Zander, A. (1985) The purposes of groups and organizations. San Francisco: Jossey-Bass.

Zanna, M.P. & Fazio, R.H. (1982) The attitude-behavior relation: Moving toward a third generation of research. In M.P. Zanna, E.T. Higgins, & C.P. Herman (Eds.), Consistency in social behavior: The Ontario symposium (Vol. 2). Hillsdale, NJ: Erlbaum.

Zimbardo, P.G. (1969) The human choice: Individuation, reason, and order versus deindividuation, impulse, and chaos. In W.J. Arnold & D. Levine (Eds.), Nebraska Symposium on Motivation, 1969. Lincoln, NE: University of Nebraska Press

Author Index

Subject Index